MostUsedWords.com presents

I0616610

French Frequency Dictionary

Advanced Vocabulary

5001-7500 Most Common French Words

Book 3

First Printing, 2018

Jolie Laide LTD
12/F, 67 Percival Street, Hong Kong

www.MostUsedWords.com

Contents

Why This Book?...4

How To Use This Dictionary 7

French English Frequency Dictionary...8

Adjectives...194

Adverbs 201

Conjunctions 202

Prepositions 203

Pronouns...204

Numerals...205

Nouns 206

Verbs 214

Alphabetical order 219

Contact, Further Reading and Resources 249

Why This Book?

Hello, dear reader.

Thank you for purchasing this book. We hope it serves you well on your language learning journey.

Not all words are created equal. The purpose of this frequency dictionary is to list the most used words in descending order, to enable you to learn a language as fast and efficiently as possible.

First, we would like to illustrate the value of a frequency dictionary. For the purpose of example, we have combined frequency data from various languages (mainly Romance, Slavic and Germanic languages) and made it into a single chart.

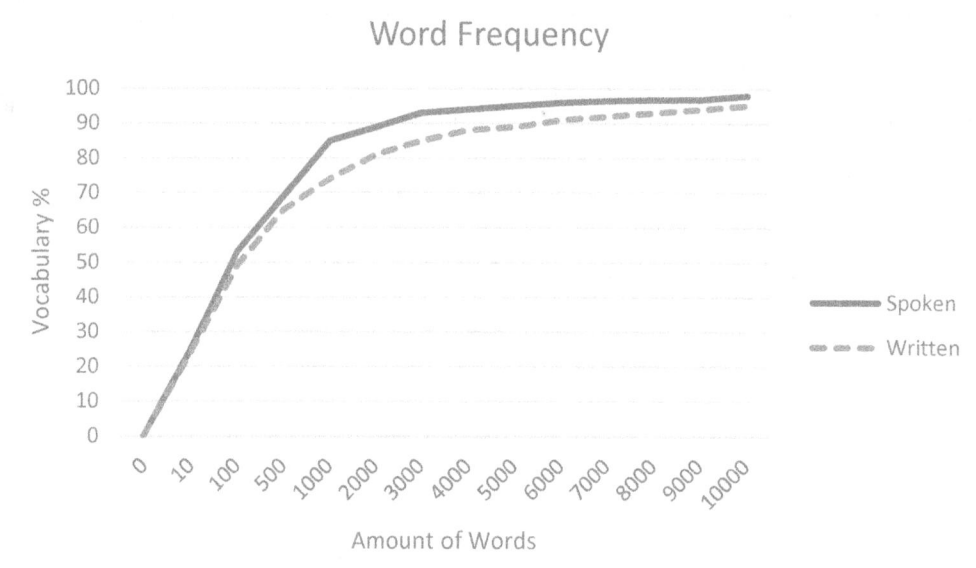

The sweet spots, according to the data seem to be:

Amount of Words	Spoken	Written
• 100	53%	49%
• 1.000	85%	74%
• 2.500	92%	82%
• 5.000	95%	89%
• 7.500	97%	93%
• 10.000	98%	95%

Above data corresponds with Pareto's law.

Pareto's law, also known as the 80/20 rule, states that, for many events, roughly 80% of the effects come from 20% of the causes.

In language learning, this principle seems to be on steroids. It seems that just 20% of the 20% (95/5) of the most used words in a language account for roughly all the vocabulary you need.

To put his further in perspective: The Concise Oxford Hachette French Dictionary lists over 175.000 words in current use, while you will only need to know 2.9% (5000 words) to achieve 95% and 89% fluency in speaking and writing. Knowing the most common 10.000 words, or 5.6%, will net you 98% fluency in spoken language and 95% fluency in written texts.

Keeping this in mind, the value of a frequency dictionary is immense. Study the most frequent words, build your vocabulary and progress naturally. Sounds logical, right?

How many words do you need to know for varying levels of fluency?

While it's important to note that it is impossible to pin down these numbers and statistics with 100% accuracy, these are a global average of multiple sources.

According to research, this is the amount of vocabulary needed for varying levels of fluency.

1. 250 words: the essential core of a language. Without these words, you cannot construct any sentence.
2. 750 words: those that are used every single day by every person who speaks the language.
3. 2500 words: those that should enable you to express everything you could possibly want to say, although some creativity might be required.
4. 5000 words: the active vocabulary of native speakers without higher education.
5. 10,000 words: the active vocabulary of native speakers with higher education.
6. 20,000 words: what you need to recognize passively to read, understand, and enjoy a work of literature such as a novel by a notable author.

Caveats & Limitations.

A frequency list is never "The Definite Frequency List."

Depending on the source material analyzed, you may get different frequency lists. A corpus on spoken word differs from source texts based on a written language.

That is why we chose subtitles as our source, because, according to science, subtitles cover the best of both worlds: they correlate to both spoken and written language.

The frequency list is based on analysis of roughly 20 gigabytes of French subtitles.

Visualize a book with almost 16 million pages, or 80.000 books of 200 pages each, to get an idea of the amount words that have been analyzed for this book. A large base text is vital in order to develop an accurate frequency list.

The raw data included over 1 million entries. The raw data has been lemmatized; words are given in their root form.

Some entries you might find odd, in their respective frequency rankings. We were surprised a couple of time ourselves. Keep in mind that the frequency list is compiled from a large amount of subtitle data, and may include words you wouldn't use yourself.

You might find non-French loanwords in this dictionary. We decided to include them, because if they're being used in subtitle translation, it is safe to assume the word has been integrated into the French general vocabulary.

We tried our best to keep out proper nouns, such as "James, Ryan, Alice as well as "Rome, Washington" or "the Louvre, the Capitol".

Some words have multiple meanings. For the ease of explanation, the following examples are given in English.

"Jack" is a very common first name, but also a noun (a jack to lift up a vehicle) and a verb (to steal something). So is the word "can" It is a conjugation of the verb "to be able" as well as a noun (a tin can, or a can of soft drink).

This skews the frequency rankings slightly. With the current technology, it is unfortunately not possible to rightly identify the correct frequency placements of above words. Luckily, these words are very few, and thus negligible in the grand scheme of things.

If you encounter a word you think you won't need in your vocabulary, just skip learning it. The frequency list includes 25 extra words to compensate for any irregularities you might encounter.

The big secret to learning language is this: build your vocabulary, learn basic grammar and go out there and speak. Make mistakes, have a laugh and learn from them.

We hope you enjoy this frequency dictionary, and that it helps you in your quest of speaking French.

How To Use This Dictionary

abbreviation	*abr*
adjective	*adj*
adverb	*adv*
article	*art*
auxiliary verb	*av*
conjunction	*con*
interjection	*int*
noun	*f(eminine), m(asculine)*
numeral	*num*
particle	*part*
phrase	*phr*
prefix	*pfx*
preposition	*prp*
pronoun	*prn*
suffix	*sfx*
verb	*vb*
singular	*sg*
plural	*pl*

Word Order

The most common translations are generally given first. This resets by every new respective part of speech. Different parts of speech are divided by ";".

Translations

We made the decision to give the most common translation(s) of a word, and respectively the most common part(s) of speech. It does, however, not mean that this is the only possible translations or the only part of speech the word can be used for.

International Phonetic Alphabet (IPA)

The pronunciation of foreign vocabulary can be tricky. To help you get it right, we added IPA entries for each entry. If you already have a base understanding of the pronunciation, you will find the IPA pronunciation straightforward. For more information, please visit www.internationalphoneticalphabet.org

French English Frequency Dictionary

Rank	French	English Translation(s)
	Part of Speech	French Example Sentence
	[IPA]	-English Example Sentence

5001 superviseur — **supervisor**
m
[sypɛʁvizœʁ]
Quant à mon superviseur, il est très incohérent, du coup le travail n'est jamais fait.
-When it comes to my supervisor, he's very inconsistent, so we never get any work done.

5002 préparé — **prepared**
adj
[pʁepaʁe]
Le Gouvernement a déjà préparé deux plans quinquennaux pour traiter la pandémie.
-The Government has already prepared two five-year plans to address the pandemic.

5003 manœuvrer — **maneuver|manipulate**
vb
[manœvʁe]
Barroso doit manœuvrer avec art entre ces propositions.
-Mr Barroso has to manoeuvre artfully between these propositions.

5004 faisable — **feasible|doable**
adj
[fəzabl]
Le sénateur LeBreton : Honorables sénateurs, nous tentons de faire ce qui est faisable.
-Senator LeBreton: Honourable senators, we are trying to achieve the doable.

5005 ampoule — **bulb|ampoule**
f
[ãpul]
Combien de gens cela prend-il de changer une ampoule ?
-How many people does it take to change a lightbulb?

5006 numérique — **digital|numerical**
adj
[nymeʁik]
L'hébreu servait de système numérique.
-Ancient Jews used Hebrew as their numerical system.

5007 consentement — **consent**
m
[kõsãtmã]
J'ai débattu avec lui jusqu'à obtenir son consentement.
-I argued him into consent.

5008 orientation — **orientation|guidance**
f
[ɔʁjãtasjõ]
Vous avez vraiment un bon sens de l'orientation.
-You have a really good sense of direction.

5009 connecter — **log on**
vb
[kɔnɛkte]
Activez le menu contextuel des objets sélectionnés et choisissez la commande Connecter.
-Open the context menu for the selected object and select the Connect command.

5010 pilotage — **control; piloting**
m; f
[pilɔtaʒ]
Pilotage intégral de DAW dans une surface de contrôle grand format extensible.
-Get powerful DAW control in an expandable large-format control surface.

5011 tracé — **route|course; tracing**
m; adj
[tʁase]
Tu ne peux pas analyser les données efficacement avant d'avoir tracé un graphique.
-You cannot analyse the data efficiently unless you draw a plot.

5012 aquarium — **aquarium**
m[akwaʁjɔm]
Voulez-vous aller à l'aquarium ? -Do you want to go to the aquarium?

5013 concession
f
[kõsesjõ]

concession|dealership

Yasugoro veut la concession du gué depuis longtemps.
-Yasugoro has been eyeing the concession at the ford for a long time.

5014 rédaction
f
[ʁedaksjõ]

writing|redaction

Le point D) (Remorques) a été adopté avec la rédaction proposée par le secrétariat.
-Section (D) (Trailers) was adopted with the wording proposed by the secretariat.

5015 diplomatique
adj
[diplɔmatik]

diplomatic

N'y aurait-il aucune possibilité de protection diplomatique pour cette société ?
-Would there be no possibility of diplomatic protection for such corporations?

5016 ravin
m
[ʁavɛ̃]

ravine

Alors qu'ils skiaient, ils eurent un accident: ils tombèrent dans un profond ravin.
-Whilst they were out skiing they had an accident: they fell down a deep ravine.

5017 venin
m
[vənɛ̃]

venom

Voici, en substance, le venin qu'il vient de cracher.
-This is the type of poison which he spouts here.

5018 immoral
adj
[imɔʁal]

immoral

Ce qui est vraiment immoral, et mérite ce qualificatif, c'est l'occupation.
-The truly immoral thing, which needs to be characterized as such, is occupation.

5019 merveilleusement
adv
[mɛʁvɛjøzmã]

wonderfully

Même merveilleusement peinte, en effet, cette pipe ne permettra jamais de fumer.
-Magnificently painted it may be, but this pipe can never be smoked.

5020 boulangerie
f
[bulãʒʁi]

bakery

Tu peux aller chercher du pain à la boulangerie, deux petites et une grosse, s'il te plait ? Et s'ils n'en ont plus, tu peux prendre quatre ficelles à la place.
-Could you please go buy bread at the baker's, two small ones and a large one please? And if they ran out, you can buy four thin baguettes instead.

5021 maquette
f
[makɛt]

model

Réaliser une maquette d'avion est intéressant.
-Making a model plane is interesting.

5022 greffer
vb
[gʁefe]

graft|engraft

Un malade à greffer sur quatre mourra avant de recevoir la greffe salvatrice.
-One in four people awaiting a donor will die before they get a transplant.

5023 écharpe
f
[eʃaʁp]

scarf

Cette écharpe est à Jacqueline.
-This scarf is Jacqueline's.

5024 sonore
f; adj[sɔnɔʁ]

sound; acoustic

Le film doublé est ennuyeux à regarder parce que la bande sonore est décalée de l'image. -The dubbed movie is annoying to watch because the audio is out of sync with the video.

5025 doctorat
m
[dɔktɔʁa]

doctorate|phD

Votre thèse de doctorat doit être écrite en anglais.
-Your PhD thesis has to be written in English.

5026 transition

transition

	f	Ma transition d'un homme vers une femme se passe bien.
	[tʁɑ̃zisjɔ̃]	-My transition from male to female is going well.
5027	**watt**	**watt**
	m	L'énergie de secours est réduite à zéro watt.
	[wat]	-Standby power is reduced to zero watt.
5028	**enchaîner**	**enchain**
	vb	Pour créer un enchaînement, cliquez sur la bordure du cadre à enchaîner.
	[ɑ̃ʃene]	-In order to create a link, click the edge of the frame you want to link.
5029	**corvée**	**corvee|chore**
	f	Ta seule corvée est de nettoyer le bol de Klaus.
	[kɔʁve]	-You're one chore is to clean Klaus's bowl.
5030	**boutique**	**shop|stall**
	f	Nous nous rendons à la boutique.
	[butik]	-We are going to the shop.
5031	**tourisme**	**tourism**
	m	Kyoto dépend de l'industrie du tourisme.
	[tuʁism]	-Kyoto depends on the tourist industry.
5032	**conservateur**	**conservative; conservative**
	adj; m	Jack est un conservateur.
	[kɔ̃sɛʁvatœʁ]	-Jack is a conservative.
5033	**pingouin**	**penguin**
	m	Je veux voir un pingouin dégobiller.
	[pɛ̃gwɛ̃]	-I just want to see a penguin throw up.
5034	**sadique**	**sadistic; sadist**
	adj; m/f	Certains sadiques font des « essais » qui englobent le harcèlement.
	[sadik]	-Some sexual sadists will go through "behavioural try-outs" that will include stalking.
5035	**lingerie**	**lingerie**
	f	Jack a essayé de convaincre Jill de mettre de la lingerie affriolante.
	[lɛ̃ʒʁi]	-Jack tried to convince Jill to put on sexy lingerie.
5036	**mutuellement**	**mutually**
	adv	Ces deux objectifs se renforcent mutuellement et ne sont pas mutuellement exclusifs.
	[mytɥɛlmɑ̃]	-Those two objectives are mutually reinforcing, not mutually exclusive.
5037	**pointure**	**size**
	f	J'ai besoin de ces chaussures en pointure dix s'il vous plait !
	[pwɛ̃tyʁ]	-I need these shoes in size ten please!
5038	**Belgique**	**Belgium**
	f	Ils sont généralement situés en Suisse, en France et aussi en Belgique.
	[bɛlʒik]	-They are generally located in Switzerland, France, and in Belgium, as well.
5039	**équiper**	**equip|provide**
	vb	Nous devons équiper le budget de l'UE en vue d'affronter le XXIe siècle.
	[ekipe]	-We need to gear the EU budget for the 21st century.
5040	**quasi**	**almost**
	adv	De la sorte, le Parlement européen est confronté à une mission quasi impossible.
	[kazi]	-As a result, the European Parliament is faced with an almost impossible task.
5041	**recommandation**	**recommendation|reference**

	f	Mon professeur mit un mot de recommandation pour moi.
	[ʁəkɔmɑ̃dasjɔ̃]	-My teacher put in a good word for me.
5042	**brève**	**breve**
	f	Cet amendement dit: «exhorte le Conseil à ne ménager aucun effort pour créer les conditions propices à une brève interruption des bombardements».
	[bʁɛv]	-The French text reads: 'exhorte le Conseil à ne ménager aucun effort pour créer les conditions propices à une brève interruption des bombardements '.
5043	**gonflé**	**inflated**
	adj	Elle a gonflé les joues.
	[gɔ̃fle]	-She expanded her cheeks.
5044	**honoraire**	**honorary; honorarium**
	adj; m	Myers (États-Unis d'Amérique) a été nommé membre honoraire du Comité.
	[ɔnɔʁɛʁ]	-Myers (United States) has been appointed as a member emeritus.
5045	**inculper**	**charge**
	vb	On ne peut pas arrêter quelqu'un et l'emprisonner sans l'inculper ni organiser de procès.
	[ɛ̃kylpe]	-You cannot charge someone and lock him up without accusing him and having a trial.
5046	**croquis**	**sketch**
	m	Faites un croquis de votre maison.
	[kʁɔki]	-Make a sketch of your house.
5047	**communion**	**Communion**
	f	Eglise veut dire communion des Saints.
	[kɔmynjɔ̃]	-The meaning of the Church is a communion of saints.
5048	**panda**	**panda**
	m	Tu es un panda.
	[pɑ̃da]	-You are a panda.
5049	**débarquement**	**landing|disembarkation**
	m	Les navires du débarquement précédent avaient chaviré.
	[debaʁkəmɑ̃]	-Boats from the prior landing turned upside down.
5050	**paragraphe**	**paragraph**
	m	Ecrivez un paragraphe sur le climat en Provence.
	[paʁagʁaf]	-Write a paragraph on the climate in Provence.
5051	**suffisant**	**sufficient**
	adj[syfizɑ̃]	En cas d'incapacité de l'un des parents, le consentement de l'autre est suffisant. -In the absence or incapacity of one parent the consent of the other shall suffice.
5052	**chatouiller**	**tickle**
	vb	On ne peut pas se chatouiller soi-même.
	[ʃatuje]	-You can't tickle yourself.
5053	**rassurant**	**reassuring**
	adj	Je crois que ce manque de transparence n' est pas rassurant pour la population.
	[ʁasyʁɑ̃]	-I do not believe that this lack of transparency is reassuring for people.
5054	**sabre**	**saber|sword**
	m	Donnez-moi mon sabre et je deviendrai...
	[sabʁ]	-Give me my sword and I will become the...
5055	**recouvrir**	**cover|re-cover**
	vb	Cela prendra-t-il du temps à recouvrir ?
	[ʁəkuvʁiʁ]	-Will it take long to recover?
5056	**évoquer**	**evoke|recall**

	vb [evɔke]	Il en va de même du mot "constitution", qui peut évoquer des choses bien différentes. -The same applies to the word "constitution" , which can also evoke quite different things.
5057	**maquereau** m [makʁo]	**mackerel|pimp** T'es son maquereau ? -Are you her pimp?
5058	**support** m [sypɔʁ]	**support|bracket** L'extrémité distale du bras support porte un siège enfant. -A child seat is supported on the distal end of the support arm .
5059	**négligence** f [negliʒãs]	**negligence|neglect** Faisons effort - en parallèle avec nos efforts pour identifier des phrases anglaises mal formées - pour ne pas perdre notre patrimoine par négligence. -Let us make an effort -in parallel with our efforts to identify ungrammatical English sentences- not to lose through neglect our patrimony.
5060	**censurer** vb [sãsyʁe]	**censor** C'en est une autre de censurer des propos politiques. -It's quite another to censor political content.
5061	**tyrannie** f [tiʁani]	**tyranny** Vous pouvez choisir n'importe quel nom qui vous plaise pour les deux types de gouvernement. J'appelle personnellement le type de gouvernement qui peut être démis « démocratie » et l'autre « tyrannie ». -You can choose whatever name you like for the two types of government. I personally call the type of government which can be removed without violence "democracy", and the other "tyranny".
5062	**carrosse** m [kaʁɔs]	**coach|carriage** Finalement, ma petite princesse a son carrosse -Finally, my little princess has her carriage.
5063	**soja** m[sɔʒa]	**soy** Quels sont les aliments que tu manges habituellement avec de la sauce de soja ? -What are some foods you usually eat with soy sauce?
5064	**diviser** vb [divize]	**divide|partition** Est interdit tout acte de nature à diviser les religions et à diviser le peuple (article 9 nouveau). -Any act liable to divide religions and divide the people is prohibited (new art. 9)
5065	**clandestin** adj [klãdɛstɛ̃]	**clandestine** Il s'agit d'un phénomène sans précédent, clandestin et qui frappe aveuglément ses victimes. -It is unconventional, clandestine, and indiscriminate with respect to its victims.
5066	**chaperon** m [ʃapʁɔ̃]	**chaperon|coping** Il était une fois, dans un petit village une petite fille qui s'appelait Petit chaperon vert. -Once upon a time, there lived in a village a little girl called Little Green Hood.
5067	**bluff** m [blœf]	**bluff** Or il apparaît que rien ce cela n'est vrai, qu'il ne s'agit que d'un bluff. -It turns out, however, that this is not true, and that it is a bluff.
5068	**blouse** f [bluz]	**gown|blouse** Je dois aller changer ma blouse. -Now I've got to change my gown.

5069	**prudemment**		**carefully**
	adv		Il est nécessaire d'avancer prudemment s'agissant de la représentation hors Siège.
	[pʁydamɑ̃]		-It was necessary to move cautiously on the question of field representation.
5070	**perpétuité**		**perpetuity**
	f		Peine capitale et réclusion à perpétuité. La peine capitale n'existe pas.
	[pɛʁpetɥite]		-Capital punishment and life imprisonment. Capital punishment does not exist.
5071	**bannir**		**banish**
	vb		C'est une façon, à mon avis, de bannir de notre vocabulaire le mot «chômage».
	[baniʁ]		-In my view, this is a way of banishing the term 'unemployment' from our vocabulary.
5072	**timing**		**timing**
	m		She was with us for only a short time and she used every minute of that time.
	[timiŋ]		-Elle n'a été parmi nous que peu de temps, mais elle en a utilisé chaque minute.
5073	**dupe**		**dupe**
	f		Votre propre client vous dupe, Pete.
	[dyp]		-You're getting duped by your client, Pete.
5074	**interrupteur**		**switch**
	m		L'interrupteur est ouvert.
	[ɛ̃tɛʁyptœʁ]		-The switch is off.
5075	**coursier**		**steed|messenger**
	m		Excusez-moi, nous cherchons un coursier...
	[kuʁsje]		-Excuse me, we're looking for a messenger.
5076	**rubis**		**ruby**
	m		Le rubis va directement dans le coffre.
	[ʁybi]		-That ruby is not going anywhere but straight down into the vault.
5077	**masquer**		**hide|mask**
	vb		L'étude de la famille en fonction de catégories peut masquer un éventail d'éléments dynamiques.
	[maske]		-Looking at the study of family in terms of categories can mask a variety of dynamics.
5078	**handicaper**		**handicap**
	vb		Nous ne devons pas nous handicaper nous-mêmes dès le départ.
	[ɑ̃dikape]		-We must not handicap ourselves from the outset.
5079	**bandeau**		**headband**
	m		C'était comme un masque de ski avec une rayure argentée au milieu et un bandeau doré.
	[bɑ̃do]		-It was like a ski mask, but shiny, with a silver zigzag up the middle and... a gold headband.
5080	**natation**		**swimming|float**
	f		Ils ont formé une équipe de natation.
	[natasjɔ̃]		-They formed a swim team.
5081	**slogan**		**slogan|tag**
	m		Le slogan pour la journée contre l'extrémisme était « Plutôt arc-en-ciel que brun ».
	[slɔgɑ̃]		-The slogan for the day dedicated to counter extremism was, "rainbow colours instead of brown."
5082	**guichet**		**window**

	m	Où est le guichet ?
	[giʃɛ]	-Where is the ticket window?
5083	**kimono**	**kimono**
	m	Elle est vraiment belle en kimono.
	[kimɔno]	-She really looks beautiful in a kimono.
5084	**équivalent**	**equivalent; equivalent**
	adj; m	Supprimer les définitions de Équivalent-lithium et Contenu d'équivalent-lithium.
	[ekivalã]	-Delete the definitions of Equivalent lithium content and Lithium-equivalent content.
5085	**prostitution**	**prostitution**
	f	La prostitution d'escorte et la prostitution au domicile de la prostituée.
	[pʁɔstitysjɔ̃]	-Escort prostitution and prostitution in the prostitute's own home.
5086	**culturel**	**cultural**
	adj	En France, son berceau, Camambert devint un phénomène culturel et social.
	[kyltyʁɛl]	-In France, its birthplace, Camambert became a cultural and social phenomenon.
5087	**diplomate**	**diplomat**
	m/f[diplɔmat]	TAY Abra, Diplomate au Ministère des Affaires Étrangères et de la Coopération. -Abra TAY, Diplomat with the Ministry of Foreign Affairs and Cooperation
5088	**locomotif**	**locomotive**
	adj	C'est quasiment une petite locomotive.
	[lɔkɔmɔtif]	-Well, it's basically a very small locomotive.
5089	**cendrier**	**ashtray**
	m	Et juste après, ils se sont assemblés sous la forme d'un cendrier.
	[sãdʁije]	-Then a moment later integrated again into the shape of an ashtray.
5090	**amendement**	**amendment**
	m	L'amendement proposé par le député de Berthier-Montcalm est recevable.
	[amãdmã]	-The amendment proposed by the hon. member for Berthier-Montcalm is in order.
5091	**gag**	**gag**
	m	C'était un gag pour vous détendre.
	[gag]	-It was just a joke to relax you.
5092	**débutant**	**beginner; novice**
	m; adj	Il s'en est bien sorti pour un débutant.
	[debytã]	-He did well for a beginner.
5093	**croquer**	**crunch|eat**
	vb	On aurait envie de... le croquer.
	[kʁɔke]	-You just want to... eat him up.
5094	**tranché**	**decided|cut**
	adj	En 2007, les médias ont relaté le cas d'un mari qui avait tranché les mains de son épouse.
	[tʁãʃe]	-In 2007, the media reported a case where a husband chopped off his wife's hands.
5095	**lunaire**	**lunar**
	adj	La Décennie lunaire internationale, par l'observateur de la Planetary Society.
	[lynɛʁ]	-"The International Lunar Decade", by the observer for the Planetary Society.
5096	**dégénérer**	**degenerate**

	vb [deʒeneʁe]	La pauvreté génère des frustrations et des révoltes qui peuvent dégénérer en conflits. -Poverty leads to frustration and revolts, which may degenerate into conflicts.
5097	**rush** m [ʁyʃ]	**rush** Jeremy contrôle le rush du déjeuner, Dieu merci. -Jeremy's got the lunch rush under control, thank God.
5098	**déchiffrer** vb [deʃifʁe]	**decipher** Il n'est pas difficile de déchiffrer le message codé: quiconque votera pour FIDESZ devra affronter la désapprobation des Russes. -It is not difficult to decipher the coded message: whoever votes for FIDESZ must face the disapproval of the Russians.
5099	**pantin** m [pɑ̃tɛ̃]	**puppet** Conclusion : tu restes un pantin. -My conclusion: you stay as a puppet.
5100	**exotique** adj[ɛgzɔtik]	**exotic** Jaffer) La danse exotique demeure une profession légale au Canada. -Dr. David Elton is a former head of political science at the University of Lethbridge, now Professor Emeritus, and also an expert on constitutional issues.
5101	**tourmenter** vb [tuʁmɑ̃te]	**torment|plague** Voilà une question qui tourmentait l'ancien député Jim Hawkes, qui fut président du comité spécial de la Chambre des communes sur la réforme électorale. -This is an issue that bedevilled former MP Jim Hawkes who chaired the House of Commons Special Committee on Electoral Reform.
5102	**ananas** m [anana]	**pineapple** S'il vous plaît, donnez-moi l'ananas le plus grand. -Please, give me the biggest pineapple.
5103	**spaghetti** m [spageti]	**spaghetti** RTAs can, however, complicate the trading environment through their "spaghetti bowl" effect. -Toutefois, ils peuvent aussi compliquer le climat commercial par leur effet «plat de spaghettis».
5104	**bison** f [bizɔ̃]	**bison** Les gens pouvaient aussi faire un tour d'essai des véhicules terrestres Bison. -They were also taking people for demonstration rides on the Bison land vehicles.
5105	**vanille** f [vanij]	**vanilla** L'économie fragile du pays était tributaire de l'exportation de la vanille et des envois de fonds des émigrants. -The country's fragile economy was dependent on exports of vanilla and emigrants' remittances.
5106	**bouillon** m [bujɔ̃]	**broth|bouillon** Voilà le bouillon de Mme Brophy. -Here's the broth for Mrs. Brophy.
5107	**secourir** vb [səkuʁiʁ]	**rescue** Le capitaine de tout navire apercevant une personne en détresse en mer doit la secourir. -The master of any ship who sees persons in distress at sea must rescue them.
5108	**hippie**	**hippy**

	f	L'objet de la culture hippie est d'éviter de se conformer aux normes sociales.
	[ipi]	-The point of hipster subculture is to avoid conforming to societal norms.
5109	**thérapeute**	**therapist**
	m/f	Rapports de Julie Patterson, thérapeute familiale, Capital Coast Health.
	[teʁapøt]	-Reports by Julie Patterson, Senior Family Therapist, Capital Coast Health.
5110	**attirant**	**attractive|appealing**
	adj	Ce que nous avons à offrir est définitivement plus attirant que ce que la Russie propose.
	[atiʁɑ̃]	-What we have on offer is definitely more attractive than what Russia is proposing.
5111	**compromettre**	**compromise**
	vb[kɔ̃pʁɔmɛtʁ]	Le chargement ne doit pas compromettre la stabilité du bateau ni la résistance de la coque. -The load shall not compromise the vessel's stability or the strength of the hull.
5112	**proprement**	**properly**
	adv	Seules les contre-mesures proprement dites entrent dans le champ du projet d'articles.
	[pʁɔpʁəmɑ̃]	-Only countermeasures properly so-called fall within the scope of the Draft articles.
5113	**réfrigérateur**	**refrigerator**
	m	Sortez les oranges du réfrigérateur.
	[ʁefʁiʒeʁatœʁ]	-Take the oranges out of the fridge.
5114	**râler**	**grumble|moan**
	vb	J'en ai marre de t'entendre râler constamment.
	[ʁale]	-I'm fed up with your constant complaining.
5115	**aviser**	**inform**
	vb	Un État peut à tout moment aviser le Greffier qu'il ne souhaite plus figurer sur la liste.
	[avize]	-A State may at any time inform the Registrar of its withdrawal from the list.
5116	**récolter**	**harvest|collect**
	vb	Du point de vue technique, il a été difficile de récolter beaucoup d'informations.
	[ʁekɔlte]	-From the technical point of view, it has been difficult to get a lot of information.
5117	**hanter**	**haunt|spook**
	vb	Le problème des réfugiés et des personnes déplacées continue de hanter l'humanité.
	[ɑ̃te]	-The problem of refugees and displaced persons continues to haunt humanity.
5118	**décence**	**decency**
	f	La décence et la simplicité n'ont aucune utilité dans ce monde.
	[desɑ̃s]	-Decency and simplicity is of no use in this world.
5119	**curry**	**curry**
	m	Je suis pas vraiment fana du curry.
	[kyʁi]	-I'm not really big on curry.
5120	**miséricordieux**	**merciful**
	adj	Il m'obtiendra clémence et grâce d'un Dieu miséricordieux.
	[mizeʁikɔʁdjø]	-May it win me mercy and favour in the sight of a compassionate God.
5121	**ressusciter**	**resurrect**

	vb [ʁesysite]	Néanmoins, à notre grand étonnement, certains tentent de ressusciter ce document. -To our astonishment, however, there are those who are attempting to resurrect this document.
5122	**moustique** m [mustik]	**mosquito** La morsure d'un chien est plus grave que la piqûre d'un moustique. -A dog bite is more serious than a mosquito bite.
5123	**redire** vb[ʁədiʁ]	**repeat** Je voudrais redire ici ce que nous avons déclaré en septembre, lors du débat général. -Here, I would like to reiterate what we said in September at the general debate.
5124	**détecter** vb [detɛkte]	**detect** En fait, le militaire en question disait que nous n'aurions même pas pu détecter cette opération par radar. -In fact the military officer said that we could not even detect that by radar.
5125	**enrichir** vb [ãʁiʃiʁ]	**enrich** Nous demeurons convaincus que leur participation contribuera à enrichir nos débats. -We are convinced that their participation will help enrich our debates.
5126	**frustration** f [fʁystʁasjõ]	**frustration** Je comprends la frustration de Jack. -I understand Jack's frustration.
5127	**morale** f [mɔʁal]	**morals|ethics** L'autorité morale est plus puissante que n'importe quelle arme. -Moral leadership is more powerful than any weapon.
5128	**tournée** f [tuʁne]	**tour|touring** La première tournée est pour la maison. -The first round is on the house.
5129	**tact** m; adj [takt]	**tact; delicate** La prochaine fois, adresse-toi à moi avec plus de tact. -Next time, speak to me more carefully.
5130	**débarrer** vb [debaʁe]	**unbar** Bon, regarde, va au char, je vais te le débarrer. -Go to the car, I'll unlock it.
5131	**associé** adj; m [asɔsje]	**associate; associate** Je me suis associé à lui. -I went into partnership with him.
5132	**meute** f [møt]	**pack** Ce quartier est comme une meute. -See, this neighborhood is like a pack.
5133	**viril** adj [viʁil]	**virile|manly** Lorsque j'étais jeune, conduire une voiture ou un camion après avoir bu de l'alcool était jugé macho et viril. -I remember when I was growing up that it was considered to be macho or manly to drink alcohol and drive a car or a truck.
5134	**mathématique** adj [matematik]	**mathematical** Le pourcentage des électeurs admissibles est un autre calcul mathématique. -The percentage of eligible voters is another mathematical calculation.
5135	**détraquer** vb [detʁake]	**break down** La Commission européenne trouve -t-elle acceptable qu'un tremblement de terre puisse détraquer le fonctionnement du barrage d'Itoiz et menacer la

centrale nucléaire d'Asco?
-Does the European Commission find it acceptable that a landslide could dislocate the operation of the Itoiz dam and threaten the Ascó nuclear power station?

5136	**antarctique**	**Antarctic**
	adj [ãtaʁktik]	La calotte glacière antarctique se divise en Antarctique Est et Antarctique Ouest. -The Antarctic icecap is divided into the East Antarctic and the West Antarctic ice sheets.
5137	**cubain**	**Cuban**
	adj [kybɛ̃]	Le système politique cubain est l'expression de la volonté populaire. -The Cuban political system is the expression of the will of the Cuban people.
5138	**réciter**	**recite**
	vb [ʁesite]	Nous avons seulement eu la force de réciter le kaddisch, la prière des morts. -We had just enough strength to recite the Kaddish — the prayer for the dead.
5139	**sournois**	**sneaky|sly**
	adj [suʁnwa]	De plus, et de manière sournoise, la Commission propose un plafonnement des aides par exploitation. -Furthermore, and in an underhand way, the Commission proposes setting a ceiling on aid per farm.
5140	**terminus**	**terminus**
	m [tɛʁminys]	Va au terminus du bus de Tsuen Wan. -Go to the Tsuen Wan Bus terminal.
5141	**insignifiant**	**insignificant**
	adj [ɛ̃siɲifjã]	L'histoire est en cours, mais les réalisations, également, sont loin d'être insignifiantes. -The story is ongoing but the achievements, likewise, are very far from being inconsiderable.
5142	**nageur**	**swimmer**
	m [naʒœʁ]	T'offusque pas, petit, mais t'es pas tres bon nageur. -No offense, kid, but you're not the best swimmer.
5143	**contremaître**	**overseer**
	m [kõtʁəmɛtʁ]	Je veux voir votre contremaître. -I want to see your supervisor.
5144	**pêche**	**fishing**
	f [pɛʃ]	Le gouvernement continue d'élaborer une stratégie concernant cette pêche. -The government is continuing to develop a strategy with regard to that fishery.
5145	**malsain**	**unhealthy**
	adj [malsɛ̃]	L'Union européenne doit elle aussi savoir qu'il est malsain de fumer. -The European Union too, should know that smoking is unhealthy.
5146	**freiner**	**curb**
	vb [fʁene]	Le premier est une procédure de décision visant à freiner les dépenses publiques. -The first is a decision rule that attempts to put a brake on government spending.
5147	**cailler**	**curdle|clot**
	vb [kaje]	Nous voulons protéger la crème caillée au même titre que les Grecs veulent défendre leur feta.

-We want to protect clotted cream just as the Greeks want to defend their feta. but to be even-handed.

5148 gitan
adj; m
[ʒitɑ̃]

Gypsy; Gypsy
Pourquoi laisser Jenny avec le gitan.
-Why she left my Jenny with the Gypsy.

5149 sanglot
m
[sɑ̃glo]

sob
Un petit sanglot et plus rien.
-A little sob and that was all.

5150 volontairement
adv
[vɔlɔ̃tɛʁmɑ̃]

willingly
Ces émissions sont volontairement exemptes de toute publicité ou parrainage.
-These broadcasts are voluntarily exempt from any publicity or sponsorship.

5151 universel
adj; m
[ynivɛʁsɛl]

universal; universal
La Banque européenne d'investissement est à présent notre outil universel.
-The European Investment Bank is now our all-purpose tool.

5152 rancard
m
[ʁɑ̃kaʁ]

date
Qui est ton rancard ce soir ?
-Who's your date tonight?

5153 décent
adj
[desɑ̃]

decent
Premièrement, l'accès à un travail décent ou, en d'autres termes, la possibilité de trouver un travail décent.
-First, access to decent work, in other words making decent work possible.

5154 dynamique
adj; f
[dinamik]

dynamic; dynamics
Jack a une personnalité dynamique.
-Jack has a dynamic personality.

5155 gouverner
vb
[guvɛʁne]

govern|steer
Le gouvernement du temps de l'apartheid prétendait gouverner au nom du christianisme.
-The previous apartheid government purported to rule in the name of Christianity.

5156 formalité
f
[fɔʁmalite]

formality
Ce n'est qu'une formalité.
-It's just a formality.

5157 tuerie
f
[tyʁi]

killing
Tous ont nié toute participation personnelle dans la tuerie.
-All of them have denied any personal participation in the killing.

5158 samba
f
[sɑ̃ba]

samba
Il ressemble parfois au mariage entre un tango argentin et une samba brésilienne.
-It sometimes resembles the combination of an Argentine tango with a Brazilian samba.

5159 épice
f
[epis]

spice
La sensibilité est comme une épice.
-Look, sensitivity is like a spice.

5160 été
m
[ete]

summer
Les chiffres sont tirés de l'horaire d'été actuel et de l'horaire d'été 1995.
-They are taken from the current summer timetable, and the summer 1995 timetable.

5161 sabotage
m[sabɔtaʒ]

sabotage
Ces plaintes de sabotage seraient donc avérées. -If he's right, then these sabotage claims could be true.

5162	**prodige**	**prodigy|wonder**
	m	Le prodige et le monstre ont les mêmes racines.
	[pʁɔdiʒ]	-The prodigy and the monster have the same roots.

5163	**truquer**	**rig|fake**
	vb	Son importance était due à la difficulté accrue de truquer les résultats.
	[tʁyke]	-Its significance was due to the increased difficulty of rigging the results.

5164	**optique**	**optical; optics**
	adj; f	Celui-ci semble plus long que celui-là mais ce n'est qu'une illusion d'optique.
	[ɔptik]	-This looks longer than that, but it is an optical illusion.

5165	**coyote**	**coyote**
	m	Josh avait raison pour le coyote.
	[kwajɔt]	-I guess Josh was right about that coyote.

5166	**rubrique**	**rubric|column**
	f	Article dans la rubrique féminine, (The Independent/L'indépendant, 13/8/04, p.
	[ʁybʁik]	-Article in the Women's Column, (The Independent/L'indépendant, 13/8/04, p. 23).

5167	**imitation**	**imitation**
	f	Est-ce une imitation ?
	[imitasjɔ̃]	-Is this fake?

5168	**nomination**	**appointment|nomination**
	f	La nomination de Mme Arbour est une nomination internationale.
	[nɔminasjɔ̃]	-The appointment of Madam Arbour is an international appointment.

5169	**mayonnaise**	**mayonnaise**
	f	Le produit présente plusieurs avantages par rapport à la mayonnaise à base d'œuf classique.
	[majɔnɛz]	-The product has several advantages over conventional egg based mayonnaise.

5170	**dandy**	**dandy; foppish**
	m; adj	À la manière des fats, il larde ses phrases de mots anglais mal digérés. Une
	[dɑ̃di]	sorte de dandy raté, auquel il manquerait la classe.
		-In the style of conceited people, he lards his sentences with ill-digested English words. A kind of failed dandy, deprived of class.

5171	**paranoïaque**	**paranoid; paranoid**
	m/f	Mon intention n'était pas de le rendre paranoïaque avec ma question.
	[paʁanɔjak]	-I do not mean to make him paranoid with my question.

5172	**stérile**	**sterile|barren**
	adj	Il ne faut pas que 2004 soit encore une année stérile pour la Conférence du
	[steʁil]	désarmement.
		-Next year — 2004 — ought not to be another blank year for the Conference on Disarmament.

5173	**gourou**	**guru**
	m	Il y a 300 ans aujourd'hui, le dixième gourou, Sri Guru Gobind Singh Ji,
	[guʁu]	créait la Khalsa.
		-On this day 300 years ago the 10th Guru Sri Guru Gobind Singh Ji created Khalsa.

5174	**émotionnel**	**emotional**
	adj[emɔsjɔnɛl]	Les deux groupes étaient unis par une émotion et une compréhension profondes. -The depth of emotion and mutual understanding between the two groups was great.

5175	**mutuel**	**mutual**

	adj [mytɥɛl]	Cette unité passe par le respect mutuel, l'acceptation mutuelle et la tolérance. -That unity requires mutual respect, mutual acceptance and tolerance.
5176	**apaiser** vb [apeze]	**appease|soothe** Nous devons apaiser ces craintes de manière conséquente et décidée. -We must work resolutely and systematically to allay those fears.
5177	**flirter** vb [flœʁte]	**flirt|spoon** Sami et Layla ont commencé à flirter. -Sami and Layla began flirting.
5178	**longuement** adv [lɔ̃gmɑ̃]	**long** La police l'aurait interrogée longuement, puis l'aurait abattue. -The police reportedly questioned her for a long time and subsequently shot her.
5179	**campement** m [kɑ̃pmɑ̃]	**camp** Juliet rassemble des informations à votre ancien campement. -Juliet is gathering information for us at your former camp.
5180	**poétique** adj [pɔetik]	**poetic** Mourir courageusement a été la dernière offrande poétique de sa vie. -To die fearlessly was the last poetic offering of his life.
5181	**recruter** vb [ʁəkʁyte]	**recruit|rush** Les pays développés sont en devoir de recruter - mais de recruter de façon responsable. -Developed countries have an obligation to recruit — but to recruit responsibly.
5182	**élevage** m [elvaʒ]	**breeding|animal husbandry** Il s'agit de l'attribution délibérée d'un brevet pour l'élevage d'êtres humains. -It amounts to deliberately awarding a patent for the breeding of human beings.
5183	**tornade** f [tɔʁnad]	**tornado** On pouvait voir des photos des divers dommages causés par la tornade. -The article had illustrations of the various damage of the tornado.
5184	**périr** vb [peʁiʁ]	**perish** Des millions d'Américains vont périr. -Tens of millions of Americans will perish.
5185	**antiquité** f [ɑ̃tikite]	**antiquity** Régulièrement, je lisais quelque chose au sujet d'une antiquité inestimable que quelqu'un trouvait dans son grenier. -Every once in a while I read about a priceless antique that someone found in their attic.
5186	**tournure** f [tuʁnyʁ]	**twist|turning** Les choses prirent soudain une mauvaise tournure. -Things took a sudden turn for the worse.
5187	**pollution** f [pɔlysjɔ̃]	**pollution** Industrialisation va souvent de pair avec pollution. -Industrialization often goes hand in hand with pollution.
5188	**imprimer** vb [ɛ̃pʁime]	**print|print out** Si vous cochez cette case, vous pouvez imprimer votre document en tant que prospectus. -Mark this option to print your document in brochure format.
5189	**dague** f [dag]	**dagger** Est-elle... Mère-grand, donne-moi ta dague. -Is she... granny, give me your dagger.

5190	**harcèlement**	**harassment|harassing**
	m	Elle a été sévèrement traumatisée par le harcèlement à l'école.
	[aʁsɛlmɑ̃]	-She's been severely traumatized by bullying at school.
5191	**trafiquant**	**trafficker**
	m	Dan a vendu de la drogue à un dangereux trafiquant de drogue.
	[tʁafikɑ̃]	-Dan sold drugs for a dangerous drug dealer.
5192	**favorable**	**favorable**
	adj	La situation actuelle semble claire et favorable.
	[favɔʁabl]	-The current situation appears to be clear and favourable.
5193	**parchemin**	**parchment|diploma**
	m	Le parchemin est de bonne qualité.
	[paʁʃəmɛ̃]	-Yes, parchment is of a fine quality.
5194	**violemment**	**violently**
	adv	On nous a violemment rappelé que la lutte contre le terrorisme nous concerne tous.
	[vjɔlamɑ̃]	-We have been violently reminded that combating terrorism is a matter for us all.
5195	**fouetter**	**whip|scourge**
	vb	À Singapour, une façon de punir les criminels est de les fouetter, ou de les frapper plusieurs fois avec une canne, sur le dos.
	[fwete]	-In Singapore, a way to punish criminals is to whip them, or hit them several strokes with a cane, on their backs.
5196	**stationnement**	**parking**
	m	J'ai moi-même payé des tas de fois des amendes pour stationnement interdit.
	[stasjɔnmɑ̃]	-I've paid parking fines a number of times myself.
5197	**surnaturel**	**supernatural; occult**
	adj; m	Il croit au surnaturel.
	[syʁnatyʁɛl]	-He believes in the supernatural.
5198	**malhonnête**	**dishonest**
	adj	C'est intolérablement malhonnête, particulièrement envers le peuple turc !
	[malɔnɛt]	-It is intolerably dishonest. It is particularly dishonest to the Turkish people.
5199	**manier**	**handle|use**
	vb	Deuxièmement, sachons manier les différentes carottes à notre disposition.
	[manje]	-Secondly, let us learn how to handle the various incentives available to us.
5200	**démence**	**dementia|madness**
	f	Je ne souffre pas de démence - j'en profite !
	[demɑ̃s]	-I don't suffer from insanity - I enjoy it!
5201	**vaudou**	**voodoo; voodoo**
	adj; m	Il s'agit sans équivoque de principes économiques qui tiennent du vaudou.
	[vodu]	-It is voodoo economics without question.
5202	**once**	**ounce**
	f	Dirigez chaque once de puissance sur le bouclier avant jusque là.
	[ɔ̃s]	-Channel every ounce of power to the forward shield until then.
5203	**Écosse**	**Scotland**
	f	La loi de 1995 sur les enfants (Écosse) définit les responsabilités et droits des parents en Écosse.
	[ekɔs]	-The Children (Scotland) Act 1995 defines parental responsibilities and rights in Scotland.
5204	**édifice**	**building|edifice**
	m	Le célèbre édifice, le Taj Mahal, est en Inde.
	[edifis]	-The famous building, the Taj Mahal, is in India.

5205	**plasma**		**plasma**
	m		Application notamment aux panneaux à plasma.
	[plasma]		-The invention particularly is applicable to plasma panels.
5206	**éventreur**		**ripper**
	m		Je me rappelle de votre affaire sur l'éventreur de Yorkshire.
	[evɑ̃tʁœʁ]		-I remember your stuff on the Yorkshire Ripper.
5207	**patin**		**skate**
	m		Il fait du patin.
	[patɛ̃]		-He is skating.
5208	**détournement**		**misappropriation**
	m		Le détournement des eaux a compromis tout cela.
	[detuʁnəmɑ̃]		-This has all been affected by the diversion of water.
5209	**observateur**		**observer; observant**
	m; adj		Tu es très observateur.
	[ɔpsɛʁvatœʁ]		-You're very observant.
5210	**axe**		**axis**
	m		La terre tourne sur son axe.
	[aks]		-The earth revolves on its axis.
5211	**pionnier**		**pioneer**
	m		C'est ce que nous appelons un pionnier.
	[pjɔnje]		-He is what we call a pioneer.
5212	**chiffon**		**cloth**
	m		Si la prise s'encrasse, essuyez-la avec un chiffon sec avant l'insertion.
	[ʃifɔ̃]		-If the plug gets dirty, wipe it off with a dry cloth before insertion.
5213	**générique**		**generic**
	adj		C'est une marque de générique rechargeable.
	[ʒeneʁik]		-It's a brand name for a generic refillable.
5214	**indiscret**		**indiscreet**
	adj		Il serait absolument indiscret de ma part d'en dire davantage.
	[ɛ̃diskʁɛ]		-It would be highly indiscreet of me to go any further.
5215	**démocratique**		**democratic**
	adj		Nous soutenons un Monténégro démocratique dans une Yougoslavie démocratique.
	[demɔkʁatik]		-We support a democratic Montenegro within a democratic Yugoslavia.
5216	**corporation**		**corporation**
	f		Le groupe ALM est une corporation.
	[kɔʁpɔʁasjɔ̃]		-Paul, The ALM Group is a corporation.
5217	**calmant**		**calming; tranquilizer**
	adj; m		Un grand nombre d'Afghanes utilisent l'opium comme médicament contre la douleur et comme calmant, y compris pour leurs enfants.
	[kalmɑ̃]		-Many Afghan women use opium as a painkiller and tranquilizer, including for their children.
5218	**déluge**		**downpour**
	m		J'ignore qui sont mes ancêtres. Nos papiers se sont perdus lors du Déluge.
	[delyʒ]		-I don't know who my ancestors are. Our papers got lost during the Flood.
5219	**douane**		**customs**
	f		Les services des douanes traitent plus de 100 millions de déclarations de douane.
	[dwan]		-The customs services deal with in excess of 100 million customs declarations.

5220	**gâter**		**spoil|pamper**
	vb		Il y a en revanche des familles riches qui gâtent leurs enfants et ont perdu toute autorité sur eux, les amenant ainsi à se compromettre dans la déviance sociale.
	[gate]		-On the other hand, some rich families indulge their children and have loose control of their children, thus driving their children to become involved in social evils.
5221	**désaccord**		**disagreement|odds**
	m		Le rapporteur invoque un "désaccord interne" pour expliquer cette situation.
	[dezakɔʁ]		-The rapporteur refers to 'internal disagreement' as the reason for this.
5222	**fourrière**		**pound**
	f		Des millions pour quelque chose qu'on donne gratuitement dans chaque fourrière d'Amérique.
	[fuʁjɛʁ]		-Millions of dollars making something they're giving away for free in every pound in America.
5223	**cosmique**		**cosmic**
	adj		Valsecchi, de l'Institut de physique cosmique et d'astrophysique spatiale (Italie).
	[kɔsmik]		-Valsecchi (Cosmic Physics and Space Astrophysics Institute, Italy).
5224	**sterling**		**sterling**
	m		Je n'avais pas plus de 3 livres sterling.
	[stɛʁliŋ]		-I had no more than three pounds.
5225	**swing**		**swing|stomp**
	m		Il était trop près quand je lui ai balancé mon swing.
	[swiŋ]		-He got too close while I was swinging.
5226	**ramoner**		**sweep**
	vb		Parce qu'il faut un ramoneur pour ramoner la cheminée.
	[ʁamɔne]		-Because you need to be a chimney sweep to sweep a chimney.
5227	**improbable**		**unlikely**
	adj		Les responsables n'estimaient-ils pas improbable une telle catastrophe ?
	[ɛ̃pʁɔbabl]		-Did those responsible not consider such a disaster to be highly improbable?
5228	**accidentellement**		**accidentally**
	adv		Les personnes empoisonnées (accidentellement ou non) doivent consulter un médecin.
	[aksidɑ̃tɛlmɑ̃]		-Persons who have been poisoned (accidentally or otherwise) must consult a doctor.
5229	**envie**		**desire**
	f		Je ne pense pas que j'ai envie de répondre à plus de tes questions pour l'instant.
	[ɑ̃vi]		-I don't think I want to answer any more of your questions right now.
5230	**perquisition**		**search**
	f		Le détective Dan Anderson est retourné à la maison de Linda armé d'un mandat de perquisition.
	[pɛʁkizisjɔ̃]		-Detective Dan Anderson returned to Linda's house armed with a search warrant.
5231	**vigueur**		**vigor|strength**
	f		Il ne leur a pas été donné suite avec suffisamment de détermination ou de vigueur.
	[vigœʁ]		-They are not being pursued with sufficient determination or vigour.
5232	**mutinerie**		**mutiny**
	f		Au cours d'un incendie provoqué le 29 juillet 1999 par une mutinerie, il était
	[mytinʁi]		enfermé dans sa cellule et n'avait eu la vie sauve que parce que d'autres

prisonniers avaient enfoncé le toit.
-During a fire on 29 July 1999 caused by a prison riot, he was locked in his cell and only managed to save himself when other prisoners broke in through the roof.

5233	**subit**	**sudden**
	adj	D'où l'accord subit et si touchant sur ce règlement pathétique.
	[sybi]	-Hence the sudden, oh-so touching agreement on this pathetic regulation.
5234	**rêveur**	**dreamer; dreamy**
	m; adj	D'accord, mais Joseph, qui était un rêveur n'a pas rêvé du Pays promis.
	[ʁɛvœʁ]	-All right, but Joseph, who was a dreamer, did not dream about the Promised Land.
5235	**hystérie**	**hysteria**
	f	Tu nous entraînes dans ton hystérie.
	[isteʁi]	-Because you include the rest of us in your hysteria.
5236	**gouffre**	**gulf**
	m	Nous sommes au bord du gouffre.
	[gufʁ]	-We're on the border of failure.
5237	**huitième**	**eighth**
	num	À l'issue de la clôture de la trente-huitième session de la Commission.
	[ɥitjɛm]	-To be held following the closure of the thirty-eighth session of the Commission.
5238	**pantoufle**	**slipper**
	f	Généralement, dans votre pantoufle de Perse.
	[pɑ̃tufl]	-Well, as a rule, it's in the toe of your Persian slipper.
5239	**moineau**	**sparrow**
	m	Alors je détesterai être le moineau.
	[mwano]	-Then I'd hate to be the sparrow.
5240	**paume**	**palm**
	f[pom]	Je peux placer la paume des mains sur le sol sans plier les genoux. -I can place the palms of my hands on the floor without bending my knees.
5241	**collant**	**tights; adhesive**
	m; adj	Ce riz est collant.
	[kɔlɑ̃]	-This rice is sticky.
5242	**chêne**	**oak**
	m	Allons trouver ce chêne rouge austral.
	[ʃɛn]	-Let's go find that southern red oak.
5243	**capitalisme**	**capitalism**
	m	Le communisme s'étant effondré, le capitalisme est maintenant accusé de vouloir "dominer le monde".
	[kapitalism]	-As communism has collapsed, capitalism is now accused of trying to "dominate the world."
5244	**critère**	**criterion**
	m	On dit que les Américains considèrent le revenu d'un homme comme critère majeur de ses capacités.
	[kʁitɛʁ]	-Americans are said to regard the amount of money a man makes as a criterion of his ability.
5245	**sédatif**	**sedative; sedative**
	adj; m	L'infirmière vous a donné un sédatif.
	[sedatif]	-The nurse gave you a sedative.
5246	**Bing!**	**Zap!**

	int	Il a pris son arme... bing, bing !
	[biŋ!]	-He shot his gun... bing, bing!
5247	**surgir**	**arise|emerge**
	vb	Il examine les problèmes ou les difficultés qui peuvent surgir dans
	[syʁʒiʁ]	l'économie internationale du jute.
		-To consider problems or difficulties which may arise in the international
		jute economy.
5248	**murmure**	**murmur**
	m	On peut entendre le murmure de l'océan.
	[myʁmyʁ]	-You can hear the sound of the ocean.
5249	**avorter**	**abort**
	vb	Dans certaines régions du pays, les parents choisissent d'avorter si l'enfant
	[avɔʁte]	est une fille.
		-In some parts of the country parents are choosing to abort if the child is
		female.
5250	**citrouille**	**pumpkin**
	f	Il a mis au point un type de semence de citrouille très spécial, la Atlantic
	[sitʁuj]	Giant.
		-He developed a most special pumpkin seed, which he labelled the Atlantic
		Giant.
5251	**surnommer**	**nickname**
	vb	Il a ajouté que la cassette avait été remise à Al-Jazira par une femme
	[syʁnɔme]	surnommée « Oum Alaa ».
		-He also stated that the tape had been given to Al-Jazeera by a woman with
		the nickname "Um Alaa".
5252	**stupidité**	**stupidity**
	f[stypidite]	La stupidité de la comptabilité électorale a injustement pénalisé mes
		fermiers. -My Euro-seat accounts stupidity has unduly penalised my farmers.
5253	**remédier**	**remedy**
	vb	Nous allons bientôt discuter de la manière dont nous pouvons remédier à
	[ʁəmedje]	cette situation.
		-We will soon be discussing how we can remedy this situation.
5254	**décret**	**decree|ordinance**
	m	Il est bien vrai que celui qui rend à chacun le sien par crainte du gibet agit
	[dekʁɛ]	par le commandement d'autrui et est contraint par le mal qu'il redoute ; on ne
		peut pas dire qu'il soit juste : mais celui qui rend à chacun le sien parce qu'il
		connaît la vraie raison des lois et leur nécessité agit en constant accord avec
		lui-même et par son propre décret, non par le décret d'autrui ; il mérite donc
		d'être appelé juste.
		-In truth, a man who renders everyone their due because he fears the
		gallows, acts under the sway and compulsion of others, and cannot be called
		just. But a man who does the same from a knowledge of the true reason for
		laws and their necessity, acts from a firm purpose and of his own accord,
		and is therefore properly called just.
5255	**sable**	**sand|grittiness**
	m	La loi sur l'extraction du sable, qui concerne la réglementation des carrières
	[sabl]	de sable.
		-The Removal of Sand Act concerning the regulation of sand quarries.
5256	**dicton**	**diction**
	m	J'adhère entièrement au fameux dicton de Talleyrand : "surtout pas trop de
	[diktɔ̃]	zèle".
		-I find myself signed up enthusiastically to the famous dictum of Talleyrand
		'surtout pas trop de zèle'.

5257	**castor**	**beaver|beaver rat**
	m	Il est intéressant de connaître l'historique du castor au sein des forces armées.
	[kastɔʁ]	-It is interesting to follow the history of the beaver within the Armed Forces.

5258	**forfait**	**package**
	m	Et on a bénéficié du forfait Argent.
	[fɔʁfɛ]	-And we did get the Silver Package.

5259	**lentille**	**lens**
	f	Elle employa une lentille grossissante.
	[lɑ̃tij]	-She used a zoom lens.

5260	**martien**	**martian**
	adj	Projet Mars Express dans le cadre duquel la Pologne contribue à l'étude de l'environnement martien et des propriétés de la poussière martienne.
	[maʁsjɛ̃]	-In the Mars Express project, Poland is contributing to the study of the Mars environment and Martian dust properties.

5261	**escalader**	**climb**
	vb	Il y a une escalade du conflit armé et le trafic de drogue demeure intense.
	[ɛskalade]	-The armed conflict is escalating and drug-trafficking is continuing on a large scale.

5262	**entrepreneur**	**entrepreneur|contractor**
	m[ɑ̃tʁəpʁənœʁ]	La société, dirigée par un entrepreneur omanais, est immatriculée aux îles Caïmanes. -The company, directed by an Omani entrepreneur, is registered in the Cayman Islands.

5263	**remerciement**	**thanks|appreciation**
	m	J'aurai un message de remerciement encore plus vif à adresser à ce Parlement.
	[ʁəmɛʁsimɑ̃]	-An even more heartfelt message of thanks is offered to this Parliament.

5264	**célébration**	**celebration**
	f	Les femmes se rendirent à la célébration, tirées à quatre épingles.
	[selebʁasjɔ̃]	-The women went to the celebration dressed to the nines.

5265	**hibou**	**owl**
	m	Protéger un hibou sans protéger la zone qui lui fournit sa nourriture et son lieu de nidification ne sert à rien.
	[ibu]	-To protect an owl without also protecting the area that provides it with food and nesting material will not do.

5266	**interruption**	**interruption**
	f	La discussion fut reprise après une courte interruption.
	[ɛ̃teʁypsjɔ̃]	-Discussion resumed after a short interruption.

5267	**rayure**	**stripe**
	f	Et soudain, je remarque une petite rayure sur le vernis.
	[ʁejyʁ]	-And all of a sudden I noticed a tiniest scratch on the finish.

5268	**inauguration**	**inauguration**
	f	À la cérémonie d'inauguration, une plaque fut inaugurée en l'honneur du fondateur.
	[inogyʁasjɔ̃]	-At the inauguration ceremony a plaque was unveiled in honor of the founder.

5269	**démanger**	**itch**
	vb	Ça me démange, maintenant !
	[demɑ̃ʒe]	-This place is making me itch.

| 5270 | **agresseur** | **aggressor; assailant** |

	m; adj	La conciliation rend l'agresseur plus agressif.
	[agʁɛsœʁ]	-Appeasement only makes the aggressor more aggressive.
5271	**mention**	**mention**
	f	Nous épluchâmes les archives de police concernant cet incident mais nous ne trouvâmes aucune mention de témoins ayant vu un grand barbu.
	[mɑ̃sjɔ̃]	-We combed police records of the incident but found no mention of witnesses seeing a tall, bearded man.
5272	**anxiété**	**anxiety**
	f	Il a des problèmes d'anxiété.
	[ɑ̃ksjete]	-He has anxiety issues.
5273	**abriter**	**shelter**
	vb	On a démoli une station-service près de chez moi pour construire un nouvel immeuble qui a d'abord abrité un magasin Beckers.
	[abʁite]	-One nearby gas station was torn down and a new building was put up, which became Beckers.
5274	**boussole**	**compass; compass**
	adj; f	Mon pays a grandement besoin d'une nouvelle boussole morale à cet égard.
	[busɔl]	-My country is badly in need of a new moral compass on this issue.
5275	**affilé**	**sharp**
	adj	Une fois la peur passée, ils vous lacèrent avec des langues affilées, alors qu'ils sont chiches à faire le bien.
	[afile]	-But once (the battle subsides and) fear departs, they assail you with sharp tongues, being avaricious for (a share in) the goods thereof (the gainings of victory).
5276	**distraction**	**distraction|entertainment**
	f	Ils verront dans ce genre d'initiative de la Commission une sorte de distraction.
	[distʁaksjɔ̃]	-They will see this kind of initiative by the Commission as a distraction.
5277	**brutalité**	**brutality**
	f	Un passant a filmé la brutalité policière à l'aide de son téléphone portable.
	[bʁytalite]	-A bystander videotaped the police beating using their cell phone.
5278	**exclusivité**	**exclusiveness**
	f	Quelqu'un a évoqué la situation en Amérique, où les périodes d'exclusivité sont plus courtes.
	[ɛksklyzivite]	-Somebody referred to the situation in America where exclusivity periods are shorter.
5279	**joyau**	**jewel**
	m	Banff est le premier joyau créé en 1885.
	[ʒwajo]	-Banff, the original jewel, was established in 1885.
5280	**rigolade**	**fun|joke**
	f	On aurait évité toute cette rigolade.
	[ʁigɔlad]	-We wouldn't have had to go through all the fun.
5281	**supplément**	**supplement**
	m	C'est un supplément.
	[syplemɑ̃]	-That's extra.
5282	**viole**	**viol**
	f	Il est vrai que l'introduction de nouveaux éléments pourrait violer le consensus.
	[vjɔl]	-It is true that the introduction of new elements could violate the consensus.
5283	**gel**	**gel|freezing**

m	Le gel occasionna beaucoup de dommages aux récoltes.
[ʒɛl]	-The frost did a lot of damage to the crops.

5284 simulation — **simulation**

f

[simylasjɔ̃]

Il faut attendre que les résidus aient convergé avant de pouvoir exploiter les résultats de la simulation.
-One must wait for the residuals to converge before being able to use the simulation's results.

5285 prédateur — **predator; predatory**

m; adj

[pʁedatœʁ]

L'appelant était un prédateur multirécidiviste.
-The appellant was a persistent predator.

5286 funèbre — **funeral**

adj

[fynɛbʁ]

Le vêtement funèbre est la dernière étape de leur purification.
-The funeral shroud is the final step in the ritual of self-purification.

5287 grincheux — **grumpy; grumbler**

adj; m

[gʁɛ̃ʃø]

Pourquoi a-t-il l'air grincheux ?
-Why does he look grumpy?

5288 bombarder — **bomb|bombard**

vb

[bɔ̃baʁde]

L'armée de l'air russe a bombardé Chkhalta, le centre administratif de l'Abkhazie.
-The Russian air force has bombarded Chkhalta, the administrative centre of Abkhazia.

5289 coussin — **cushion**

m

[kusɛ̃]

Merde, mon coussin en épeautre germe.
-Damn, my wheat pillow is sprouting.

5290 émouvoir — **move|stir**

vb

[emuvwaʁ]

C'est une chose qui ne peut manquer d'émouvoir, où que l'on se trouve dans le monde.
-That is something that cannot fail to move anyone, wherever in the world they may be.

5291 reconduire — **renew**

vb

[ʁəkɔ̃dɥiʁ]

Nous voudrions reconduire, pour trois ans, l'accord passé avec les Îles Salomon.
-We are currently aiming to renew the FPA with the Solomon Islands for another three years.

5292 boyau — **casing**

m

[bwajo]

L'invention concerne aussi un procédé de production d'un boyau alimentaire.
-It is also object of the invention to provide a process for producing a food casing.

5293 publiquement — **publicly**

adv

[pyblikmɑ̃]

Les décisions des tribunaux disciplinaires sont toujours prononcées publiquement.
-Judgments passed by disciplinary courts are always announced publicly.

5294 croisement — **crossing**

m

[kʁwazmɑ̃]

Il existe assurément des possibilités de croisement des compétences et de renforcement mutuel entre les deux dossiers.
-Useful cross-fertilisation and mutual reinforcement do certainly exist between the two files.

5295 Madone — **Madonna**

f

[madɔn]

Quand l'église de la Madone s'est écroulée.
-When the church of the Madonna collapsed.

5296 haler — **tow**

	vb	Le plan de montage consistait à haler l'extrémité supérieure par tracteur sur une distance de quelque 3,000 pieds, et au moyen d'un câble de halage relié à un treuil installé au sommet, pour les 10,000 pieds restants.
	[ale]	-The erection plan was to haul up the high end some 3,000 feet by means of a tractor and pull up the remaining 10,000 feet by means of a hauling cable attached to a winch to be installed at the top.
5297	**relativement**	**relatively**
	adv	C'est la décision qu'a prise un pays relativement petit et relativement riche.
	[ʁəlativmɑ̃]	-It is a relatively small and a relatively wealthy country.
5298	**tribune**	**gallery**
	f	Cette importante tribune possède un secrétariat permanent.
	[tʁibyn]	-There is a permanent secretariat for that important forum.
5299	**parquet**	**parquet**
	m	Les lames du parquet grincent un peu lorsqu'on marche dessus.
	[paʁkɛ]	-The floorboards creak a bit when you walk across them.
5300	**intimider**	**intimidate|frighten**
	vb	Si le but principal était d'intimider, l'effet produit était en réalité l'inverse.
	[ɛ̃timide]	-If the main objective was to intimidate, the effect actually achieved was the opposite.
5301	**carabine**	**carbine**
	f	Martineau avait le pistolet à air comprimé et Tremblay la carabine.
	[kaʁabin]	-Martineau had the pellet pistol and Tremblay had the rifle.
5302	**choquant**	**shocking**
	adj	Ce qui s'est passé en Hongrie avec le programme LEADER est tout à fait choquant.
	[ʃɔkɑ̃]	-What has happened in Hungary concerning the LEADER programme is quite shocking.
5303	**viking**	**viking**
	m	Autant que je sache, le Viking ne s'est pas vu refuser l'accès à un port de refuge.
	[vikiŋ]	-As far as I know, the Viking was not denied access to a port of refuge.
5304	**boulet**	**ball|drag**
	m	Quel boulet !
	[bulɛ]	-What a drag!
5305	**démocrate**	**democrat; democratic**
	m/f; adj	Monsieur Poettering, quelle est la différence entre un démocrate chrétien et un démocrate européen?
	[demɔkʁat]	-Mr Poettering, what is the difference between a Christian Democrat and a European Democrat?
5306	**tempérament**	**temperament|temper**
	m	Jack essayait de contrôler son propre tempérament violent.
	[tɑ̃peʁamɑ̃]	-Jack was trying to control his own violent temper.
5307	**expulsion**	**expulsion|deportation**
	f	L'expulsion proprement dite doit être précédée d'un arrêté d'expulsion.
	[ɛkspylsjɔ̃]	-Prior to the actual deportation as described above, there should be an order for deportation.
5308	**obéissance**	**obedience**
	f	L'obéissance de tous à des règles, même absurdes, assure à la société une cohésion plus grande.
	[ɔbeisɑ̃s]	-The obedience of everyone to rules, even absurd ones, promotes a greater cohesion within society.
5309	**technicien**	**technician**

m
[tɛknisjɛ̃]

On demanda au technicien de fabriquer une boîte imperméable à la lumière.
-The tech was asked to make a light-tight box.

5310 **maternité** **maternity**

f

[matɛʁnite]

Le congé maternité est une indemnité disponible dans la plupart des pays, à l'exception des États-Unis d'Amérique.
-Paid maternity leave is a benefit available in almost all countries, except the United States.

5311 **superstition** **superstition**

f

[sypɛʁstisjõ]

Mais ce courant de pensée est proche de la superstition pure et simple.
-But this school of thought is bordering on outright superstition.

5312 **illustre** **illustrious|illustrated**

adj

[ilystʁ]

C'est ce qu'illustre la situation aux États-Unis.
-We had this illustrated in the United States.

5313 **battement** **beat|beating**

m

[batmã]

Et comme nous le savons aujourd'hui, un battement d'ailes de papillon à Strasbourg peut parfois provoquer un séisme à plusieurs milliers de kilomètres.
-As we now know, the beating of a butterfly's wings in Strasbourg may sometimes unleash a hurricane thousands of miles away.

5314 **popularité** **popularity**

f

[pɔpylaʁite]

Il mérite sa popularité.
-He is deservedly popular.

5315 **magistrat** **magistrate**

m

[maʒistʁa]

Le magistrat sera là dans quelques jours.
-The magistrate will be here in a few days.

5316 **radeau** **raft**

m

[ʁado]

Les garçons ont construit un radeau.
-The boys built a raft.

5317 **dépendance** **dependence|outbuilding**

f

[depãdãs]

La dépendance énergétique du Maroc reste très élevée.
-Morocco still has a very high level of energy dependence.

5318 **ouïr** **hear**

vb

[wiʁ]

Les yeux ne peuvent le voir et les oreilles, l'ouïr.
-What Tao is, the eyes cannot see and the ears cannot hear.

5319 **fleuriste** **florist**

m

[flœʁist]

Le sénateur Lynch-Staunton: Qui est le fleuriste ?
-Senator Lynch-Staunton: Who is the florist?

5320 **lucide** **lucid|rational**

adj

[lysid]

Mais après le constat lucide, doivent venir le projet et la stratégie.
-But after the lucid statement must come the project and the strategy.

5321 **mosquée** **mosque**

f

[mɔske]

Un dispensaire, le cimetière de la ville et une mosquée ont également subi des dommages.
-A health clinic was also damaged as was the cemetery of the town and a mosque.

5322 **casque** **helmet**

m

[kask]

J'ai même réussi à comprendre votre dernière demande de nous en tenir à notre temps de parole sans me servir du casque.
-I was even able to understand your last request to keep to our speaking time without using headphones.

5323 **fragment** **fragment|piece**

	m		McVeigh a inclus ce fragment dans son analyse.
	[fʁagmã]		-McVeigh included this nine millimeter shell fragment in his analysis.

5324 sonar — sonar

m

[sɔnaʁ]

Le sonar a détecté un sous-marin russe dans les environs.
-Sonar picked up a Russian sub nosing around.

5325 piocher — pickax

vb

[pjɔʃe]

J'essaye juste d'en piocher un.
-I'm not. I'm just trying to pick one.

5326 caniveau — gutter

m[kanivo]

Ils vidèrent des bouteilles de vin de Bordeaux dans le caniveau devant les caméras de télévision, en criant des slogans contre la France qui refusait la guerre en Iraq. -Before TV cameras, they emptied bottles of Bordeaux wine into the gutter - crying out slogans against the France that had rejected the war in Iraq.

5327 mourant — dying

adj

[muʁã]

Je comprends que toute personne mourant d'une insuffisance rénale soit désespérée.
-I appreciate that anyone dying of kidney failure will be desperate.

5328 astucieux — clever | astute

adj

[astysjø]

Il restait sept minutes au très astucieux et érudit député d'Ottawa-Vanier.
-The astute and erudite hon. member for Ottawa-Vanier had seven minutes remaining.

5329 vil — vile | base

adj

[vil]

Et ils le vendirent à vil prix: pour quelques dirhams comptés. Ils le considéraient comme indésirable.
-And they sold him for a paltry price – a few silver coins – so little did they value him.

5330 paf — high; bam!

adj; int

[paf]

Alors, vice-présidente, président... paf.
-So, vice president, president... bam.

5331 agrandir — enlarge | extend

vb

[agʁãdiʁ]

Cette fenêtre d' aperçu vous permet de réduire et d' agrandir l' affichage.
-The preview allows you to enlarge or reduce the view using the mouse.

5332 nouveauté — novelty

f

[nuvote]

Cette nouveauté devrait accélérer la procédure.
-This novelty is expected to make the proceedings more expedient.

5333 éclipser — eclipse | outshine

vb

[eklipse]

Nous ne devons pas laisser ces vues extrêmes éclipser celles de la majorité.
-We must not allow these extreme views to overshadow those of the majority and the mainstream.

5334 décennie — decade

f

[deseni]

Cette décennie a été exceptionnelle dans l'histoire des télécommunications.
-By any measure, this decade has been a remarkable one in the history of telecommunications.

5335 hilarant — hilarious

adj

[ilaʁã]

Il est tout simplement hilarant de parler d'un manque de préparation à nos frontières orientales lorsque l'on voit la perméabilité de nos frontières méridionales.
-To speak about a lack of preparation at our eastern borders when seeing the permeability of our southern borders is simply hilarious.

5336 baril — barrel | crater

	m	Le prix du baril de pétrole a dépassé la barre psychologique des 50 dollars.
	[baʁil]	-The price of a barrel of oil has exceeded the psychological barrier of USD 50.
5337	**littéraire**	**literary**
	adj	Le droit à la protection scientifique littéraire ou artistique.
	[liteʁɛʁ]	-The right to protection of scientific, literary and artistic production.
5338	**renvoi**	**return|reference**
	m[ʁɑ̃vwa]	Un renvoi au site Internet pertinent suffit. -A reference to the relevant website should be sufficient.
5339	**brandir**	**brandish**
	vb	Depuis le 1er mars 2000, il est interdit de brandir ou de montrer une arme en public.
	[bʁɑ̃diʁ]	-On 1 March 2000, a ban was imposed on brandishing/display of weapons in public.
5340	**cartel**	**cartel|coalition**
	m	Je comprends le fonctionnement du cartel.
	[kaʁtɛl]	-I understand how the cartel is running now.
5341	**couché**	**lying down; abed**
	adj; adv	Il a été dit que nul ne laisse d'empreinte dans le sable en restant couché.
	[kuʃe]	-It has been said that no one leaves footprints in the sands of time by lying down.
5342	**lacet**	**shoelace**
	m	En passant devant un immeuble résidentiel habité par des Albanais, le défunt Aleksandar s'arrêta un instant pour nouer les lacets de ses chaussures.
	[lasɛ]	-While passing alongside a block of flats inhabited by Albanians, the late Aleksandar stopped for a moment to tie lace on his tennis shoes.
5343	**ingénieux**	**ingenious**
	adj	Tout cela est plutôt ingénieux, mais bien trop transparent pour que vous puissiez réussir.
	[ɛ̃ʒenjø]	-That is all rather ingenious, but much too transparent for you to be able to succeed in this.
5344	**financement**	**funding**
	m	Nous avons perdu tout notre financement.
	[finɑ̃smɑ̃]	-We lost all of our funding.
5345	**compenser**	**compensate|offset**
	vb	Il a donc ajusté la somme demandée pour compenser ce risque de surestimation.
	[kɔ̃pɑ̃se]	-The Panel has therefore adjusted the claim to offset such risk of overstatement.
5346	**difficilement**	**with difficulty**
	adv	Le sénateur Prud'homme aurait difficilement pu éviter l'engagement politique.
	[difisilmɑ̃]	-It would have been hard for Senator Prud'homme to avoid a life of politics.
5347	**distinction**	**distinction**
	f	Le problème cité n'en est pas un, mais il y en a dans la partie lecture qui vous demandent de faire la distinction entre pronoms relatifs et adverbes relatifs.
	[distɛ̃ksjɔ̃]	-The problem quoted isn't one, but there are problems in the reading section that ask you to distinguish relative pronouns from relative adverbs.
5348	**entourage**	**entourage**
	m	Elle l'a trouvé difficile de s'adapter à son nouvel entourage.
	[ɑ̃tuʁaʒ]	-She found it difficult to adapt herself to her new entourage.

5349	**consolation**	**consolation|comforting**
	f[kɔ̃sɔlasjɔ̃]	Le leader du gouvernement ne peut-elle offrir aucun réconfort, aucune consolation ? -Is there any comfort or solace that the Leader of the Government can offer?
5350	**diffuser**	**broadcast|spread**
	vb [difyze]	Et ils étaient si terriblement inquiets qu'ils voulaient diffuser cette information sur-le-champ. -And it was this tremendous concern that caused them to circulate the information immediately.
5351	**truand**	**hoodlum**
	m [tʁyɑ̃]	Peut-être que la sauce truand contient des morceaux de gangsters morts. -For all we know, the mobster sauce contains actual chunks of deceased mobsters.
5352	**contribuer**	**contribute**
	vb [kɔ̃tʁibɥe]	La Bulgarie est convaincue que les soldats de la paix peuvent contribuer au travail de prévention. -Bulgaria is convinced that peacekeepers can contribute to the work of prevention.
5353	**vétéran**	**veteran; old**
	m; adj [veteʁɑ̃]	Mon oncle est vétéran de la guerre du Viêtnam. -My uncle is a veteran of the Vietnam War.
5354	**amnésie**	**amnesia**
	f [amnezi]	Amnésie signifie « perte de mémoire ». -Amnesia means "loss of memory".
5355	**vacarme**	**racket|noise**
	m [vakaʁm]	Ne fais donc pas un tel vacarme ! -Don't make such a racket!
5356	**annulation**	**cancellation|annulment**
	f [anylasjɔ̃]	In the case in question, the courts cannot annul the disputed decision. -Or, dans le cas d'espèce, le juge judiciaire ne peut annuler l'acte attaqué.
5357	**avatar**	**avatar**
	m [avataʁ]	L'Américain James Cameron a dépensé pour son film "Avatar" l'équivalent du programme "Culture" de l'Union européenne pour la période 2007-2013. -The American film maker James Cameron spent on his film 'Avatar' the equivalent of the European Union's 'culture' programme for the 2007-2013 period.
5358	**mercenaire**	**mercenary; mercenary**
	adj; m [mɛʁsənɛʁ]	La définition de mercenaire en droit international est hautement problématique. -As such, the definition of mercenary in international law is highly problematic.
5359	**constance**	**constancy**
	f [kɔ̃stɑ̃s]	La question de la constance réelle, de la constance budgétaire exigera un compromis. -We will have to reach a compromise on the question of real constancy, budgetary constancy.
5360	**tonneau**	**barrel|ton**
	m [tɔno]	Son estomac assoiffé d'alcool semble sans fond comme le tonneau des Danaïdes. -His stomach, thirsty for alcohol, seemed bottomless, like the Danaids' barrel.
5361	**tendrement**	**tenderly|fondly**

adv
[tãdʁəmã]
Voici pourquoi aujourd'hui Notre-Dame tendrement a fait valoir que ce grand et beau vénération de Sa Heart.
-Here is why today Our Lady has tenderly claimed this great and wonderful veneration of Her Heart.

5362 **assurément**　　**certainly**

adv
[asyʁemã]
Cela étant, les résultats passés ne garantissent assurément pas les résultats futurs.
-Past performance is assuredly no guarantee of future results, however.

5363 **vinaigrer**　　**souse**

vb
[vinegʁe]
Ça fait beaucoup de vinaigre balsamique.
-That is a lot of balsamic vinegar.

5364 **pancarte**　　**placard**

f
[pãkaʁt]
Beaucoup de gens défilaient avec la photo du leader disparu affichée sur une pancarte.
-Many waved placards bearing a picture of the lost leader.

5365 **suture**　　**suture**

f
[sytyʁ]
Sami a reçu vingt points de suture.
-Sami was given twenty stitches.

5366 **voyant**　　**seer; clairvoyant**

m; adj
[vwajã]
J'ai ri aux éclats en le voyant.
-I burst out laughing when I saw him.

5367 **boiteux**　　**lame|limping; lame person**

adj; m/f
[bwatø]
Le ministère a lui-même déclaré que ce processus était boiteux.
-The department itself referred to it as a process that was flawed.

5368 **pie**　　**magpie**

f
[pi]
On dirait une pie qui construit son nid.
-You're like a magpie building a nest.

5369 **orgue**　　**organ**

m
[ɔʁg]
L'orgue se mit à jouer.
-The organ started to play.

5370 **sifflement**　　**whistling|hiss**

m
[sifləmã]
Nous fûmes éveillés, au point du jour, par le sifflement d'un train.
-We were roused at daybreak by the whistle of a train.

5371 **damner**　　**damn**

vb
[dane]
Comme dans une tragédie grecque, le sauveur est également le damné.
-As in a Greek tragedy, the saviour is also the damned.

5372 **piètre**　　**poor|mediocre**

adj
[pjɛtʁ]
Ils reçoivent une piètre compensation destinée à étouffer leur opposition et leurs protestations.
-They receive paltry compensation which is intended to stifle their opposition and protests.

5373 **réconcilier**　　**reconcile**

vb
[ʁekɔ̃silje]
Il est difficile de reconcilier cela avec les besoins d'un système de gestion efficace.
-This is difficult to reconcile with the needs of an effective management system.

5374 **hurlement**　　**howl|yell**

m
[yʁləmã]
Pourquoi ces hurlements hystériques ?
-Why all this howling, hysterical sorrow?

5375 **étagère**　　**shelf**

| | f | | La nacelle métallique doit être en contact direct avec l'étagère métallique de l'étuve. |
| | [etaʒɛʁ] | | -The metal container must be in direct contact with the metal shelf of the drying oven. |

5376 **exploration** — **exploration**
f
[ɛksplɔʁasjɔ̃]
Est-il nécessaire d'élargir la connaissance de l'Homme à travers l'exploration de l'espace ?
-Is it necessary to expand human knowledge with space exploration?

5377 **espérance** — **hope|expectation**
f
[ɛspeʁɑ̃s]
Une espérance de paix, une espérance de fraternité, une espérance de progrès.
-Hope for peace, hope for fraternity, hope for progress.

5378 **escouade** — **squad**
f
[ɛskwad]
Bien. Je vais moi-même mener une escouade terrestre au réacteur.
-Very well. I'll lead a ground squad to the reactor myself.

5379 **cachot** — **dungeon**
m
[kaʃo]
Il a en outre visité la prison centrale et le cachot du commissariat de police.
-He also visited the central prison and the holding cell at the police station.

5380 **charpentier** — **carpenter**
m
[ʃaʁpɑ̃tje]
Il est bon charpentier.
-He is a good carpenter.

5381 **bikini** — **bikini**
m
[bikini]
Je veux pas mouiller mon bikini.
-I don't want to get my bikini wet.

5382 **utérus** — **uterus**
m
[yteʁys]
Quand j'étais dans l'utérus de ma mère, je regardai à travers le nombril de ma mère la maison dans laquelle j'allais naître, et pensai : « Jamais je n'irai là-bas. »
-When I was inside my mother's womb, I looked through my mother's navel at the house where I would be born and I thought: "No way I'm going there".

5383 **logiciel** — **software**
m
[lɔʒisjɛl]
De quelle sorte de logiciel se sert Jack habituellement ?
-What kind of software does Jack usually use?

5384 **geisha** — **geisha**
f
[ʒiza]
Voici Kobana, notre troisième grande geisha.
-This here is Kobana, our third great geisha.

5385 **argile** — **clay**
f
[aʁʒil]
Jack a façonné l'argile et en a fait un vase.
-Jack worked the clay into a vase.

5386 **clarté** — **clarity|lightness**
f
[klaʁte]
Je me sentis nu dans un monde étrange. Je ressentis peut-être ce qu'un oiseau peut ressentir dans la clarté de l'air, sachant que le faucon bat des ailes au-dessus et va plonger.
-I felt naked in a strange world. I felt as perhaps a bird may feel in the clear air, knowing the hawk wings above and will swoop.

5387 **ogre** — **ogre**
m[ɔgʁ]
Jemaine, on dirait un ogre travaillant dans une bibliothèque. -Jemaine, they say an ogre works in the library.

5388 **chouchou** — **pet**
m
[ʃuʃu]
Je ne voulais pas être son chouchou.
-I didn't want to be her pet.

5389	**gland**	**glans**
	m	L'écureuil enfila son casque de gland.
	[glɑ̃]	-The squirrel put his acorn helmet on.
5390	**redonner**	**restore|give back**
	vb	« On devrait pouvoir juste faire le service communautaire et redonner quelque chose à la collectivité.
	[ʁədɔne]	-"We shoud be able to just do community service and give back to the community."
5391	**pétition**	**petition**
	f	Ils sont à l'origine de la pétition, la plus importante jamais rassemblée en Europe.
	[petisjɔ̃]	-They initiated the petition, which is the largest petition ever raised in Europe.
5392	**coiffer**	**style**
	vb	Le mouvement du Crédit Social était alors actif et pouvait encore coiffer le NPD aux urnes.
	[kwafe]	-This was a time when the Social Credit movement was active and could still out-perform the NDP at the polls.
5393	**délinquant**	**offender; delinquent**
	m; adj	Il faut envoyer ce message au délinquant.
	[delɛ̃kɑ̃]	-That message has to be sent to the offender.
5394	**emballage**	**packing|wrap**
	m	L'emballage alimentaire réduit la détérioration de la nourriture.
	[ɑ̃balaʒ]	-Food packaging reduces spoilage.
5395	**merlin**	**marlin|poleaxe**
	m	L'utilisation du merlin, de la masse et de la puntilla est interdite par la Convention.
	[mɛʁlɛ̃]	-The use of a pole-axe, hammer or puntilla is prohibited by the Convention.
5396	**crécher**	**chum**
	vb	Il est organisé des services de crèche et de garderie pour les parents qui travaillent en milieu urbain.
	[kʁeʃe]	-Day-care centre services are provided to working parents living in urban communities.
5397	**migraine**	**migraine**
	f	Pas étonnant que tu aies la migraine, avec ce que tu as bu hier soir.
	[migʁɛn]	-No wonder you've got a headache; the amount you drank last night.
5398	**dictature**	**dictatorship**
	f	La dictature du marché unique débouche inéluctablement sur la dictature d'une réglementation unique.
	[diktatyʁ]	-The dictatorship of the single market inevitably results in the dictatorship of a single regulation.
5399	**caprice**	**fancy**
	m	Imagine-la calcinée, pour mon caprice.
	[kapʁis]	-Picture it reduced to ash at my whim.
5400	**cirer**	**wax**
	vb	Je leur avais dit de ne pas le cirer.
	[siʁe]	-I thought I told them not to wax this.
5401	**impardonnable**	**unforgivable**
	adj	Ce serait un retournement de situation impardonnable qui nous couvrirait tous d'opprobre.
	[ɛ̃paʁdɔnabl]	-That would be an unforgivable reversal and bring shame on all of us.
5402	**renverse**	**inverse**

f

[ʁɑ̃vɛʁs]

Nous avons donc renversé la charge de la preuve.
-So we have shifted the burden of proof.

5403 **salement** **dirtily**

adv

[salmɑ̃]

Tu dois vouloir "jouer salement".
-You have to be willing to play dirty.

5404 **croître** **grow**

vb

[kʁwatʁ]

Au-delà de cette partie centrale, la largeur de l'éprouvette doit croître progressivement.
-Beyond this central part the width of the test-piece must increase progressively.

5405 **bouseux** **hick**

adj

[buzø]

Pour moi, "bouseux" signifie une splendide absence de classe.
-For the record, my definition of "redneck": a glorious absence of sophistication.

5406 **tolérance** **tolerance**

f

[tɔleʁɑ̃s]

La tolérance à l'égard d'ambiguïtés est nécessaire à l'apprentissage d'une langue.
-The tolerance of ambiguities is necessary in learning a language.

5407 **extraction** **extraction**

f

[ɛkstʁaksjɔ̃]

Y aurait-il une autre solution que l'extraction ?
-Is there any other way besides extraction?

5408 **zodiaque** **zodiac**

m

[zɔdjak]

Chacun est nommé par un signe du zodiaque.
-Each was known only by a sign of the zodiac.

5409 **expansion** **expansion**

f

[ɛkspɑ̃sjɔ̃]

L'expansion de l'univers s'accélère.
-The expansion of the universe is speeding up.

5410 **artère** **artery**

f

[aʁtɛʁ]

Heureusement, la morsure de requin n'a pas touché d'artère majeure.
-Fortunately, the shark bite didn't hit any major arteries.

5411 **hobby** **hobby**

m

[ɔbi]

The political hobby of the eurocrats may well cost money but it will leave us empty-handed.
-Le hobby politique des eurocrates peut bien coûter de l'argent, mais il ne nous apportera rien.

5412 **affreusement** **frightfully**

adv

[afʁøzmɑ̃]

Ces deux domaines - les normes comptables et Bâle II - sont affreusement compliqués.
-Both areas - the accounting standards and Basel II - are hideously complicated.

5413 **scrupule** **scruple|compunction**

m[skʁypyl]

Ils exploitent sans scrupule les enfants aussi bien que d'autres personnes. -They used children, as they used others, without scruple.

5414 **dynastie** **dynasty**

f

[dinasti]

La dynastie des Timurides s'est vite emparée du pouvoir.
-Power passed swiftly to the Timurid dynasty established by Tamerlane.

5415 **millénaire** **millennium|millennial; millenary**

m; adj

[milenɛʁ]

Les objectifs de développement du millénaire ont pour but de réduire la faim, la pauvreté et la maladie.
-The Milennium Development Goals aim to reduce hunger, poverty and disease.

5416	**pieux**	**pious|devout**
	adj	Concernant l'emploi, nous avons entendu des voeux pieux et de belles
	[pjø]	paroles.
		-On employment we have heard pious words, pious words and pious words.

5417	**ravitaillement**	**refueling**
	m	Le bateau de ravitaillement est notre seule chance.
	[ʁavitajmã]	-The supply ship was our only chance.

5418	**narrateur**	**narrator**
	m	Et le lendemain, votre ami et humble narrateur... était un homme libre.
	[naʁatœʁ]	-And the very next day, your friend and humble narrator...... was a free man.

5419	**galop**	**gallop**
	m	Le cheval traversait les champs au galop.
	[galo]	-The horse ran through the fields.

5420	**boucan**	**racket|din**
	m	Selon le dictionnaire officiel du néerlandais, le bruit est: un son dur et
	[bukã]	désagréable, notamment le tintamarre, le tapage, le chambard, le vacarme et
		le boucan.
		-According to the Dutch official dictionary, noise is defined as a harsh,
		unpleasant sound, including background noise, din, racket, roar and
		commotion.

5421	**éduquer**	**educate|teach**
	vb	Nous ne pouvons ignorer le fait qu'il nous faut éduquer nos enfants, surtout
	[edyke]	les filles.
		-We cannot ignore the need to educate our children, especially the girl child.

5422	**délégation**	**delegation**
	f	Ma délégation souhaite remercier l'Ambassadeur Levitte de son exposé
	[delegasjõ]	détaillé.
		-My delegation would also like to thank Ambassador Levitte for his
		comprehensive briefing.

5423	**candidature**	**application|candidacy**
	f	J'ai retiré ma candidature.
	[kãdidatyʁ]	-I withdrew my application.

5424	**subconscient**	**subconscious**
	adj	Elle symbolise peut-être quelque chose dans son subconscient profond.
	[sypkõsjã]	-Perhaps it symbolises something deep in her subconscious, as the
		psychiatrist believes.

5425	**sacoche**	**pannier**
	f[sakɔʃ]	Pédaler avec la sacoche, c'est comme transporter un éléphant. -Pedalling
		with the bag is like carrying an elephant on your back.

5426	**navigateur**	**navigator**
	m	La seule extension qui plante dans mon navigateur est Flash.
	[navigatœʁ]	-The only plug-in that crashes on my browser is Flash.

5427	**jogging**	**jogging**
	m	Après un jogging comme ça, on aime fumer une petite cigarette.
	[dʒɔgiŋ]	-After a jogging like this, we like to smoke a nice little cigarette.

5428	**médaillon**	**medallion**
	m	J'essayais de comprendre le médaillon.
	[medajõ]	-Look, I was just trying to figure out the medallion.

5429	**ardeur**	**ardor|heat; vehement**
	f; adj	Cela doit même intensifier notre ardeur pour la bonne application et
	[aʁdœʁ]	l'universalisation du Traité.

-It should even more reignite our fervour to contribute to the full implementation and universalization of that Convention.

5430	**sanctifier**		**sanctify**
	vb		Notre Père qui est au Ciel, que Ton nom soit sanctifié.
	[sɑ̃ktifje]		-Our Father, who art in heaven...... hallowed be Thy name.

5431	**guetter**		**await**
	vb		Le danger les guette sans relâche.
	[gete]		-Danger lurks around every corner.

5432 **crevé**   **flat|all in|tired**
adj
[kʁəve]
Soit on reste et on crève, soit on sort... et on crève !
-We either stay and snuff it or we all go -- and snuff it!

5433 **charlatan**   **charlatan|quack**
m
[ʃaʁlatɑ̃]
Quel charlatan !
-What a phony!

5434 **vertébral**   **vertebral**
adj
[vɛʁtebʁal]
Implant vertébral intersomatique composite facilitant la fusion de vertèbres adjacentes.
-A composite interbody vertebral implant for facilitating fusion of adjacent vertebrae.

5435 **lanterne**   **lantern**
vb
[lɑ̃tɛʁn]
Ces cheveux blonds luisent comme une lanterne.
-You know, that blond hair of yours stands out like a lantern.

5436 **ultra-**   **ultra-**
pfx
[yltʁa-]
C'est la caricature d'une Europe ultra libérale que je combats.
-It is the distortion of an ultra-liberal Europe that I am resisting.

5437 **hautement**   **highly**
adv
[otmɑ̃]
Le sujet de ce rapport est à la fois hautement spécifique et hautement complexe.
-The subject of this report is both highly specific and highly complex.

5438 **camer**   **dope**
vb
[kame]
Ses vrais parents doivent se camer.
-Besides, his birth parents are probably crackheads.

5439 **innombrable**   **innumerable**
adj[inɔ̃bʁabl]
D'innombrables conseillers ont apporté un soutien logistique à l'opposition ukrainienne. -Innumerable advisors have given logistical support to the opposition in Ukraine.

5440 **appelant**   **appellant; appellant**
adj; m
[aplɑ̃]
Tous les détenus peuvent appeler leur avocat au prix d'une communication ordinaire.
-All prisoners have the ability to call legal representatives at the standard call costs.

5441 **impensable**   **unthinkable**
adj
[ɛ̃pɑ̃sabl]
Un État constitutionnel est impensable sans système judiciaire indépendant.
-A constitutional state is unthinkable without an independent judicial system.

5442 **foule**   **crowd|host**
f
[ful]
En entrant dans le musée, ils auraient été bousculés par une foule en colère.
-As they entered the museum, they were reportedly jostled by an angry crowd.

5443 **gouvernail**   **rudder**

	m	Sans compter que le gouvernail est bloqué.
	[guvɛʁnaj]	-On top of that, the rudder's jammed.
5444	**guitariste**	**guitarist**
	m/f	Il vous faut un meilleur guitariste.
	[gitaʁist]	-Well, I think you guys need a better guitarist.
5445	**démonter**	**disassemble|dismantle**
	vb	À l'arrivée, on nous a entraînés pendant une semaine à tirer et à démonter des AK-47.
	[demɔ̃te]	-On arrival, we were trained for a week to shoot and dismantle AK-47 guns.
5446	**jaguar**	**jaguar**
	m	Une femme vient d'appeler pour signaler avoir vu un jaguar.
	[ʒagwaʁ]	-A woman just called in a sighting of a jaguar.
5447	**sortilège**	**spell**
	m	Heureusement, un sortilège très simple chasse l'épouvantard.
	[sɔʁtilɛʒ]	-Luckily, a very simple charm exists to repel a boggart.
5448	**soucoupe**	**saucer**
	f	J'ai été enlevé et inséminé par des loups qui ont atterri avec leur soucoupe volante dans ma cour.
	[sukup]	-I was abducted and impregnated by wolves who landed their flying saucer in my backyard.
5449	**palestinien**	**Palestinian**
	adj	Premièrement, il faut reconnaître un État palestinien.
	[palɛstinjɛ̃]	-First, there must be recognition of a Palestinian state.
5450	**israélien**	**Israeli**
	adj	Elle ignorait que Bethléem était sous contrôle israélien.
	[isʁaeljɛ̃]	-She would have no idea that Bethlehem at that time was under Israeli control.
5451	**fibre**	**fiber|staple**
	f	Des filtres en fibre de verre imprégnés d'un hydrocarbure fluoré doivent être utilisés.
	[fibʁ]	-Fluorocarbon coated glass fiber filters are required.
5452	**fréquent**	**frequent**
	adj	Et ceci malgré le manque fréquent de soutien de la part des États membres.
	[fʁekã]	-And this was done notwithstanding the frequent lack of support in Member States.
5453	**présager**	**predict|foresee**
	vb	Rien ne laissait pourtant présager une issue heureuse.
	[pʁezaʒe]	-Things did not bode well for the summit.
5454	**improviser**	**improvise**
	vb	Je pense, mais on ne peut pas l'improviser comme cela, dans l'hémicycle.
	[ɛ̃pʁɔvize]	-I agree, however we cannot simply improvise in this way in the Chamber.
5455	**questionner**	**question**
	vb	Nous avons voulu attirer l'attention sur ce point, afin de le questionner.
	[kɛstjɔne]	-We seek to highlight that point in order to query it.
5456	**prestige**	**prestige**
	m	Le prestige du Parlement en sort agrandi.
	[pʁɛstiʒ]	-Parliament's prestige is enhanced at the end of this period.
5457	**douillet**	**cozy|soft**
	adj	Le foyer européen, qui, pour le moment, ne semble peut-être pas très chaleureux et douillet, doit être ouvert à nos pays voisins dans la mesure où ils satisfont aux exigences requises.
	[dujɛ]	

-The European home, which does not at the moment perhaps feel so warm and cosy, must be open to our neighbouring countries when they fulfil the necessary requirements.

5458	**simplicité**	**simplicity**
	f	Et le rapport von Wogau souligne cette solennité avec élégance et simplicité.
	[sɛ̃plisite]	-And the von Wogau report underlines that solemnity with elegance and simplicity.

5459	**étranglé**	**strangled**
	adj	Ce pays est complètement déstabilisé, étranglé littéralement par la Fédération de Russie.
	[etʁɑ̃gle]	-The country is completely destabilised, literally strangled by the Russian Federation.

5460	**tombeur**	**ladykiller**
	m	Le plus gros tombeur de Scottsdale.
	[tɔ̃bœʁ]	-Wife? This guy was the biggest stud in Scottsdale, Arizona.

5461	**prévisible**	**predictable**
	adj	Une présence internationale soutenue sera nécessaire dans un avenir prévisible.
	[pʁevizibl]	-A sustained international presence will be necessary for the foreseeable future.

5462	**recueillir**	**collect|gather**
	vb	Cela signifie que pour être élu, un candidat devra recueillir au moins 96 voix.
	[ʁəkœjiʁ]	-That means that to be elected, a candidate needs to gather at least 96 affirmative votes.

5463	**intercepter**	**intercept**
	vb[ɛ̃tɛʁsɛpte]	Avoir les moyens de faire des patrouilles nocturnes et d'intercepter des missions. -Be able to conduct night-time patrols and intercept missions.

5464	**criminalité**	**criminality**
	f	Schengen est un mécanisme qui a été inventé pour lutter contre la criminalité.
	[kʁiminalite]	-Schengen is a mechanism that was invented to fight against criminality.

5465	**coéquipier**	**team mate**
	m	Mon ancien coéquipier, Red Kelly, m'a raconté comment il avait été pressenti pour être candidat du Parti libéral aux élections fédérales de 1962.
	[koekipje]	-My former teammate, Red Kelly, tells the story of when he was first approached to run as a Liberal Party candidate for member of Parliament in 1962.

5466	**imminent**	**imminent**
	adj	En cas de danger imminent, l'accord du Chancelier fédéral suffit.
	[iminɑ̃]	-In case of imminent danger, the consent of the Federal Chancellor is sufficient.

5467	**dixième**	**tenth**
	num	Un antibiotique sur trois et un médicament sur dix, au niveau mondial, sont des faux.
	[dizjɛm]	-Worldwide, one antibiotic in three and one medicine in ten are counterfeit.

5468	**bossu**	**hunchback; hunchbacked**
	m; adj	Tu diras une prière pour moi dans cette église du bossu.
	[bɔsy]	-Say a prayer for me in that hunchback's church.

5469	**traîneau**	**sled|drag**
	m	Défaisons les fournitures et étendons-le sur le traîneau.
	[tʁɛno]	-Okay, let's unpack the supplies and get him on the sled.

5470 cadence — **pace**
f
[kadãs]
D'abord, le gouvernement a ralenti sa cadence de nominations.
-First, the government has slowed the pace of appointments.

5471 symphonie — **symphony**
f
[sɛ̃fɔni]
Chère Europe, la symphonie est la même et elle sonne toujours plus faux.
-Good old Europe; the symphony plays on, more out of tune than ever.

5472 vison — **mink**
m
[vizɔ̃]
Elle portait un manteau de vison.
-She was wearing a mink coat.

5473 rédiger — **rewrite**
vb
[ʁediʒe]
Il faudrait donc en priorité revoir et rédiger à nouveau ces descriptifs de poste.
-A priority should therefore be to have job descriptions reviewed and rewritten.

5474 rouiller — **rust**
vb
[ʁuje]
Ils doivent regarder les voitures rouiller.
-They probably sit around and watch the cars rust.

5475 ouvertement — **openly**
adv [uvɛʁtəmã]
Le ministre des Finance a abordé cette affaire ouvertement et honnêtement hier. -The Minister of Finance addressed this matter openly and honestly yesterday.

5476 shilling — **shilling**
m
[ʃiliŋ]
On te donnera un shilling au commissariat.
-There will be a shilling for you back at the station.

5477 réviser — **revise|review**
vb
[ʁevize]
Deuxièmement, la Commission propose de réviser la procédure disciplinaire.
-Second, the Commission proposes to overhaul the disciplinary procedure.

5478 protéine — **protein**
f
[pʁɔtein]
Lesdites compositions contiennent un polysaccharide et/ou une protéine.
-The compositions of the invention contain a polysaccharide and/or protein.

5479 maintenance — **maintenance**
f
[mɛ̃tnãs]
Nos serveurs seront hors ligne le 20 octobre pour la maintenance prévue.
-Our server will be offline on October 20th for scheduled maintenance.

5480 dilemme — **dilemma**
m
[dilɛm]
Il y a toujours un dilemme entre l'aide humanitaire et la dimension politique.
-There is always a dilemma between humanitarian aid and the political dimension.

5481 colon — **colon|settler**
m
[kɔlɔ̃]
Chez les hommes, c'était les poumons (26 %), l'estomac (8 %) et le colon (8 %).
-In males the commonest killers were lung (26%), stomach (8%), and colon (8%).

5482 intolérable — **intolerable**
adj
[ɛ̃tɔleʁabl]
C'est intolérable, et la Russie est dans la mauvaise voie avec une telle politique.
-That is intolerable, and Russia is on the wrong track with such a policy.

5483 sculpture — **sculpture|sculpting**
f
[skyltyʁ]
Équipement de deux ateliers de sculpture et de vannerie (formation et production);

-Equipment of two training and production workshops in sculpture and basketry.

5484	**chaudière**	**boiler**
	f	La chaudière comporte une ou plusieurs surfaces.
	[ʃodjɛʁ]	-The boiler includes one or more generally cross sectional areas.
5485	**collaborer**	**collaborate**
	vb	L'UNESCO, le FNUAP et l'OMS vont collaborer à l'harmonisation des messages.
	[kɔlabɔʁe]	-UNESCO, UNFPA and WHO will collaborate in the harmonization of messages.
5486	**percher**	**perch|hang**
	vb	Et viennent se percher sur son épaule.
	[pɛʁʃe]	-And come perch on his shoulder.
5487	**joujou**	**toy**
	m	Je prendrai soin de votre joujou.
	[ʒuʒu]	-I'll take care of your toy for you.
5488	**fluide**	**fluid; fluid**
	adj; m	C'est réellement un environnement fluide qui requiert une adaptation constante.
	[flɥid]	-It is quite literally a fluid environment that calls for constant adaptation.
5489	**clairon**	**bugle**
	m	Je n'ai pas amené mon clairon.
	[klɛʁɔ̃]	-I didn't bring my bugle.
5490	**biberon**	**baby bottle**
	m	Le biberon présente une base élargie assurant une stabilité.
	[bibʁɔ̃]	-The baby bottle is provided with an enlarged base for stability.
5491	**gaspillage**	**waste|wastage**
	m	Ceci entraîne un gaspillage d' argent, de personnel et une moindre efficacité.
	[gaspijaʒ]	-This leads to wastage, wastage of money, wastage of manpower and wastage of efficiency.
5492	**dictateur**	**dictator**
	m	La populace était sous le charme des caprices du dictateur.
	[diktatœʁ]	-The populace was in thrall to the dictator's whims.
5493	**carcasse**	**carcass**
	f	Je viendrais récupérer ta carcasse au matin.
	[kaʁkas]	-I'll come and pick up your carcass in the morning.
5494	**implant**	**implant**
	m	Mais j'ai un implant contraceptif...
	[ɛ̃plɑ̃]	-But I'm on this birth control implant.
5495	**parallèle**	**parallel; parallel**
	adj; m/f	Malheureusement, on peut établir un parallèle avec la Conférence du désarmement.
	[paʁalɛl]	-Unfortunately, there is a parallel in the Conference on Disarmament.
5496	**manucure**	**manicure**
	f	Et je reconnais votre manucure Tahiti Sunset.
	[manykyʁ]	-And I appreciate your Tahiti Sunset manicure.
5497	**anxieux**	**anxious|worried**
	adj	Ne sois pas si anxieux !
	[ɑ̃ksjø]	-Don't be so worried!
5498	**cadenas**	**padlock**

m
[kadna]

C'est là un message très important : pas de clef unique mais un cadenas à combinaison.
-That is a very important message: no single key, but a combination lock.

5499 blasphémer — **blaspheme**

vb
[blasfeme]

Falun Gong prend les dehors d'une religion pour mieux blasphémer contre la religion.
-Falun Gong has assumed the outward trappings of a religion in order to better blaspheme against religion.

5500 clavier — **keyboard**

m
[klavje]

Que vous ai-je dit à propos de l'alimentation au-dessus du clavier ?
-What did I tell you about eating over the keyboard?

5501 imprévu — **unexpected; contingency**

adj; m[ɛ̃pʁevy]

Ce plan décrit la procédure à suivre en cas de sinistre, c'est-à-dire si un événement imprévu venait à interrompre le cours normal des opérations de l'Office. -The disaster recovery plan is meant to describe how the Agency is to deal with potential disaster, which is an unforeseen event that makes the continuation of normal functions impossible.

5502 virilité — **virility|manhood**

f
[viʁilite]

Et dans certains cas, nous associons clairement la prise d'alcool au sex appeal et à la virilité.
-And we especially associate alcohol intake with sex appeal and manhood, in some cases.

5503 bungalow — **bungalow**

m
[bɛ̃galo]

J'ai été élue au comité des chambres du bungalow 12.
-I've been elected to the Rooms Committee, Bungalow 12.

5504 estimation — **estimate|rating**

f
[ɛstimasjɔ̃]

Cela coûtera trente mille yens selon la plus faible estimation.
-It will cost thirty thousand yen at the lowest estimate.

5505 alphabet — **alphabet**

m
[alfabɛ]

Nicolas veut dire que la romanisation de l'alphabet cyrillique est aussi belle que le soleil, qui brûle les yeux quand on le regarde.
-Nicolas means that romanization of the Cyrillic alphabet is as beautiful as the sun, which burns your eyes when you look at it.

5506 olympique — **Olympic**

adj
[ɔlɛ̃pik]

La Trêve olympique est au coeur même de la philosophie du Mouvement olympique.
-The Olympic Truce goes right to the heart of the philosophy of the Olympic Movement.

5507 bonne — **housemaid**

f
[bɔn]

L'une des victimes a été conduite à Singapour sous prétexte d'être employée comme bonne.
-One of the victims was brought into Singapore under the pretext of finding a job as a maid.

5508 dépêche — **dispatch|telegram**

f
[depɛʃ]

Dépêche-toi, ou tu seras en retard.
-Hurry up, or you'll be late.

5509 truie — **sow**

f
[tʁɥi]

C'est la peau d'une truie.
-This is the hide of a sow.

5510 tourbillon — **vortex|whirlwind**

m
[tuʁbijɔ̃]

Cap sur le centre du tourbillon.
-Set a course for the centre of the vortex.

5511	**sanglant**		**bloody**
	adj		Jusqu'à maintenant, elle s'est répétée dans un contexte sanglant et tragique.
	[sãglã]		-Thus far these repetitions have been nothing but bloody and tragic.
5512	**irruption**		**irruption**
	f		En effet, cette irruption massive de l'information dans notre société modifie de façon radicale la notion de droits d'auteur et de droits voisins.
	[iʁypsjõ]		-Indeed, this massive irruption of information into our society is radically modifying the concept of author's rights and related rights.
5513	**monétaire**		**monetary**
	adj[mɔnetɛʁ]		Une politique monétaire dûment complaisante n'est pas une politique monétaire laxiste. -Appropriate accommodating monetary policy is not lax monetary policy. '
5514	**verger**		**orchard**
	m		Ma maison comporte un verger.
	[vɛʁʒe]		-My house has a orchard.
5515	**diarrhée**		**diarrhea**
	f		Il n'y a pas que la diarrhée qui peut conduire un homme aux toilettes.
	[djaʁe]		-There's more than diarrhea that drives a man to the toilet.
5516	**schéma**		**schema|diagram**
	m		Je vous explique avec un schéma.
	[ʃema]		-Let me explain it with a diagram.
5517	**plaine**		**plain**
	f		Dans la plaine dominent des nomades peul et touareg.
	[plɛn]		-On the plains, the Peul and Tuareg nomads are dominant.
5518	**lutin**		**pixie|leprechaun; impish**
	m; adj		On dirait un petit lutin en complet-veston.
	[lytɛ̃]		-He looks more like a little leprechaun in a business suit.
5519	**chemisier**		**blouse**
	m		Aimez-vous ce chemisier ?
	[ʃəmizje]		-Do you like this blouse?
5520	**oracle**		**oracle**
	m		Ils auraient au moins pu consulter l'oracle.
	[ɔʁakl]		-Well! The least they could have done is consult the oracle.
5521	**holocauste**		**holocaust**
	m		L'holocauste nucléaire dépassera l'entendement.
	[ɔlokost]		-There will be a nuclear holocaust beyond imagination.
5522	**rudement**		**roughly|harshly**
	adv		Jusqu'à présent, l'hiver en Afghanistan n'a pas été aussi rude qu'on le craignait.
	[ʁydmã]		-So far, the winter in Afghanistan has not been as harsh as had been feared.
5523	**raisonnement**		**reasoning**
	m		Je ne comprends pas ce raisonnement.
	[ʁɛzɔnmã]		-I don't understand this reasoning.
5524	**déshonneur**		**disgrace**
	m		La mort est préférable au déshonneur.
	[dezɔnœʁ]		-Death is preferable to dishonor.
5525	**traditionnel**		**traditional**
	adj		Ils n'ont pas nécessairement, au départ, tout le bagage traditionnel que cela prend.
	[tʁadisjɔnɛl]		-They do not necessarily have all it traditionally takes right from the start.
5526	**gnôle**		**hooch**

	f	Je vends seulement de la gnôle tous les autres jeudis.
	[ɲol]	-I'm only selling hooch every other Thursday.
5527	**hypothèque**	**mortgage**
	f	Une seconde hypothèque sur Piedmont Place.
	[ipɔtɛk]	-That's a second mortgage on piedmont place.
5528	**fertile**	**fertile|fruitful**
	adj[fɛʁtil]	Ensemble, ils ont préparé le terrain pour une discussion fertile aujourd'hui. - Together they have set the stage for a fruitful discussion today.
5529	**mendiant**	**beggar; begging**
	m; adj	Nous ne voulons plus être un État mendiant.
	[mãdjã]	-We no longer want to be a beggar State.
5530	**contredire**	**contradict**
	vb	Je dois d'ailleurs fortement contredire à ce sujet l'interlocuteur qui m'a précédé.
	[kɔ̃tʁədiʁ]	-I must emphatically contradict the previous speaker on this point.
5531	**taillé**	**tailored**
	adj	Je n'ai pas mon costume taillé parfaitement sur mesure.
	[taje]	-I don't have my perfectly tailored tux.
5532	**contempler**	**contemplate**
	vb	On peut parler, analyser... contempler.
	[kɔ̃tãple]	-Now, we can talk, analyze... contemplate.
5533	**stellaire**	**stellar**
	adj	Une fois l'amas stellaire traversé, vous pourrez retourner sur vos vaisseaux.
	[stelɛʁ]	-Once we get through the star cluster, you will be returned to your designated ships.
5534	**excursion**	**excursion|trip**
	f	Combien coûte cette excursion par personne ?
	[ɛkskyʁsjɔ̃]	-How much is this tour per person?
5535	**polir**	**polish|buff**
	vb	Elle venait de la nécessité pour le premier ministre de polir son image internationale à l'occasion d'une conférence internationale, il y a deux ans.
	[pɔliʁ]	-No, it started from the need of the Prime Minister to polish his international stature at an international conference two years ago.
5536	**application**	**application**
	f	L'histoire ne finit pas là pour autant. Pour pouvoir s'enregistrer auprès de l'application, on attend d'un greffon qu'il ait une fonction d'initialisation que l'application appellera.
	[aplikasjɔ̃]	-The story doesn't end here, however. To register itself with the application, a valid plugin is expected to have an initialization function which the application will call.
5537	**imperméable**	**impermeable; waterproof**
	adj; m	Qui est la fille avec l'imperméable jaune ?
	[ɛ̃pɛʁmeabl]	-Who's the girl in a yellow raincoat?
5538	**relaxer**	**relax**
	vb	Avant de rentrer, je prendrais bien un verre pour relaxer.
	[ʁəlakse]	-Before going home, I have a few drinks to relax.
5539	**croisade**	**crusade**
	f	Finalement, la réforme a été réduite à une croisade pour la compression d'effectifs.
	[kʁwazad]	-Reform was subverted into a crusade for downsizing and retrenchment.
5540	**redresser**	**straighten|redress**

		vb[ʁədʁese]	La MONUC tente de redresser la situation, mais ils ne respectent pas le calendrier établi. -MONUC is trying to correct the situation, but they are not following the timetable.

5541 effrayant — scary|frightening
adj
[efʁɛjã]
Le naufrage du au large des côtes flamandes en a été un exemple effrayant.
-The off the Flemish coast was a chilling example of this.

5542 cabot — pooch|mutt
m
[kabo]
C'est un cabot, juste comme moi.
-He's a mutt, just like me.

5543 emmerdeur — pain in the neck
m
[ãmɛʁdœʁ]
Tu es un véritable emmerdeur.
-You're a real pain in the ass.

5544 calamar — squid
m
[kalamaʁ]
Il était également le plus grand chasseur de calamar au monde.
-He was also the world's foremost squid hunter.

5545 maturité — maturity
f
[matyʁite]
L'âge ne conduit pas à la maturité, à moins que vous ne soyez un fromage.
-Age doesn't lead to maturity, unless you're a cheese.

5546 renommée — renown
f
[ʁənɔme]
Ce roman améliora encore sa renommée.
-The novel added to his reputation.

5547 sphère — sphere|globe
f
[sfɛʁ]
D'antiques ruines extraterrestres, dans les postes avancés éloignés de la sphère de l'espace humain, hantèrent de nombreuses générations.
-Ancient alien ruins in faraway outposts of the Human Space Sphere spooked many generations.

5548 plongeon — dive|plunge
m
[plɔ̃ʒɔ̃]
Je vais te montrer un beau plongeon.
-I am going to show you a nice dive.

5549 superstitieux — superstitious
adj
[sypɛʁstisjø]
C'est ce qui arrive aux lieutenants superstitieux.
-Same thing's been known to happen to superstitious lieutenants.

5550 hésitation — hesitation
f
[ezitasjɔ̃]
Elle n'avait aucune hésitation à être violente envers ses enfants.
-She has no qualms about being violent towards her children.

5551 fâcheux — annoying; meddler
adj; m/f
[faʃø]
Vous savez peut-être... un fâcheux incident à Fort Griffin.
-Well, perhaps you've heard, we had an unfortunate incident in Fort Griffin...

5552 rival — rival; rival
adj; m
[ʁival]
Anne n'a pas de rival au tennis.
-Ann is second to none in tennis.

5553 jockey — jockey
m
[ʒɔkɛ]
Mesdames et messieurs, changement de jockey.
-Ladies and gentlemen, we have a change of rider.

5554 plomberie — plumbing
f
[plɔ̃bʁi]
Ils avaient un petite entreprise de plomberie.
-Her parents had a small plumbing business.

5555 introduction — introduction|listing

	f	Qu'as-tu écrit dans l'introduction ?
	[ɛ̃tʁɔdyksjɔ̃]	-What did I write in the introduction?
5556	**liqueur**	**liqueur**
	f	Cette liqueur a un goût unique.
	[likœʁ]	-This liquor has a taste all of its own.
5557	**aboyer**	**bark**
	vb	La surprise a été que le chien était bien là, mais qu'il n'aboyait pas.
	[abwaje]	-The surprise was that the dog was there and did not bark.
5558	**déléguer**	**delegate|devolve**
	vb	Dans la pratique, la Cour populaire suprême peut déléguer cette fonction à une haute Cour.
	[delege]	-Nevertheless, in practice, the Supreme People's Court can delegate this function to a high court.
5559	**fabricant**	**manufacturer**
	m	Donc on devrait trouver le fabricant facilement.
	[fabʁikã]	-Meaning it shouldn't be too hard to find the manufacturer.
5560	**paranoïa**	**paranoia**
	f	La paranoïa est symptomatique d'un enlèvement.
	[paʁanɔja]	-Paranoia is one of the telltale signs of an abduction.
5561	**hormis**	**except for**
	prp	Je ne veux personne ici hormis les démineurs et les légistes.
	[ɔʁmi]	-I don't want anybody here except the bomb squad and forensics.
5562	**indéfiniment**	**indefinitely**
	adv	Ce tribunal ne pourra certainement pas poursuivre son travail indéfiniment.
	[ɛ̃definimã]	-Certainly, this tribunal will not be able to continue its work indefinitely.
5563	**rédemption**	**redemption**
	f	Parce qu'il s'agit de cela: de la réalité de la rédemption du Christ.
	[ʁedãpsjɔ̃]	-For this is the matter under consideration: the reality of the redemption of Christ.
5564	**duper**	**fool|deceive**
	vb	Nous ne devons pas nous laisser duper par la reprise.
	[dype]	-We must not let the recovery fool us.
5565	**rai**	**streak**
	m	Il y a un rai de lumière qui filtre par là.
	[ʁɛ]	-A ray of light coming from in there.
5566	**cuisiné**	**cooked**
	adj	Ce matin-là, l'accusé a pris un couteau dans la cuisine et il a attaqué sa mère.
	[kɥizine]	-That morning, the accused got a knife from the kitchen and attacked his mother.
5567	**poulain**	**foal**
	f	Le poulain pourrait valoir une fortune.
	[pulɛ̃]	-The foal could be worth a great deal.
5568	**veuf**	**widower**
	m	Un veuf peut recevoir une pension de veuf s'il s'occupe au moins d'un enfant à charge.
	[vœf]	-A widower's pension is provided to a widower, if he is looking after at least one dependent child.
5569	**retomber**	**drop|relapse**
	vb [ʁətɔ̃be]	Le pays risque néanmoins de retomber petit à petit dans une situation de conflit. -There was a risk, however, that the country was slowly sliding back into conflict.

5570	**moniteur**	**monitor**
	m	Si le véhicule se déplace à une vitesse supérieure ou en marche arrière, le moniteur peut être utilisé pour afficher le champ de vision d'autres caméras montées sur le véhicule.
	[mɔnitœʀ]	-In case the vehicle is moving with higher speed or moving backwards the monitor can be used to display the field of vision of other cameras mounted to the vehicle.
5571	**mouler**	**mold|press**
	vb	Je suis très craintif devant des gouvernements qui essaient de mouler et de façonner notre culture.
	[mule]	-I am very apprehensive about government trying to shape and mould culture.
5572	**comprimer**	**compress|jam**
	vb	Il va aussi comprimer, briser et tasser la couche plus dure de sédiments sous-jacents.
	[kɔ̃pʀime]	-The nodule collector will compress, break up and squeeze the harder underlying sediment layer.
5573	**déménagement**	**move|removal**
	m	Ce déménagement visait environ 1000 personnes.
	[demenaʒmɑ̃]	-There were 1,000 people involved in the move.
5574	**spécifique**	**specific**
	adj	Je souhaiterais recevoir une analyse spécifique d'une réalité spécifique.
	[spesifik]	-I would like to know the specific analysis of the specific reality.
5575	**expertise**	**expertise|valuation**
	f	Une expertise crédible des enregistrements devrait être menée.
	[ɛkspɛʀtiz]	-A credible expertise of the recordings should be carried out.
5576	**hypocrisie**	**hypocrisy**
	f	Il y a des gens qui réussissent à cacher même leur hypocrisie.
	[ipɔkʀizi]	-There are men who manage to hide even their own hypocrisy.
5577	**nostalgie**	**nostalgia**
	f	Monsieur le Président, une vague de nostalgie de mon grand-père me voila les yeux.
	[nɔstalʒi]	-Mr President, tears of nostalgia for my grandfather clouded my eyes.
5578	**décorateur**	**decorator**
	m	Le décorateur a recommencé neuf fois.
	[dekɔʀatœʀ]	-I had the decorator redo it nine times.
5579	**marguerite**	**daisy**
	f	Auriez-vous une marguerite pour moi ?
	[maʀɡəʀit]	-Would you have a daisy for me?
5580	**dissuader**	**deter|put off**
	vb	Dissuader les délinquants, et quiconque, de commettre des infractions.
	[disɥade]	-To deter the offender and other persons from committing offences.
5581	**trot**	**trot**
	m[tʀo]	J'ai appris a passer du trot au petit galop. -I learned to go from a trot to a canter.
5582	**douteux**	**doubtful**
	adj	Les socialistes en Albanie jouent malheureusement toujours un jeu douteux.
	[dutø]	-Unfortunately, the socialists in Albania are still playing a dubious role.
5583	**anatomie**	**anatomy**

f

[anatɔmi]

Les femmes sont plus vulnérables à l'infection que les hommes en raison de leur anatomie.

-Women are more vulnerable to infection than men, given their anatomy.

5584 fournisseur — **supplier|contractor**

m

[fuʁnisœʁ]

Constatations Le fournisseur du programme est un établissement autorisé.

-Findings The evidence indicates that the provider of the program is a permitted institution.

5585 alerter — **alert|warn**

vb

[alɛʁte]

Mais ils sont mal placés pour alerter la population canadienne.

-But these people are not in a position to alert the Canadian public about these shortfalls.

5586 compétent — **competent**

adj

[kɔ̃petã]

Le Groupe de travail et son Président très compétent méritent notre haute estime.

-The Working Group and its very able Chairman deserve our high appreciation.

5587 engrais — **fertilizer**

m

[ãgʁɛ]

Les engrais en particulier manquent cruellement.

-Fertilizer in particular has been in short supply.

5588 vocal — **vocal**

adj

[vɔkal]

L'alerte sonore doit consister en un signal sonore continu ou intermittent ou un message vocal.

-Audible warning shall be by continuous or intermittent sound signal or by vocal information.

5589 psychiatrie — **psychiatry**

f

[psikjatʁi]

J'ai fait dermatologie et psychiatrie.

-All I've done are dermatology and psychiatry.

5590 cochonnerie — **junk**

f

[kɔʃɔnʁi]

Ouais, cette cochonnerie ne confirme qu'une chose.

-Yep, this junk means only one thing.

5591 rejet — **rejection**

m

[ʁəʒɛ]

Le Gouvernement andorran veut réaffirmer son rejet actif du terrorisme.

-The Government of Andorra wishes to reaffirm its active rejection of terrorism.

5592 tonic — **tonic**

m

[tɔnik]

Vous m'avez toujours injecté comme un tonic.

-You always affected me like a tonic.

5593 orthographe — **spelling**

f

[ɔʁtɔgʁaf]

Sa rédaction est très bonne bien qu'elle comporte quelques fautes d'orthographe.

-Her composition is very good except for a few errors in spelling.

5594 lâcheté — **cowardice**

f

[laʃte]

Tu confonds lâcheté et retraite stratégique.

-You're confusing cowardice with a tactical retreat.

5595 attente — **waiting|expectation**

f

[atãt]

Mais les salles d'attente de Bruxelles sont grandes et les délais, incertains.

-But the Brussels waiting rooms are large, and waiting times uncertain.

5596 charitable — **charitable**

adj

[ʃaʁitabl]

La nuit passe dans l'espoir que l'aube suivante sera plus charitable pour ces gens et leurs enfants, qui toutes les nuits sanglotent de terreur. »

-The night passes in the hope that we will see a new dawn that will be more merciful to those people and to their children, who spend their nights weeping in terror."

5597	**apogée**	**apogee|peak**
	m	Il était alors à l'apogée d'une brillante carrière dans les affaires.
	[apɔʒe]	-He was then at the peak of a brilliant career in business.

5598	**amertume**	**bitterness|grief**
	f	Même aujourd'hui, plusieurs décennies après la guerre froide, il y a encore beaucoup d'amertume entre les Allemands et les Russes, en particulier dans les zones qui avaient été occupées par l'Union soviétique.
	[amɛʁtym]	-Even now, many years after the cold war, there is still much bitterness between Germans and Russian, especially in areas which were occupied by the Soviet Union.

5599	**dégainer**	**unsheathe**
	vb	Il ne s'agit pas d'être les premiers à dégainer.
	[degene]	-This is not about being the first to draw.

5600	**nettement**	**clearly|sharply**
	adv	Les saisies d'héroïne ont nettement augmenté aussi dans les pays d'Asie centrale.
	[nɛtmã]	-Large increases in heroin seizures were also noted by countries in Central Asia.

5601	**fiasco**	**fiasco|failure**
	m	Personne n'a été puni pour le fiasco.
	[fjasko]	-No one was punished for the fiasco.

5602	**lustre**	**chandelier|luster**
	m	Elles ont été une parfaite farce et n'ont servi à rien d'autre qu'à donner un lustre civil à la junte militaire.
	[lystʁ]	-They were an utter farce and served no purpose other than to give a civilian gloss to the military junta.

5603	**réforme**	**reform**
	f	Réforme ou casse-toi !
	[ʁefɔʁm]	-Shape up or ship out!

5604	**caraïbe**	**Caribbean**
	adj	Des rapports seront établis avec l'élément caraïbe du Réseau informatique des petits États insulaires en développement.
	[kaʁaib]	-Linkages will be established with the Caribbean component of the Small Island Developing States Network.

5605	**truite**	**trout**
	f	Les myes et la truite comptent pour presque 50 % de la production totale.
	[tʁɥit]	-Clams and trout represent almost 50% of the total production.

5606	**frousse**	**jitters**
	f	J'ai la frousse.
	[fʁus]	-I'm jittery.

5607	**déclin**	**decline**
	m[deklɛ̃]	Le pic pétrolier, événement basé sur la théorie de Hubbert, est le point du temps auquel le taux maximal d'extraction pétrolière est atteint, après quoi, on s'attend à ce que le taux de production entre en déclin final. -Peak oil, an event based on Hubbert's theory, is the point in time when the maximum rate of petroleum extraction is reached, after which the rate of production is expected to enter terminal decline.

5608	**collectionner**	**collect**

vb
[kɔlɛksjɔne]

Plus tard, quand j'étais un peu plus vieux, j'ai commencé à collectionner les timbres.
-Later, when I got a little older, I started collecting stamps.

5609 **diffusion** **diffusion|distribution**

f

[difyzjɔ̃]

Une dernière recommandation concerne la diffusion des connaissances.
-Last but not least, a final recommendation deals with diffusion of knowledge.

5610 **trame** **weave**

f

[tʁam]

La première trame est une trame focalisée, alors que la seconde trame est une trame non focalisée.
-The first frame is a focused frame and the second frame is an unfocused frame.

5611 **éclaireur** **scout**

m

[eklɛʁœʁ]

Vous pourrez rentrer au poste avec l'éclaireur.
-You and the scout can catch up with the detail, head back to post.

5612 **porcelaine** **porcelain**

f

[pɔʁsəlɛn]

La porcelaine pourrait facilement s'y être mélangée.
-The porcelain could have easily gotten mixed in there.

5613 **paupière** **eyelid**

f

[popjɛʁ]

Une paupière s'ouvrit en grand.
-An eyelid opens wide.

5614 **poliment** **politely**

adv

[pɔlimɑ̃]

La Commission est poliment invitée à continuer à oeuvrer dans cette direction.
-We would politely request the Commission to take further action in this direction.

5615 **opium** **opium**

m

[ɔpjɔm]

Il faut remédier au trafic d'opium.
-The opium trade needs to be dealt with.

5616 **soufrer** **sulfur|sulphurize**

vb

[sufʁe]

Toutefois, le grain est un aliment et nous devons lui accorder un traitement qui diffère légèrement de celui que nous réservons au charbon ou au soufre ou à la potasse.
-However, grain is food and we have to treat it a bit different than we do coal or sulphur or potash.

5617 **Pérou** **Peru**

m

[peʁu]

Ils ont bâti leur empire au Pérou il y a environ cinq cents ans.
-They built their empire in Peru about five hundred years ago.

5618 **bûcher** **pyre|slave; log**

m; vb

[byʃe]

Rite hindou qui voulait que les veuves s'immolaient sur le bûcher funéraire de leur mari.
-The former Hindu practice of a widow immolating herself on her husband's funeral pyre.

5619 **collectif** **collective**

adj[kɔlɛktif]

La sécurité internationale est un problème collectif qui exige une action collective. -International security is a collective concern requiring collective engagement.

5620 **remorque** **trailer**

f

[ʁəmɔʁk]

La superstructure a la forme d'une remorque transportable.
-The superstructure is configured in the form of a transportable trailer.

5621 **dégoût** **disgust**

	m	Nous observons tous les jours avec incrédulité et dégoût les massacres et la destruction.
	[degu]	-We watch daily in disbelief and disgust the slaughter and destruction.
5622	**cupidité**	**greed**
	f	Ce n'est pas la cupidité, la cupidité individuelle, qui a été le facteur décisif.
	[kypidite]	-It is not greed, individual greed, which was the decisive factor.
5623	**global**	**overall|global**
	adj	Les projets d'infrastructure sont souvent régis par un accord global de concession.
	[glɔbal]	-Infrastructure projects are often governed by an global concessionary agreement.
5624	**brosser**	**brush**
	vb	Ce que ces gens racontent est bien différent du tableau que le député vient de brosser.
	[bʁɔse]	-They are telling a very different story than the picture he just finished painting.
5625	**métis**	**metis; colored**
	m; adj	Il y avait beaucoup de commissaires aux traités qui disaient qu'ils ne pouvaient déterminer qui était Métis et qui était Indien.
	[metis]	-We have many of the treaty commissioners talking about how they could not tell who is a half-breed and who is an Indian.
5626	**terrien**	**earthling|landlubber**
	m	Il dut choisir entre « Terrien » et « Terran » pour leur gentilé.
	[teʁjɛ̃]	-He had to choose between "Earthling" and "Terran" for their demonym.
5627	**tripoter**	**tamper|paw**
	vb	Tripoter les chiffres, cela veut dire qu'on joue avec les chiffres sur tous les plans.
	[tʁipɔte]	-To fiddle with the figures means to manipulate them on all fronts.
5628	**fascinant**	**fascinating**
	adj	Monsieur le Président, quelle déclaration fascinante de la part d'un autre libéral.
	[fasinɑ̃]	-Speaker, a purely riveting statement from another Liberal.
5629	**vertueux**	**virtuous**
	adj	Il vise à former un citoyen vertueux, modèle de rectitude, de modération et de tolérance.
	[vɛʁtɥø]	-It aims to create a virtuous citizen, a model of rectitude, moderation and tolerance.
5630	**magot**	**hoard|loot**
	m	Vous et votre magot sortirez du coup indemnes.
	[mago]	-You and your loot will emerge unharmed.
5631	**lisse**	**smooth|sleek**
	adj	C'est lisse comme le derrière d'un nouveau-né.
	[lis]	-It's as smooth as a baby's bottom.
5632	**hisser**	**hoist|pull up**
	vb	J'aimerais hisser la voile et te ramener.
	[ise]	-I wish I could hoist my sail and take you in.
5633	**routier**	**truck; teamster**
	vb; m	Ce péage routier injustifié en est la compensation financière.
	[ʁutje]	-The unjustified charging of a road toll is the financial compensation.
5634	**caractéristique**	**characteristic; characteristic**
	adj; f	Ce n'est pas du tout caractéristique.
	[kaʁakteʁistik]	-It's not at all typical.

5635	**algue**	**alga; algoid**
	f; adj	L'invention concerne un procédé et un système de récupération de caroténoïdes mélangés de l'algue Dunaliella salina.
	[alg]	-A process and system are disclosed for recovering mixed carotenoids from the alga Dunaliella salina.
5636	**gamma**	**gamma**
	f	Micro-ondes directes, radiations gamma, signaux radio...
	[gama]	-A tuned microwave beam, gamma radiation, a radio signal.
5637	**opérationnel**	**operational**
	adj	Cependant, ils ne représentent pas suffisamment l'environnement opérationnel réel.
	[ɔpeʁasjɔnɛl]	-However, it does not sufficiently replicate the actual operating environment.
5638	**créativité**	**creativity**
	f	La créativité européenne est soutenue par une tradition culturelle brillante.
	[kʁeativite]	-European creativity is supported by Europe's brilliant cultural tradition.
5639	**fesse**	**buttock|bottom**
	f	Elle a un hématome sur la fesse droite.
	[fɛs]	-She has a hematoma on her right cheek.
5640	**astuce**	**trick|cunning**
	f	Mais, c'est tout de l'astuce et du chiqué.
	[astys]	-But that's all his craft and artfulness.
5641	**méditation**	**meditation**
	f	La méditation ne coûte rien mais ça prend du temps.
	[meditasjɔ̃]	-Meditation doesn't cost anything, but it takes time.
5642	**notamment**	**in particular**
	adv	Elles concernent notamment l'extension du rôle et du champ d'activité de la BEI.
	[nɔtamɑ̃]	-A particular priority here will be extending the role and activities of the EIB.
5643	**courtier**	**broker**
	m	Ça doit nous mener au courtier.
	[kuʁtje]	-That should lead us back to the broker.
5644	**oseille**	**money|dough**
	m	Prends l'oseille et tire-toi !
	[ozɛj]	-Take the money and run.
5645	**mâcher**	**chew|gum**
	vb[maʃe]	De toute évidence, ce gouvernement est incapable de marcher et de mâcher de la gomme en même temps. -This is a government that cannot walk and chew bubble gum at the same time.
5646	**cane**	**cane**
	vb	Mais très vite, tu auras des béquilles, puis une cane.
	[kan]	-But in a few weeks we'll have you up on crutches, then we'll get you a cane.
5647	**clouer**	**nail|tack**
	vb	Je vais clouer la fenêtre fermée.
	[klue]	-I'll go nail the window shut.
5648	**commotion**	**shock|concussion**
	f	Votre ami a eu une commotion nécessitant des sutures.
	[kɔmosjɔ̃]	-Your friend suffered a Grade 2 concussion and required some stitches.
5649	**seigneurie**	**lordship**

	f [sɛɲœʁi]	En 1346 et en 1355, les Grimaldi font l'acquisition des seigneuries et fiefs de Menton et Roquebrune. -In 1346 and 1355, the Grimaldis took over the seigniories and fiefs of Menton and Roquebrune.
5650	**apte** adj [apt]	**apt** C'est seulement pour cette raison que je me sens apte à voter en faveur du rapport. -It is only for this reason that I felt able to vote in favour of the report.
5651	**motard** m [mɔtaʁ]	**outrider** Par rapport à son homologue casqué, un motard non muni d'un casque court un risque 40 % plus élevé d'être atteint mortellement à la tête. -Compared to a helmeted rider, an un-helmeted rider is 40 per cent more likely to incur a fatal head injury.
5652	**combiner** vb [kɔ̃bine]	**combine|compound** Certains députés européens souhaitent combiner à terme les deux stratégies. -Certain MEPs wish to combine these strategies in the long run.
5653	**pressing** m [pʁesiŋ]	**dry cleaning** Aucune idée, je rapporte leur pressing. -I don't know, I'm just returning their dry cleaning.
5654	**OVNI** abr [oveɛni]	**UFO** Nous avons immédiatement perdu de vue l'OVNI. -We lost sight of the UFO right away.
5655	**admirateur** m [admiʁatœʁ]	**admirer** L'honorable Tommy Banks : Honorables sénateurs, je suis un grand admirateur des talents. -Tommy Banks: Honourable senators, I am a great admirer of talent.
5656	**gaufrer** vb [gofʁe]	**emboss** L'approche préférée consiste à gaufrer ces zones de liaisons. -The preferred approach is to emboss these bond areas.
5657	**zoom** m [zɔ̃]	**zoom** Utilisez le zoom cartographique qui se trouve sur la gauche pour effectuer un zoom avant ou arrière. -Use the maps zoom controls found on the left side to zoom in or out of the map.
5658	**travestir** vb [tʁavɛstiʁ]	**travesty** Ce serait un travesti de justice que de permettre aux auteurs d'actes de terrorisme de se rallier à la lutte contre le terrorisme. -It would be a travesty of justice to allow the perpetrators of terrorism to join the fight against terrorism.
5659	**percé** adj [pɛʁse]	**perforated** Un bloc de bois de 95 mm de diamètre et de 25 mm d'épaisseur percé d'un trou central pour maintenir le détonateur. -Wood block, 95 mm diameter and 25 mm thick, with a hole drilled through the centre to hold the detonator.
5660	**imprudent** adj [ɛ̃pʁydɑ̃]	**imprudent|unwise** Ce serait aussi imprudent et irresponsable que d'entamer une autre série de déficits. -This would be as imprudent and irresponsible as incurring another round of deficits.
5661	**pâtir** vb [patiʁ]	**suffer** Ce serait une grande honte si ce document devait pâtir de ce problème. -It would be a great shame if this document had to suffer from this problem.

5662	**modestie**		**modesty**
	f		Sir Charles a orné le bureau du chef d'État avec grâce, dignité et modestie.
	[mɔdɛsti]		-Sir Charles adorned the office of head of State with grace, dignity and humility.
5663	**potable**		**potable**
	adj		Le droit à l'eau potable est directement lié à la vie des personnes.
	[pɔtabl]		-The right to drinkable water is directly linked to the right to life.
5664	**conserve**		**preserve**
	f		Elles mettent du poisson en conserve.
	[kɔ̃sɛʁv]		-They put fish in tin cans.
5665	**laverie**		**laundry|laundromat**
	f		Y a-t-il des détergents dans la laverie ?
	[lavʁi]		-Are there any detergents in the laundry?
5666	**méchanceté**		**wickedness**
	f		Esaïe 33 parle de la colère de Dieu contre la méchanceté.
	[meʃɑ̃ste]		-Isaiah 33 speaks of God's consuming anger against wickedness.
5667	**recrutement**		**recruitment|recruiting**
	m		Recrutement illicite et dissimulation des motifs véritables du recrutement
	[ʁəkʁytmɑ̃]		-Unlawful recruitment and representation that such recruitment is for lawful purposes
5668	**raffiner**		**refine**
	vb		(Note : Pour raffiner votre recherche, ajoutez au filtre plus d'une catégorie.)
	[ʁafine]		-(Note: To refine your search, add more than one category to the filter.)
5669	**lieue**		**league**
	f		Suivez le passage sur une lieue.
	[ljø]		-Follow the narrow passage for another league.
5670	**horde**		**horde**
	f		La désintégration de la Horde d'Or a donné naissance à un grand nombre d'États.
	[ɔʁd]		-The break-up of the Golden Horde led to the formation of a large number of States.
5671	**canton**		**canton**
	m		En 1807, Robert Morrison, le premier missionnaire protestant Britannique en Chine, arriva à Canton.
	[kɑ̃tɔ̃]		-In 1807, Robert Morrison, the first British Protestant missionary to China arrived in the Canton region.
5672	**urne**		**urn**
	f		Cette urne était pleine de feuilles.
	[yʁn]		-Wasn't this urn filled with leaves? Why, yes.
5673	**rotation**		**rotation**
	f		Ensuite, nous suivrons la rotation proportionnelle habituelle.
	[ʁɔtasjɔ̃]		-After that, we will follow the usual proportional rotation.
5674	**flagrant**		**flagrant|blatant**
	adj		L'exemple le plus flagrant de cette perversion concerne les fonds structurels.
	[flagʁɑ̃]		-The most flagrant example of this perversion concerns the Structural Funds.
5675	**instructeur**		**instructor**
	f		L'identité des témoins est révélée au magistrat instructeur.
	[ɛ̃stʁyktœʁ]		-The identity of the witness is disclosed to the examining magistrate.
5676	**conjurer**		**conjure**

vb
[kɔ̃ʒyʁe]

Mr Barroso has tried to carry out a sleight of hand, but he is not a good conjurer.
-Barroso a tenté un tour de passe-passe, mais il n'est pas bon prestidigitateur.

5677 accordéon — **accordion**

m
[akɔʁdeɔ̃]

La forme ondulée en accordéon constitue le principal avantage de la présente invention.
-The wavy accordion shape is the main advantage of this invention.

5678 insolence — **insolence**

f
[ɛ̃sɔlãs]

Ses manières relèvent de l'insolence.
-His manner partakes of insolence.

5679 paddy — **paddy**

m
[padi]

L'humidité du paddy séché ne doit pas dépasser 14 %.
-The moisture content of the dried paddy rice may not exceed 14 %.

5680 glacier — **glacier**

m
[glasje]

J'y ai visité une petite ville appelée Ilulissat, et juste au nord d'Ilulissat se trouve un glacier.
-I visited a small town there called Ilulissat, and just north of Ilulissat is a glacier.

5681 projeter — **project**

vb
[pʁɔʒte]

Le cinquième projet avait pour objet un terminal de soufre liquide (le «projet soufre»).
-The fifth project was the Liquid Sulphur Terminal Project (the "Sulphur Project").

5682 fainéant — **lazy; lounger**

adj; m
[feneã]

Jack n'est pas un enfant fainéant.
-Jack isn't a lazy child.

5683 stratégique — **strategic**

adj[stʁateʒik]

Le Secrétariat s'est efforcé de restructurer ces activités de manière stratégique. -The PTS has taken measures to reshape strategically these outreach activities.

5684 chevet — **bedside**

m
[ʃəvɛ]

Laissez-moi dire une prière à son chevet.
-Let me say a prayer by her bedside.

5685 homosexualité — **homosexuality**

f
[omosɛksɥalite]

Cette émission aborde les questions de la grossesse chez les adolescentes et de l'homosexualité.
-This TV show tackles issues of teenage pregnancy and homosexuality.

5686 supplice — **torture|ordeal**

m
[syplis]

Ce supplice consiste à couvrir la tête d'un sac en plastique jusqu'à l'asphyxie.
-This form of torture consists in covering the head with a plastic bag to cause asphyxia.

5687 concerto — **concerto**

m
[kɔ̃sɛʁto]

Elle compare l'effet de son entraînement à un élève de piano qui progresse dans sa capacité de jouer un air simple à exécuter un concerto.
-She likens the impact of his training to a piano student progressing from the ability to play a simple tune to performing a concerto.

5688 transe — **trance**

f
[tʁãs]

Il déambule aux alentours, en transe.
-He is wandering around in a trance.

5689 cratère — **crater**

	m	Sur la Lune, il y a un cratère qui porte le nom d'Albert Einstein.
	[kʁatɛʁ]	-There is a crater on the Moon named after Albert Einstein.
5690	**courtois**	**courteous**
	adj	Je vous demanderai donc, Monsieur le Président du Conseil européen: "Où sont les galanteries courtoises ?
	[kuʁtwa]	-I ask you now, Mr President of the European Council: 'Where are the courtly gallantries?
5691	**clodo**	**bum**
	m	J'ai supporté financièrement un clodo du golf.
	[klɔdo]	-I'm supporting him as a golf bum.
5692	**concret**	**concrete; concrete**
	adj; m	Il est concret, assez concret pour les missions à accomplir.
	[kɔ̃kʁɛ]	-It is concrete, concrete enough for the tasks that have to be tackled.
5693	**expérimenter**	**experiment|experience**
	vb	Comment les gens vivant dans ces pays pourraient -ils donc véritablement expérimenter l'Europe des citoyens?
	[ɛkspeʁimɑ̃te]	-How are the people there supposed to experience the people's Europe in situ?
5694	**citerne**	**tank**
	f	ADR : Ajouter "conteneur-citerne ou caisse mobile citerne" après "citerne démontable".
	[sitɛʁn]	-ADR: Add "tank-container or tank swap body" after "demountable tank".
5695	**grabuge**	**mayhem**
	m[gʁabyʒ]	Mais elle ne fera pas de grabuge. -And she won't make mayhem.
5696	**stupéfiant**	**narcotic; amazing**
	m; adj	C'est tout simplement stupéfiant.
	[stypefjɑ̃]	-This is simply amazing.
5697	**arctique**	**Arctic**
	adj	Ce cadre constitue la base d'une gestion responsable de l'océan Arctique.
	[aʁktik]	-This framework provides a foundation for responsible management of the Arctic ocean.
5698	**scooter**	**scooter**
	m	Pour ma part, je n'opterai pas pour un scooter; tout ce que je veux, c'est un vélo de meilleure qualité.
	[skɔte]	-I will not settle for a scooter, though; all I want is a better bike.
5699	**crotte**	**dung**
	f	Une crotte au singulier, sous le tabouret.
	[kʁɔt]	-There was a dropping, singular, under the cork-topped stool.
5700	**sévèrement**	**severely**
	adv	Les gens ont sévèrement critiqué la tour Eiffel lors de sa construction.
	[sevɛʁmɑ̃]	-People severely criticized the Eiffel Tower during its construction.
5701	**démontrer**	**demonstrate|reveal**
	vb	Elle continue de démontrer que la paix et la justice ne sont pas contradictoires.
	[demɔ̃tʁe]	-It continues to demonstrate that peace and justice are not contradictory terms.
5702	**boulanger**	**baker**
	m	Comme boulanger, monsieur le Président, vous pouvez sûrement en témoigner.
	[bulɑ̃ʒe]	-As a baker, Mr. Speaker, I am certain you can answer to that.
5703	**infaillible**	**infallible**

adj
[ɛ̃fajibl]

Devant l'éventualité de tels abus, aucune législation ne peut être 100 % infaillible.
-Against the possibility of such abuses no legislation can ever be totally foolproof.

5704 **souple** — **flexible|soft**

adj
[supl]

L'AGCS est un instrument souple, à condition seulement d'être utilisé avec souplesse.
-The GATS is a flexible instrument, but only if it is used in a flexible way.

5705 **confronter** — **confront**

vb
[kɔ̃fʁɔ̃te]

Vouloir réformer pose toujours un défi car cela nous oblige à confronter le statu quo.
-Reform is always a challenge, as it requires us to confront the status quo.

5706 **dévotion** — **devotion**

f
[devɔsjɔ̃]

Pour les sauver, Dieu veut établir dans le monde la dévotion à mon Cœur immaculé.
-To save them, God wishes to establish in the world devotion to my Immaculate Heart.

5707 **naval** — **naval**

adj[naval]

There should be no naval blockade or other intervention, including ground troops. -Pas de blocus naval et pas d'autre intervention, incluant des troupes terrestres.»

5708 **manifestant** — **demonstrator; riotous**

m; adj
[manifɛstɑ̃]

Un manifestant a lancé un cocktail Molotov et l'antenne a pris feu.
-A demonstrator threw a Molotov cocktail and the antenna caught fire.

5709 **label** — **label**

m
[labɛl]

Je démarre mon propre label Will.
-I'm starting my own label, Will.

5710 **sornette** — **fiddlestick**

f
[sɔʁnɛt]

Monsieur le Président, il suffit de présenter des faits pour donner une idée du genre de sornettes que débite le Parti réformiste.
-Speaker, if anybody wants any example of the kind of nonsense that is being spouted by the Reform Party, let us simply respond by facts.

5711 **escale** — **stop**

f
[ɛskal]

Ce navire fait escale à Hong Kong.
-The liner stopped at Hong Kong.

5712 **bousculer** — **hustle**

vb
[buskyle]

Le Parlement se fait bousculer pour approuver sans discussion ce que veut le gouvernement.
-This is parliament being railroaded into rubber stamping what the government wants.

5713 **punaise** — **bug**

f
[pynɛz]

Il est en train d'observer la punaise.
-He's watching the bug.

5714 **oriental** — **Oriental**

adj
[ɔʁjɑ̃tal]

Le Partenariat Oriental crée aussi de vastes possibilités de collaboration.
-An Eastern Partnership can be the arena for such promising cooperation.

5715 **transpirer** — **sweat|transpire**

vb
[tʁɑ̃spiʁe]

59 % des femmes et 68 % des hommes pratiquent pendant leurs loisirs une activité physique les amenant à transpirer au moins une fois par semaine.
-59% of women and 68% of men practice a physical activity to the point of perspiration during their leisure time at least once a week.

5716 **basque** — **Basque; Basque**

adj; f
[bask]

Madame la Présidente, je suis basque et membre du parti nationaliste basque.
-Madam President, I am a Basque and I belong to the Basque Nationalist party.

5717 **maigrir**
vb
[meɡʁiʁ]

slim | become thin
Elle a essayé diverses méthodes pour maigrir.
-She has tried various methods of slimming down.

5718 **atrocité**
f
[atʁɔsite]

atrocity | outrage
Nous sommes tombés amoureux de l'atrocité.
-We fell in love with atrocity.

5719 **mécano**
m
[mekano]

mechanic
Incroyable, elle couchait avec le mécano.
-Unbelievable, she was sleeping with the mechanic.

5720 **cirage**
m[siʁaʒ]

wax | polish
Il a même mangé du cirage. -He even ate the shoe polish.

5721 **ardent**
adj
[aʁdã]

ardent | burning
C'est là le souhait ardent de la communauté internationale.
-This is the ardent hope and expectation of the international community.

5722 **effroyable**
adj
[efʁwajabl]

frightful | appalling
Nous ne changerons pas le comportement effroyable des dictateurs par nos seules paroles.
-We will not change the appalling behaviour of the dictators by words alone.

5723 **fondateur**
m
[fõdatœʁ]

founder
L'université porte le nom de son fondateur.
-The university bears the name of its founder.

5724 **démolition**
f
[demɔlisjõ]

demolition
Je pourrais forcer la démolition du temple.
-I could've forced the demolition of the temple.

5725 **tabouret**
m
[tabuʁɛ]

stool
Si tu veux atteindre le placard du haut tu dois monter sur un tabouret.
-If you stand on this stool, you can reach the top of the closet.

5726 **perspicace**
adj
[pɛʁspikas]

perceptive | perspicacious
Les critères de sélection devraient être sensés et leur application perspicace.
-The criteria for this selection should be sound and their application insightful.

5727 **paternel**
adj; m
[patɛʁnɛl]

paternal; pater
Mon grand-père paternel était Joe Keeper, qui a représenté le Canada au Jeux olympiques de 1912.
-My paternal grandfather was Joe Keeper who represented Canada at the 1912 Olympics.

5728 **diminuer**
vb
[diminɥe]

decrease | reduce
Le règlement de la question du statut doit renforcer la stabilité régionale, et non la diminuer.
-The resolution of status will enhance regional stability, not detract from it.

5729 **auditeur**
m; adj
[oditœʁ]

auditor; auditorial
L'exactitude du calcul est confirmée par un auditeur externe.
-The correctness of the calculation shall be confirmed by an external auditor.

5730 **défensive**

defensive

adj
[defɑ̃siv]

Toute blessure de couteau sur la main d'une victime est considérée défensive.
-Every knife would on a stabbing victim's hand is considered defensive.

5731 **biographie**
f
[bjɔgʁafi]

biography

Il a consacré les dernières années de sa vie à écrire sa biographie.
-He devoted the last years of his life to writing his autobiography.

5732 **prescrire**
vb
[pʁɛskʁiʁ]

prescribe

Dans ces cas, c'est l'autorité de surveillance qui doit prescrire la rectification.
-In such cases, the correction must be prescribed by the supervisory authority.

5733 **conditionné**
adj
[kɔ̃disjɔne]

conditioned

C'est précisément cette démarche qui conditionne la réussite du marché intérieur.
-This is precisely the approach that guarantees the success of the internal market.

5734 **atome**
m
[atom]

atom

Ceci signifie fondamentalement qu'un atome peut émettre un photon.
-This basically means that an atom can emit a photon.

5735 **destructeur**
adj; m
[dɛstʁyktœʁ]

destructive; destroyer

Il ne fait aucun doute qu'un tremblement de terre est un phénomène destructeur.
-There is no doubt that an earthquake is a destructive phenomenon.

5736 **intestin**
adj; m
[ɛ̃tɛstɛ̃]

intestine; intestine

Le duodenum est un segment de l'intestin grêle.
-The duodenum is a section of the small intestine.

5737 **molécule**
f
[mɔlekyl]

molecule

Une molécule d'eau se compose de deux atomes d'hydrogène et d'un atome d'oxygène.
-A molecule of water is made up of one oxygen and two hydrogen atoms.

5738 **saveur**
f
[savœʁ]

flavor|taste

L'échec est le condiment qui donne au succès sa saveur.
-Failure is the condiment that gives success its flavor.

5739 **inculpation**
f
[ɛ̃kylpasjɔ̃]

charge

De plus, l'inculpation et la sommation forment habituellement deux actes distincts et séparés.
-Furthermore, a charge and a summons are usually found in two separate and distinct instruments.

5740 **orgie**
f
[ɔʁʒi]

orgy

Si vous êtes invité à votre première orgie, n'apparaissez simplement pas nue.
-If you get invited to your first orgy, don't just show up naked.

5741 **ivoire**
m
[ivwaʁ]

ivory

Ces questions sont: qui est à proprement parler un citoyen de la Côte d'Ivoire ?
-These are questions such as: who exactly is a citizen of the Ivory Coast?

5742 **crampe**
f
[kʁɑ̃p]

cramp

En nageant, j'ai eu une crampe à la jambe.
-While I was swimming, I got a cramp in my leg.

5743 **dock**
m
[dɔk]

dock

Chercher une serviette sous le dock.
-Searching for a suitcase under the dock.

5744 **sabot**

shoe|hoof

	m [sabo]	L'empreinte a été laissée par un sabot pour genou-cheville-pied orthosis. -The footprint was left by a shoe used for knee-ankle-foot orthosis.
5745	**style** m [stil]	**style|design** Écrit en style simple, tel qu'il est, son papier est facile à lire. -Written in plain style, as it is, his paper is easy to read.
5746	**ruche** f[ʁyʃ]	**hive** D'après les statistiques officielles, il y a 17 291 apiculteurs au Portugal, avec 38 203 ruchers et 562 557 colonies. -According to official statistics, there are 17 291 beekeepers in Portugal, with 38 203 hives and 562 557 colonies.
5747	**kiosque** m [kjɔsk]	**kiosk|newsstand** Arrêtez-vous au kiosque pour acheter le journal. -Stop at the newsstand to buy the paper.
5748	**brusque** adj [bʁysk]	**sudden|brusque** En général, on me reprocherait plutôt d'être trop brusque avec les députés qui souhaitent présenter une motion de procédure. -I am usually accused of being too brusque with Members who want to make a point of order.
5749	**pleurnicher** vb [plœʁniʃe]	**whimper|snivel** Il suffit de soupirer, de se lamenter et de pleurnicher pour obtenir de l'argent [...] et si l'on proteste le moindrement, on passe pour étroit d'esprit. -You sigh and you whine and you snivel, and you get the money... and if you say anything about it, you're a bigot.
5750	**rouvrir** vb [ʁuvʁiʁ]	**reopen** Ces catastrophes ont poussé les autorités à rouvrir le pays à l'aide extérieure. -These disasters pressured the authorities to reopen the country to outside aid.
5751	**picoler** vb [pikɔle]	**drink|booze** Hors du bureau, ces filles ont pas peur de picoler. -Once you get those girls out of the office, they aren't afraid to drink.
5752	**souche** f [suʃ]	**strain|stump** La souche humaine de la maladie est appelée Creutzfeldt-Jakob. -The human strain of the mad cow disease is called Creutzfeldt-Jakob.
5753	**inflation** f [ɛ̃flasjɔ̃]	**inflation** On a prévu quatre pour cent d'inflation pour cette année. -Four percent inflation is forecast for this year.
5754	**australien** adj; m [ɔstʁaljɛ̃]	**Australian; digger** Jiro communique avec son correspondant australien. -Jiro communicates with his pen pal in Australia.
5755	**allégeance** f [aleʒɑ̃s]	**allegiance** Dans beaucoup de cas, l'allégeance tribale prend le pas sur l'allégeance nationale. -Tribal allegiance in many instances supersedes national allegiances.
5756	**poilu** adj [pwaly]	**hairy** Mais dans les dessins de Crumb, tu ressembles à un singe poilu... avec plein de vagues de puanteur qui émanent de ton corps. -But then, the way Crumb draws you... you look like a hairy ape, with all these... wavy, stinky lines undulating off your body.
5757	**réincarnation** f [ʁeɛ̃kaʁnasjɔ̃]	**reincarnation** Crois-tu à la réincarnation ? -Do you believe in reincarnation?
5758	**essentiellement**	**essentially; essentiality**

	adv; nn[esɑ̃sjɛlmɑ̃]	Le parti d'en face dit essentiellement qu'il est opposé à l'égalité fondamentale. -What that group is saying basically is that it is opposed to fundamental equality.

5759 avide — **eager | greedy**

adj
[avid]

Cela signifie que le grand peuple d'Amérique et de plusieurs nations européennes doit obéir aux exigences et aux souhaits d'un petit nombre de personnes avides et invasives.
-That means that the great people of America and various nations of Europe need to obey the demands and wishes of a small number of acquisitive and invasive people.

5760 minorité — **minority | infancy**

f
[minɔʁite]

Rien ne semble plus surprenant à ceux qui considèrent les affaires humaines d'un œil philosophique que la facilité avec laquelle la multitude est gouvernée par une minorité; et la soumission implicite par laquelle les hommes renoncent à leurs propres sentiments et passions pour ceux de leurs gouvernants.
-Nothing appears more surprising to those, who consider human affairs with a philosophical eye, than the easiness with which the many are governed by the few; and the implicit submission, with which men resign their own sentiments and passions to those of their rulers.

5761 anus — **anus**

m
[anys]

Puis on pince les parties privées des garçons, en particulier l'anus et les testicules ou le pénis.
-Private parts of boys, especially the anus and testicles/penis, are squeezed.

5762 cocu — **cuckold; cheated on**

m; adj
[kɔky]

Tu te figures que tout le monde est cocu...
-You imagine that everybody is deceived...

5763 vaillant — **valiant | brave**

adj
[vajɑ̃]

Hall a posé l'acte le plus vaillant et le plus courageux qui soit — il a risqué sa vie pour sauver quelqu'un.
-Hall did the most valiant and brave thing any one person could do — he put his own life at risk to save another.

5764 hospice — **hospice**

m
[ɔspis]

Les gens à l'hospice sont en phase terminale.
-I mean, the people in the hospice are terminally ill.

5765 twist — **twist**

m
[twist]

Celui-ci peut t'apprendre le twist.
-This Sam Adams will teach you the twist.

5766 considérable — **considerable | significant**

adj
[kɔ̃sideʁabl]

C'est là un handicap considérable pour le développement de l'enfant au Libéria.
-This situation is a major bottleneck to the development of children in Liberia.

5767 publicitaire — **advertiser; advertising**

m/f; adj
[pyblisitɛʁ]

C'est juste un coup publicitaire à peu de frais.
-That's just a cheap publicity stunt.

5768 instruire — **instruct | educate**

vb[ɛ̃stʁɥiʁ]

Les enfants ont le droit de s'instruire et de jouir d'un niveau de vie convenable. -Children have the right to an education and to an adequate standard of living.

5769 orchidée — **orchid**

	f	Saul a mis une orchidée dans ses cheveux.
	[ɔʁʃide]	-Saul has already got an orchid behind his ear.

5770 rentable — **profitable|cost-effective**
adj
[ʁɑ̃tabl]
Le SGDDI est conçu pour assurer une gestion efficace et rentable de l'information.
-RDIMS is designed to provide effective and cost-effective information management.

5771 contaminer — **contaminate**
vb
[kɔ̃tamine]
Le plomb, en se décomposant dans l'environnement, peut contaminer le sol et l'eau.
-When it decomposes in the environment, lead can contaminate soil and water.

5772 plongeur — **diver**
m
[plɔ̃ʒœʁ]
Il est bon plongeur.
-He is good at diving.

5773 plausible — **plausible**
adj
[plozibl]
Nothing could be further removed from a plausible causal connection with terrorism than religion.
-Rien n'est moins vraisemblable que d'établir un lien de cause à effet plausible entre la religion et le terrorisme.

5774 ardoise — **slate**
f
[aʁdwaz]
Nous utilisons 27300kg d'ardoise Japonaise.
-We're using 60,000 pounds of Japanese slate.

5775 panthère — **panther**
f
[pɑ̃tɛʁ]
Lorsque j'affirme avoir tué une panthère sans autre secours qu'un couteau, cela signifie que je n'avais pas de chiens avec moi et, que je ne me suis pas servi de carabine.
-When I said that I had killed a panther with nothing but a knife, this means that I did not have any dogs with me and that I did not use a rifle.

5776 anguille — **eel; anguine**
f; adj
[ɑ̃gij]
Mais, il y a aussi l'anguille d'élevage aux Pays-Bas avec une production de 3 800 tonnes.
-On top of that, though, came eel farming in the Netherlands, with production of 3 800 tonnes.

5777 infliger — **impose|mete**
vb
[ɛ̃fliʒe]
Ce phénomène est l'un des pires maux que des individus puissent infliger à autrui.
-Human trafficking is one of the worst wrongs which people can inflict on others.

5778 sérénité — **serenity**
f
[seʁenite]
Çà et là, l'eau brillait comme l'argent et, au-delà, la terre s'élevait en d'ondulantes collines bleues et s'évanouissaient ainsi dans la sérénité du ciel.
-Here and there water shone like silver, and beyond, the land rose into blue undulating hills, and so faded into the serenity of the sky.

5779 radiateur — **radiator**
m[ʁadjatœʁ]
Ne mets pas le portefeuille sur le radiateur. -Don't put the wallet on the top of the heater.

5780 respectueux — **respectful**
adj
[ʁɛspɛktɥø]
Il est nécessaire d'établir un dialogue respectueux entre les diverses religions et civilisations.
-There is a need for respectful dialogue among various religions and civilizations.

5781	**rite** m [ʁit]	**rite** Elle est constituée essentiellement d'Arabes musulmans de rite malékite. -It consists essentially of Muslim Arabs of the Malikite rite.
5782	**potence** f [pɔtãs]	**gallows** On a décapité son cadavre et ceux de ses comparses, et on les a enterrés sous la potence. -His body and those of his henchmen were beheaded and buried under the gallows.
5783	**étincelle** f [etẽsɛl]	**spark** Cet événement fut l'étincelle qui a mené à l'explosion yougoslave des années 1990. -That was the spark that led to the Yugoslav explosion of the 1990s.
5784	**tablier** m [tablije]	**apron** Mon père s'est promis de raccrocher le tablier pour ses soixante ans ! -My father promised himself that he'd hang up his apron at sixty.
5785	**trio** m [tʁijo]	**trio** En tant que dernier pays du trio, nous allons assurer une transition sans heurt vers le prochain trio. -As the final country in the trio we will ensure a smooth transition to the next trio.
5786	**charabia** m [ʃaʁabja]	**gibberish** La théorie de la relativité d'Einstein, pour moi, c'est du charabia. -Einstein's theory of relativity is gibberish to me.
5787	**jeton** m [ʒətɔ̃]	**token** Ledit dispositif comprend un processeur conçu pour générer une demande de détection de connexion comprenant un jeton. -The device includes a processor configured to generate a connection detection request including a token.
5788	**bobard** m [bɔbaʁ]	**lie** Il va falloir un gros bobard, et je suis pas douée pour ça. -It's gonna require a really big lie and I'm terrible at that.
5789	**flair** m [flɛʁ]	**flair** Un chien a un flair très développé. -A dog has a sharp sense of smell.
5790	**craie** f [kʁɛ]	**chalk** Ce n'est pas facile d'écrire avec une craie. -It is not easy to write in chalk.
5791	**actualité** f [aktɥalite]	**actuality** Il lit le journal pour suivre l'actualité. -He reads the newspaper in order to keep up with the times.
5792	**socialisme** m [sɔsjalism]	**socialism** Socialisme ou barbarie. -Socialism or barbarism.
5793	**ingrédient** m [ẽgʁedjã]	**ingredient** Une meilleure coopération avec l' OSCE sera un ingrédient majeur en la matière. -Improved cooperation with the OSCE will be a vital ingredient in this.
5794	**clarifier** vb [klaʁifje]	**clarify** De notre point de vue, l'Organisation doit clarifier sa position sur ce sujet. -In our view, there is a need to clarify our Organization's position on this subject.

5795	**stimulant** adj; m [stimylã]	**stimulating; stimulant** Ce sera beaucoup plus stimulant qu'ici. -It is far more stimulating there than in here.
5796	**désobéir** vb [dezɔbeiʁ]	**disobey** Ils sont obligés de désobéir à de tels ordres et de porter plainte à cet effet. -They were obliged to disobey such orders and lodge the corresponding complaints.
5797	**solidarité** f [sɔlidaʁite]	**solidarity** Mais il ne pourra y avoir de solidarité budgétaire sans solidarité fiscale. -There can, however, be no budget solidarity without fiscal solidarity.
5798	**octave** m [ɔktav]	**octave** Une bande passante instantanée inférieure à une demi-octave. -An instantaneous bandwidth of less than half an octave.
5799	**waters** m [wate]	**bathroom|can** Il est l'heure d'écouter le type des waters. -It's time to listen to the bathroom guy.
5800	**gouine** f [gwin]	**dyke** Tu ferais pourtant une bonne gouine. -I still maintain you'd make a good dyke.
5801	**bambou** m [bãbu]	**bamboo** Les produits en bambou seront vendus sur le marché national et international. -The bamboo products will be sold on both the domestic and the international market.
5802	**indication** f [ɛ̃dikasjɔ̃]	**indication** Il n'y avait aucune indication que quoi que ce soit clochait. -There was no indication that anything was wrong.
5803	**pornographie** f [pɔʁnɔgʁafi]	**pornography** La pornographie, particulièrement la pornographie juvénile, est-elle un sujet de préoccupation ? -Is pornography, particularly child pornography, a concern?
5804	**missionnaire** adj; m [misjɔnɛʁ]	**missionary; missionary** Votre paroisse entend suivre son patron et célèbre aujourd'hui sa journée missionnaire. -Your parish intends to follow its Patron Saint, and today celebrates its mission day.
5805	**fente** f [fãt]	**slot|slit** Cette coupe réceptrice comprend également une fente ou rainure à travers laquelle passe une tige de support. -The receiver cup also includes a slot or groove through which a support rod passes.
5806	**meneur** m [mənœʁ]	**leader** Jack n'a pas ce qu'il faut pour être un meneur. -Jack doesn't have what it takes to be a leader.
5807	**semence** f [səmãs]	**seed|seeds** De la semence pourrie nous vient le fruit nourrissant. -From the rotten seed comes to us the nutritious fruit.
5808	**mât** m [ma]	**mast** Le mât cassa et notre navire commença à dériver. -The mast broke and our ship went adrift.
5809	**tramway**	**streetcar**

	m	La ville a décidé de supprimer le tramway.
	[tʁamwɛ]	-The city has decided to do away with the streetcar.
5810	**accélérateur**	**accelerator**
	m	As-tu déjà, dans ta voiture et après un long moment sans conduite, appuyé
	[akseleʁatœʁ]	par inadvertance sur le frein et sur l'accélérateur ?
		-Have you ever got in your car after a long absence and got the brake mixed up with the accelerator?
5811	**furie**	**fury|she-cat**
	f	La furie de la nature ne fait pas la distinction entre pays développés et pays
	[fyʁi]	en développement.
		-Nature's fury does not distinguish between developing and developed countries.
5812	**prévision**	**forecast**
	f	Tu devrais toujours économiser de l'argent en prévision de périodes de
	[pʁevizjõ]	vaches maigres.
		-You should always save money for a rainy day.
5813	**camouflage**	**camouflage**
	m	Le chasseur portait des vêtements de camouflage.
	[kamuflaʒ]	-The hunter wore camouflage clothing.
5814	**impair**	**odd; faux pas**
	adj; m	Un nombre pair multiplié par un nombre impair donne un nombre pair. Un
	[ɛ̃pɛʁ]	nombre impair multiplié par un nombre impair donne un nombre impair.
		-Even times odd is even, odd times odd is odd.
5815	**intituler**	**title**
	vb	L'article était intitulé: Une patriote âgée sermonne Nortel.
	[ɛ̃tityle]	-The headline read: Elderly Patriot scolds Nortel.
5816	**gadget**	**gadget**
	m	L'Enviromod est un gadget pré-programmé.
	[gadʒɛt]	-I mean, an Enviromod is just a preprogrammed gadget.
5817	**psychique**	**psychic**
	adj	Il peut y avoir lieu à l'internement compulsif des porteurs d'anomalie
	[psiʃik]	psychique.
		-Internment may be ordered for minors suffering from mental disorders.
5818	**tempe**	**temple**
	f	Ils ont ensuite torturé le père, le frappant à la tempe avec la crosse d'un
	[tɑ̃p]	pistolet jusqu'à ce qu'il perde connaissance.
		-The soldiers then tortured the father, hitting him on the temple with a pistol butt until he lost consciousness.
5819	**motiver**	**motivate**
	vb[mɔtive]	Je comprends le contexte qui peut motiver certains commentaires impromptus. -I understand the background that would motivate certain off-the-cuff comments.
5820	**brick**	**brig**
	m	Une nouvelle carte marine et un nouveau compte rendu de l'expédition du
	[bʁik]	brick El Activo ont été découverts.
		-A new chart and a new report from the expedition of the brig El Activo have been discovered.
5821	**prolonger**	**extend|prolong**
	vb	Le gouvernement n'a fait que prolonger ce transfert pour une période de
	[pʁɔlõʒe]	quatre ans.
		-This government has only delivered a four-year extension to this transfer.
5822	**débauche**	**debauchery**

	f [deboʃ]	Le fait de tenir des tripots, lieux de débauche ou débits de boissons clandestins. --Running dens for gambling, debauchery or consumption of alcoholic drinks.
5823	**gogo** m [gɔgo]	**sucker** Il y a un gogo qui naît chaque minute. -There's a sucker born every minute.
5824	**fiesta** f [fjɛsta]	**shindig** On fera une fiesta ce soir. -We're going to have a fiesta tonight.
5825	**rougir** vb [ʁuʒiʁ]	**blush|go red** C'est magnifique de le voir rougir. -It is nice to see him blush.
5826	**séduction** f [sedyksjɔ̃]	**seduction** La séduction devient intéressante lorsque l'un des protagonistes se fait désirer. -Courtships get interesting when one of the two plays hard to get.
5827	**brésilien** adj [bʁeziljɛ̃]	**Brazilian** La montée de l'intolérance préoccupe gravement le Gouvernement brésilien. -The sentiment of growing intolerance is a serious concern for the Brazilian Government.
5828	**coroner** m [kɔʁɔnɛʁ]	**coroner** Le Coroner a refusé de formuler toute recommandation à l'égard de cette affaire. -The Coroner declined to make any recommendations in regard to this matter.
5829	**huissier** m [ɥisje]	**bailiff** Donnez ces lunettes à l'huissier. -What? - Give those glasses to the bailiff.
5830	**attache** f [ataʃ]	**clip** Je n'attache pas une grande importance à son opinion. -I don't make much of his opinion.
5831	**éruption** f [eʁypsjɔ̃]	**eruption|rash** Le volcan est, cette année, entré deux fois en éruption. -The volcano has erupted twice this year.
5832	**piment** m [pimã]	**spice** Ne vous frottez jamais les yeux après avoir coupé un piment. -Never rub your eyes after cutting a hot pepper.
5833	**incliner** vb [ɛ̃kline]	**tilt|incline** Nous avons besoin de l'incliner sur le côté. -We need to tilt her on her side.
5834	**investigation** f [ɛ̃vɛstigasjɔ̃]	**investigation|inquiry** Le Ministère de la Justice des États-Unis et le Bureau fédéral d'investigation (FBI) ont pris pour cible des musulmans américains lors d'opérations d'infiltration abusives menées dans le cadre de la lutte antiterroriste et basées sur des critères d'identité religieuse et ethnique, ont affirmé Human Rights Watch et l'Institut des droits de l'homme. -The US Justice Department and the Federal Bureau of Investigation (FBI) have targeted American Muslims in abusive counterterrorism "sting operations" based on religious and ethnic identity, Human Rights Watch and Human Rights Institute said.

5835	**politiquement**	**politically**
	adv	Il peut en sortir affaibli militairement, mais politiquement renforcé.
	[pɔlitikmã]	-Possibly it will come out debilitated militarily, but strengthened politically.

5836	**illégalement**	**illegally**
	adv	Il instituera une interdiction d'investir sur des biens illégalement expropriés.
	[ilegalmã]	-It will provide for a ban on investments in illegally expropriated property.

5837	**cloner**	**clone**
	vb	Elle est vraiment une figure marquante du Parti libéral, un symbole que j'aimerais pouvoir cloner.
	[klɔne]	-She is truly an icon in the Liberal Party, an icon I could only wish to clone.

5838	**tige**	**stem|spindle**
	f	« Jack a offert à Jill une boite de pralines et une rose à longue tige pour son anniversaire. » « C'est vraiment mignon. »
	[tiʒ]	-"Jack gave Jill a box of chocolates and one long-stemmed rose for her birthday." "That's really sweet."

5839	**lugubre**	**dismal|lugubrious**
	adj	Quoi qu'il en soit, même cette lugubre raison économique ne justifie pas un massacre de cette ampleur.
	[lygybʁ]	-Yet even this dismal economic justification for culling on such a scale does not stand up.

5840	**gigolo**	**gigolo**
	m	Notre maison été détenu par un gigolo.
	[ʒigɔlo]	-Your brownstone used to be owned by a gigolo.

5841	**tourment**	**torment**
	m	Un jouet pour Joffrey à la torture ou la reine Cersei au tourment.
	[tuʁmã]	-A plaything for Joffrey to torture or Queen Cersei to torment.

5842	**affectation**	**assignment|allocation**
	f	Je pensais que cette affectation devait être temporaire.
	[afɛktasjõ]	-I just thought this assignment was supposed to be temporary.

5843	**bobine**	**coil|reel**
	f	L'ensemble bobine comprend une cavité.
	[bɔbin]	-The coil assembly is provided with a cavity.

5844	**placement**	**investment|placement**
	m	Le placement dans les familles est privilégié par rapport au placement en institution.
	[plasmã]	-Priority is given to placement in families rather than placement in institutions.

5845	**tocard**	**tacky; loser**
	adj; m	Ce tocard a engagé un certain Rosie, qui connaît sans doute Darius.
	[tɔkaʁ]	-That loser hired somebody named Rosie who probably knows Darius.

5846	**harmonica**	**harmonica**
	m	C'est le premier joueur reconnu de blues à l'harmonica.
	[aʁmɔnika]	-He's the first acknowledged master of the country blues harmonica.

5847	**pilier**	**pillar|pier**
	m	Il s'appuya contre le pilier et contempla la Statue de la Liberté.
	[pilje]	-He leaned against the pillar and gazed at the Statue of Liberty.

5848	**neutraliser**	**neutralize|negative**
	vb	Elle a entrepris de neutraliser, politiquement et physiquement, cette autre communauté.
	[nøtʁalize]	-It had undertaken to neutralize, politically and physically, the other community.

5849 compréhensif   **comprehensive**

[kɔ̃pʁeɑ̃sif]

Nous saluons cet examen compréhensif qui devrait devenir un exercice périodique.
 -We welcome this comprehensive assessment, which should become a regular exercise.

5850 croquette   **croquette**

f
[kʁɔkɛt]

L'invention concerne également des aliments pour animaux comportant une croquette sous la forme d'un noyau saupoudré avec des principes actifs.
 -An animal feed comprising a kibble in the form of a core dusted with active ingredients.

5851 argenterie   **silverware**

f
[aʁʒɑ̃tʁi]

Quand je sors, elle compte l'argenterie.
 -When I leave, she counts the silverware.

5852 coffret   **case**

m
[kɔfʁɛ]

Ensemble compresseur comprenant un boîtier et un coffret électrique.
 -A compressor assembly including a housing and a terminal box is provided.

5853 banjo   **banjo**

m
[bɑ̃ʒo]

Pour devenir un joueur professionnel de banjo, il faut passer des milliers d'heures à pratiquer.
 -To become a professional banjo player, you need to spend thousands of hours practicing.

5854 neuvième   **ninth**

num
[nœvjɛm]

Ce neuvième rapport est soumis conformément aux résolutions susmentionnées.
 -This ninth report is submitted in accordance with the aforementioned resolutions.

5855 shampooing   **shampoo**

m
[ʃɑ̃powɛ̃g]

Être chauve présente au moins un avantage - on économise beaucoup en shampooing.
 -Being bald has at least one advantage - you save a lot on shampoo.

5856 sangler   **strap**

vb
[sɑ̃gle]

Ne pas sangler la personne âgée à son lit.
 -Do not strap the elderly person in bed.

5857 stagiaire   **trainee**

m/f
[staʒjɛʁ]

Il emploie treize personnes occupant 7,9 postes et comprend un poste de stagiaire juridique.
 -It employs thirteen persons occupying 7.9 posts, including a legal trainee's post.

5858 délicatesse   **delicacy|sensitivity**

f
[delikatɛs]

C'est une impardonnable faute de délicatesse.
 -Running away from a ghost is an unforgiveable lack of delicacy.

5859 cerner   **invest|bestow**

vb
[sɛʁne]

Et Allah ne cesse de cerner (par Sa science) ce qu'ils font.
 -God indeed encompasses (with His Knowledge) all that they do.

5860 trèfle   **clover|shamrock**

m
[tʁɛfl]

Je laisse du trèfle pousser sur les bords.
 -I am allowing clover to grow on the edges.

5861 donjon   **dungeon**

m
[dɔ̃ʒɔ̃]

Je surveille la porte du donjon.
 -Okay. I've got eyeballs on the dungeon door.

5862 belge   **Belgian**

adj
[bɛlʒ]

Une mention honorable a été décernée à Yolande Mukagasana, Rwandaise de nationalité belge née au Rwanda en 1954.
-Moreover, the jury also awarded an Honourable Mention to Yolande Mukagasana, a Rwandan-Belgian woman born in Rwanda in 1954.

5863 **aval**

m; adj
[aval]

approval; down-stream

À notre avis, l'aval de l'opposition devrait être obligatoire.
-We believe the opposition's approval should be mandatory.

5864 **alimenter**

vb
[alimɑ̃te]

feed

L'instabilité politique continuait d'alimenter l'instabilité économique.
-Political instability continued to feed economic instability.

5865 **barbu**

adj; m
[baʁby]

bearded; bearded man

Dessin 4: Un homme barbu portant un turban, debout avec un halo en forme de croissant de lune au-dessus de la tête.
-Drawing 4: A bearded man wearing a turban, standing with a halo shaped like a crescent moon over his head.

5866 **mitraillette**

f
[mitʁajɛt]

submachine gun

Un individu serait descendu du véhicule et aurait ouvert le feu sur les deux hommes avec une mitraillette.
-A man allegedly alighted from the vehicle and opened fire on the two men with a submachine gun.

5867 **requérir**

vb
[ʁəkeʁiʁ]

require

La Norvège regrette vivement que cette pratique odieuse continue de requérir notre attention.
-Norway strongly regrets the fact that this abhorrent practice continues to require our attention.

5868 **agressivité**

f
[agʁesivite]

aggressiveness

La consommation abusive de drogues peut conduire à l'impulsivité et à l'agressivité.
-Abusing drugs can lead to impulsivity and aggression.

5869 **cambrioler**

vb
[kɑ̃bʁijɔle]

burgle|rob

Pas besoin de cambrioler de banque.
-Now I don't actually have to rob banks.

5870 **remboursement**

m
[ʁɑ̃buʁsəmɑ̃]

reimbursement|refund

Je veux un remboursement.
-I want a refund.

5871 **couvercle**

m
[kuvɛʁkl]

lid

Ce couvercle est si serré que je ne peux l'ouvrir.
-This lid is so tight I can't open it.

5872 **acquitter**

vb
[akite]

pay|discharge

Il salue les efforts déployés par tous pour s'acquitter du mandat de la COCOVINU.
-It appreciates the great efforts that all are making to fulfil UNMOVIC's mandate.

5873 **épuisement**

m
[epɥizmɑ̃]

exhaustion|depletion

Je meurs d'épuisement.
-I'm dying of exhaustion.

5874 **pesant**

adj
[pəzɑ̃]

cumbersome

Wang a affirmé qu'il était innocent de toutes les charges pesant contre lui.
-Mr. Wang claimed that he was innocent of all charges levelled against him.

5875 **égyptien**

Egyptian

adj
[eʒipsjɛ̃]

Le Rapporteur spécial remercie le Gouvernement égyptien pour sa réponse.
-The Special Rapporteur would like to thank the Egyptian Government for its reply.

5876 **encens**
m
[ɑ̃sɑ̃]

incense

Trouve de l'encens pour les offrandes rituelles.
-Get some incense for sacrificial offerings.

5877 **aération**
f
[aeʁasjɔ̃]

aeration

Les avantages de l'aération sont illustrés et décrits.
-The benefits of aeration are shown and described for each season of the year.

5878 **casserole**
f
[kasʁɔl]

pan

Cette casserole avec des trous dedans.
-You know, that pan with the holes in it.

5879 **manchot**
m; adj
[mɑ̃ʃo]

penguin; one-handed

C'est un manchot empereur comme les autres.
-He's a regular emperor penguin.

5880 **nabot**
m; adj
[nabo]

runt; dwarfish

Je crois m'en prendre à un nabot malingre.
-I am messing with a pencil-neck midget, I believe.

5881 **ravoir**
vb
[ʁavwaʁ]

get back

Monsieur le Président, je suis très heureux de souligner que les contribuables vont ravoir les 30 milliards de dollars qui leur appartiennent à juste titre.
-Speaker, I am very glad to underline that the taxpayers are going to get back the $30 billion that rightfully belongs to them.

5882 **incognito**
adv; m[ɛ̃kɔɲito]

incognito; incognito

Oui, mais il viendra incognito. -Yes, though he'll be coming incognito.

5883 **symbolique**
adj
[sɛ̃bɔlik]

symbolic|nominal

Nous nous réjouissons de cette décision, qui revêt une valeur symbolique incontestable.
-We are delighted with this decision, which is of unquestionable symbolic value.

5884 **protestation**
f
[pʁɔtɛstasjɔ̃]

protest|outcry

Lever les mains est devenu un symbole de protestation.
-Raised hands have become a symbol of protest.

5885 **stabilité**
f
[stabilite]

stability|steadiness

La politique budgétaire sera déterminante pour la stabilité macroéconomique.
-Fiscal policy will be the key element of a sound macroeconomic stability.

5886 **flan**
m
[flɑ̃]

flan|pudding

Vous avez sûrement mangé trop de flan.
-Maybe you shouldn't have had all that pudding.

5887 **boudin**
m
[budɛ̃]

black pudding|blood sausage

Il est autorisé en France et nous le trouvons dans le boudin, par exemple.
-It is authorised in France and used in black pudding, for example.

5888 **marqué**
adj
[maʁke]

marked

Mais ce texte est bien trop marqué par un esprit fédéraliste.
-However, its federalist tendencies are rather too pronounced.

5889 **cuvette**
f
[kyvɛt]

bowl|basin

Votre fils Flynn a été vu buvant dans la cuvette des toilettes.
-Your son Flynn has been observed drinking from a toilet bowl.

5890 **convertir**

convert

	vb [kɔ̃vɛʁtiʁ]	Elle aimait les hommes gras, elle décida donc de se convertir au Bouddhisme. -She loved fat men, so she decided to convert to Buddhism.
5891	**composé** adj; m [kɔ̃poze]	**compound; compound** Le film alimentaire est composé de polyéthylène. -Cling film is made from polyethylene.
5892	**mélancolique** adj; m/f [melɑ̃kɔlik]	**melancholy; melancholiac** J'espère que ce ne sera pas un effort inutile, car un penseur de mon pays disait que l'effort inutile mène à la mélancolie et, à cette heure tardive, je ne tiens pas à devenir mélancolique. -I hope it will not be a wasted effort, because a thinker from my country used to say that wasted effort leads to melancholy, and at this time of night I do not want to get melancholic.
5893	**importuner** vb [ɛ̃pɔʁtyne]	**bother** Bien que ce soit un fait bien établi, les autres ont toujours du mal à comprendre que le but n'est pas d'importuner les transporteurs routiers. -Although that is a well-known fact, it was still difficult to make others see that this is not about pestering lorries.
5894	**domination** f [dɔminasjɔ̃]	**domination** Vous parlez de domination du marché, domination potentielle. -You talk about market domination, potential domination.
5895	**blocage** m[blɔkaʒ]	**blocking** Aucun problème avec le blocage nerveux. -There's no problem with the nerve block.
5896	**caissier** m [kesje]	**cashier** L'acheteur doit aller en personne chez le Caissier pour régler le matériel. -The buyer must go to the Cashier's Office in person to pay for the equipment.
5897	**rôder** vb [ʁode]	**prowl|lurk** Ceux qui cherchent à promouvoir la transparence devraient cesser de rôder dans les couloirs, d'enregistrer et de filmer leurs collègues secrètement. -Those who seek to promote transparency should cease to skulk in the corridors and secretly record and film their colleagues.
5898	**sceller** vb [sele]	**seal|embed** À moins d'un changement de dernière minute, la proposition de Londres risque bien de sceller un échec cuisant. -Unless there are last-minute changes, London's proposal is liable to set the seal on a resounding failure.
5899	**carré** adj; m [kaʁe]	**square; square** Un carré a quatre côtés égaux. -A square has four equal sides.
5900	**dôme** m [dom]	**dome** Les anneaux compromettent peut-être l'intégrité du dôme. -It's possible the rings compromise the dome's integrity.
5901	**saboter** vb [sabɔte]	**sabotage** D'un autre côté, exiger l'unanimité peut saboter des mesures par ailleurs impératives. -On the other hand, the requirement of unanimity can sabotage imperative actions.
5902	**fané** adj [fane]	**withered|dry** J'ai couru. J'ai dévoué ma vie entière à courir une fleur qui, à peine atteinte, avait déjà fané.

-I ran. I devoted my entire life to running to a flower that had already wilted when I reached it.

5903	**torchon**	**tea towel**
	m	Mayuko a essuyé la table avec un torchon.
	[tɔʁʃɔ̃]	-Mayuko wiped a table with a cloth.

5904	**inimaginable**	**unimaginable**
	adj	Il ne faut pas supposer pour autant que la volonté délibérée de ce faire est inimaginable.
	[inimaʒinabl]	-Nevertheless, it should not be assumed that such wilfulness is unimaginable.

5905	**rapidité**	**speed|rapidity**
	f	J'étais stupéfait par la rapidité de sa réaction.
	[ʁapidite]	-I was stunned by the speed of its reaction.

5906	**probation**	**probation**
	f	Probation (especially adult probation) and other non-institutional measures.
	[pʁɔbasjɔ̃]	-Probation et autres mesures non privatives de liberté (notamment probation des adultes).

5907	**pascal**	**pascal; paschal**
	m; adj[paskal]	Le pascal est une unité de mesure utilisée dans les pressions barométriques. -Pascal is a unit of measurement used in barometric pressure.

5908	**exorcisme**	**exorcism**
	m	La cérémonie reproduit l'exorcisme originel.
	[ɛgzɔʁsism]	-The ceremony is a reenactment of the original exorcism.

5909	**zèle**	**zeal**
	m	Vous mettez toute l'opération en danger avec votre... zèle.
	[zɛl]	-You put our entire operation at risk of exposure with your... zeal.

5910	**sandale**	**sandal**
	f	Enlève tes sandales: car tu es dans la vallée sacrée Tuwa.
	[sɑ̃dal]	-So take off your sandals, for you are in the sacred valley of Tuwa.

5911	**pli**	**fold|ply**
	m	Il y a un pli rebelle sur ma chemise que je n'arrive simplement pas à avoir avec le fer à repasser.
	[pli]	-There's a pesky wrinkle on my shirt that I just can't get the iron to remove.

5912	**avancement**	**advancement|promotion**
	m	Mon avancement dépend de sa décision.
	[avɑ̃smɑ̃]	-My promotion hangs on his decision.

5913	**descendant**	**descending; descendant**
	adj; m	Attention à la marche en descendant les escaliers.
	[desɑ̃dɑ̃]	-Watch your step in going down the stairs.

5914	**pâtée**	**mash|food**
	f	Si tu me ressers de cette pâtée, je devrais la balancer à la poubelle.
	[pate]	-If you keep serving up this sort of mash, I'm going to have to keep spitting it in the bin.

5915	**propice**	**suitable**
	adj	L'utilisation abusive de pièces d'identité n'est pas toujours propice à une société durable.
	[pʁɔpis]	-The improper use of ID does not always prove conducive to a sustainable society.

5916	**oppression**	**oppression**
	f	George Eliot est subtilement subversive : il y a des nécessiteux dans tous les bords et ses personnages féminins collaborent à une oppression mutuelle
	[ɔpʁesjɔ̃]	

détaillée de manière exquise.
-George Eliot is subtly subversive: there are have-nots on every fringe, and her women collaborate in exquisitely detailed mutual oppression.

5917 affectueux — **affectionate**
adj
[afɛktɥø]
A tous, mes affectueux encouragements et l'assurance de mes prières.
-To all, my affectionate encouragement and the assurance of my prayers.

5918 morbide — **morbid**
adj
[mɔʁbid]
Je pense que les députés réformistes ont une fascination morbide pour ce genre de faits.
-There is a morbid fascination that Reform members seem to have with dragging these issues before the House of Commons.

5919 déserter — **desert**
vb[dezɛʁte]
Durant leur séjour aux États-Unis, ils ont été harcelés, ont fait l'objet d'interrogatoires abusifs et ont été incités à déserter. -During their captivity they were harassed, interrogated harshly and urged to desert.

5920 cortège — **procession**
m
[kɔʁtɛʒ]
Son cortège nuptial arrive de Manikpur.
-Her wedding procession is coming all the way from Manikpur...

5921 dépouiller — **strip|skin**
vb
[depuje]
La véritable erreur, les véritables torts sont du côté de ceux qui ont voulu dépouiller les États de leurs prérogatives régaliennes.
-The real mistake and the real errors lie with those who sought to strip the Member States of their sovereign powers.

5922 noyade — **drowning**
f
[nwajad]
Ces personnes ont été sauvées de la noyade par notre équipe de patrouille maritime maltaise.
-In fact these people were saved from drowning by our Maltese maritime patrol team.

5923 mentalité — **mentality**
f
[mãtalite]
C'est la mentalité des athlètes.
-Well, that's the athlete's mentality.

5924 denteler — **indent**
vb
[dãtle]
Le manchon protecteur est souple et conçu pour transmettre, à la partie de la paroi cardiaque, une force sur celle-ci, au moyen de l'élément de commande, de manière à denteler la partie de la paroi cardiaque.
-The protective sheath is flexible and operable to transmit, to the heart wall portion, a force thereon by the actuator element for indenting the heart wall portion.

5925 véranda — **veranda|porch**
f
[veʁãda]
Sergent-chef, livrez vos armes sous la véranda et une brigade les récupérera.
-Now, sergeant major, if you leave your weapons on the veranda I'll send a squad to collect them.

5926 bonder — **cram**
vb
[bɔ̃de]
La semaine dernière, nous avons vu des trains bondés de réfugiés sans carte d'identité ni bien.
-Last week we saw the crowded trains crammed with refugees without identity cards or belongings.

5927 manipulation — **handling|rigging**
f
[manipylasjɔ̃]
L'accessoire doit être réutilisable et permettre une manipulation intensive et automatique de tels tonneaux.
-The appliance must be reusable and allows an intensive and automatic handling of such barrels.

5928 côtelette — **chop**
f
[kɔtlɛt]
Cette côtelette de veau aurait une ligne autour du coin.
-No. That veal chop would have a line around the corner.

5929 gaucher — **left-hander; left-handed**
m; adj
[goʃe]
Le sénateur Mahovlich: Et c'est en plus un gaucher.
-Senator Mahovlich: And he is a southpaw.

5930 croiseur — **cruiser**
m [kʁwazœʁ]
Le croiseur est retourné en orbite. -Sir, the cruiser's returned to orbit.

5931 tram — **tram|car**
m
[tʁam]
Alors que j'attendais le tram, j'ai assisté à un accident.
-While I was waiting for the streetcar, I witnessed a traffic accident.

5932 motion — **motion**
f
[mɔsjɔ̃]
Il y a eu deux-cent-quinze suffrages en faveur de la motion et quinze contre.
-There were 215 votes for the motion and 15 votes against it.

5933 confrontation — **showdown**
f
[kɔ̃fʁɔ̃tasjɔ̃]
Tout le monde sait que la Guerre Froide est une confrontation entre deux pays.
-Everybody knows that Cold War is the confrontation between two nations.

5934 talisman — **talisman**
m
[talismɑ̃]
Consacriamo nous à Madonna moyens d'engager elle-même et de ne pas trouver, dans le présent, une sorte d'amulette ou de talisman en chance.
-Consacriamo us to Madonna means to bind her and not find, in this, a kind of talisman or amulet lucky.

5935 uranium — **uranium**
m
[yʁanjɔm]
Enriched uranium means uranium containing a greater mass percentage of uranium-235 than 0.72%.
-Uranium enrichi, l'uranium contenant un pourcentage en masse d'uranium 235 supérieur à 0,72%.

5936 vortex — **vortex**
m
[vɔʁtɛks]
Il faut désamorcer ce vortex à puissance négative.
-We'll all regret it if we don't deal with this negative power vortex.

5937 branlette — **hand job**
f
[bʁɑ̃lɛt]
Tu lui as déjà fait une branlette.
-You already gave him a hand job.

5938 extension — **extension|expansion**
f
[ɛkstɑ̃sjɔ̃]
Elle attribue, pour chaque extension, un numéro d'ordre, dénommé numéro d'extension.
-It shall assign a serial number to each extension, to be known as the extension number.

5939 catin — **trollop|whore**
f
[katɛ̃]
La mort de cette catin d'Anne Boleyn est providentielle.
-The death of whore Anne Boleyn is perhaps providential.

5940 désarmer — **disarm**
vb
[dezaʁme]
Nous ne pouvons désarmer ou rendre compte de mesures de désarmement alors que nous avons déjà désarmé.
-We cannot disarm or report on disarmament of those that are already disarmed.

5941 décapiter — **decapitate**
vb
[dekapite]
On se rappellera qu'Henri VIII, par un simple décret, pouvait faire décapiter n'importe qui en Angleterre.

-You will remember that Henry VIII could, by decree, order that anyone in England be beheaded.

5942 délice — **delight**
m[delis]
J'ai eu l'occasion de voyager avec elle, et ce fut un pur délice. -I also had the occasion to travel with her, which was an absolute delight.

5943 indifférence — **indifference**
f
[ɛ̃difeʁɑ̃s]
L'indifférence de la population est évidente et ô combien compréhensible. -The indifference of the population is obvious and entirely understandable.

5944 pif — **conk|snitch**
m
[pif]
Méfie-toi, tu vas t'écorcher le pif. -Be careful, Matt, or you're going to cut the nose right off of you.

5945 compensation — **compensation**
f
[kɔ̃pɑ̃sasjɔ̃]
La solution est claire: il y a soit compensation financière, soit compensation sous une autre forme. -That is an obvious solution: either financial compensation or compensation in some other form.

5946 recoudre — **sew|sew up**
vb
[ʁəkudʁ]
Donc ils doivent recoudre le trou. -So they're going to sew up the hole.

5947 maritime — **maritime**
adj
[maʁitim]
Mars tomberait sur le droit maritime... -Well, technically, Mars would be under maritime laws.

5948 méditer — **meditate|think**
vb
[medite]
Au moins à la salle d'étude, je peux méditer. -At least in study hall I can meditate.

5949 endurance — **endurance|stamina**
f
[ɑ̃dyʁɑ̃s]
Vous devez avoir beaucoup d'endurance pour être un athlète olympique. -You have to have a lot of stamina to be an Olympic athlete.

5950 cobaye — **guinea pig**
m
[kɔbaj]
Dans le cas d'espèce, nous avons d'une certaine manière servi de cobaye. -In this particular case, we have in a way been a guinea pig.

5951 reddition — **surrender**
f
[ʁedisjɔ̃]
Je viens négocier les conditions de votre reddition. -I'm here to negotiate the terms of your surrender.

5952 adolescence — **adolescence**
f
[adɔlesɑ̃s]
Je ne me suis pas senti comme ça depuis mon adolescence. -I haven't felt like this since I was a teenager.

5953 azur — **azure**
m
[azyʁ]
Les touristes, sur la Côte d'Azur, sont cambriolés par des voleurs qui les gazent pendant qu'ils dorment. -Tourists on the Azure Coast are being robbed by thieves who gas them as they sleep.

5954 puéril — **childish**
adj
[pɥeʁil]
C'est puéril et indigne de la vision européenne des pères fondateurs. -This is childish and unworthy of the founding fathers' European vision.

5955 précoce — **precocious**
adj
[pʁekɔs]
Dépistage précoce en vue d'une intervention rapide en faveur des enfants handicapés. -Early identification of and early intervention for children with disabilities.

5956 forain — **showman**

	m	Alors il vient à nous, comme d'habitude, ce bon à rien de forain.
	[fɔʁɛ̃]	-So he comes to us, as usual, the good-for-nothing showman.
5957	**jupon**	**petticoat**
	m[ʒypɔ̃]	Tu examines tout ce qui porte jupon. -You look at everything in a skirt.
5958	**marraine**	**godmother**
	f	Elle est ma marraine.
	[maʁɛn]	-She's my godmother.
5959	**romantisme**	**romanticism**
	m	Et ils disent que le romantisme est mort.
	[ʁɔmɑ̃tism]	-And they say romance is dead.
5960	**cornichon**	**gherkin|nincompoop**
	m	Donc, bois ton jus de cornichon.
	[kɔʁniʃɔ̃]	-So, drink your pickle juice.
5961	**capitaliste**	**capitalist; capitalistic**
	m/f; adj	Le modèle économique capitaliste n'est pas efficace en réduisant la pauvreté.
	[kapitalist]	-The capitalist economic model was not effective at resolving poverty.
5962	**diplomatie**	**diplomacy**
	f	Cette diplomatie de proximité constitue un outil efficace de la diplomatie préventive.
	[diplɔmasi]	-This diplomacy of proximity is a useful tool of preventive diplomacy.
5963	**gibbon**	**gibbon**
	m	Elle est plus proche d'un gibbon que de moi.
	[ʒibɔ̃]	-In relation, she's closer to a gibbon than she is to me.
5964	**pudeur**	**modesty**
	f	Exquise pudeur d'une vraie jeune fille.
	[pydœʁ]	-The exquisite modesty of a true maiden.
5965	**récréation**	**recreation|recess**
	f	Toutes les cours de récréation ont leur tyran.
	[ʁekʁeasjɔ̃]	-Every playground has its bully.
5966	**fracas**	**crash|smash**
	m	De vieux antagonismes en sommeil se sont réveillés avec comme moyens d'expression privilégiés, le fracas des armes et un mépris pour les normes humanitaires.
	[fʁaka]	-Dormant antagonisms have been reawakened, with the primary manifestation being the clash of arms and disdain for fundamental humanitarian norms.
5967	**tee**	**tee**
	m	Tu as une tache sur ton tee-shirt.
	[ti]	-You've got a spot on your shirt.
5968	**plutonium**	**plutonium**
	m	a) Le plutonium, excepté le plutonium composé à 80 % ou plus de plutonium 238;
	[plytɔnjɔm]	-(a) Plutonium except plutonium whose isotopic composition includes 80 percent or greater plutonium-238.
5969	**contrer**	**counteract**
	vb	Cela permettrait de contrer les actions terroristes promptement et efficacement.
	[kɔ̃tʁe]	-This would allow us to counter terrorist actions swiftly and efficiently.
5970	**cité**	**city-state; city**

	f; adj[site]	Le rapporteur a cité une phrase de Cicéron qui s'adapte effectivement à un parlementaire. -The rapporteur quoted Cicero, which is appropriate for a Member of Parliament.
5971	**rationnel** adj; m [ʁasjɔnɛl]	**rational; rational** On dit « rationnel » un nombre qui s'exprime en tant que fraction de deux entiers relatifs. -Numbers that can be expressed as fractions of two whole numbers are called rational numbers.
5972	**vibrer** vb [vibʁe]	**vibrate|thrill** On est allés les voir... et vibrer de toute notre âme pour la victoire des nôtres. -We went to see them... and vibrate with all the energy of our soul for the victory of our team.
5973	**luxure** f [lyksyʁ]	**lust** Baruch Spinoza disait que l'avarice, l'ambition et la luxure ne sont rien d'autre qu'une sorte de folie. -Baruch Spinoza said that avarice, ambition and lust, are nothing but a species of madness.
5974	**lavabo** m [lavabo]	**sink** J'adore être lavé dans un lavabo. -I love being bathed in the sink.
5975	**platine** m; f [platin]	**platinum; deck** Ces immeubles respecteront-ils la norme écologique or ou platine ? -Will they be built to the gold or platinum standard of the greenest lead standard?
5976	**patriotisme** m [patʁijɔtism]	**patriotism** C'est là un patriotisme espagnol et un patriotisme européen. -That is Spanish patriotism and it is also European patriotism.
5977	**choléra** m [kɔleʁa]	**cholera** La Guinée-Bissau continuait de faire face à d'importantes épidémies de choléra. -Guinea-Bissau continues to face significant outbreaks of cholera.
5978	**titan** m [titã]	**titan** Elle aurait un titan pour allié. -She'd have a titan for an ally.
5979	**licencier** vb [lisãsje]	**dismiss|fire** J'ai licencié tout le personnel et j'ai embauché Jack. -I fired the whole staff and hired Jack.
5980	**prestation** f [pʁɛstasjɔ̃]	**benefit** Je suis satisfaite de sa prestation. -I'm pleased with his performance.
5981	**conservatoire** m [kɔ̃sɛʁvatwaʁ]	**conservatory** Ici le Dr Summerland du conservatoire Williams. -This is Dr. Summerland from the Williams Conservatory.
5982	**pénal** adj[penal]	**penal** Le Code pénal de 1860 est l'instrument fondateur de la notion de responsabilité pénale. -The main statute that creates penal liability is the Pakistan Penal Code of 1860.
5983	**administrateur** m [administʁatœʁ]	**administrator** J'ai parlé à l'administrateur. -I have spoken with the administrator.
5984	**graffiti**	**graffiti**

m
[gʁafiti]
Les textes des graffiti anti-hongrois sont tout aussi choquants.
-Equally shocking are the texts of anti-Hungarian graffiti.

5985 veston   **jacket**

m
[vɛstɔ̃]
Je remarque que le leader parlementaire du Parti réformiste a remis son veston.
-I notice that the House leader for the Reform Party has put his jacket on.

5986 miniature   **miniature; miniature**

adj; f
[minjatyʁ]
Certains considèrent dès lors la Belgique comme une Europe en miniature.
-There are some who therefore say that Belgium is Europe in miniature.

5987 peseta   **peseta**

f
[peseta]
Le dollar américain aurait pu se jouer de la peseta, avec quel impact économique ?
-The US dollar could have played games with the peseta, and what economic effects might that have had?

5988 brièvement   **briefly**

adv
[bʁijɛvmɑ̃]
Ces critiques seront brièvement examinées au début du présent rapport.
-These criticisms will be briefly considered at the outset of the present report.

5989 indemne   **unscathed**

adj
[ɛ̃dɛmn]
Celui-ci en est sorti indemne mais un garde du corps a été tué et 21 personnes ont été blessées.
-General Dostum escaped unharmed although 1 body guard was killed and 21 people were injured.

5990 louange   **praise**

f
[lwɑ̃ʒ]
Louange à Dieu et paix et bénédiction sur son prophète,
-Praise be to God and Prayers and Peace be upon the Last of the Prophets.

5991 amélioration   **improvement**

f
[ameljɔʁasjɔ̃]
Il permet l'amélioration des prix: sans amélioration des prix, le compromis n'est pas réalisable.
-It allows price improvement: without price improvement the compromise is not workable.

5992 licorne   **unicorn**

f
[likɔʁn]
La licorne est un monstre fabuleux.
-The unicorn is a fabulous monster.

5993 refléter   **reflect**

vb
[ʁəflete]
La composition du personnel du Secrétariat doit refléter la diversité de ses Membres.
-The composition of the Secretariat's staff must reflect the diversity of its membership.

5994 sucrerie   **suger refinery**

f[sykʁəʁi]
Fernandes, concerne les problèmes spécifiques aux Açores, notamment la sucrerie Sinaga. -Raised by Mr Freitas and Mr Fernandes, the matter concerns the problems specific to the Azores and, in particular, to the Sinaga sugar refinery.

5995 paisiblement   **peacefully**

adv
[peziblǝmɑ̃]
Or, toutes ces manifestations se sont déroulées paisiblement.
-All these demonstrations disbanded themselves peacefully.

5996 élémentaire   **elementary**

adj
[elemɑ̃tɛʁ]
Loi sur l'enseignement préscolaire, élémentaire, secondaire, supérieur et autre.
-Act on preschool, elementary, secondary, higher professional and other education.

5997	**mœurs**	**manners**
	fpl	Ô temps, ô mœurs !
	[mœʁ]	-Oh the times! Oh the customs!
5998	**miteux**	**shabby|seedy**
	adj	Il traîne dans les night-clubs miteux.
	[mitø]	-Always in some seedy nightclub.
5999	**idiotie**	**idiocy**
	f	Idiot utile ou inutile, peu importe, je connais, j'ai autant lu Lénine que vous,
	[idjɔsi]	Monsieur.
		-Whether what was said was 'useful' or 'useless' idiot is scarcely relevant.
6000	**verbal**	**verbal; verbal**
	adj; m	Refus de reconnaître Israël, antisémitisme verbal, rhétorique agressive.
	[vɛʁbal]	-Refusal to recognise Israel; Iran's verbal anti-Semitism; aggressive
		rhetoric.
6001	**fanatique**	**fanatic; fanatic**
	adj; m/f	Les intellectuels fanatiques antioccidentaux de gauche ont connu un déclin
	[fanatik]	collectif lorsque le communisme s'est effondré.
		-The anti-Western intellectual cranks of the Left suffered a collective
		breakdown when Communism collapsed.
6002	**décisif**	**decisive**
	adj	À cet égard, le nouveau millénaire sera décisif pour notre planète et ses
	[desizif]	habitants.
		-In that sense, the new millennium would be decisive for the planet and
		humankind.
6003	**maquiller**	**make up**
	vb	Disons que la technique a essayé de maquiller la politique.
	[makije]	-Let us say there has been an attempt to put technical make-up on the
		political face.
6004	**alligator**	**alligator**
	m	Peux-tu distinguer un alligator d'un crocodile ?
	[aligatɔʁ]	-Can you tell an alligator from a crocodile?
6005	**peloter**	**grope**
	vb	Tu vas laisser ce truand de merde peloter ta femme comme ça ?
	[pəlɔte]	-You're gonna let this friggin ' goombah grope your woman like that?
6006	**frustrer**	**frustrate**
	vb[fʁystʁe]	Le contraire reviendrait à frustrer les espoirs et les ambitions annoncées. -In
		this case, the expectations and ambitions announced in the end will be
		frustrated.
6007	**brutalement**	**brutally**
	adv	Quinze des 70 otages ont été brutalement assassinés par les terroristes.
	[bʁytalmã]	-Fifteen of the 70 hostages were brutally murdered by the terrorists.
6008	**percée**	**breakthrough**
	f	Un membre de la délégation de l'ATNUTO a qualifié cet accord de percée.
	[pɛʁse]	-This was characterized by a member of the UNTAET delegation as a
		breakthrough.
6009	**pénitence**	**penance**
	f	Ce serait une meilleure pénitence de nettoyer la poêle.
	[penitãs]	-You know, a better penance would be to clean the frying pan.
6010	**partition**	**partition|score**
	f	Il ne saurait y avoir ni partition, ni monoethnicité, ni structures parallèles.
	[paʁtisjõ]	-There can be no partition, no mono-ethnicity and no parallel structures.

6011	**torride**	**torrid**
	adj	C'était une nuit torride que je n'ai pu m'endormir avant minuit.
	[tɔʁid]	-It was such a hot night that I could not sleep till midnight.
6012	**sensass**	**sensational**
	adj	C'est censé être sensass.
	[sɑ̃sas]	-It's supposed to be wild.
6013	**toupet**	**nerve|cheek**
	m	N'ayez pas le toupet de toucher quoi que ce soit !
	[tupɛ]	-Don't you have the nerve to touch anything.
6014	**bijouterie**	**jewelry|jewelry store**
	f	Dans cette bijouterie, il y a de jolies boucles d'oreilles.
	[biʒutʁi]	-In this jewelry store there are some pretty earrings.
6015	**châle**	**shawl**
	m	Je tricote un châle pour mon neveu.
	[ʃal]	-I knitted a shawl for my nephew.
6016	**gémir**	**moan|wail**
	vb	Cessons donc de gémir et de dire que nous n'avons pas de politique commune.
	[ʒemiʁ]	-So let us stop moaning that we do not have a common policy.
6017	**larbin**	**stooge|flunkey**
	m	Oui, je suis un larbin.
	[laʁbɛ̃]	-Yeah, I'm a stooge.
6018	**pastèque**	**watermelon**
	f	Ma fille aime les fruits d'été comme les cerises, la pastèque et les pêches.
	[pastɛk]	-My daughter likes summer fruits, such as cherries, watermelons and peaches.
6019	**curieusement**	**funnily**
	adv	Curieusement, le Conseil ne semble pas vouloir se référer à cet article.
	[kyʁjøzmɑ̃]	-Curiously, the Council does not seem to want to refer to this article.
6020	**habileté**	**skill|cleverness**
	f	Il devait son succès autant à son habileté qu'à son application.
	[abilte]	-He owed his success to both ability and industry.
6021	**navet**	**turnip**
	m[navɛ]	Pas la peine d'avoir peur d'un navet. -No use getting scared of a turnip.
6022	**météorite**	**meteorite**
	f	Pas même un gros météorite en fer produirait un champ pareil.
	[meteɔʁit]	-And not even a big nickel iron meteorite could produce a field as intense as this.
6023	**camelot**	**hawker**
	m	Un camelot crie dans le vide.
	[kamlo]	-A peddler shouts in the void.
6024	**pomper**	**pump**
	vb	Le problème, en Saskatchewan, c'est que nous essayons de pomper du brut très lourd.
	[pɔ̃pe]	-The problem in Saskatchewan is that it is very heavy crude that we are trying to pump.
6025	**infrarouge**	**infrared**
	adj	Il faut sûrement disposer d'un détecteur infrarouge pour déceler une attaque imminente.
	[ɛ̃fʁaʁuʒ]	-Surely, an infrared detector is required to detect pending attack.
6026	**léguer**	**will**

	vb	Quel monde voulons-nous en effet léguer à nos enfants et petits-enfants ?
	[lege]	-What kind of world do we want to leave to our children and grandchildren?

6027 nappe — **tablecloth**
f
[nap]
Emmy plia la nappe en deux.
-Emmy folded the napkin in half.

6028 juteux — **juicy**
adj
[ʒytø]
Je vous souhaite également un bon appétit tout à l'heure, devant un steak bien juteux!
-I trust that you will all now go and enjoy a nice juicy steak!

6029 duquel — **whose; whereof**
prn; con
[dykɛl]
Ouvrez le document à partir duquel vous souhaitez copier l' image.
-Open the document from which you want to copy the graphic object.

6030 savourer — **enjoy|glory**
vb
[savuʁe]
L'heure est venue de savourer notre victoire et de nous préparer pour l'avenir.
-To conclude, we must relish the victory and prepare for the future.

6031 sombrer — **sink**
vb
[sɔ̃bʁe]
In reality, the portrait may well be more sombre than that painted here.
-Dans les faits, le portrait risque d'être nettement plus sombre que celui brossé ici.

6032 emprisonnement — **imprisonment**
m
[ɑ̃pʁizɔnmɑ̃]
Sanction : 25 ans d'emprisonnement (en cas de négligence grave : 15 ans d'emprisonnement).
-Penalty: Imprisonment for 25 years (in the case of recklessness: imprisonment for 15 years).

6033 fat — **smug person**
m
[fa]

6034 glissant — **sliding|slippery**
adj[glisɑ̃]
Le sol est glissant, vieux. -This floor is slippery, man.

6035 régaler — **regale|feast**
vb
[ʁegale]
De temps en temps, le Sénat pouvait se régaler de ses paroles, que je n'ai jamais oubliées.
-Every once in a while, we heard him regale this Senate, and I remember his words to this day.

6036 mascotte — **mascot**
f
[maskɔt]
Voyez-vous... pendant le combat, ils ont tous sorti leur mascotte, comme des gosses.
-You know... during the fight; they all held up their mascots; like kids.

6037 spécialiser — **specialize**
vb
[spesjalize]
Il semble se spécialiser en rapports techniques difficiles, mais le fait toujours très bien.
-He seems to specialize in technical, difficult reports but always does it very well.

6038 engendrer — **generate|give rise to**
vb
[ɑ̃ʒɑ̃dʁe]
La violence ne peut qu'engendrer rancoeurs et ressentiments et perpétuer la violence.
-Violence can only beget bitterness and resentment and perpetuate violence.

6039 valeureux — **valorous|gallant**
adj
[valœʁø]
Notre Constitution elle-même fait référence à nos valeureux alliés en Europe.
-Our very Constitution makes reference to our gallant allies in Europe.

6040	**soucieux**	**concerned**
	adj	Cela nous rend amers, inquiets et soucieux et, c'est le bon endroit pour le dire.
	[susjø]	-This leaves us bitter, worried and anxious, and this is the place to say so.
6041	**désign**	**design**
	m	Une adéquation entre ces éléments et le design est nécessaire.
	[dezɪɲ]	-A suitable relationship between these elements and design has to be established.
6042	**superstar**	**superstar**
	m	Une superstar venait voir notre petite troupe.
	[sypɛʁstaʁ]	-A superstar was coming to see our little troupe.
6043	**hiérarchie**	**hierarchy**
	f	Ce sont deux choses séparées, différentes dans la hiérarchie morale, dans la hiérarchie du mal.
	[jeʁaʁʃi]	-They are two different things, different in the moral hierarchy and in the hierarchy of evil.
6044	**tôle**	**sheet metal|slammer**
	f	La présente invention concerne un ensemble matrice d'emboutissage de tôle.
	[tol]	-The present invention provides a sheet metal drawing die assembly.
6045	**incapacité**	**inability|disability**
	f	Je fus dans l'incapacité de venir en raison de la pluie.
	[ɛ̃kapasite]	-I wasn't able to come because of the rain.
6046	**sénile**	**senile**
	adj[senil]	Chérie, quand je commencerai à être sénile... tu seras très occupée avec tes petits-enfants. -When I'm showing my senility, darling... you'll be occupying your time with your grandchildren.
6047	**pinceau**	**brush**
	m	J'ai légèrement orienté votre pinceau.
	[pɛ̃so]	-Well, I did guide the brush a little bit.
6048	**gronder**	**scold|rumble**
	vb	J'ai vu sa mère le gronder.
	[gʁɔ̃de]	-I saw his mother scold him.
6049	**iceberg**	**iceberg**
	m	Les passagers dormaient dans leurs cabines lorsque le navire percuta un immense iceberg.
	[ajsbɛʁg]	-The passengers were asleep in their cabins when the ship hit a huge iceberg.
6050	**squaw**	**squaw**
	f	He says you'd make a fine squaw.
	[ska]	-Il dit que tu ferais une bonne squaw.
6051	**moralement**	**morally**
	adv	Cibler délibérément et sans discrimination des civils est moralement répugnant.
	[mɔʁalmɑ̃]	-The deliberate and indiscriminate targeting of civilians is morally repugnant.
6052	**microscope**	**microscope**
	m	Il regardait au microscope.
	[mikʁɔskɔp]	-He was looking through a microscope.
6053	**barder**	**bard**
	vb	La Gaelic Society d'Écosse, An Comunn Gàidhealach, a désigné Lewis MacKinnon nouveau barde écossais.
	[baʁde]	

-An Comunn Gàidhealach, the Gaelic Society of Scotland, has crowned Lewis MacKinnon the newest Scottish bard.

6054	**morue**	**cod**
	f	Les députés savent que les stocks de morue ont beaucoup diminué.
	[mɔʁy]	-Members know that cod stocks are down the toilet.
6055	**humblement**	**humbly**
	adv	Je demande humblement aux représentants de faire preuve de compréhension et de coopération.
	[ɛ̃bləmɑ̃]	-I humbly request the cooperation and understanding of representatives.
6056	**riposter**	**hit back|retaliate**
	vb	Nous devons riposter sans délai et ne pas nous en tenir à des paroles ou à des écrits.
	[ʁipɔste]	-We must retaliate swiftly and not be content with spoken or written protests.
6057	**hostilité**	**hostility**
	f	Cela suscitera la violence, l'extrémisme et l'hostilité des populations arabes.
	[ɔstilite]	-This will generate violence, extremism and hostility among the Arab peoples.
6058	**dévaliser**	**rob|raid**
	vb	Il a dit que la Commission était en train de dévaliser les domaines principaux.
	[devalize]	-He said that the Commission was raiding the main areas.
6059	**contradiction**	**contradiction**
	f	L'amour est une grande contradiction. Vous ne pouvez pas vivre sans, mais en même temps elle vous blessera.
	[kɔ̃tʁadiksjɔ̃]	-Love is a great contradiction. You cannot live without it but at the same time you will be hurt by it.
6060	**allergie**	**allergy**
	f	L'allergie est la maladie endémique de notre temps.
	[alɛʁʒi]	-Allergy is the endemic disease of our time.
6061	**infernal**	**infernal; fiend**
	adj; m	En bout de ligne, il s'est finalement agi de savoir si l'alliance, qui avait recouru à d'autres moyens, ne devait pas simplement se retirer et laisser les choses suivre leur cours infernal.
	[ɛ̃fɛʁnal]	-At the end of the day the question became whether the alliance which had tried other means should simply stand back and let events take their infernal course.
6062	**entité**	**entity**
	f	Lesdites deux entités peuvent comprendre une entité hôte.
	[ɑ̃tite]	-The at least two entities may include a host entity.
6063	**valide**	**valid|available**
	adj	L'acceptation expresse d'une réserve non valide n'est elle-même pas valide.
	[valid]	-The explicit acceptance of a non-valid reservation is not valid either.
6064	**probabilité**	**probability**
	f	Il y avait une forte probabilité de son succès.
	[pʁɔbabilite]	-There was a strong likelihood of his succeeding.
6065	**mobilier**	**suite**
	m	UEA, Fédération européenne des fabricants de mobilier: Furniture in Europe.
	[mɔbilje]	-UEA European Furniture Manufacturers Federation: Furniture in Europe.
6066	**amusement**	**fun**

	m	J'écoute ces commentaires souvent avec beaucoup d'amusement.
	[amyzmã]	-I often listen to the comments with considerable amusement.
6067	**guéri**	**recovered**
	adj	Jésus ne le toucha pas mais cet homme fut guéri et ses péchés furent
	[geʁi]	pardonnés.
		-Jesus did not touch him but the man was healed and his sin forgiven.
6068	**encercler**	**circle|surround**
	vb	Les troupes de Fort Myer ont traversé le Potomac d'urgence et sont venues
	[ãsɛʁkle]	encercler le vaisseau.
		-Troops have been rushed across the Potomac River from Fort Myer and
		have thrown a cordon around the ship.
6069	**carter**	**housing|casing**
	m	On peut ainsi réaliser un carter de configuration unitaire.
	[kaʁtɛʁ]	-As a result, the housing may be made of a unitary construction.
6070	**quincaillerie**	**hardware**
	f	Il y a, à la quincaillerie, de nombreux trucs utiles.
	[kɛ̃kajʁi]	-There are many useful appliances in the hardware store.
6071	**porcherie**	**pigsty**
	f[pɔʁʃəʁi]	Mon bureau est une porcherie ! -My office is a pigsty!
6072	**rabais**	**discount**
	m	Pouvez-vous m'accorder un rabais ?
	[ʁabɛ]	-Can you give me a discount?
6073	**épicer**	**spice**
	vb	Maintenant, pour épicer le tout.
	[epise]	-Now, to spice it up.
6074	**posture**	**posture**
	f	Ainsi en va-t-il de la double posture du Représentant permanent du Pakistan.
	[pɔstyʁ]	-An example is the twofold position taken by the Permanent Representative
		of Pakistan.
6075	**refiler**	**palm off**
	vb	En fin de compte, les deux en viennent à se refiler la responsabilité, de sorte
	[ʁəfile]	qu'il ne se passe rien.
		-The bottom line is that they both end up passing the buck and nothing gets
		done.
6076	**pointu**	**sharp**
	adj	Cela suggère que Sarah est tombée sur quelque chose de pointu.
	[pwɛ̃ty]	-That suggests Sarah fell into something sharp.
6077	**raffut**	**racket**
	m	Qu'est-ce que c'est que ce raffut ?
	[ʁafy]	-What is all this rumpus about?
6078	**effectif**	**effective**
	adj	On aimerait instaurer un couvre-feu, effectif immédiatement.
	[efɛktif]	-We'd like to institute the curfew, effective immediately.
6079	**dû**	**due**
	adj	Ne vous excusez jamais de réclamer votre dû.
	[dy]	-Don't ever apologize for asking for what you're owed.
6080	**béat**	**smug**
	adj	Toujours aussi béat, vous penser était plus intelligent que moi.
	[bea]	-Always so smug, thinking you were smarter than me.
6081	**taille**	**size|height**

	f	Nous avons la même taille.
	[taj]	-We're the same size.
6082	**dune**	**dune**
	f	C'est juste après cette dune.
	[dyn]	-Come on, it's right over this dune.
6083	**mémorable**	**memorable**
	adj	Monsieur le Président, on dirait que la 35e session de l'OACI sera
	[memɔʁabl]	mémorable.
		-Mr President, it looks like the 35th ICAO Meeting will be a memorable one.
6084	**sentinelle**	**sentinel**
	f	À l'échelon municipal, le Gouvernement a renforcé le programme
	[sɑ̃tinɛl]	«Sentinelle».
		-At the municipal level, the Government had strengthened the Sentinel programme.
6085	**restauration**	**restoration|restaurant**
	f	Quel est ton restaurant de restauration rapide préféré?
	[ʁɛstɔʁasjɔ̃]	-What is your favourite fast-food restaurant?
6086	**coûteux**	**expensive**
	adj	Cela signifie que le processus sera très coûteux et prendra beaucoup de
	[kutø]	temps.
		-This means that the process will be both very costly and time-consuming.
6087	**estropié**	**crippled; cripple**
	adj; m	L'estropié, vous savez que vous le tenez... si vous restez à distance et que
	[ɛstʁɔpje]	vous l'épuisez.
		-With a cripple, you know you've got him... if you keep your distance and wear him down.
6088	**rider**	**wrinkle|ruffle**
	vb	Le temps n'a rien fait d'autre que te rider.
	[ʁide]	-Time hasn't done a thing but wrinkle you.
6089	**récupération**	**recovery|retrieval**
	f	Procédés de récupération et de retraitement de plastiques rigides mélangés.
	[ʁekypeʁasjɔ̃]	-The present invention relates to methods for the recovery and processing of mixed rigid plastics.
6090	**égoïsme**	**selfishness**
	m	It is a symbol of solidarity and of overcoming national egoism.
	[egɔism]	-C'est le symbole de la solidarité et du dépassement de l'égoïsme national.
6091	**biais**	**bias|angle**
	m	Ces biais sont lisibles dans la problématique actuelle des indicateurs.
	[bjɛ]	-These areas of bias are obvious in the current problem regarding indicators.
6092	**glacial**	**glacial**
	adj	Je comprends les conditions qui prévalent dans la mer Baltique et les
	[glasjal]	conditions glaciales auxquelles elle a fait référence.
		-I understand the conditions that prevail in the Baltic Sea and the freezing conditions she referred to.
6093	**discrimination**	**discrimination**
	f	Nous poursuivrons nos efforts pour éliminer la discrimination raciale.
	[diskʁiminasjɔ̃]	-We shall continue our efforts to eradicate racial discrimination.
6094	**héberger**	**accommodate|harbor**
	vb	Le FIDA a été choisi pour héberger le Mécanisme mondial selon la décision
	[ebɛʁʒe]	24/COP.1.
		-IFAD was selected as the host institution for the GM in decision 24/COP.1.

6095	**sceptique**	**skeptical; skeptic**
	adj; m/f	Le grand humaniste français Michel de Montaigne était un sceptique.
	[sɛptik]	-The great French humanist Michel de Montaigne was a sceptic.
6096	**tatouer**	**tattoo**
	vb	Alors il s'est fait tatouer un putain de diable hilare sur la fesse.
	[tatwe]	-So he got this fucking great laughing devil tattooed right on his arse.
6097	**fief**	**fief|fee**
	m[fjɛf]	Ces deux-la sont les antiquités du fief. -Those two here are the antiquities of the fief.
6098	**carpe**	**carp**
	f	La longévité de la carpe n'est pas affectée par l'agitation du mille-pattes.
	[kaʁp]	-The carp's longevity is unmolested by the turmoil of the millipede.
6099	**volt**	**volt**
	m	Les tensions différentielles peuvent être relativement faibles, de l'ordre de moins de 1 volt par exemple, ceci assurant un fonctionnement à faible puissance.
	[vɔlt]	-The differential voltages can be relatively low, such as less than 1 volt, thus providing low power operation.
6100	**mess**	**mess**
	m	Il refroidissait au mess des artilleurs.
	[mɛs]	-It was cooling over at the artillery mess.
6101	**équation**	**equation**
	f	C'est stable parce que toutes les racines de cette équation sont négatives.
	[ekwasjɔ̃]	-It's stable because all the roots of this equation are negative.
6102	**allumage**	**ignition**
	m	L'autre thermo-élement est couplé au brûleur d'allumage du dispositif thermo-électrique de sécurité.
	[alymaʒ]	-The other thermoelement is coupled to the ignition burner of the security thermoelectric device.
6103	**supposition**	**assumption|guess**
	f	Or une telle supposition ne reposerait sur aucun fondement scientifique.
	[sypozisjɔ̃]	-However, there is no scientific basis for this assumption.
6104	**durable**	**lasting|enduring**
	adj	Paix durable et développement socioéconomique durable sont intimement liés.
	[dyʁabl]	-Durable peace and sustainable socio-economic development are inextricably linked.
6105	**mélancolie**	**melancholy**
	f	C' est pourquoi il y a une touche de mélancolie dans l' air aujourd' hui.
	[melãkɔli]	-That is why there is a touch of melancholy in the air today.
6106	**civière**	**litter|stretcher**
	f	Elle ne voulait pas se faire porter sur une civière; elle ne voulait aucune aide.
	[sivjɛʁ]	-She would not be taken on a stretcher — she wanted no assistance.
6107	**aggraver**	**aggravate**
	vb	La politique de décentralisation menée par le Gouvernement ne peut qu'aggraver cette tendance.
	[agʁave]	-The Government's decentralization policy would only aggravate that tendency.
6108	**finesse**	**fineness|delicacy**
	f	Cela manque de finesse.
	[finɛs]	-That lacks subtlety.

6109	**receveur**	**recipient | conductor**
	m	L'invention concerne une bobine inductive pour un canal auditif d'un patient receveur.
	[ʁəsəvœʁ]	-An inductive coil arrangement is described for an ear canal of a recipient patient.

6110	**libéral**	**liberal**
	adj	De plus, la création monétaire publique est compatible avec une économie libérale.
	[libeʁal]	-Moreover, the public creation of money would be compatible with a free market economy.

6111	**expirer**	**expire | breathe out**
	vb	Le délai de garantie de 60 mois devait expirer en juin 1990.
	[ɛkspiʁe]	-The 60-month guarantee period was to expire in June 1990.

6112	**corsé**	**spicy**
	adj	Ce 23 juillet, en Corse, la canicule a été exceptionnelle: 44 degrés, un air très sec, un sirocco très fort.
	[kɔʁse]	-On 23 July, in Corsica, the heat was exceptional: 44 degrees, very dry air and a very strong sirocco wind.

6113	**épouvantail**	**scarecrow**
	m	Je ne peux pas faire fuir les oiseaux. Je ne suis pas un épouvantail.
	[epuvãtaj]	-I cannot scare the birds away. I am not a scarecrow.

6114	**rand**	**rand**
	m	L'unité monétaire est le rand (R), qui compte 100 cents.
	[ʁã]	-The unit of currency is the rand (R), which is divided into 100 cents.

6115	**skier**	**ski**
	vb	Un ancien président de la commission des budgets et un ancien rapporteur général étaient partis skier.
	[skje]	-A former chairman of the Committee on Budgets and a former general rapporteur went on a skiing holiday.

6116	**fiscal**	**tax**
	adj	La présidence du Conseil économique et fiscal a été transférée au Premier Ministre.
	[fiskal]	-Chairmanship of the Economic Fiscal Council was transferred to the Prime Minister.

6117	**animateur**	**animator**
	m	L'un d'eux est devenu animateur à Walt Disney Studios.
	[animatœʁ]	-One of the two is now an animator with Walt Disney Studios.

6118	**justicier**	**justiciary | vigilante**
	m	Pas plus qu'un justicier qui fête Halloween tous les soirs.
	[ʒystisje]	-Yeah, but, then again, so does a vigilante who thinks every day is Halloween.

6119	**paroi**	**wall**
	f	Si on creusait dans cette paroi...
	[paʁwa]	-But if we burrowed through this wall here...

6120	**expérimental**	**experimental**
	adj	Un enseignement expérimental utilise comme véhicule les langues maternelles.
	[ɛkspeʁimãtal]	-Experimental education uses the mother tongue as the medium of instruction.

6121	**ogive**	**warhead**
	f	Observez ce test de la première ogive nanobotique.
	[ɔʒiv]	-Watch this test of the world's first nanomite warhead.

6122	**vessie**	**bladder**
	f [vesi]	J'ai eu une infection de la vessie le mois dernier. -I had a bladder infection last month.
6123	**mascarade**	**masquerade**
	f [maskaʁad]	Excuse-moi de t'imposer cette mascarade. -I'm so sorry to make you go through this charade.
6124	**répression**	**repression**
	f [ʁepʁesjɔ̃]	Pas de répression spéciale contre les partis illégaux. -No special repression against the illegal parties or their leaders.
6125	**sosie**	**double**
	f [sozi]	Santos n'était pas juste un sosie... -Santos wasn't just a look-alike...
6126	**aristocrate**	**aristocrat**
	m/f [aʁistɔkʁat]	C'est un aristocrate. -He's an aristocrat.
6127	**séquence**	**sequence**
	f [sekɑ̃s]	Comment puis-je extraire le son d'une séquence vidéo ? -How can I extract the audio from a video clip?
6128	**comparable**	**comparable**
	adj [kɔ̃paʁabl]	Il n'existait aucun indicateur comparable pour les droits civils et politiques. -No comparable indicators existed in the area of civil and political rights.
6129	**annexe**	**annex|schedule**
	f [anɛks]	Je sais que ça n'y ressemble pas, mais je me suis vraiment débarrassé de nombreuses choses provenant de la pièce annexe. -I know it doesn't look like it, but I've actually gotten rid of a lot of stuff out of the spare room.
6130	**intrépide**	**intrepid|bold**
	adj [ɛ̃tʁepid]	Il s'agit d'un diplomate intrépide qui nous a dit la vérité telle qu'il la ressentait. -He is a fearless diplomat who told us the truth as he saw it.
6131	**brochure**	**brochure**
	f [bʁɔʃyʁ]	Peut-il nous envoyer une brochure ? -Could he send us a brochure?
6132	**ignorant**	**ignorant; ignoramus**
	adj; m [iɲɔʁɑ̃]	Je suis honteusement ignorant et je ne peux simplement plus le tolérer d'avantage. -I am disgracefully ignorant and I simply cannot tolerate it any longer.
6133	**tigresse**	**tigress**
	f [tigʁɛs]	Comme lui vous avez tenté de résister aux petits marquis de ce Parlement et aux tigresses de bandes dessinées du Colisée de notre Assemblée. -Like Pombal, you tried to resist the petty dignitaries of this Parliament and the cartoon tigresses of this Coliseum-style Assembly.
6134	**géographie**	**geography**
	f [ʒeɔgʁafi]	Ses connaissances en géographie sont insuffisantes. -His knowledge of geography is insufficient.
6135	**excessif**	**excessive|overdone**
	adj [ɛksesif]	Il n'est pas excessif de dire que c'est un génie. -It is not too much to say that he is a genius.
6136	**banquette**	**bench|seat**
	f [bɑ̃kɛt]	Donc... cette banquette est libre. -So... I guess this seat is free

6137	**envergure**	**span**
	f	Il est le premier politicien d'envergure nationale à avoir été nommé dans un scandale de corruption qui s'avère grandissant.
	[ãvɛʁgyʁ]	-He is the first national politician to be named in a widening corruption scandal.

6138	**fondement**	**foundation**
	m	La désobéissance est le vrai fondement de la liberté. Ceux qui obéissent doivent être esclaves.
	[fɔ̃dmã]	-Disobedience is the true foundation of liberty. The obedient must be slaves.

6139	**libellule**	**dragonfly**
	f	La libellule effleurait l'eau.
	[libelyl]	-The dragonfly was skimming across the water.

6140	**inondation**	**flood**
	f	L'histoire d'une grande inondation est très répandue dans la mythologie mondiale.
	[inɔ̃dasjɔ̃]	-The story of a great flood is very common in world mythology.

6141	**benne**	**dumpster|tub**
	f	Trouvée dans une benne derrière votre immeuble.
	[bɛn]	-Picked it up in a dumpster behind your building.

6142	**interférence**	**interference**
	f	Avec la boîte, aucune interférence possible.
	[ɛ̃tɛʁfeʁãs]	-No, there can't be any interference with the box.

6143	**antibiotique**	**antibiotic; antibiotic**
	adj; m	C'est un antibiotique plus puissant.
	[ãtibjɔtik]	-I've given him a shot of a stronger antibiotic.

6144	**présentateur**	**presenter**
	m	Le présentateur fit allusion à la corruption dans le monde politique.
	[pʁezãtatœʁ]	-The speaker hinted at corruption in the political world.

6145	**préservatif**	**condom; preservative**
	m; adj	Avez-vous utilisé un préservatif ?
	[pʁezɛʁvatif]	-Did you use a condom?

6146	**implication**	**involvement**
	f	Nous devons renforcer notre implication en Irak, et cette implication doit être mieux organisée.
	[ɛ̃plikasjɔ̃]	-We must step up our involvement in Iraq, and this involvement must be better organised.

6147	**bistrot**	**pub**
	m	Jack a été invité à venir prendre un bock au bistrot du coin.
	[bistʁo]	-Jack was invited to come and have a beer at the local bistro.

6148	**insinuer**	**insinuate|suggest**
	vb	Monsieur le Président, j'espère que je n'ai pas enfreint le Règlement, mais il se trouve que le député de York-Sud-Weston ne cesse d'insinuer que le reste d'entre nous ne travaille pas.
	[ɛ̃sinɥe]	-Mr. Speaker, I hope I was not out of order but the member for York South-Weston keeps alluding to the fact that the rest of us do not work.

6149	**véritablement**	**truly|actually**
	adv [veʁitabləmã]	Le terrorisme mondial ne connaît pas de frontières et ses réseaux sont véritablement transnationaux. -Global terrorism recognizes no territorial boundaries, and its networks are veritably trans-national.

6150	**filou**	**trickster**

| | m | Je le connais ce Zamyslovski, c'est un filou. |
| | [filu] | -I've met this Zamyslovsky, he's a crook. |

6151 querelle — **quarrel|feud**
f
[kəʁɛl]
L'occasion nous est donnée d'éviter que cette querelle ne s'éternise, et nous devons la saisir.
 -We are afforded the opportunity to avoid eternalizing this feud and we should seize it.

6152 rossignol — **nightingale**
m
[ʁɔsiɲɔl]
J'ai entendu un rossignol japonais.
 -I heard a Japanese nightingale.

6153 victorieux — **victorious**
adj
[viktɔʁjø]
Mais nous sommes sortis victorieux de cette terrible tempête de feu et d'acier.
 -Nevertheless, we came through that terrible storm of fire and steel to ultimate victory.

6154 caniche — **poodle**
m
[kaniʃ]
Le caniche McGinty est en chaleur.
 -I heard that the McGintys' poodle was in heat.

6155 aplomb — **aplomb**
m
[aplɔ̃]
Cette tâche que tu accomplis avec tellement d'aplomb, même quand l'immeuble où tu travailles explose.
 -A task that you handle with such aplomb, even when the building where you work explodes around you.

6156 bluffer — **bluff**
vb
[blyfe]
Voilà des années qu'on nous parle donc d'expériences et que les États attribuent au compte-gouttes quelques aumônes pour bluffer l'opinion publique.
 -For years we have been told of such experiments and the Member States grant a handful of pittances in order to fool public opinion.

6157 olivier — **olive**
m
[ɔlivje]
Ils ont planté du jasmin et un olivier.
 -They've planted jasmine and an olive.

6158 saignant — **bleeding**
adj
[sɛɲɑ̃]
Peu après avoir été emmené dans l'autre bureau, le requérant a été retrouvé à l'extérieur de la pièce, blessé et saignant à trois endroits à la jambe droite.
 -Shortly after the complainant had been brought into the other office, he was found outside the office with three bleeding injuries on his right lower leg.

6159 athée — **atheist; atheistic**
m/f; adj
[ate]
L'Europe chrétienne est en train de perdre la bataille contre une Europe socialiste et athée.
 -Christian Europe is losing the battle against a socialist and atheist Europe.

6160 forum — **forum**
m [fɔʁɔm]
J'ai vu votre nom et vos publications sur un forum en anglais et j'ai pris la liberté de lire votre profil. -I saw your name and posts in an English forum and took the liberty of reading your profile.

6161 mythologie — **mythology**
f
[mitɔlɔʒi]
Loisirs Musique classique; lecture (histoire, astronomie, mythologie gréco-romaine).
 -Hobbies: Classical music; reading (History, Astronomy, Greek Mythology, Roman Mythology.

6162 traducteur — **translator**

	m [tʁadyktœʁ]	Le traducteur est un traître. -The translator is a traitor.
6163	**borgne** adj [bɔʁɲ]	**one-eyed** Mais il s'agit d'une indépendance borgne, sélective. -However, it is a one-eyed, selective independence.
6164	**masturbation** f [mastyʁbasjɔ̃]	**masturbation** Mythes et préjugés : Mythes liés à la masturbation, pudeur, honte et crainte. -Myths and preconceived ideas: myths on masturbation, modesty, shame and fear.
6165	**brûlant** adj [bʁylɑ̃]	**burning** Pendant 60 secondes, on expose le réservoir à la flamme du carburant brûlant librement. -For 60 seconds the tank must be exposed to the flame from the freely burning fuel.
6166	**percuter** vb [pɛʁkyte]	**ram** Les auteurs de cet acte se sont servi de passagers innocents pour percuter des avions contre des bâtiments, afin de faire le plus grand nombre possible de victimes. -The perpetrators used innocent passengers to crash aircraft into buildings, so as to take the largest possible number of human lives.
6167	**encourageant** adj [ɑ̃kuʁaʒɑ̃]	**encouraging** Le taux des projets de coopération technique approuvés est encourageant. -The rate of technical cooperation approvals was an encouraging indicator.
6168	**dingo** m; adj [dɛ̃go]	**dingo; nuts** J'entends un dingo manger votre bébé. -Hey, I think I hear a dingo eating your baby.
6169	**limer** vb [lime]	**file** On peut se limer les ongles avec. -I can file my nails with it.
6170	**taquiner** vb [takine]	**tease** On ne doit pas taquiner ces hommes-là. -It's not right to tease these men.
6171	**démasquer** vb [demaske]	**unmask|expose** Nous devons démasquer ces pays qui, par le commerce, aident et sortent d'affaire ce régime corrompu. -We need to expose those countries that aid and bail out this corrupt regime with trade.
6172	**démoniaque** adj; m/f [demɔnjak]	**demonic; demoniac** Nous savons aujourd'hui que ce plan démoniaque a échoué. -Today, we know that he failed in his demonic plan.
6173	**épine** f [epin]	**thorn** Juste comme une épine plantée dans la gorge. -Just as a thorn stuck in one's throat.
6174	**antre** m [ɑ̃tʁ]	**den** On ne peut capturer le petit du tigre qu'en pénétrant dans son antre. -One may only catch the tiger cub by entering the tiger's den.
6175	**scélérat** m; adj [seleʁa]	**scoundrel; miscreant** Je réponds qu'on peut sourire tant qu'on voudra et être tout de même un scélérat. -I say in reply that one may smile and smile and still be a villain.
6176	**rouble**	**ruble**

m
[ʁubl]

Je peux justifier chaque rouble, si tu veux.
-I can account for every rouble, if you want.

6177 **ventilation** — **ventilation**

f
[vãtilasjõ]

Un module à ventilation d'injection / évacuation est prévu.
-A module with balanced ventilation is provided.

6178 **troublant** — **disturbing**

adj
[tʁublã]

Je tiens à présent à évoquer brièvement un moment troublant de ces négociations.
-I should now like to say a few words on a disturbing moment in these negotiations.

6179 **méprisable** — **contemptible**

adj
[mepʁizabl]

C'est un personnage méprisable qui essaie par tous les moyens de plier la loi à sa botte.
-He is a sad figure who tries to have complete control over the law.

6180 **inhumain** — **inhuman**

adj
[inymɛ̃]

Vu le mépris froid et inhumain dont ils ont fait preuve pour la vie d'innocents, on peut en être sûr.
-Their calculated and callous disregard for innocent human lives ensures that.

6181 **racket** — **racketeering**

m
[ʁakɛ]

Ceci résume le racket du marché du rosé.
-This sums up the racket in the rosé market.

6182 **clic** — **click|snip**

m
[klik]

Achat confortable sur un clic de souris.
-Purchase in a comfortable manner, per mouse click.

6183 **solder** — **settle**

vb
[sɔlde]

Je pourrais solder ma dette avec... quelque chose mieux que l'argent.
-I could settle the debt with... something better than money.

6184 **notoire** — **notorious**

adj
[nɔtwaʁ]

Pourtant, on lui attribue souvent à tort un euroscepticisme notoire.
-And yet it is still too often known falsely for its notorious Euro-sceptics.

6185 **martinet** — **swift**

m
[maʁtinɛ]

As-tu déjà vu un martinet ?
-Have you ever seen a swift?

6186 **guérisseur** — **healer**

m[geʁisœʁ]

Le plus souvent, elles sont soignées à la maison ou confiées aux soins d'un guérisseur. -They are more often treated at home or taken to a traditional healer.

6187 **lotus** — **lotus**

m
[lɔtys]

Les temples sur Mars sont décorés avec des fleurs de lotus.
-The temples on Mars are decorated with lotus flowers.

6188 **daim** — **suede**

m
[dɛ̃]

Vernie, mate, daim bleu.
-Shiny, matte finish, blue suede.

6189 **immature** — **immature**

adj
[imatyʁ]

Je suis immature, je suis égoïste, un parfait imbécile.
-I'm immature, I'm unthoughtful, I'm a friggin' idiot.

6190 **sangsue** — **leech**

f
[sãsy]

Le premier petit lien avec le tueur démange et pique comme une sangsue.
-The first small bond to the killer itches and stings like a leech.

6191 **analyste** — **analyst**

	m/f [analist]	Bibliothèque du Parlement : Raphaelle Deraspe, analyste; Sonya Norris, analyste. -Library of Parliament: Raphaelle Deraspe, Analyst; Sonya Norris, Analyst.
6192	**décalage** m [dekalaʒ]	**lag|shift** J'ai un méchant décalage horaire. -I've got a bad case of jet lag.
6193	**cochonner** vb [kɔʃɔne]	**pig** Ils sont bons qu'à cochonner la piste ! -They're spics! Look at them, greasing up the floor.
6194	**galactique** adj [galaktik]	**galactic** Sur leur trajet vers la Terre (qui dure de 15 à 50 heures), le nuage et les ondes magnétiques modulent le flux des rayons cosmiques galactiques et le rendent anisotrope. -On the way to Earth (15-50 hours), the magnetic cloud and shock modulate the galactic cosmic ray (GCR) flux, making it anisotropic.
6195	**stéréo** f [steʁeo]	**stereo** John doit faire sans chaîne stéréo pour l'instant. -John has to do without a stereo for the time being.
6196	**string** m [stʁiŋ]	**string|thong** Peut-être devrais-je ramener mon string ailleurs. -Well, perhaps I should take my thong elsewhere.
6197	**germer** vb [ʒɛʁme]	**germinate** Une de ces formes consiste à adopter l'hypothèse malheureuse selon laquelle aucune religion ne porte en elle le germe de la haine. -A form of this is the unfortunate pronouncement that not a single religion harbours a germ of hatred.
6198	**tromperie** f [tʁɔ̃pʁi]	**deception** L'UE est fondée sur la déformation de la réalité, la tromperie et les mensonges. -The EU is founded on misrepresentation, deceit and lies.
6199	**ventilateur** m [vãtilatœʁ]	**fan** L'une des pales du ventilateur s'est détachée et s'est brisée contre le mur. -One of the fan blades broke loose and shattered against the wall.
6200	**feuilleton** m [fœjtɔ̃]	**serial** Il est dans la chambre, il regarde un feuilleton espagnol. -He's in our den, watching a Spanish soap opera.
6201	**révérence** f [ʁeveʁãs]	**reverence|bow** Ils assistèrent avec révérence à la cérémonie solennelle dans l'église. -They watched the solemn ceremony in the church with awe.
6202	**conformément** adv [kɔ̃fɔʁmemã]	**in step** Celles-ci fonctionnent de façon autonome, conformément aux principes coopératifs. -They have been rendered autonomous according to the cooperative principles.
6203	**kaiser** m [kajzɛʁ]	**Kaiser** A mains nues avec le kaiser lui-même. -Hand to hand with the kaiser himself.
6204	**poulailler** m [pulaje]	**hen house** Les poules sont dans le poulailler. -The hens are in the chicken coup.
6205	**Saturne**	**Saturn**

	m [satyʁn]	La théorie scientifique que j'aime le plus est que les anneaux de Saturne sont entièrement composés de bagages perdus. -The scientific theory I like the best is that the rings of Saturn are composed entirely of lost luggage.
6206	**renouveler** vb [ʁənuvle]	**renew** Aujourd'hui, au XXIe siècle, nous devons renouveler l'esprit de l'effort commun. -Today in the twenty-first century we need to renew our spirit of common effort.
6207	**mécontent** adj [mekɔ̃tɑ̃]	**dissatisfied|unhappy** Elles craignent que la proposition ne devienne une charte des mécontents. -They fear it will become a unhappy charter.
6208	**canari** m [kanaʁi]	**canary** Cette région a d'ailleurs été comparée au canari dans la mine. -The region has been compared to a canary in a mine.
6209	**faucher** vb [foʃe]	**mow|reap** Nos pensées vont aujourd'hui à ces hommes fauchés à la fleur de l'âge. -Our thoughts can only go out to them today as they were cut down in the prime of life.
6210	**prohibition** f [pʁɔibisjɔ̃]	**prohibition** L'État est pleinement garant de cette prohibition. -The State has established full guarantees in respect of that prohibition.
6211	**fusiller** vb [fyzije]	**shoot** Ça me fait penser qu'on devrait vous fusiller dans cette tenue. -Come to think of it, we shall have to shoot you dressed like that.
6212	**chimiste** m [ʃimist]	**chemist** Je vais en particulier parler de la carrière de Suzanne Adams, une brillante chimiste. -Suzanne Abrams, a brilliant chemist.
6213	**variété** f[vaʁjete]	**variety|choice** Strictement parlant, le bambou est une variété d'herbe. -Strictly speaking, the bamboo is a kind of grass.
6214	**feindre** vb [fɛ̃dʁ]	**pretend|put on** Nous feignons en permanence de nous intéresser aux droits de l'homme, mais nos actes sont sans rapport avec nos paroles. -We always pretend to care about human rights, but we do not act on the basis of what we say.
6215	**manette** f [manɛt]	**lever|controller** Veuillez connecter une manette. -Please connect a controller.
6216	**cascade** f [kaskad]	**cascade** Son érosion peut devenir irréversible et aboutir à une cascade de prolifération. -Its erosion could become irreversible and result in a cascade of proliferation.
6217	**zinc** m [zɛ̃g]	**zinc** Ce revêtement empêche la corrosion du métal et autres matières ferreuses ou métalliques plus précieuses que le zinc. -The coating inhibits corrosion of steel and other ferrous or metal materials more noble than zinc.
6218	**externe**	**external; extern**

adj; m/f
[εkstεʁn]

Cette couleur concerne la face externe du cornet.
-This color refers to the outer face of the cornet.

6219 **hybride** **hybrid; crossbred**

m; adj
[ibʁid]

C'est un hybride.
-This is a hybrid.

6220 **superficiel** **superficial**

adj
[sypεʁfisjεl]

Tête de filet laissée en place ou enlevée; Niveau de parage du gras superficiel.
-Specify: rib numbers to be frenched and length of frenching required.

6221 **hamster** **hamster**

m
[amstεʁ]

Gina a été vraiment malade à cause du hamster.
-Gina got really sick because of the hamster.

6222 **magnétophone** **tape recorder**

m
[maɲetɔfɔn]

Son appareil photo et son magnétophone auraient été confisqués.
-His camera and tape-recorder were reportedly confiscated.

6223 **déserteur** **deserter**

m
[dezεʁtœʁ]

Je devais juste réprimander un lâche déserteur.
-I simply 'ad to reprimand the cowardly deserter.

6224 **tapage** **noise|fuss**

m
[tapaʒ]

Nous avons une année de plus de ce tapage en réserve.
-We have another year of this din in store for us.

6225 **polaire** **polar**

adj
[pɔlεʁ]

Il a été noté que le satellite QSAT réaliserait des observations du plasma polaire.
-It was noted that the QSAT satellite would perform polar plasma observations.

6226 **charlot** **clown**

m[ʃaʁlo]

Aux auditeurs de ce charlot : Nick est hors zone de l'amitié. -Okay, for all those who listen to this clown... Nick Persons will never be in the friend zone.

6227 **éminent** **eminent|learned**

adj
[eminã]

À cet égard, nous notons avec intérêt la proposition du Secrétaire général visant à créer un groupe de haut niveau de personnalités éminentes.
-In this connection, we note with interest the Secretary-General's proposal to establish a high-level panel of eminent personalities.

6228 **impératif** **imperative**

m
[ɛ̃peʁatif]

Il est impératif que tu finisses pour dimanche.
-It is imperative for you to finish by Sunday.

6229 **incompréhensible** **incomprehensible**

adj
[ɛ̃kɔ̃pʁeãsibl]

Il est tout à fait injuste et incompréhensible qu'un tribunal rende un tel jugement.
-It is utterly wrong and incomprehensible for a court to pronounce such a sentence.

6230 **escargot** **snail**

m
[εskaʁgo]

Attention ! Tu marches sur un escargot.
-Careful! You're stepping on a snail.

6231 **inaperçu** **unseen**

adj
[inapεʁsy]

Il est donc évident que beaucoup d'infractions passent inaperçues.
-Obviously much impaired driving crime goes unreported and undetected.

6232 **pulsion** **drive|pulse**

f — Une forte pulsion électromagnétique peut les mettre K.O.
[pylsjɔ̃] -We also found that a strong electromagnetic pulse... can knock them out.

6233 **parcelle** **parcel|plot**
f De même, les coûts par parcelle peuvent varier entre des centaines et des
[paʁsɛl] milliers de córdobas.
-Similarly, the costs per manzana [1.75 acre lot] can run into the thousands of córdobas.

6234 **encouragement** **encouragement**
m Un énorme cri d'encouragement s'éleva de la foule.
[ãkuʁaʒmã] -A mighty cheer burst from the crowd.

6235 **disperser** **disperse|spread**
vb La police a également fait un usage excessif de la force pour disperser les
[dispɛʁse] manifestants.
-Excessive force was also used by PNTL in trying to disperse the protesters.

6236 **tablette** **tablet**
f Cette tablette contient l'adresse d'une station-relais.
[tablɛt] -This tablet has the address of an off-world relay station.

6237 **rhinocéros** **rhinoceros**
m À Sao Paulo en 58, le candidat avec le plus de voix fut un rhinocéros qui
[ʁinɔseʁɔs] s'appelait Cacareco.
-In São Paulo in '58, the candidate with the most votes was a rhinoceros named Cacareco.

6238 **musclé** **muscular**
adj[myskle] Préférez-vous qu'il soit grand, mince, musclé, petit ou est-ce que ça n'a pas d'importance ? -Would you rather he was tall, thin, muscular, small... or you don't mind how he's built?

6239 **clebs** **mutt**
m Retiens ton clebs ou j'en fais des merguez.
[klɛb] -Control your dog or I'll turn it into sausage.

6240 **balayage** **scanning**
m L'invention concerne également une technique de balayage aléatoire.
[balɛjaʒ] -Using the random scanning technique, the light efficiency is nearly doubled than that of the prior art.

6241 **perplexe** **puzzled**
adj En fait, il n'y aura pas de stupéfaction perplexe, car la raison de cette
[pɛʁplɛks] hystérie est claire.
-In fact, there will be no bemused amazement, for the reason for this hysteria is clear.

6242 **pèlerin** **pilgrim**
m On doit fabriquer un pèlerin en feutre.
[pɛlʁɛ̃] -We have to make a pilgrim out of felt.

6243 **monture** **mount**
f Le diamant était enchâssé dans une monture d'or.
[mɔ̃tyʁ] -The diamond was set in a gold ring.

6244 **mulet** **mule|mullet**
m Mon ami a disparu comme un mulet gris dans le brouillard.
[mylɛ] -My friend disappeared like a grey mule in the fog.

6245 **fatigant** **tiring|fatiguing**
adj Ce voyage a dû être fatigant, je vous ferai donc grâce de remarques
[fatigã] supplémentaires.
-It was a tiring trip, so I shall make no further preliminary remarks.

6246	**génocide**	**genocide**
	m	Le génocide est probablement le comble de l'horreur et l'Holocauste a été un
	[ʒenɔsid]	génocide.
		-Genocide is probably the ultimate horror and the Holocaust was genocide.
6247	**relancer**	**revive**
	vb	En finir avec la monoculture du maïs et relancer la polyculture pour
	[ʁəlɑ̃se]	combattre l'uniformisation des paysages et des sols
		-Stop maize monoculture, and reestablish multiple cropping, to combat the
		loss of landscape and soil diversity.
6248	**originaire**	**native**
	adj	Originaire de Rivière-du-Loup, (Joseph) Charles Stein naît le 6 juillet 1912.
	[ɔʁiʒinɛʁ]	-(Joseph) Charles Stein, a native of Rivière-du-Loup, was born on July 6,
		1912.
6249	**présentable**	**presentable**
	adj	Une forme encore présentable mais un contenu très déficitaire.
	[pʁezɑ̃tabl]	-The form is just about presentable, but is very much lacking in content.
6250	**seller**	**saddle**
	vb	Son nouveau roman est devenu un best-seller.
	[sele]	-Her new novel has become a best seller.
6251	**moisson**	**harvest**
	m[mwasɔ̃]	La Ligue des États arabes pense que les enfants sont la moisson de demain. -
		The Arab League believes that children are the harvest of the future.
6252	**apéritif**	**aperitif**
	m	Juste à temps pour un apéritif.
	[apeʁitif]	-You're just in time for an aperitif.
6253	**mijoter**	**simmer**
	vb	Comme beaucoup d'entre nous, je suis toujours curieuse de voir ce que
	[miʒɔte]	Thelma est en train de mijoter.
		-I am always watching to see what Thelma is up to, as many of us do.
6254	**prodigieux**	**prodigious**
	adj	La Chine et l'Inde développent leur secteur universitaire de manière
	[pʁɔdiʒjø]	prodigieuse.
		-China and India are developing their university sector in an extraordinary
		way.
6255	**norme**	**standard**
	f	La folie est quelque chose de rare chez les individus, mais dans les groupes,
	[nɔʁm]	les partis, les peuples, les âges, c'est la norme.
		-Madness is something rare in individuals — but in groups, parties, peoples,
		ages it is the rule.
6256	**garderie**	**nursery**
	f	Je suis arrivé en retard au travail car j'ai dû déposer ma fille à la garderie.
	[gaʁdəʁi]	-I got to work late because I had to drop my daughter off at the day-care
		center.
6257	**prescription**	**prescription**
	f	On espérait renouveler sa prescription aujourd'hui.
	[pʁɛskʁipsjɔ̃]	-We were just hoping to refill her prescription today.
6258	**goudron**	**tar**
	m	Cigarette produisant une quantité réduite de goudron.
	[gudʁɔ̃]	-A cigarette in which the amount of tar produced during smoking is
		reduced.
6259	**contraint**	**constrained**

adj
[kɔ̃tʁɛ̃]
Ce phénomène contraint de nombreux enfants à abandonner l'école.
-Many children are constrained to abandon school as a consequence of such phenomenon.

6260 **séisme** **earthquake**

m
[seism]
Il s'est produit après cela, en été, un événement inattendu, le séisme en Turquie.
-Later, in the summer, something unexpected happened: the earthquake in Turkey.

6261 **résident** **resident**

m
[ʁezidɑ̃]
Au plus, un résident de Richmond gagnera le loto.
-At most, one resident of Richmond will win the lottery.

6262 **réhabilitation** **rehabilitation**

f
[ʁeabilitasjɔ̃]
Les prisons sont, par euphémisme, dénommées centres de réhabilitation.
-Prisons are euphemistically called rehabilitation centers.

6263 **distant** **distant**

adj[distɑ̃]
On l'a qualifié d'aristocratique et de distant, en somme on a dit que ce n'était pas vraiment un homme du peuple. -It was all black and white, agree or disagree, like or dislike, patrician and aloof — in short, he could not really be considered as a man of the people.

6264 **thermique** **thermal**

adj
[tɛʁmik]
Ledit transducteur retrouve son état d'origine par refroidissement thermique.
-The transducer returns to its original state by a process of thermal cooling.

6265 **bûcheron** **lumberjack**

m
[byʃʁɔ̃]
Jack est bûcheron.
-Jack is a lumberjack.

6266 **indestructible** **indestructible**

adj
[ɛ̃dɛstʁyktibl]
Malheureusement, c'est la réalité; l'indestructible Izzy nous a quittés.
-Sadly, it is true: The indestructible Izzy is gone.

6267 **mesquin** **mean|shabby**

adj
[mɛskɛ̃]
Je trouve cela un peu mesquin, sans compter que nous donnons une mauvaise image.
-I find this somewhat petty-minded, quite apart from the fact that it gives us a bad image.

6268 **initiation** **initiation**

f
[inisjasjɔ̃]
Ainsi commença mon initiation aux secrets d'Avalon.
-And so began my initiation into the secrets of Avalon.

6269 **prêcher** **preach|sermonize**

vb
[pʁeʃe]
S'ils pensent que le système est mauvais, ils devraient prêcher par l'exemple.
-If they think it is a wrong system they should practise what they are preach.

6270 **régisseur** **steward**

m
[ʁeʒisœʁ]
Ce système de commande comporte un régisseur global, un prédicteur de passerelle et de nombreux régisseurs locaux.
-The control system includes a global controller, a bridge predictor and many local controllers.

6271 **tracas** **hassle; worry**

m; adj
[tʁaka]
Pas de tracas.. Ce n'est qu'une petite arnaque.
-No hassle. It's an easy hustle.

6272 **brigand** **brigand**

m
[bʁigɑ̃]
Plusieurs régions sont nettement dangereuses et infestées de bandits et de brigands.
-Several regions are visibly insecure, infested with bandits and outlaws.

6273	**transparent**	**transparent|clear**
	adj	Le mécanisme sera simple, opportun, efficient, efficace et transparent.
	[tʁɑ̃spaʁɑ̃]	-Their mechanism will be simple, timely, efficient, effective and transparent.
6274	**frappant**	**striking**
	adj	Il existe un consensus frappant entre les pays développés et les pays en développement.
	[fʁapɑ̃]	-There is a striking consensus among the developed and developing countries.
6275	**balançoire**	**swing**
	f[balɑ̃swaʁ]	Ma fille adore faire de la balançoire. -My daughter loves to go on the swing.
6276	**paralysie**	**paralysis**
	f	Jennifer Talon peut provoquer la paralysie.
	[paʁalizi]	-Jennifer Talon had the ability to induce paralysis.
6277	**filature**	**spinning**
	f	Comme une sorte d'une roue, la filature.
	[filatyʁ]	-Like some kind of a wheel, spinning.
6278	**captivité**	**captivity**
	f	Tout porte à penser qu'elles sont toujours vivantes et en captivité.
	[kaptivite]	-There was every reason to believe that they were still alive and in captivity.
6279	**cordonnier**	**shoemaker**
	m	C'est l'heure de fermer boutique, cordonnier.
	[kɔʁdɔnje]	-Time to close up the shop, shoemaker.
6280	**cottage**	**cottage**
	m	Perhaps tomorrow, I'll come by the cottage.
	[kɔtaʒ]	-Peut-être que demain je passerai à la villa.
6281	**canular**	**hoax**
	m	Est-ce un canular ?
	[kanylaʁ]	-Is this some kind of hoax?
6282	**pharmaceutique**	**pharmaceutical**
	adj	Elle concerne enfin une composition pharmaceutique contenant ladite protéine ou un analogue.
	[faʁmasøtik]	-Finally, the invention relates to a pharmaceutical composition containing said protein or an analog.
6283	**satin**	**satin|demon**
	m	Une peau couleur acajou, douce comme du satin.
	[satɛ̃]	-Skin the color of mahogany... soft as satin.
6284	**tiède**	**lukewarm**
	adj	Mon pays n'a jamais été tiède dans la lutte contre le terrorisme.
	[tjɛd]	-My country has never been lukewarm in the fight against terrorism.
6285	**confisquer**	**confiscate|condemn**
	vb	Il continue de coloniser et de confisquer illégalement ce territoire.
	[kɔ̃fiske]	-It continues to colonize and illegally confiscate that territory.
6286	**invalide**	**invalid; invalid**
	adj; m/f	La réponse est non : l'invalider ne changerait pas la validité de l'acte ou de son résultat.
	[ɛ̃valid]	-The answer is no: declaring it invalid would not change the validity of the act or its result.
6287	**pinte**	**pint**
	f	En Angleterre, le serveur nous demanda : "-Combien de bière désirez-vous,
	[pɛ̃t]	une demi pinte ou bien une pinte ?". N'ayant aucune idée de ce que ça

pouvait représenter, nous lui demandâmes de nous montrer les verres.
-In England the waiter asked us, "How much beer would you like, a half pint or a pint?" Having no idea how much that would be, we asked him to show us the glasses.

6288	**robuste**	**robust|sturdy**
	adj[ʁɔbyst]	Il est essentiel d'avoir un mécanisme robuste pour surveiller et évaluer l'impact. -A robust mechanism for monitoring and assessing impact is essential.
6289	**déterrer**	**dig|unearth**
	vb	Leurs corps ont été déterrés dans la nuit du samedi 18 mai au dimanche 19 mai 2002 et amenés à une destination inconnue.
	[deteʁe]	-Their bodies were dug up the night of 18/19 May 2002 and taken to an unknown destination.
6290	**éventualité**	**eventuality**
	f	Un budget conditionnel a donc été prévu pour faire face à une telle éventualité.
	[evɑ̃tɥalite]	-The budget therefore includes a contingency to cover these costs.
6291	**laveur**	**mop**
	m	Tu vois le raton laveur ?
	[lavœʁ]	-Do you see the raccoon?
6292	**chevelure**	**hair**
	f	Pendant un moment, j'ai cru que j'écoutais Trent Lott ou Newt Gingrich avec une chevelure plus foncée.
	[ʃəvlyʁ]	-I thought for a moment it was Trent Lott speaking or Newt Gingrich with darker hair.
6293	**énergétique**	**energetics; energizing**
	f; adj	Il y aura une crise énergétique dans l'avenir proche.
	[enɛʁʒetik]	-There will be an energy crisis in the near future.
6294	**illuminer**	**illuminate|floodlight**
	vb	Cette organisation est le phare qui peut illuminer notre chemin.
	[ilymine]	-This Organization is the beacon that can illuminate that path.
6295	**conforme**	**compliant**
	adj	Cette situation n'est pas conforme aux dispositions de la circulaire susmentionnée.
	[kɔ̃fɔʁm]	-This situation is not compliant with the terms of the aforementioned bulletin.
6296	**tract**	**leaflet**
	m	L'authenticité de ce tract est également douteuse.
	[tʁakt]	-The authenticity of the tract has also been questioned.
6297	**suer**	**sweat**
	vb	Pas assez de place à Philadelphie pour suer un bon coup.
	[sɥe]	-Not enough space to run around in Philly, work up a decent sweat.
6298	**couchette**	**bed**
	f	Dans le tiroir de la couchette.
	[kuʃɛt]	-In the drawer beside the bed.
6299	**entrave**	**obstacle|interference**
	f	Sur le plan légal, il n'existe aucune entrave à l'éducation des filles.
	[ɑ̃tʁav]	-Legally, there is no impediment to the education of girls.
6300	**réceptionniste**	**receptionist**
	m/f	Il est donc proposé de créer un poste d'agent local pour un réceptionniste à plein temps.
	[ʁesɛpsjɔnist]	-It is therefore proposed to establish a local post for a full-time receptionist.

6301	**Soudan**	**Sudan**
	m[sudɑ̃]	On peut rejoindre Roberts au Soudan. -We can hook up with Roberts in the Sudan.
6302	**retraiter**	**reprocess**
	vb [ʁətʁete]	Nous ne sommes pas autorisés à les retraiter. -We are not allowed to reprocess it.
6303	**corridor**	**corridor**
	m [kɔʁidɔʁ]	On laisse quelques lumières dans le corridor. -We always keep a few lights burning out in the corridor.
6304	**dénicher**	**unearth**
	vb [deniʃe]	Quand elles le seront, la concurrence dénichera celles qui conduisent leurs affaires d'une manière contraire aux intérêts des consommateurs. -After this deregulation, competition will ferret out those businesses that conduct their affairs in a manner inconsistent with consumer interests.
6305	**bouée**	**buoy**
	f [bwe]	Florence a été pour moi une bouée de sauvetage dans la mer de la vie. -Florence was for me a life buoy in the sea of life.
6306	**expédier**	**send|dispatch**
	vb [ɛkspedje]	Les Américains voulaient expédier du plutonium au Canada pour s'en débarrasser. -The Americans wanted to ship plutonium to Canada in order to dispose of it.
6307	**tuberculose**	**tuberculosis**
	f [tybɛʁkyloz]	De nos jours, peu de gens souffrent de tuberculose. -These days few people suffer from tuberculosis.
6308	**afficher**	**display**
	vb [afiʃe]	Sélectionnez cette option pour ne pas afficher de bordure visible autour du Frame. -Mark this option if the floating frame is not to have a visible border.
6309	**diesel**	**diesel**
	m [djezɛl]	Moteurs diesel et véhicules équipés d'un moteur diesel -Diesel engines and vehicles equipped with a diesel engine
6310	**maçon**	**mason**
	m [masɔ̃]	C'est au pied du mur que l'on connait le maçon. -It is at the foot of the wall that we know the mason.
6311	**internat**	**internship|boarding school**
	m [ɛ̃tɛʁna]	Vous pourriez le mettre en internat. -You could send him off to boarding school.
6312	**collectionneur**	**collector**
	m [kɔlɛksjɔnœʁ]	C'était également un fin collectionneur et un sportif passionné. -He was also an astute art collector and an avid sportsman.
6313	**palmier**	**palm**
	m [palmje]	Attends quelques secondes et ton palmier disparaîtra. -Just wait a couple of seconds and your palm tree will completely disappear.
6314	**incurable**	**incurable**
	adj[ɛ̃kyʁabl]	Ironie du destin, cet homme qui, pendant 50 ans, a voué un culte à la bonne forme physique reçut en 2006 un diagnostic de la maladie neurologique incurable appelée syndrome de l'X fragile. -In a cruel twist of fate for one who was a physical fitness devotee for over 50 years, Peter was diagnosed in 2006 with an untreatable neurological condition known as Fragile X.
6315	**sabbat**	**Sabbath**

m
[saba]

Pour ce second groupe, la Loi rend l'observance du sabbat financièrement onéreuse.
-For this second group, the Act made the observance of the Sabbath financially onerous.

6316 **étreindre**　　**embrace|grasp**

vb
[etʁɛ̃dʁ]

Peu à peu, d'une étreinte à une autre.
-Gradually, from embrace to embrace.

6317 **lotion**　　**lotion**

f
[losjɔ̃]

J'ai besoin de lotion pour les mains.
-I need hand lotion.

6318 **déduction**　　**deduction**

f
[dedyksjɔ̃]

Le Comité a appliqué cette déduction dans le calcul de l'indemnité recommandée.
-The Panel has applied such a deduction in calculating the compensation recommended.

6319 **calorie**　　**calorie**

f
[kalɔʁi]

C'est la calorie qui est l'unité utilisée par les consommateurs avertis dans leurs calculs.
-The calorie is the unit that informed consumers use in their calculations.

6320 **épinard**　　**spinach**

m
[epinaʁ]

Faut que j'arrête les épinards.
-Better lay off the spinach.

6321 **imprimerie**　　**printing house**

f
[ɛ̃pʁimʁi]

D'autres activités de l'industrie de base, comme la fabrication de caoutchouc et de papier, l'imprimerie et l'industrie de la rayonne, ont vu leurs installations sabotées.
-Other basic industry activities, such as rubber and paper production, the printing industry and the rayon industry, were the objects of sabotage at several facilities.

6322 **putois**　　**skunk**

m
[pytwa]

King était un putois de première classe.
-King was a skunk of the first order.

6323 **repli**　　**withdrawal|fold**

m
[ʁəpli]

L'invention concerne un système et des procédés de messagerie de repli.
-A system and methods for fallback messaging are disclosed.

6324 **embouteillage**　　**bottling**

m
[ãbutɛjaʒ]

Des embouteillages peuvent se former quotidiennement sur les tronçons du réseau définis ci-dessus.
-Bottlenecks can occur on a daily basis on the sections of the network defined above.

6325 **périlleusement**　　**perilously**

adv[peʁijøzmã]

Les valeurs et les principes qui nous sont si chers semblent être des rêves distants dans le contexte des horreurs qui se produisent dans des endroits reculés pour certains, mais périlleusement proches pour d'autres. -The values and principles we hold so dear seem to be distant dreams against the backdrop of horrors occurring in places remote for some, but dangerously close to others.

6326 **hydraulique**　　**hydraulic; hydraulics**

adj; f
[idʁolik]

C'est l'énergie hydraulique qui actionne la roue.
-Water power turns the wheel.

6327 **grimer**　　**make up|disguise**

	vb	J'ai dû me grimer pour quitter le palais sans escorte.
	[gʁime]	-I had to disguise myself. I'm not permitted to leave the palace unescorted.

6328 gerbe — sheaf

f

[ʒɛʁb]

Je sais que ça ne fait pas le poids contre un rib steak et des pois et une gerbe chaude de pain de mais.

-I know it probably doesn't compete with rib steak and beans and... a hot sheaf of cornbread.

6329 logo — logo

m

[lɔgo]

Vous devez mettre notre logo sur le lecteur vidéo.

-Okay, look, you have to put our logo in the viewer. That's it.

6330 sondage — survey|poll; probing

m; adj

[sɔ̃daʒ]

En raison du manque de données, le sondage a été arrêté.

-In the absence of sufficient data, the survey was given up.

6331 échéance — term

f

[eʃeɑ̃s]

Comment est-ce que je vais pouvoir arriver à rencontrer l'échéance pour ce document ?

-How can I make the deadline for this document?

6332 rétablissement — recovery|restoration

m

[ʁetablismɑ̃]

Le rétablissement du pays va exiger un engagement de la communauté internationale.

-Restoring the country will require the commitment of the international community.

6333 inséparable — inseparable

adj

[ɛ̃sepaʁabl]

Le processus politique est inséparable de la situation sur le terrain.

-The political process is inseparable from the situation on the ground.

6334 débrancher — unplug

vb

[debʁɑ̃ʃe]

Toute personne qui n'est pas débranchée... est un agent en puissance.

-That means that anyone we haven't unplugged...... is potentially an agent.

6335 infect — foul|vile

adj

[ɛ̃fɛkt]

If you have truck with countries of this sort, then what they do is infect you.

-Quand on travaille avec des pays de cet acabit, il est facile de se laisser infecter.

6336 contesté — disputed

adj

[kɔ̃tɛste]

Cela n'a jamais été contesté, et ce non plus pour la Banque centrale européenne.

-Not that this was ever disputed for the European Central Bank.

6337 piller — plunder|loot

vb[pije]

Des Libériens traversent régulièrement la frontière pour piller ainsi la zone. -Liberians have regularly crossed the border to loot the area in this manner.

6338 pieuvre — octopus

f

[pjœvʁ]

C'est une pieuvre déchaînée qui lance ses tentacules meurtriers dans toutes les directions.

-It is a frantic octopus sending its deadly tentacles in all directions.

6339 incompétence — incompetence

f

[ɛ̃kɔ̃petɑ̃s]

La violence est la dernière extrémité de l'incompétence.

-Violence is the last refuge of incompetence.

6340 pharmacien — pharmacist

m

[faʁmasjɛ̃]

Tu devrais demander conseil à un pharmacien avant de prendre ce médicament.

-You should ask a pharmacist for his advice before taking this medicine.

6341 bûche — log

f
[byʃ]

Une bûche peut rester dix ans dans une rivière, mais elle ne deviendra jamais un crocodile.
-A log may remain in the water for ten years, but it will never become a crocodile.

6342 téléspectateur — **viewer**

m
[telespɛktatœʁ]

Un téléspectateur aimerait vérifier la validité de ces affirmations.
-A viewer would like to verify the validity of these statements.

6343 inutilement — **uselessly**

adv
[inytilmɑ̃]

N'avez -vous pas le sentiment de charger la barque inutilement?
-Do you not feel that this is an extra burden that serves no purpose?

6344 humanitaire — **humanitarian**

adj
[ymanitɛʁ]

Le 31 mars 2004, l'auteur a demandé à être considéré comme un cas humanitaire.
-On 31 March 2004, the author applied for consideration on compassionate grounds.

6345 body — **body**

m
[bɔdi]

Le body art est une expérience intime.
-Body art's this really personal experience.

6346 chenille — **caterpillar**

f
[ʃǝnij]

Oh, une chenille !
-Oh look, a caterpillar!

6347 léser — **injure**

vb
[leze]

Cette loi ne vise en aucun cas à léser les bailleurs.
-In no case, this Act purports to harm lessors.

6348 égocentrique — **egocentric; egomania**

adj; m/f
[egosɑ̃tʁik]

Jack est impulsif et égocentrique.
-Jack is impulsive and self-centered.

6349 aisément — **easily**

adv
[ezemɑ̃]

Les particules sont ensuite aisément collectées dans un dépoussiéreur électrostatique.
-The particles are then easily collected in an electrostatic precipitator.

6350 voûter — **stoop|vault**

vb
[vute]

Mais tu ne dois pas te voûter.
-And you... but you don't have to slouch.

6351 progéniture — **offspring**

f
[pʁɔʒenityʁ]

Les parents peuvent transmettre bien des maladies à leur progéniture.
-Parents can pass many diseases on to their offspring.

6352 oasis — **oasis**

f
[ɔazis]

Le Président a rappelé qu'un comité conjoint de coordination avec OASIS avait été établi.
-The Chairperson reminded that a Joint Coordination Committee with OASIS was in place.

6353 somnambule — **somnambulist; somnambulistic**

m; adj
[sɔmnɑ̃byl]

Le fait de découvrir que j'étais somnambule m'a déçu énormément.
-What a disappointment to discover I was a sleepwalker.

6354 bienfaiteur — **benefactor; benefactor**

adj; m
[bjɛ̃fɛtœʁ]

Ce projet a reçu un financement d'un bienfaiteur privé en Chine, M. Luo Hong.
-This project received funding from a private benefactor in China, Mr. Luo Hong

6355 inexplicable — **inexplicable**

108

adj
[inɛksplikabl]
Cependant,» inexplicable» devient de plus en plus la norme dans ce Parlement.
-However, ' inexplicable ' is becoming more and more the norm in this House.

6356 **gymnastique** **gymnastics; gymnastic**
f; adj
[ʒimnastik]
Il est bon en gymnastique.
-He is good at gymnastics.

6357 **brouiller** **blur|scramble**
vb
[bʁuje]
Loin d'élucider la question, ces grandes affirmations contribuent plutôt à brouiller les pistes.
-These broad allegations about the nexus often obscure more than they reveal.

6358 **pommade** **ointment**
f
[pɔmad]
Il n'y a plus de pommade.
-There's no more ointment.

6359 **oculaire** **ocular; ocular**
adj; m
[ɔkylɛʁ]
Un télescope ayant une ouverture nominale de 20 mm et un pouvoir grossissant compris entre 10 et 30, équipé d'un oculaire réglable comprenant un réticulaire.
-A telescope with an aperture nominally 20 mm and a magnification between 10 and 30, fitted with an adjustable eyepiece incorporating a reticular.

6360 **remplacement** **replacement|displacement**
m
[ʁãplasmã]
En cas de défaillance, nous garantissons le remplacement gratuit du processeur de mots.
-Should the word processor go wrong, we guarantee to replace it free of charge.

6361 **Coran** **Koran**
m
[kɔʁã]
C'est une façon rhétorique d'exprimer les choses par rapport au texte du Coran.
-It is a rhetorical way of expression relative to the saying of the Koran.

6362 **cascadeur** **stuntman**
m[kaskadœʁ]
Le cascadeur, Rick, ses empreintes sont partout dessus. -The stuntman, Rick, his prints are all over it.

6363 **publication** **publication|issue**
f
[pyblikasjõ]
Le magazine Look a arrêté sa publication.
-The magazine Look is no longer being published.

6364 **inverser** **reverse**
vb
[ɛ̃vɛʁse]
Ce qui, à son tour, pourrait inverser la logique actuelle des avantages du désarmement.
-That, in turn, could reverse the current logic of the advantages of disarmament.

6365 **tournevis** **screwdriver**
m
[tuʁnəvi]
Auriez-vous un tournevis par hasard ?
-Have you such a thing as a screwdriver by chance?

6366 **prune** **plum**
f
[pʁyn]
On m'a mis une prune.
-I got fined.

6367 **voyeur** **voyeur**
m
[vwajœʁ]
On dirait que le voyeur a trafiqué la fenêtre.
-Now, looks like the peeper jimmied the window open.

6368 **sketch** **sketch**

m
[skɛtʃ]

Ça vient du sketch "lucha libre brunch buffet".
-It was from the "lucha libre brunch buffet" sketch.

6369 **chacal** — **jackal**

m
[ʃakal]

Qui peut oublier qu'il a accueilli et offert l'asile à Carlos le Chacal et à Oussama Ben Laden ?
-Who can forget that it hosted and gave safe haven to both Carlos the Jackal and Osama bin Laden?

6370 **scalpel** — **scalpel**

m
[skalpɛl]

S'il te chope avec le scalpel, c'est toi qui es cuit.
-If he catches you with that scalpel, you're the one that's history.

6371 **obèse** — **obese**

adj
[ɔbɛz]

Plus de la moitié des adultes néo-zélandais étaient trop gros ou obèses en 1997.
-In 1997, over half of all adult New Zealanders were overweight or obese.

6372 **lister** — **list**

vb
[liste]

Cette pratique, qui s'écarte de celle consistant à lister des articles spécifiques, porte le nom de « clause attrape-tout ».
-Compared with the practice of listing specific items, this approach is known as "catch-all" controls.

6373 **aluminium** — **aluminum**

m
[alyminjɔm]

Les plaques avant et arrière en aluminium sont fixées aux blocs d'aluminium en nids-d'abeilles.
-Front and rear aluminium plates are attached to the aluminium honeycomb blocks.

6374 **équipée** — **escape**

f
[ekipe]

Chaque pièce est équipée d'un grand bureau.
-Each room is equipped with large desks.

6375 **infantile** — **infantile**

adj
[ɛ̃fɑ̃til]

Taux de mortalité infantile dans les localités urbaines et rurales
-Infantile mortality rate in urban and rural localities.

6376 **funéraire** — **funerary**

adj
[fyneʁɛʁ]

Rite hindou qui voulait que les veuves s'immolaient sur le bûcher funéraire de leur mari.
-The former Hindu practice of a widow immolating herself on her husband's funeral pyre.

6377 **livret** — **book**

m
[livʁɛ]

Hier je suis tombé sur une copie du livret de famille de mon père.
-Yesterday I stumbled across a copy of my father's family register.

6378 **attribuer** — **assign|attribute**

vb
[atʁibɥe]

Il appartient à chaque gouvernement d'attribuer cette responsabilité.
-It remains the prerogative of each government to assign this responsibility.

6379 **épicier** — **grocer**

m
[episje]

J'ai accumulé des dettes chez le marchand de riz et chez l'épicier.
-I built up some debts at the rice seller and at the grocer.

6380 **digérer** — **digest**

vb
[diʒeʁe]

Je prendrai le temps nécessaire pour digérer les détails de votre réponse.
-I will take time to digest the detail in your answer.

6381 **biblique** — **biblical**

adj
[biblik]

Monsieur le Cardinal, chers membres de la Commission biblique pontificale !
-Your Eminence, Dear Members of the Pontifical Biblical Commission,

6382	**recréer**		**recreate**
	vb		Il faut recréer les conditions propres à rendre confiance au consommateur européen.
	[ʁəkʁee]		-We must recreate the right conditions for winning back consumer confidence in Europe.
6383	**dégoûtant**		**disgusting**
	adj		Je ne dirai rien de plus, mais je suis dégoûtée - nous devons tous être dégoûtés - par cette barbarie.
	[degutɑ̃]		-I will say no more, but I am disgusted - we must all be disgusted - at this savagery.
6384	**jaser**		**gossip|blab**
	vb		Pourvu qu'il n'aille pas jaser.
	[ʒaze]		-I hope he won't gossip.
6385	**poivrot**		**boozer; rummy**
	m; adj		C'était un vrai poivrot.
	[pwavʁo]		-He was a real drunkard.
6386	**suspecter**		**suspect**
	vb		Cela pousse les non-musulmans à suspecter les musulmans de leur être généralement favorables.
	[syspɛkte]		-This causes non-Muslims to suspect that Muslims are generally in sympathy with them.
6387	**marchander**		**haggle|bargain**
	vb		Nous ne voulons pas non plus marchander le financement de programmes pluriannuels déjà approuvés.
	[maʁʃɑ̃de]		-Neither do we wish to haggle over the financing of multi-annual programmes that have already been approved.
6388	**dérober**		**steal**
	vb[deʁɔbe]		Un proverbe ancien du Myanmar dit que l'éducation est un trésor que personne ne peut dérober. -There is an old Myanmar proverb that says that education is the pot of gold that no one can steal.
6389	**sagement**		**wisely**
	adv		Cette sage recommandation n'est, malheureusement, guère respectée par les États.
	[saʒmɑ̃]		-Unfortunately, the States paid little heed to this wise recommendation.
6390	**mangeur**		**eater**
	m		C'est un gros mangeur.
	[mɑ̃ʒœʁ]		-He is a big eater.
6391	**directif**		**directive**
	adj		Il faudra pour cela que les gouvernements jouent un rôle plus directif dans l'économie.
	[diʁɛktif]		-This will require a more directive role for Government in the economy.
6392	**vénérer**		**revere|worship**
	vb		Ils le vénèrent comme un ancêtre qui mérite toute leur fierté.
	[veneʁe]		-They revere him as an ancestor deserving of their pride.
6393	**calvaire**		**ordeal**
	m		Edna, un calvaire s'achève, mais le prochain vous attend.
	[kalvɛʁ]		-Well, Edna, one ordeal is over, the next is all ready and waiting for you.
6394	**ménager**		**household; spare**
	adj; vb		Le volume de travail ménager est essentiellement fonction du stade de l'existence.
	[menaʒe]		-Doing household work is centrally dependent on the life phase of the person.

6395 détection — **detection**
f
[detɛksjɔ̃]
L'invention relève de la détection qualitative et/ou quantitative d'analytes.
-The present invention relates to the field of qualitative and/or quantitative detection of analytes.

6396 blanchir — **whiten|launder**
vb
[blɑ̃ʃiʁ]
Il signale aussi qu'une source aurait affirmé qu'on utilisait les sociétés d'État pour «blanchir les fonds fédéraux».
-It reports a source saying that Crown corporations were used to "launder federal funds."

6397 roulant — **rolling**
adj
[ʁulɑ̃]
Le véhicule roulant à vive allure glissa et s'enfonça tête la première dans l'arrière d'un camion avant que son conducteur n'ait pu dire Jack Robinson.
-The speeding vehicle skidded and crashed head-on into the rear-end of a truck before the driver could say Jack Robinson.

6398 auxiliaire — **auxiliary; auxiliary**
adj; m
[ɔksiljɛʁ]
Un grand voilier avec un moteur diesel auxiliaire.
-It's a big sailboat with an auxiliary, a diesel engine.

6399 inonder — **flood|inundate**
vb
[inɔ̃de]
Les produits chinois inondent sans cesse le marché et ils continueront à l'inonder de plus en plus.
-Chinese products are constantly flooding the market and will flood it more and more.

6400 muffin — **muffin**
m[myfɛ̃]
Je veux un muffin anglais. -I want an English muffin.

6401 orge — **barley**
f
[ɔʁʒ]
Peux-tu distinguer de l'orge du blé au premier coup d'œil ?
-Can you tell barley from wheat at first sight?

6402 classement — **classification**
m
[klasmɑ̃]
Il en résultera une amélioration du respect du classement approprié.
-As a result the enforcement of a correct classification will be improved.

6403 assigner — **assign**
vb
[asiɲe]
Cliquez ici pour assigner les paramètres choisis à une transition.
-To assign the selected settings to a slide transition, click here.

6404 ajuster — **adjust|tighten**
vb
[aʒyste]
Proposition de la Communauté européenne visant à ajuster le Protocole de Montréal;
-Proposal by the European Community for adjustment of the Montreal Protocol.

6405 épaisseur — **thickness**
f
[epɛsœʁ]
Je ne peux lire un livre de cette épaisseur en une semaine.
-I cannot read such a thick book in a week.

6406 gaieté — **cheerfulness**
f
[gete]
Nous lui souhaitons, pour les années qui viennent, de garder son enthousiasme et sa gaieté.
-We wish for him that in the years to come his enthusiasm and cheerfulness never wane.

6407 aptitude — **aptitude|fitness**
f
[aptityd]
Les aveugles développent parfois une aptitude compensatoire à sentir la proximité des objets autour d'eux.
-Blind people sometimes develop a compensatory ability to sense the proximity of objects around them.

6408 **séducteur** — seducer; seductive
m; adj
[sedyktœʁ]
Tu tentes de faire passer ce pauvre Jones pour un séducteur.
-You're trying to turn poor Jones into a seducer.

6409 **nigaud** — simpleton; stupid
m; adj
[nigo]
Expliquez ça au nigaud, veux-tu?
-Explain it to the simpleton, would you?

6410 **provocation** — provocation
f
[pʁɔvɔkasjõ]
Malheureusement, les autres parties persistent dans cette logique de provocation.
-Unfortunately, the other parties have persisted in this course of provocation.

6411 **vigilant** — vigilant | watchful
adj
[viʒilã]
Le Conseil de sécurité demeurera vigilant pour qu'il n'y ait pas d'impunité.
-The Security Council will remain vigilant to ensure that there is no impunity.

6412 **bavardage** — chat | chatting
m
[bavaʁdaʒ]
Désolé, chérie, il n'y a aucun moyen que je puisse prendre toute une soirée pour un bavardage autour de cocktails.
-Sorry honey, there's just no way I can take a whole evening of cocktail party chitchat.

6413 **couplet** — verse
m
[kuplɛ]
Si tu pouvais ralentir vers la fin du couplet.
-If you were to slow it down as we head out of the verse...

6414 **rimer** — rhyme
vb
[ʁime]
Pourtant, l'AIEA prétend, sans rime ni raison, que mon gouvernement viole les accords internationaux.
-Nevertheless, with no rhyme or reason, the IAEA claims that my Government is in violation of international agreements.

6415 **amazone** — amazon
f
[amazon]
Pour ce faire, le programme est arrivé jusqu'en Amazone.
-To include these segments, the programme has reached the Amazon.

6416 **cosaque** — Cossack
m
[kɔzak]
Depuis 2001, il n'y a pas de programmes fédéraux de soutien aux organisations cosaques.
-No federal programmes to support Cossack organizations have existed since 2001.

6417 **matraquer** — club | cosh
vb
[matʁake]
Quand on parle de cette loi, on peut parler en toute légitimité d'une loi matraque.
-This legislation can legitimately be referred to in terms of a bludgeon or big stick legislation.

6418 **commandant** — commander; commanding
m; adj
[kɔmãdã]
La commande de passage en faisceaux de croisement doit commander simultanément l'extinction du ou des feux-route.
-The control for changing over to the passing beam(s) shall switch off the driving beam(s) simultaneously.

6419 **diabète** — diabetes
m
[djabɛt]
Aujourd'hui, un Canadien sur quatre est atteint de diabète ou de prédiabète.
-Today, one in four Canadians either have diabetes or pre-diabetes.

6420 **manœuvre** — maneuver | move
f
[manœvʁ]
Le gouvernement slovaque tente une manœuvre de rattrapage.
-The Slovak Government is trying to carry out an overtaking manoeuvre.

6421	**justesse**	**accuracy|appropriateness**
	f	On dit, avec justesse, que le temps est le remède contre la colère.
	[ʒystɛs]	-It is said that, rightly so, that time is anger's medicine.
6422	**cannibale**	**cannibal; cannibal**
	adj; m/f	Je vais te motiver, Baleine, à en raccourcir la bite de tous les cannibales du Congo !
	[kanibal]	-I will motivate you, Private Pyle...... if it short-dicks every cannibal on the Congo!
6423	**incompétent**	**incompetent**
	adj	Enfin, l'auteur réaffirme qu'il a été jugé par un tribunal incompétent.
	[ɛ̃kɔ̃petã]	-Finally, the author reiterates that he was tried by an incompetent tribunal.
6424	**chambellan**	**chamberlain**
	m	En tant que chambellan de Tatebayashi montre-toi plus responsable.
	[ʃãbelã]	-As Tatebayashi's chamberlain, show more responsability.
6425	**brigadier**	**brigadier**
	m	Mon associé, le brigadier Pike, trouvera trois chasseurs à réaction.
	[bʁigadje]	-My partner, Brigadier Pike, knows where to find three jet fighters.
6426	**valve**	**valve**
	f[valv]	Ça pousse probablement sur la valve. -It's probably pushing in on the valve.
6427	**adhésif**	**adhesive; adhesive**
	adj; m	L'adhésif à employer sera la résine époxy de type H9940 ou équivalent.
	[adezif]	-The adhesive to be used shall be an Epoxy Resin type H9940 or equivalent.
6428	**guérilla**	**guerrilla**
	f	Nos agents de maintien de la paix seraient entraînés dans une guerre de guérilla.
	[geʁija]	-Our peacekeepers would be sucked into a guerrilla war.
6429	**urbain**	**urban**
	adj	Application aux véhicules ferroviaires de transport urbain.
	[yʁbɛ̃]	-The invention is applicable to urban transportation railway vehicles.
6430	**sauvagement**	**savagely**
	adv	Le rapport décrit notamment comment l'une d'elles a été sauvagement torturée.
	[sovaʒmã]	-The report described in particular how one of them had been savagely tortured.
6431	**caféine**	**caffeine**
	f	Je suis devenu accro à ma dose quotidienne de caféine.
	[kafein]	-I have grown dependent on my daily dose of caffeine.
6432	**sachet**	**bag**
	m	Ce matériau est respectueux de l'environnement et le sachet peut être fabriqué à faibles coûts.
	[saʃɛ]	-This material is environmentally friendly and the bag can be produced at low cost.
6433	**jargon**	**jargon**
	m	Parallèlement, il devrait être facile à lire, sans trop de jargon technique.
	[ʒaʁgɔ̃]	-At the same time, it should be easy to read, without too much technical jargon.
6434	**périscope**	**periscope**
	m	On va en lâcher une pile dans son périscope.
	[peʁiskɔp]	-I reckon we'll just drop a pile right down his periscope.
6435	**acclamation**	**acclamation|cheer**

	f	La Déclaration a été adoptée par acclamation à la dernière séance de la réunion.
	[aklamasjɔ̃]	-The Declaration was adopted by acclamation at the final session of the meeting.
6436	**rincer**	**rinse**
	vb	En cas d'ingestion, rincer la bouche de la victime avec de l'eau (uniquement
	[ʁɛ̃se]	si elle est consciente).
		-If swallowed, rinse mouth with water (only if the person is conscious).
6437	**organique**	**organic**
	adj	Elle se spécialise en chimie organique.
	[ɔʁganik]	-She majors in organic chemistry.
6438	**densité**	**density**
	f	L'invention concerne une cigarette double densité biodégradable.
	[dɑ̃site]	-The present invention relates to a biodegradabale dual density cigarette.
6439	**moisir**	**mold**
	vb[mwaziʁ]	Il ne faut pas laisser moisir le foin sinon il devient tout simplement dangereux. -Hay should not be allowed to go mouldy, since this makes it downright dangerous.
6440	**trébucher**	**stumble|stagger**
	vb	Ce sont les défis indistincts qui nous font trébucher quand ils se manifestent.
	[tʁebyʃe]	-It is the vague ones that we stumble over when they manifest themselves.
6441	**béquille**	**crutch**
	f	Il sera plus autonome sans béquille.
	[bekij]	-He'll be more self-reliant without a crutch.
6442	**resserrer**	**tighten**
	vb	Kenney a entrepris de resserrer la définition de ce qu'est un Canadien.
	[ʁəseʁe]	-Kenney set out to tighten the definition of what it means to be a Canadian.
6443	**cruche**	**jug|pitcher**
	f	On a fait que jeter quelques cendres dans une cruche.
	[kʁyʃ]	-Dumped a couple of ashtrays into a jug.
6444	**filon**	**vein**
	m	On dirait que nous avons trouvé le filon.
	[filɔ̃]	-Looks like we hit the vein.
6445	**visionnaire**	**visionary; visionary**
	adj; m	Ce type de messages, cependant, ne caractérise les dernières années de
	[vizjɔnɛʁ]	visionnaire.
		-This kind of messages, however, would only characterized the last years of visionary.
6446	**modification**	**modification**
	f	Date de dernière modification de cette page : le 03/11/2010.
	[mɔdifikasjɔ̃]	-Date of last revision of this page: 2010-11-03
6447	**gluant**	**sticky|slimy**
	adj	C'est gluant !
	[glyɑ̃]	-It's sticky.
6448	**récif**	**reef**
	m	En septembre 2001, le MV Tokelau s'est échoué sur un récif de l'atoll de
	[ʁesif]	Nukunonu.
		-In September 2001, the MV Tokelau ran aground on a reef at Nukunonu atoll.
6449	**footballeur**	**footballer**

	m [futbɔlœʁ]	Osher, qui rêvait de devenir footballeur, ne sait pas qu'il a perdu une jambe. -Osher, who dreamed of becoming a soccer player, does not yet know that he has lost one of his legs.
6450	**obstruction** f [ɔpstʁyksjõ]	**obstruction|blockage** Complicité de meurtre, conspiration, obstruction. -We're talking about accessory to murder, conspiracy, obstruction.
6451	**steward** m [stəwaʁ]	**steward** I was a chief steward. -J'étais premier intendant.
6452	**enflure** f[ãflyʁ]	**swelling** Juste du sang, de l'enflure, des ecchymoses. -There's been bleeding, swelling, bruises...
6453	**défectueux** adj [defɛktɥø]	**defective|deficient** Les systèmes de classification des emplois sont défectueux, voire inexistants. -Job classification systems are defective, if they exist.
6454	**rugby** m [ʁygbi]	**rugby** Nous jouions au rugby. -We were playing rugby.
6455	**capteur** m [kaptœʁ]	**sensor** Globalement, le capteur doit être économique à fabriquer. -Overall, the sensor is intended to be inexpensive to produce.
6456	**shooter** vb [ʃɔte]	**shoot|shoot up** Je vais me shooter et je reviens. -I'll be right back after I shoot up.
6457	**commerçant** m; adj [kɔmɛʁsã]	**merchant; trading** Un commerçant est une personne qui achète et qui vend de la marchandise. -A merchant is a person who buys and sells goods.
6458	**friandise** f [fʁijãdiz]	**delicacy|treat** Qui aboie jusqu'à ce qu'on lui lance une friandise. -Keeps barking until someone tosses it a treat.
6459	**déplaisant** adj [deplɛzã]	**unpleasant|distasteful** Je trouve que c'est déplaisant: cela n'a rien à voir avec le système PNR. -I find that distasteful: it has nothing to do with PNR.
6460	**orthodoxe** adj [ɔʁtɔdɔks]	**orthodox** Au sein des membres de cette commission, seule l'Église orthodoxe est représentée. -Only the Orthodox Church is represented among the members of the commission.
6461	**sauterelle** f [sotʁɛl]	**grasshopper** La sauterelle fit un grand bond. -The locust made a big jump.
6462	**fossile** adj; m [fɔsil]	**fossil; fossil** La dépendance de l'énergie fossile est un obstacle à notre développement durable. -Dependency on fossil fuel is an obstacle to our sustainable development.
6463	**coupant** adj; m [kupã]	**cutting; bolter** Au moment de la rentrée atmosphérique, ces charges s'enflamment, coupant le réservoir. -Upon re-entry, these charges ignite, cutting the tank.
6464	**amnésique**	**amnesic; amnesiac**

m/f; adj
[amnezik]

Probablement que le plus grand amnésique de tous, c'est l'actuel premier ministre, l'ancien chef de l'opposition.
-The one with the most serious case of amnesia of all is probably the former Leader of the Opposition, the current Prime Minister.

6465 **accessible**

adj
[aksesibl]

accessible|reachable

Sinon, cela restera un luxe accessible à certains de nos citoyens seulement.
-Otherwise this will remain an affordable luxury for only some of our citizens.

6466 **pourpre**

adj[puʁpʁ]

purple

Fait attention, idiote aux cheveux pourpre. -Be careful you purple haired imbecile!

6467 **radieux**

adj
[ʁadjø]

radiant|bright

C'est bien embêtant tout de même, ces femmes qui, du fond de leur cuisine, ou des comptes de leur ménage, refusent l'avenir radieux de l'euro.
-It is really very annoying that these women, from the depths of their kitchens or household accounts, are rejecting the radiant future of the euro.

6468 **doter**

vb
[dɔte]

endow

L'idée était de doter Strasbourg d'une université de classe mondiale.
-The idea was to endow Strasbourg with a world-class university.

6469 **saccager**

vb
[sakaʒe]

sack|ransack

Quatre personnes auraient été tuées et des églises baptistes auraient été saccagées.
-Four people were said to have been killed and Baptist churches ransacked.

6470 **approchant**

adj
[apʁɔʃã]

approaching

On pourrait éviter complètement une telle situation en approchant la question sous un autre angle.
-It could be completely avoided by approaching it from a different position.

6471 **supériorité**

f
[sypeʁjɔʁite]

superiority

La politique de dissuasion nucléaire ou de supériorité militaire persiste encore.
-The policy of nuclear deterrence or of military superiority still remains.

6472 **camisole de force**

f
[kamizɔl də fɔʁs]

straightjacket

La "contrainte sévère" signifie qu'il est fait usage d'une camisole de force ou d'un brancard.
-"Severe coercion" means the use of a straightjacket or stretcher.

6473 **attirance**

f
[atiʁãs]

attraction

Dan a de l'attirance pour Linda.
-Dan was attracted to Linda.

6474 **bannière**

f
[banjeʁ]

banner

Souvenons-nous que c'est un homme de cet État qui, le premier, a planté la bannière du parti républicain à la Maison-Blanche, un parti fondé sur les valeurs d'autonomie, de liberté individuelle et d'unité nationale.
-Let's remember that it was a man from this state who first carried the banner of the Republican Party to the White House, a party founded on the values of self-reliance and individual liberty and national unity.

6475 **rivaliser**

vb
[ʁivalize]

compete

Nous devons pouvoir rivaliser avec eux pour assurer notre prospérité.
-We must be able to compete with them to ensure our future prosperity.

6476 **redressement**

m
[ʁədʁɛsmã]

recovery|redress

Le redressement est facilité par la politique macroéconomique prudente du Gouvernement.

-The recovery was facilitated by prudent macroeconomic policies that the Government continued to implement.

| 6477 | **matinal** | **morning** |
| adj[matinal] | |

Cela s'explique par un certain manque d'expérience et par l'heure matinale. -It is because of a lack of experience and the early morning hour.

6478 **semelle** **sole**
f
[səmɛl]

Ce steak est aussi dur que de la semelle.
 -This steak is as tough as shoe's sole.

6479 **penderie** **wardrobe**
f
[pɑ̃dʁi]

Je suspendis mon manteau dans la penderie de l'entrée.
 -I hung my coat in the hall closet.

6480 **fièrement** **proudly**
adv
[fjɛʁmɑ̃]

Le Canada y était fièrement représenté par 113 athlètes, entraîneurs et bénévoles.
 -Canada was proudly represented by 113 athletes, coaches and volunteers.

6481 **approximativement** **approximately**
adv
[apʁɔksimativmɑ̃]

La coupe doit être nette et approximativement perpendiculaire à l'axe longitudinal.
 -The cut must be clean and approximately perpendicular to the longitudinal axis.

6482 **purgatoire** **purgatory**
m
[pyʁgatwaʁ]

Cass a ramené des Léviathans du purgatoire.
 -Then Cass brought in a bunch of Leviathans from Purgatory.

6483 **bascule** **rocker|weighing machine**
f
[baskyl]

Le Gouvernement fédéral met à disposition des crédits dont le montant représente le coût du remplacement d'un pont à bascule (89 millions d'euros).
 -The Federal Government is making a basic sum amounting to the cost of replacing a bascule bridge available (€89 million).

6484 **racisme** **racism**
m
[ʁasism]

Les Étasuniens noirs continuaient à endurer le racisme.
 -Black Americans continued to suffer from racism.

6485 **pupille** **pupil**
f
[pypij]

Les nerfs crâniens et les réflexes de la pupille semblent normaux, compte tenu du traumatisme.
 -Cranial nerves and pupil reflex looks normal, considering the trauma.

6486 **terrier** **terrier**
m
[teʁje]

Il était croisé berger australien et terrier.
 -He was a mixture of Australian sheep and terrier.

6487 **substitut** **surrogate|substitute**
m
[sypstity]

Ces derniers temps, on aperçoit un emploi de plus en plus fréquent du terme "simpliste" comme substitut au mot "simple". De tels solécismes, qui sont sans doute motivés par le désir de paraître érudit, appauvrissent la langue.
 -Recently "simplistic" is being used more and more often as a substitute for "simple." Such solecisms--presumably driven by a desire to appear learned--impoverish the language..

6488 **hélice** **propeller|screw**
f
[elis]

Le filet s'est emmêlé dans l'hélice.
 -The net got entangled in the screw.

6489 **surprenant** **surprising**
adj
[syʁpʁənɑ̃]

Nous trouvons donc surprenant que cela ne soit pas mentionné dans le rapport.

-We therefore find it surprising that there is no mention of them in the report.

6490 agricole — **agricultural**
adj
[agʁikɔl]
Pourcentage de salariées dans le secteur non agricole qui sont des femmes (OIT).
-Share of women in wage employment in the non-agricultural sector (ILO) 12.

6491 carat — **carat**
m
[kaʁa]
Au moins un carat, il brille comme tout.
-A carat, at least. It sparkles like a virgin's teardrop.

6492 indulgence — **indulgence**
f
[ɛ̃dylʒɑ̃s]
Je remercie la Chambre et mes collègues pour leur indulgence.
-I thank the House and my colleagues for their indulgence.

6493 délégué — **delegate; vicarious**
m; adj
[delege]
J'ai le délégué suédois ici.
-I've got the Swedish delegate in here.

6494 raie — **ray | parting**
f
[ʁɛ]
Rencontrer une raie est une expérience inoubliable.
-Encountering a ray is a terrific experience.

6495 proue — **bow | head**
f
[pʁu]
La proue l'a transperce mais elle s'est soudée.
-The bow drilled through her, but she sealed herself right up.

6496 dédicace — **dedication**
f
[dedikas]
Pas besoin de lire la dédicace.
-You don't have to read the dedication.

6497 sponsor — **sponsor**
m
[spɔ̃sɔʁ]
Tu vas devenir mon sponsor pour IETI.
-You get to be my sponsor for y. E. T. I.

6498 somptueux — **sumptuous | magnificent**
adj
[sɔ̃ptɥø]
Je vous présente... ma somptueuse assistante, Miss Van Eyck.
-Let me introduce my gorgeous assistant, Miss Van Eyck.

6499 injecter — **inject**
vb
[ɛ̃ʒɛkte]
L'accusée devait injecter une overdose à la victime et s'injecter ensuite la même dose.
-The female accused was to inject the male victim with an overdose of drugs and then inject herself.

6500 héroïsme — **heroism**
m
[eʁɔism]
Patten peut enterrer leur héroïsme, nous veillerons à le faire vivre.
-Mr Patten may bury their heroism, we will see to it that their heroism still lives.

6501 aboutir — **lead**
vb
[abutiʁ]
Nous avons exploré ensemble toutes les possibilités en vue d'aboutir à un consensus.
-Collectively, we explored all possibilities to reach a consensus.

6502 trombone — **trombone; annoyed**
m; adj
[tʁɔ̃bɔn]
Jouez-vous du trombone ?
-Do you play the trombone?

6503 participant — **participant; participating**
m; adj
[paʁtisipɑ̃]
Le participant fit deux faux départs.
-The contestant made two false starts.

6504 absorber — **absorb**

	vb	
	[apsɔʁbe]	Le marché du travail est incapable d'absorber ces enfants après réadaptation.
		-The labour market is unable to absorb these children after rehabilitation.

6505 évadé — **escape; evader; escaped**
f; m; adj
[evade]
Le contre-amiral, suspendu, a été assigné à résidence mais s'est évadé.
-The Rear Admiral was suspended and kept under house arrest, and subsequently escaped.

6506 envahisseur — **invader**
m
[ãvaisœʁ]
La pluie faisait échouer chaque envahisseur.
-It was the rain that defeated every invader.

6507 contamination — **contamination**
f
[kɔ̃taminasjɔ̃]
Patron, la menace de contamination est minimale.
-Boss, the threat of contamination is minimal.

6508 enfouir — **bury**
vb
[ãfwiʁ]
Nous ne pouvons pas continuer à nous enfouir la tête dans le sable.
-That statistic speaks volumes; we cannot continue to bury our heads in the sand.

6509 passeur — **ferryman | smuggler**
m
[pasœʁ]
Le passeur a été arrêté à l'aéroport.
-The drug smuggler was arrested at the airport.

6510 inaccessible — **inaccessible**
adj
[inaksesibl]
La protection des civils dans une zone aussi étendue et inaccessible constitue un énorme défi.
-The protection of civilians in such a huge and inaccessible area is a major challenge.

6511 verset — **verse**
m
[vɛʁsɛ]
Chapitre et verset sur le révérend Rick.
-So... chapter and verse on the Reverend Rick.

6512 exclusivement — **exclusively**
adv
[ɛksklyzivmã]
La responsabilité de leur intégration n'incombe pas exclusivement aux autorités.
-Responsibility for integration does not lie entirely with the authorities.

6513 masturber — **masturbate**
vb
[mastyʁbe]
Faire des maths, c'est la seule façon socialement acceptable de se masturber en public.
-Doing math is the only socially acceptable way to masturbate in public.

6514 compas — **compass**
m
[kɔ̃pa]
Charles Walcot a enquêté sur le compas magnétique des pigeons.
-Charles Walcot investigated the magnetic compass bearing sense in pigeons.

6515 suceur — **nozzle**
m
[sysœʁ]
Je dois travailler près de connard suceur.
-I have to work around that douche nozzle?

6516 charmeur — **charmer; charming**
m; adj[ʃaʁmœʁ]
Oui, c'est tout à fait Finlay: sans âge, éternellement jeune, divertissant, le charmeur par excellence. -A spark of nature's fire, yes, that was Finlay: ageless, timeless, a charmer and an entertainer par excellence.

6517 faisceau — **beam**
m
[fɛso]
On obtient ainsi un faisceau de forme quasi-rectangulaire.
-Therefore, a beam mode of a nearly rectangular shape is obtained.

6518 unanimité — **unanimity**

	f [ynanimite]	L'unanimité - ou, comme c'est le cas aujourd'hui - la quasi-unanimité, n'est pas une garantie de liberté. -Unanimity - or, as we have it today - virtual unanimity is no guarantee of freedom.
6519	**déshonorer** vb [dezɔnɔʁe]	**dishonor** Madame le Président, comme prévu, ce Parlement s'est une nouvelle fois déshonoré. -Madam President, as expected, this Parliament has once again brought disgrace on itself.
6520	**entamer** vb [ɑ̃tame]	**start|launch** La foi c'est entamer la première marche, même lorsqu'on ne voit pas la totalité de l'escalier. -Faith is taking the first step, even when you don't see the whole staircase.
6521	**regorger** vb [ʁəgɔʁʒe]	**abound** Les tribunaux regorgent des dossiers de litiges fonciers. -The courts are overflowing with cases of land disputes, and killings by both sides are not uncommon.
6522	**dépanner** vb [depane]	**repair|debug** Le logiciel du détecteur de mouvement sera impossible à analyser ou dépanner sur site. -There shall be no way to analyse or debug the motion sensor software in the field.
6523	**pèlerinage** m; vb [pɛlʁinaʒ]	**pilgrimage; streak** Quel est le but d'une vie de pèlerinage ? -What's the purpose of a life of pilgrimage?
6524	**dégoter** vb [degɔte]	**find|dig up** Laissez-moi vous dégoter la clé. -Let me get you the key.
6525	**ressaisir** vb [ʁəseziʁ]	**catch** Je sais que c'est encore le début, mais nous devons absolument nous ressaisir. -I know it is still the beginning, but we really need to get our act together.
6526	**élaborer** vb [elabɔʁe]	**elaborate|design** Elaborer une convention internationale pour la protection contre le pollupostage. -Elaborate an international convention for protection against SPAM.
6527	**amabilité** f [amabilite]	**kindness** Le plus frappant étaient son humilité, sa distinction et son amabilité. -What was most striking about him was his humility, grace and kindness.
6528	**affoler** vb [afɔle]	**panic** Je ne veux pas l'affoler avant d'avoir des preuves. -Hollings. I don't want to spook him until we have got enough evidence.
6529	**inestimable** adj [inɛstimabl]	**invaluable|inestimable** Cette ressource présentera un intérêt inestimable pour la communauté internationale. -This resource will be of invaluable use to the international community.
6530	**vigne** f [viɲ]	**vine** Dans les années à venir, la vigne donnera beaucoup de raisin. -In the years to come, the vine will give many grapes.
6531	**consommer** vb [kɔ̃sɔme]	**consume|use** La population russe commence à consommer davantage de légumes, de fruits et de baies.

-The population of Russia has begun to consume more vegetables, fruit and berries.

6532	**gui**	**mistletoe**
	m	Vous... allez m'embrasser sous le gui.
	[gi]	-You are going to kiss me under the mistletoe.
6533	**fondamental**	**fundamental; fundamental**
	adj; m	C'est un problème fondamental, mais un problème fondamental pour les États membres.
	[fɔ̃damɑ̃tal]	-That is a fundamental problem, but it is a fundamental problem for the Member States.
6534	**révision**	**revision**
	f	Selon une révision de recherches antérieures, un haut niveau de consommation de chocolat peut réduire le risque de maladies coronariennes et d'accident vasculaire cérébral.
	[ʁevizjɔ̃]	-According to a review of previous research, high levels of chocolate consumption can reduce the risk of coronary heart disease and stroke.
6535	**récital**	**recital**
	m	Quand donneront-elles un récital ?
	[ʁesital]	-When will they give a concert?
6536	**fatalité**	**fatality**
	f	La canicule n'est pas une fatalité et ses conséquences macabres n'étaient pas inéluctables.
	[fatalite]	-The heatwave is not fate and its gruesome repercussions were not unavoidable.
6537	**météore**	**meteor**
	m	Le météore ne doit donc pas être loin.
	[meteɔʁ]	-Then the meteor can't be far off.
6538	**skipper**	**skipper**
	m	The skipper can never be held responsible for the nature of the goods or the contents of the loading unit.
	[skipe]	-Le capitaine ne peut jamais être tenu pour responsable de la nature des marchandises et du contenu de l'unité de chargement.
6539	**insuline**	**insulin**
	f	Should the use of insulin have been forbidden 75 years ago?
	[ɛ̃sylin]	-Aurait-il fallu interdire il y a soixante-quinze ans l'utilisation de l'insuline ?
6540	**roche**	**rock**
	f	Le phare, le rocher, le restaurant, les trois tombent juste.
	[ʁɔʃ]	-The lighthouse, the rock and the restaurant all fit the doubloon.
6541	**localisation**	**location|tracking**
	f[lɔkalizasjɔ̃]	La localisation est donc indispensable à une diffusion plus large. -Localization is therefore indispensable for a wider dissemination.
6542	**méfiant**	**suspicious|distrustful**
	adj	Les déplacés restent cependant très méfiants à son égard.
	[mefjɑ̃]	-Internally displaced persons remain deeply distrustful of the police, however.
6543	**délivrance**	**deliverance|release**
	f	Le Seigneur est le Dieu de la délivrance, et Jésus délivre.
	[delivʁɑ̃s]	-The Lord is the God of deliverance and Jesus delivers.
6544	**nuptial**	**nuptial|wedding**
	adj	Il est l'heure de boire le vin nuptial...
	[nypsjal]	-Time to drink the nuptial wine...

6545 **ligoter**
vb
[ligɔte]

bind|tie up

Sur ordre du général Yav, Freddy Loseke est ligoté et reçoit cent cinquante coups de fouets.
-On the same day General Yav called for Freddy Loseke to be tied up and given 150 lashes.

6546 **redoute**
f
[ʁədut]

redoubt

Un ministère public européen n' est pas un instrument qu' il faille redouter.
-The European Public Prosecutor' s Office is nothing to be afraid of.

6547 **lunette**
f
[lynɛt]

lens

Cela signifie qu'elle examine le présent et envisage l'avenir à travers la lunette du passé.
-It implies that UNCTAD looks at the present and into the future through the lens of the past.

6548 **étiquette**
f
[etikɛt]

label|etiquette

Lis attentivement l'étiquette.
-Read the label carefully.

6549 **purger**
vb
[pyʁʒe]

purge|bleed

Ramener progressivement la pression de l'eau à zéro et purger le pneumatique.
-Decrease, progressively, the pressure of the water to zero and drain the tyre.

6550 **indulgent**
adj
[ɛ̃dylʒɑ̃]

indulgent|forgiving

Il n'est pas dans la nature d'un Détraqueur de se montrer indulgent.
-It is not in the nature of a dementor to be forgiving.

6551 **incarner**
vb
[ɛ̃kaʁne]

embody|personify

Un acte unilatéral ne peut exister dans un vide; il doit s'incarner dans une forme.
-A unilateral act could not exist in a vacuum; it needed a form to embody it.

6552 **basculer**
vb
[baskyle]

toggle|tip

Je vous le demande aussi, Monsieur Reinfeldt: faites basculer les chefs d'État et de gouvernement !
-I ask the same of you, Mr Reinfeldt: shake up the Heads of State or Government!

6553 **réconciliation**
f
[ʁekɔ̃siljasjɔ̃]

reconciliation

Il signifie « Connaissance bienveillance réconciliation ».
-It means "Knowledge, understanding, reconciliation".

6554 **régal**
m
[ʁegal]

treat

Quel régal de trouver quelqu'un de cultivé dans cette maison.
-What a treat to find someone cultured in this house.

6555 **jardinage**
m
[ʒaʁdinaʒ]

gardening

Le jardinage a toujours été considéré comme un travail partagé.
-Gardening has always, according to the communities been regarded as a shared role.

6556 **mousquetaire**
m
[muskətɛʁ]

musketeer

Elle pourrait être le 3eme mousquetaire.
-She could be the third musketeer.

6557 **coalition**
f
[kɔalisjɔ̃]

coalition

La coalition internationale contre le terrorisme international est enterrée.
-The international coalition against international terrorism is being undermined.

6558 **flirt**

flirting

m
[flœʁt]

Le flirt est un rituel italien.
-Flirting's a ritual in Italy.

6559 **présidentiel** **presidential**

adj
[pʁezidãsjɛl]

Un conseiller présidentiel coordonne désormais l'élaboration des politiques ethniques.
-A presidential adviser now coordinates the formulation of ethnic policies.

6560 **rosbif** **roast beef**

adj
[ʁɔsbif]

Un rosbif sans sauce est nu.
-A roast beef without sauce is naked.

6561 **psychose** **psychosis**

f
[psikoz]

Cecilie Larsen souffre d'une profonde psychose.
-Cecilie Larsen is suffering from a very deep psychosis.

6562 **synagogue** **synagogue**

f
[sinagɔg]

Sur intervention des autorités centrales, la synagogue aurait été restituée à ses propriétaires.
-When the central authorities intervened, the synagogue was restored to its owners.

6563 **judo** **judo**

m
[ʒydo]

David Douillet started practicing judo very young.
-David Douillet débute très jeune la pratique du judo.

6564 **aboiement** **bark**

m
[abwamã]

Je n'entends pas d'aboiement.
-I don't hear barking.

6565 **renifler** **sniff|smell**

vb
[ʁənifle]

Je l'ai entendue renifler.
-I heard her sniffle.

6566 **régional** **regional**

adj
[ʁeʒjɔnal]

Ces ateliers ont été suivis par un atelier régional et un séminaire régional.
-These workshops were followed by a regional workshop and a regional seminar.

6567 **crypte** **crypt**

f
[kʁipt]

On l'a largué dans sa crypte.
-We dumped him in his crypt.

6568 **cheeseburger** **cheeseburger**

m[ʃizbyʁʒe]

Je lui envoie un cheeseburger virtuel. -I'm going to send her a virtual cheeseburger.

6569 **bouddhiste** **Buddhist**

adj
[budist]

Le Kazakhstan est situé au carrefour des cultures islamique, chrétienne et bouddhiste.
-Kazakhstan is at the crossroads of Islamic, Christian and Buddhist cultures.

6570 **prêteur** **lender**

m
[pʁɛtœʁ]

Le taux de remboursement pour la première tranche du prêt est évalué à 98 %.
-The loan recovery rate from the first tranche of the loan is estimated at 98%.

6571 **crique** **creek**

f
[kʁik]

Être dans une crique sans pagaie.
-To be up a creek without a paddle.

6572 **collaborateur** **collaborator|contributer**

m
[kɔlabɔʁatœʁ]

Vous êtes un collaborateur, recherché pour meurtre.
-You're on the run, a collaborator, wanted for murder.

6573	**teinture**	**dyeing**
	f	Ladite imprégnation est effectuée de préférence dans des machines de teinture sur bobine croisée.
	[tɛ̃tyʁ]	-The saturation is preferably carried out in cheese dyeing machines.

6574	**malaria**	**malaria**
	f	L'initiative Roll Back Malaria permettra de renforcer la lutte contre le paludisme.
	[malaʁja]	-The Roll Back Malaria initiative will strengthen the campaign against malaria.

6575	**barré**	**crossed**
	adj	Il m'a barré le chemin.
	[baʁe]	-He blocked my way.

6576	**palpiter**	**throb|palpitate**
	vb	Parce que j'aime voir palpiter les veines de tes tempes !
	[palpite]	-Because I love to see those veins in your temple throb.

6577	**divorce**	**divorce**
	m	Aucun motif spécifique n'est prévu pour le mari qui souhaite divorcer.
	[divɔʁs]	-No grounds are laid down in respect of a husband who wishes to obtain a divorce.

6578	**empoisonnement**	**poisoning**
	m	Ces derniers sont également responsables de l'empoisonnement des terres.
	[ãpwazɔnmã]	-The settlers are also responsible for poisoning the land.

6579	**grignoter**	**nibble**
	vb	Tu n'as pas quelque chose à grignoter ?
	[gʁiɲɔte]	-Have you got anything to nibble?

6580	**piston**	**piston|valve**
	m	Un piston annulaire secondaire est également fourni pour assurer le déverrouillage.
	[pistɔ̃]	-A secondary annular piston is also provided to guarantee unlocking.

6581	**couronnement**	**coronation|crowning**
	m[kuʁonmã]	Dr Logue... assistera au couronnement. -Dr. Logue... will be attending the Coronation.

6582	**élimination**	**elimination**
	f	Tout gouvernement responsable doit avoir pour objectif l'élimination du déficit.
	[eliminasjɔ̃]	-Any responsible government must have as its goal the elimination of the deficit.

6583	**bibliothécaire**	**librarian**
	m	Aucun des mercenaires n'était bibliothécaire, à plus forte raison indépendant.
	[biblijɔtekɛʁ]	-Not one of the convicted mercenaries is a librarian, let alone an independent one.

6584	**concorde**	**concord|amity**
	f	Le processus électoral va se poursuivre dans un climat apaisé et de concorde nationale.
	[kɔ̃kɔʁd]	-The electoral process will continue in a climate of national peace and harmony.

6585	**havre**	**haven**
	m	Le monde serait -il devenu tout d'un coup un havre de paix et de prospérité ?
	[avʁ]	-Has the world suddenly become a haven of peace and prosperity?

6586	**crasseux**	**filthy|grimy**
	adj	Ils sont crasseux, mais c'est ce que j'ai trouvé de mieux.
	[kʁasø]	-They're a dirty-looking lot, but it's the best I could fiind.

6587	**viseur**	**viewfinder**
	m	Chaque fois que je regarde dans le viseur, j'espère voir Shizuru.
	[vizœʁ]	-Every time I peer into the viewfinder, I pray that I'll see Shizuru.
6588	**dense**	**dense**
	adj	Grâce à ce réseau dense, les enfants peuvent accéder facilement aux bibliothèques.
	[dɑ̃s]	-Thanks to the dense service network, children have easy access to libraries.
6589	**secousse**	**shock|shake**
	f	Peut-être qu'il voulait lui donner une petite secousse, musclé.
	[səkus]	-Maybe he wanted to give him a shake, muscle him around a little.
6590	**élastique**	**elastic; rubber band; elasticy**
	adj; m; f	Ils ont déclaré: [...] nous pensons qu'on a étiré l'élastique jusqu'à la limite.
	[elastik]	-They have said:...we now believe the elastic band has been stretched as far as it can go.
6591	**tulipe**	**tulip**
	f	Un petit conseil... abandonne la tulipe.
	[tylip]	-Piece of advice - lose the tulip.
6592	**verrouillage**	**locking**
	m	En tout cas, parallèlement, se met en place un verrouillage du système.
	[veʁujaʒ]	-In any event, a deadlock is being imposed on the system at the same time.
6593	**allégation**	**allegation**
	f[alegasjɔ̃]	Le Gouvernement n'a fourni aucune réponse concernant cette allégation générale. -No response was received from the Government regarding this general allegation.
6594	**propulsion**	**propulsion**
	f	La propulsion repose sur une combustion à pression constante.
	[pʁɔpylsjɔ̃]	-The propulsion relies on constant pressure combustion (CDWE).
6595	**cappuccino**	**cappuccino**
	m	Si je puis m'exprimer ainsi, nous n'apprécions pas toujours le cappuccino.
	[kapyksino]	-To use a figure of speech, cappuccino is not always good for us.
6596	**vietnamien**	**Vietnamese; Vietnamese**
	adj; m	C'est un prénom vietnamien courant.
	[vjɛtnamjɛ̃]	-Dong is a common Vietnamese name.
6597	**esquiver**	**dodge|avoid**
	vb	Je ne pense pas que quiconque ait l'intention d'esquiver le débat sur cette question, bien au contraire.
	[ɛskive]	-I do not think that anyone is trying to dodge the issue in this respect, quite the opposite.
6598	**syphilis**	**syphilis**
	f	La syphilis, la trichomoniase et la gonorrhée sont les MST les plus fréquentes.
	[sifilis]	-Syphilis, trichomoniasis and gonorrhoea are prevailing among the STIs.
6599	**repeindre**	**repaint**
	vb	Nous devons repeindre la grange.
	[ʁəpɛ̃dʁ]	-We need to repaint the barn.
6600	**poignée**	**handle|handful**
	f	On me dit que les francs-maçons ont une poignée de main secrète.
	[pwaɲe]	-I hear the Freemasons have a secret handshake.
6601	**incorrigible**	**incorrigible**
	adj	Les garçons de la catégorie incorrigible pouvaient être confinés durant une période indéfinie d'au moins deux ans.
	[ɛ̃kɔʁiʒibl]	

-Boys in the incorrigible category could be confined for an indefinite period of not less than two years.

6602 progression — **progression**
f
[pʁɔgʁesjɔ̃]
La progression de la vérification est indiquée dans une barre de progression.
-A progress bar shows how far the check has progressed.

6603 mouette — **seagull**
f
[mwɛt]
Le lac Har Us Nuur offre un habitat idéal pour les canards sauvages, les oies, les tétras, les perdrix et les mouettes, ainsi que pour les mouettes reliques et les goélands argentés, plus rares.
-Lake Khar Us Nuur is a perfect habitat for wild ducks, geese, wood grouse, partridges and seagulls, including the rare relict gull and herring gull.

6604 nudité — **nudity**
f
[nydite]
La nudité de la femme est l'œuvre de Dieu.
-The nakedness of woman is the work of God.

6605 souiller — **soil|defile**
vb
[suje]
Le fait de souiller ou de profaner des sépultures ou des cimetières.
-Defile or desecrate graves or cemeteries.

6606 coopérative — **cooperative|cooperation**
f
[kɔɔpeʁativ]
Voyons un peu les retombées de cette gouvernance coopérative.
-Let us look at the benefits derived from this cooperative form of governance.

6607 vengeur — **avenger; vengeful**
m; adj
[vɑ̃ʒœʁ]
Tu comptes sur le vengeur ailé pour te délivrer du mal, n'est-ce pas, mon ami ?
-You're counting on the Winged Avenger to deliver you from evil...... aren't you, my friend?

6608 tenace — **tenacious|persistent**
adj
[tənas]
Tenace, il pourchassa les soldats ennemis en retraite et réussit à en capturer un.
-Not giving up, he chased the retreating group, managing to capture one of the enemy.

6609 girafe — **giraffe**
f
[ʒiʁaf]
Une girafe allonge le cou pour aller chercher de la nourriture.
-A giraffe extends its neck to get food.

6610 brio — **brillance**
m
[bʁijo]
Monsieur Schultz, je n'ai pas interrompu une intervention empreinte de brio et je vous ai laissé dépasser votre temps de parole.
-Mr Schulz, I did not interrupt you in a speech which was distinguished by its brilliance and I allowed you to exceed your time.

6611 extrémité — **end|extremity**
f
[ɛkstʁemite]
La flèche théorique à l'extrémité de la poutre est de 2 cm.
-The calculated deflection at the end of the beam is 2 cm.

6612 omettre — **omit|pass over**
vb
[ɔmɛtʁ]
Néanmoins, la déclaration ne doit pas omettre d'évoquer la Constitution.
-However, the declaration must not fail to talk about the Constitution.

6613 pillage — **looting|pillage**
m
[pijaʒ]
Les mercenaires interviennent dans ce pillage et exécutent une grande part des opérations délictueuses.
-Mercenaries take part in the plundering and carry out many of the criminal operations.

6614 insomnie — **insomnia**

f
[ɛ̃sɔmni]

Tous deux avaient eu une nuit agitée, le vieillard par l'insomnie, la jeune fille par des rêves délicieux.
-Both had had a restless night, the old man due to insomnia, and the young girl due to delicious dreams.

6615 **voilier**

m
[vwalje]

yacht

Thomas rêvait d'avoir un voilier.
-Thomas dreamed of having a sailboat.

6616 **brancard**

m
[bʁɑ̃kaʁ]

stretcher

On soulève alors le brancard, avec le patient.
-The stretcher is then lifted with the patient.

6617 **alignement**

m[aliɲmɑ̃]

alignment

Appareil et procédé d'alignement d'images comportant typiquement deux vues perspectives. -Apparatus and method for the alignment of images in which, typically, two perspective views are provided.

6618 **canneler**

vb
[kanle]

groove

La présente invention concerne un procédé pour produire du carton ondulé et un procédé pour coller un élément à canneler sur un revêtement au moyen d'adhésifs thermofusibles grâce à la technique d'encollage en rideau.
-The present invention is directed to a method for the manufacture of corrugated board and to a method for gluing a fluting medium to a liner by means of hot-melt adhesives using curtain coating technique.

6619 **inciter**

vb
[ɛ̃site]

encourage|incite

Ceci devrait nous rappeler nos lacunes et nous inciter à mettre fin à l'érosion du mandat de la Conférence.
-This should remind us of our shortcomings and impel us to make efforts to stop the erosion of this Conference's mandate.

6620 **pertinent**

adj
[pɛʁtinɑ̃]

relevant|pertinent

La Commission considère que le rapport révisé est à la fois concis, pertinent et constructif.
-The Commission regards the revised report as concise, to the point and constructive.

6621 **mortier**

m
[mɔʁtje]

mortar

Pendant l'injection, le mortier est conduit sous basse pression dans le trou foré.
-During injection, the mortar is fed into the bore hole under low pressure.

6622 **verbe**

m
[vɛʁb]

vb

Au paragraphe 6, le verbe « réaffirme » devrait être utilisé au lieu de « note ».
-In paragraph 6, the verb "reaffirms" should be used in preference to "notes".

6623 **métallique**

adj
[metalik]

metallic

l'élimination définitive sans danger et économiquement avantageuse du mercure métallique.
-The safe and economically advantageous final disposal of metallic mercury.

6624 **ravisseur**

m
[ʁavisœʁ]

abductor|ravisher

Plusieurs villageois ont été témoins de l'incident et ont confirmé l'identité du ravisseur.
-Some villagers witnessed the incident and confirmed the identity of the abductor.

6625 **spore**

spore

	f	Mieux connu sous le nom de spore.
	[spɔʁ]	- Better known as your basic spore.
6626	**nectar**	**nectar**
	m	Il devient dès lors possible de mélanger différentes sortes de nectar, sans
	[nɛktaʁ]	qu'un nectar ne soit présent à plus de 50 %.
		-It then becomes possible to mix different sorts of nectar, without more than
		50% of a nectar being present.

6627 **forage** — **drilling | digging**

m[fɔʁaʒ] — La présente invention peut être appliquée au forage de puits pétroliers. -The present invention may be applied to the drilling of oil wells.

6628 **stockage** — **storage | stocking**

m
[stɔkaʒ] — Conteneur convenant particulièrement au stockage de matériau plastique granulé brut.
 -A container particularly suited for the storage of granular plastic raw material.

6629 **pâturage** — **pasture | grazing**

m
[patyʁaʒ] — Les vaches mangent l'herbe du pâturage.
 -Cows are eating grass in the meadow.

6630 **lourdement** — **heavily**

adv
[luʁdəmã] — Les personnes les plus lourdement impliquées nient toujours leur participation.
 -The people who were most heavily implicated still denied their participation.

6631 **underground** — **underground; underground**

adj; m
[ɛ̃dɛʁgʁun] — An underground ventilated system for storing nuclear waste materials.
 -La présente invention porte sur un système ventilé souterrain qui permet de stocker des matières de déchets nucléaires.

6632 **damnation** — **damnation**

f
[danasjɔ̃] — Ils volent les uns des autres de porter les uns les autres à la damnation.
 -They steal from each other to bring each other to damnation.

6633 **approprier** — **appropriate**

vb
[apʁɔpʁije] — La gauche européenne avait tenté de s'approprier l'idée de taxation des transactions financières.
 -The European left tried to take sole credit for the idea of taxing financial transactions.

6634 **grandement** — **sorely**

adv
[gʁãdmã] — J'apprécie grandement votre conseil.
 -I greatly appreciate your advice.

6635 **licenciement** — **termination | redundancy**

m
[lisãsimã] — Des dispositifs spéciaux protègent les femmes enceintes contre le licenciement.
 -There are special protection mechanisms against the dismissal of pregnant employed women.

6636 **terne** — **dull | drab**

adj
[tɛʁn] — Comme l'heure des questions ici, je la trouve terne, interminable et monocorde.
 -Like Question Time here I find it dull, long-winded and lacking in sparkle.

6637 **extermination** — **extermination**

f
[ɛkstɛʁminasjɔ̃] — This will result in the gradual extermination of the Polish nation.
 -Cette situation aboutira à l' extermination progressive de la nation polonaise.

6638 **amont** — **uphill**

	adv [amɔ̃]	Ensuite, les conditions de placement ont été définies de façon plus stricte en amont. -Secondly, the conditions of placement are more rigorously established upstream.
6639	**apparent** adj[apaʁɑ̃]	**apparent | obvious** Dans d'autres États, il peut toujours faire valoir ses droits à l'encontre d'un acquéreur apparent. -In other States, the lessor may always be able to claim its right against an ostensible purchaser.
6640	**pétale** m [petal]	**petal** Le dernier pétale de rose est tombé. -The last rose petal has fallen.
6641	**sarcastique** adj [saʁkastik]	**sarcastic** Comme l'a déclaré un commentateur sarcastique, "le meilleur tribunal russe est à Strasbourg". -As one sarcastic commentator said: 'The best Russian court is in Strasbourg'.
6642	**bactérie** f [bakteʁi]	**bacterium** Cette bactérie est résistante à la pénicilline. -This bacterium is resistant to penicillin.
6643	**chiche** adj; int [ʃiʃ]	**stingy; I dare you** Alors je vous dirai: chiche, voilà un beau dossier pour le faire ! -So I would say to you: there is a good area for you to work on - go on, I dare you!
6644	**sanguinaire** adj [sɑ̃ginɛʁ]	**bloody** C'est la justification du dictateur sanguinaire qui veut aujourd'hui assujettir ces populations. -Such is the justification of the bloodthirsty dictator who wants to subdue these people.
6645	**pian** m [pjɑ̃]	**yaws** Un projet pilote a été engagé dans le district de Koraput (Orissa) dans le cadre du Programme d'éradication du pian en 1996-1997. -Under the Yaws Eradication Programme a pilot project is started on Koraput district in Orissa in 1996-97.
6646	**lacté** adj [lakte]	**milky** Par ailleurs, j'approuve la décision de faire également figurer dans le règlement le yaourt à boire et les boissons lactées. -I also welcome the decision to also include drinking yoghurt and milk-based beverages in the regulation.
6647	**palier** m [palje]	**bearing** Est également présenté un palier de culbuteur. -A bearing assembly for mounting within a rocker arm is also disclosed.
6648	**rigide** adj [ʁiʒid]	**rigid | inflexible** Elle concluait que les forces de police de la Bosnie-Herzégovine étaient rigides et mal préparées pour l'avenir. -It concluded that the police forces of Bosnia and Herzegovina are both rigid and unprepared for the future.
6649	**intouchable** adj [ɛ̃tuʃabl]	**untouchable** Le traité de Nice, selon lui, devait être considéré comme intouchable. -The Treaty of Nice was to remain in place.
6650	**amplement** adv [ɑ̃pləmɑ̃]	**amply** Les causes foncières de cette situation ont été amplement exposées. -The underlying causes of this situation have been amply articulated.

6651 véreux   **shady|dubious**
adj[veʁø]
Dans le cadre de cette tolérance, les fruits éclatés ou véreux sont limités à 2 %. -Within this tolerance, not more than 2 per cent may consist of dubious or worm-eaten fruit.

6652 impec   **impeccable**
adj
[ɛ̃pɛk]
Ah superbe, c'est impec.
-Oh great, it's impeccable.

6653 huile   **oil|big shot**
f
[ɥil]
Pourquoi elle met de l'huile d'olive sur ses cils ?
-Why does she apply olive oil on her lashes?

6654 aérodrome   **aerodrome**
m
[aeʁodʁom]
Ray a prévu un assaut à l'aérodrome de London East.
-Ray's planned a raid at the London East aerodrome.

6655 sacrilège   **sacrilege; sacrilegious**
m; adj
[sakʁilɛʒ]
En paiement du meurtre sacrilège de Troïlus, mon fils.
-Payment for the sacrilege of murdering Troilus, my son.

6656 jasmin   **jasmine**
m
[ʒasmɛ̃]
La révolution de jasmin avait essentiellement pour base la dignité et la justice.
-The Jasmine Revolution was very much about dignity and equity.

6657 cidre   **cider**
m
[sidʁ]
D'après l'amendement proposé, cet additif permettrait la tenue de la mousse du cidre.
-It would be used, under the proposed amendment to the list, to retain the head or foam on cider.

6658 pondre   **lay**
vb
[pɔ̃dʁ]
Créés à partir de poulets trop vieux pour pondre.
-Originally created from old chickens that could no longer lay eggs,

6659 défaillance   **failure**
f
[defajɑ̃s]
Ce qui rend la vieillesse difficile à supporter, ce n'est pas la défaillance des facultés, qu'elles soient mentales ou physiques, mais le poids des souvenirs.
-What makes old age hard to bear is not the failing of one's faculties, mental and physical, but the burden of one's memories.

6660 scolarité   **schooling**
f
[skɔlaʁite]
Depuis octobre 2000, plus de 264 000 jours de scolarité ont été perdus au total.
-Since October 2000 more than 264,000 school days have been lost.

6661 salami   **salami**
m
[salami]
Merci pour le salami. Délicieux.
-Thanks for the salami, it's terrific.

6662 monarchie   **monarchy**
f
[mɔnaʁʃi]
Le Vatican est une monarchie absolue dont le roi est élu.
-The Vatican is an absolute monarchy with an elected king.

6663 détonation   **detonation**
f
[detɔnasjɔ̃]
Nous nous trouvions dans le salon lorsque nous avons entendu la détonation.
-We were in the living room when we heard the gunshot.

6664 yaourt   **yogurt**
m[jauʁ]
Manger du yaourt à la fourchette est assez difficile. -Eating yogurt with a fork is somewhat difficult.

6665 échappement   **exhaust|escapement**

m
[eʃapmã]

Une ramification latérale est en communication avec le passage d'échappement principal.
-A side branch is in communication with the main exhaust passageway.

6666 **pailleté** **jeweled**

adj
[pajte]

Je ne peux pas porter de slip pailleté et me pavaner devant Frank Rich.
-I can't wear jeweled panties and strut out in front of Frank Rich.

6667 **cil** **eyelash**

m
[sil]

L'appareil comprend un corps principal, sur lequel est disposé un cil artificiel.
-The apparatus includes a main body, upon which an artificial eyelash is disposed.

6668 **électricien** **electrician**

m
[elɛktʁisjɛ̃]

L'électricien était employé au titre de l'assistance temporaire depuis 19 mois.
-The electrician had been on general temporary assistance for the past 19 months.

6669 **crucifier** **crucify**

vb
[kʁysifje]

Et aujourd'hui, ils seraient prêts à le crucifier !
-And today they are ready to crucify Gaddafi!

6670 **éther** **ether**

m
[etɛʁ]

Le procédé consiste à utiliser un alpha-amino éther pour piéger les mercaptans.
-The method involves using an alpha-amino ether to scavenge the mercaptans.

6671 **patrimoine** **heritage**

m
[patʁimwan]

À ses yeux, cette domination constitue une menace pour le patrimoine de l'humanité. Et fait peser sur elle un risque plus grave encore : voir cette « langue unique » déboucher sur une « pensée unique » obsédée par l'argent et le consumérisme.
-In his view, the domination by English is a threat to the heritage of humanity. It poses an even worse risk: This "single language" will lead to a "single thought" obsessed with money and consumerism.

6672 **gourmand** **greedy|gourmand; gourmand**

adj; m
[guʁmã]

Je suis gourmand.
-I'm greedy.

6673 **lobe** **lobe**

m
[lɔb]

Les enfants en dessous de l'âge de huit ans n'ont pas un lobe frontal assez développé, ce qui pourrait être la cause du fait qu'il ne leur soit pas possible de distinguer la réalité de la fantaisie. Certains d'entre eux peuvent par exemple croire qu'il y a des monstres dans leur armoire ou sous leur lit. Ils ne peuvent aussi parfois pas distinguer les rêves de la réalité.
-Children below the age of 8 have an underdeveloped frontal lobe that might cause them to be unable to separate reality from fantasy. Some of them might believe that there are monsters in their closet or under the bed for example. They are also sometimes unable to distinguish dreams from reality.

6674 **pensionnat** **boarding school**

m[pɑ̃sjɔna]

Sean rentre de son pensionnat bientôt. -Sean's coming home from boarding school soon.

6675 **dentier** **denture**

m
[dɑ̃tje]

Ça correspond sûrement avec les marques de dentier trouvées par Zack.
-They'll probably match the denture marking Zack found.

6676 **insolite** **unusual**

	adj [ɛ̃sɔlit]	Nous vivons une époque insolite qui exige des réponses exceptionnelles. -These are unusual times demanding exceptional responses.
6677	**irréel**	**unreal**
	adj [iʁeɛl]	"Champion... " " plus tu deviens toi, plus tout devient irréel. " -He said, " Champ... the more real you get, the more unreal it's gonna get
6678	**esquimau**	**Eskimo; Eskimo**
	adj; m [ɛskimo]	Le courlis esquimau, un des oiseaux les plus rares du Canada, vit aussi dans cette région. -It is also the home of one of the rarest birds in Canada, the Eskimo curlew.
6679	**flaque**	**puddle**
	f [flak]	Il existe des liens entre divers facteurs, et une goutte lancée dans une flaque d'eau provoque un gros effet de vague. -Various factors are interlinked, and one drop in a pool of water has a big ripple effect.
6680	**embarrasser**	**embarrass|bother**
	vb [ãbaʁase]	Ce n'est pas non plus un projet de loi qui vise à embarrasser certains groupes d'intérêt. -This is not a bill to embarrass some private interest groups.
6681	**envol**	**flight**
	m [ãvɔl]	En bas, le pont d'envol avec la navette. -That's the flight deck down there - with the shuttle craft.
6682	**fourniture**	**supply**
	f [fuʁnityʁ]	Fourniture de soutien aux terroristes et aux organisations terroristes. -Providing support to terrorists or terrorist organizations.
6683	**largage**	**dropping**
	m [laʁgaʒ]	Tu étais sur la zone de largage. -You were in the drop zone.
6684	**néné**	**tit**
	m [nene]	J'ai adoré quand Susan Sarandon léchait le néné de Catherine. -Oh, I loved that bit when Susan Sarandon was slurping on Catherine thingy's titty.
6685	**myrtille**	**blueberry**
	f [miʁtij]	C'est là que ma mère faisait une tarte à la myrtille chaque dimanche. -You know what? That's just where my mom made a blueberry pie every Sunday.
6686	**affût**	**carriage**
	m [afy]	Gardez l'œil à l'affût ! -Keep an eye out.
6687	**préjudice**	**prejudice|injury**
	m [pʁeʒydis]	La victime peut demander réparation pour le préjudice matériel et pour le préjudice moral. -The victim can claim compensation for both material damage and psychological suffering.
6688	**élargir**	**broaden|stretch**
	vb [elaʁʒiʁ]	Premièrement, l'OTAN et l'ONU devraient élargir la portée de leur dialogue. -First, NATO and the United Nations should seek to broaden their areas of dialogue.
6689	**babouin**	**baboon**
	m [babwɛ̃]	On dirait un babouin dans un placard a minuit. -Looks like a baboon in a closet at midnight.
6690	**phoque**	**seal**

m
[fɔk]

Allons d'abord examiner le phoque.
-First, we'll go check the seal.

6691 **piquant**
adj; m
[pikɑ̃]

spicy; spiciness
Au Japon aussi, on aime le piquant.
-In Japan too, we like spicy.

6692 **triché**
adj
[tʁiʃe]

cheated
J'ai joué et triché aux cartes mais il y a une chose que je ne fais pas.
-And I gamble and I cheat at cards, but there is one thing I do not do.

6693 **insuffisant**
adj
[ɛ̃syfizɑ̃]

insufficient|inadequate
Eurocontrol s' est avéré un mécanisme insuffisant pour gérer le trafic aérien.
-Eurocontrol has proven to be inadequate as a mechanism for managing air traffic.

6694 **impuissance**
f
[ɛ̃pɥisɑ̃s]

impotence|helplessness
Le destin de Jack et Jill hantait sans cesse l'auteur, accablé par sa propre impuissance à en assumer le poids.
-The destiny of Jack and Jill ceaselessly haunted the author, weighed down by his own powerlessness to assume it.

6695 **controverse**
f
[kɔ̃tʁɔvɛʁs]

controverse
Cela a suscité beaucoup de controverse.
-That was the subject of a lot of controversy.

6696 **déballer**
vb
[debale]

unpack
Elle est en train de déballer son cadeau d'anniversaire.
-She is unwrapping her birthday present.

6697 **péniche**
f
[peniʃ]

barge|houseboat
Péniche remorquée ou barge de poussage (barge) désigne un bateau sans propulsion propre.
-Barge means a vessel that has no propulsion of its own.

6698 **fixement**
adv
[fiksəmɑ̃]

fixedly
J'étais curieux de savoir pourquoi les gens m'avaient regardé fixement.
-I was curious to know why people had been staring at me.

6699 **rasage**
m
[ʁazaʒ]

shaving
Utilises-tu un après-rasage ?
-Do you use aftershave?

6700 **déduire**
vb
[dedɥiʁ]

deduct|deduce
Les honorables sénateurs pourront en déduire ce qu'ils voudront.
-Honourable senators can deduce from that what they may.

6701 **cinquantaine**
num; f
[sɛ̃kɑ̃tɛn]

fifties; middle age
Il a la cinquantaine bien tassée.
-He's in his late fifties.

6702 **trésorier**
m[tʁezɔʁje]

treasurer
Il travaille comme trésorier pour l'armée. -He works as a kind of treasurer for the military.

6703 **imbattable**
adj
[ɛ̃batabl]

unbeatable
Toutefois, nous avons formé une équipe imbattable.
-However, we were an unbeatable team.

6704 **optimisme**
m
[ɔptimism]

optimism
Toutefois, certains facteurs cruciaux permettent un optimisme prudent.
-But there are a few important factors that give rise to cautious optimism.

6705 **gracieux**
adj
[gʁasjø]

gracious|graceful
Cela produit effectivement un mouvement doux et gracieux.
-So what that effectively does is produces a smooth and graceful motion.

6706 **gazelle** **gazelle**
f
[gazɛl]
Le Groupe de Travail soutient l'inclusion de la Gazelle de Mongolie en Annexe II.
-The Working Group endorses the inclusion of the Mongolian gazelle in Annex II.

6707 **méfiance** **mistrust**
f
[mefjɑ̃s]
Ceci a engendré davantage de peur et de méfiance.
-This has bred more fear and mistrust.

6708 **marmotter** **mutter**
vb
[maʁmɔte]
Tu aurais dû le dire au lieu de marmotter.
- You should have said it to him, instead of mumbling away.

6709 **guidage** **guidance**
m
[gidaʒ]
Le guidage est constitué de sections reliées entre elles de manière articulée.
-The guide consists of hingedly interconnected sections.

6710 **consommateur** **consumer**
m
[kɔ̃sɔmatœʁ]
Le but de la publicité est de familiariser le consommateur avec le nom d'un produit.
-The purpose of advertising is to familiarize consumers with the name of a product.

6711 **rogue** **rogue**
adj
[ʁɔg]
Diefenbaker n'était pas le seul «rogue», ou le seul coquin, sous son microscope.
-Mr. Diefenbaker was not the only rogue under his microscope.

6712 **persister** **persist|continue**
vb
[pɛʁsiste]
Nous devons persister, encore et encore, et nous ne gagnerons pas la lutte.
-We must persist and continue to persist and we will not win the battle at any point.

6713 **extorsion** **extortion**
f
[ɛkstɔʁsjɔ̃]
Recherché pour 3 autres braquages, extorsion et kidnapping.
-He's wanted in connection with three other bank robberies... extortion and kidnapping.

6714 **compléter** **complete|complement**
vb
[kɔ̃plete]
Ces arrangements ne doivent pas remplacer le TNP, ils doivent le compléter.
-Such arrangements, however, should complement rather than substitute for the NPT.

6715 **patiner** **skate**
vb[patine]
Plusieurs joueurs de hockey de la Ligue nationale auraient intérêt à patiner aussi vite qu'elle. -Many an NHL player should skate as fast as she does.

6716 **équilibrer** **balance|trim**
vb
[ekilibʁe]
50 milliards pour équilibrer la balance des paiements des États membres qui ne font pas partie de la zone euro.
-EUR 50 billion for non-Eurozone European Union Member States for payments and to equilibrate the balance of payments.

6717 **lustrer** **polish**
vb
[lystʁe]
Intolerance sullied that diamond and made it lose its lustre.
-L'intolérance souille ce diamant et lui fait perdre son lustre.

6718 **crucifix** **crucifix**
m
[kʁysifi]
Un rappeur sans bling-bling est comme un pape sans crucifix.
-A rapper without bling is like a pope without a crucifix.

6719 **écœurer** **disgust**
vb
[ekœʁe]
La grande majorité des Sahraouis sont écoeurés par la façon dont il gère leur cause.

-The great majority of Saharans were disgusted with its management of their cause.

6720	**aveugler**	**blind**
	vb	Il a plutôt pour objectif d'aveugler les citoyens avec de la science.
	[avœgle]	-Rather, it is designed to blind people with science.
6721	**prêtresse**	**priestess**
	f	Il est trop tard pour prier, prêtresse.
	[pʀɛtʀɛs]	-Too late for prayer, priestess.
6722	**héréditaire**	**hereditary**
	adj	L'hémophilie héréditaire transmise par la femme est également un problème majeur.
	[eʀediteʀ]	-Hemophilia that transmits from women by heredity is also a major problem.
6723	**logis**	**dwelling**
	m	Il protège notre logis, mon fils.
	[lɔʒi]	-He's guarding our home, son.
6724	**préméditer**	**premeditate**
	vb	En outre, aux termes de l'article 4 du Statut, il n'est pas nécessaire que les actes de génocide aient été longuement prémédités.
	[pʀemedite]	-Further, article 4 of the Statute does not require that the genocidal acts be premeditated over a long period.
6725	**marmiter**	**strafe**
	vb	Ça s'est mis à marmiter tous azimuts.
	[maʀmite]	-Heavy shelling had begun.
6726	**pègre**	**underworld**
	f	Les organisations criminelles ne sont pas le simple produit de la pègre.
	[pɛgʀ]	-Criminal organizations are not purely creatures of the underworld.
6727	**serbe**	**Serbian; Serbian**
	adj; m	Mme Raskovic-Ivic a mentionné la Constitution serbe et le programme de négociation serbe.
	[sɛʀb]	-Raskovic-Ivic mentioned the Serbian Constitution and the Serbian platform.
6728	**figurant**	**extra|dummy**
	m	Il ne joue pas un rôle de figurant dans ce processus.
	[figyʀã]	-It is not a bit-part player in the process.
6729	**autonomie**	**autonomy**
	f	On entend beaucoup parler... d'autonomie personnelle.
	[ɔtɔnɔmi]	-Now, we hear a lot of talk... about personal autonomy.
6730	**cameraman**	**cameraman**
	m	Sentez-moi ça, monsieur le cameraman.
	[kamʀamã]	-Have a smell of that, mister cameraman.
6731	**fraîcheur**	**freshness|coolness**
	f	Je me redressai dans la fraîcheur du matin, essayant de me rappeler comment j'étais parvenu là.
	[fʀɛʃœʀ]	-I sat up in the freshness of the morning, trying to remember how I had got there.
6732	**albanais**	**Albanian; Albanian**
	adj; m|mpl	Quelque 275 000 personnes, tant Albanais que Serbes, souffrent actuellement.
	[albanɛ]	-There are 275,000 people suffering, both of Albanian and Serbian background.

6733	**nicher**	**nest**
	vb	Il cause toujours des ravages chez les oiseaux et les aigles à tête blanche qui aiment nicher dans la région des Grands Lacs.
	[niʃe]	-It is still causing havoc for the birds and the bald eagles which like to nest in the Great Lakes area.

6734	**affaiblir**	**weaken|reduce**
	vb	C'est un instrument important et il ne faut pas en affaiblir l'impact.
	[afebliʁ]	-It is an important instrument, and we should not dilute the impact of it.

6735	**synthèse**	**synthesis**
	f	Application: préparation intermédiaire synthèse chirale.
	[sɛ̃tɛz]	-The method may be used to prepare an intermediate for chiral synthesis.

6736	**tâter**	**feel**
	vb	C'est pour eux une façon économique de tâter le pouls de la population.
	[tate]	-In doing so the governments are able to get a feeling in public opinion for much cheaper.

6737	**surpasser**	**surpass|excel**
	vb	En second lieu, il est clair que l'Asie a surpassé le reste du monde.
	[syʁpase]	-Second, it is clear that Asia has outperformed the rest of the world.

6738	**proportion**	**proportion|rate**
	f	On trouve une forte proportion d'immigrants parmi la main-d'œuvre de ces usines.
	[pʁɔpɔʁsjɔ̃]	-One finds a large proportion of immigrants among the workforce in these factories.

6739	**initier**	**initiate**
	vb	L'approche initiée à l'ONU a été adoptée et développée en particulier par la Cour interaméricaine des droits de l'homme.
	[inisje]	-The approach pioneered within the United Nations setting was adopted and further developed by the Inter-American Court of Human Rights in particular.

6740	**touristique**	**tourist**
	adj[tuʁistik]	Navire à passagers destiné à fournir une expérience touristique complète aux passagers. -A passenger ship intended to provide passengers with a full tourist experience.

6741	**beige**	**beige; beige**
	adj; m	C'est comme écouter une communication de TED sur la couleur beige.
	[bɛʒ]	-This is like listening to a TED talk by the color beige.

6742	**diffus**	**diffuse**
	adj	Au Togo, a-t-il dit, l'insécurité était un phénomène temporel et diffus.
	[dify]	-In Togo, he said, insecurity was a temporal, diffuse phenomenon.

6743	**amnistie**	**amnesty**
	f	Ils vous accordent l'amnistie complète.
	[amnisti]	-Sam, they'll give you full amnesty...

6744	**chasteté**	**chastity**
	f	Sa ceinture de chasteté a déclenché le détecteur métallique à l'aéroport.
	[ʃastəte]	-Her chastity belt set off the metal detector at the airport.

6745	**tanière**	**lair**
	f	Il est aussi interdit de détruire sa résidence, sa tanière ou son nid.
	[tanjɛʁ]	-Also, no person shall destroy its residence, its den or its nest.

6746	**télégraphe**	**telegraph**
	m	Allez vous poster près du télégraphe.
	[telegʁaf]	-Go down and stand by the telegraph.

6747	**affrontement**	**confrontation**
	m	Cette politique conduirait à un affrontement stérile.
	[afʁɔ̃tmã]	-Such an approach would lead to a sterile confrontation.

6748	**fendre**	**split|slit**
	vb	Puis quand le ciel se fendra et deviendra alors écarlate comme le cuir rouge.
	[fãdʁ]	-And finally when the heaven is split open, and it becomes rosy like red leather!

6749	**magnéto**	**magneto**
	f	En cas de réduction de la puissance des feux, cela présentera un avantage considérable en ce qui concerne la conception de la magnéto et le système de régulation de la recharge de la batterie.
	[maɲeto]	-In the case of reduction in wattage of lamps, it will be of considerable advantage in designing the magneto, and system for regulating battery charging.

6750	**buste**	**bust**
	m	Une était intéressée par un buste de Frederic Remington.
	[byst]	-One expressed interest in a Frederic Remington bust.

6751	**tri**	**sorting**
	m	Je traiterai tout d'abord du tri visant à ne garder que les prises de valeur élevée de crevette nordique.
	[tʁi]	-I will deal first with the high-grading of northern shrimp.

6752	**lépreux**	**leper; leper**
	adj; m	Et je guéris l'aveugle-né et le lépreux, et je ressuscite les morts, par la permission d'Allah.
	[lepʁø]	-And I heal the blind from birth and the leper, and I revive the dead, by God's leave.

6753	**irréprochable**	**unexceptionable**
	adj[iʁepʁɔʃabl]	Je suis persuadée que la grande majorité des membres du Parlement européen s'acquitte de ses fonctions d'une manière moralement irréprochable. -I believe that the vast majority of the Members of the European Parliament perform their duty in a morally unexceptionable manner.

6754	**observatoire**	**observatory**
	m	Il construit un observatoire astronomique pour étudier les étoiles.
	[ɔpsɛʁvatwaʁ]	-He built an observatory to study the stars.

6755	**marquise**	**marquise**
	f	Monseigneur, permettez-moi de vous présenter la marquise.
	[maʁkiz]	-My lord, allow me to introduce you the Marquise.

6756	**triompher**	**triumph**
	vb	Comme eux, nous sommes déterminés à triompher des forces qui nous ont infligé cette épreuve.
	[tʁijɔ̃fe]	-Like them, we are determined to overcome the forces that inflicted this ordeal upon us.

6757	**brevet**	**patent|certificate**
	m	Un brevet est une propriété importante.
	[bʁəvɛ]	-A patent right is an important property.

6758	**claquette**	**tap**
	f	Ballet, claquette, et apparemment country.
	[klakɛt]	-Ballet, tap, and apparently country dancing.

6759	**traverse**	**crossing|going through**
	f	Ne traverse pas la rue !
	[tʁavɛʁs]	-Don't cross the street!

6760 **monotone** **monotone**

adj

[mɔnɔtɔn]

Un régime alimentaire monotone et déséquilibré en termes de protéines, vitamines et minéraux demeure la cause de l'anémie des femmes enceintes et de la naissance d'enfants de faible poids.
-A diet that is unvaried and is unbalanced in terms of proteins, vitamins, and minerals remains the cause of anaemia in pregnant women and of low-birth-weight babies.

6761 **larve** **larva**

f

[laʁv]

Arachnocampa Luminosa - c'est la larve d'une mouche.
-Arachnocampa luminosa - it's the larva of a fly.

6762 **sucette** **lollipop|pacifier**

f

[sysɛt]

Lèche la sucette !
-Lick the lollipop!

6763 **cuiller** **spoon**

f

[kyje]

Je suis juste venu te rendre ta grande cuiller.
-I just came to give you your big spoon back.

6764 **autonome** **autonomous**

adj

[otonom]

Comparaison du salaire mensuel moyen du travailleur par région autonome.
-Comparison of the Average Monthly Salary per Worker in the Autonomous Regions.

6765 **continental** **continental**

adj

[kɔ̃tinãtal]

The African continent is the least developed continent in the world.
-Le continent africain est le continent le moins avancé au monde.

6766 **mutilé** **mutilated**

adj[mytile]

Ce groupe assassine et mutile les adultes aussi bien que les enfants. -The group has killed, maimed or mutilated children as well as adults.

6767 **lambeau** **shred**

m

[lãbo]

Le couplage de la ligne à l'ensemble canule consiste en un lambeau de perfusion.
-Coupling the line to the cannula assembly is an infusion flap.

6768 **souligner** **emphasize|underline**

vb

[suliɲe]

Je dois souligner que la participation des provinces est entièrement volontaire.
-I must emphasize that the participation of the provinces is completely voluntary.

6769 **judicieux** **wise|sound**

adj

[ʒydisjø]

Il était généreux pour ses amis, en leur donnant des conseils judicieux basés sur un bon jugement.
-He was generous with his friends in that he would give them good advice based on sound judgment.

6770 **compote** **compote**

f

[kɔ̃pɔt]

Je lui donnerai une compote et un yaourt.
-Don't worry, I'll feed him compote or yogurt.

6771 **réalisme** **realism**

m

[ʁealism]

Elle s'efforcera de concilier ambition et réalisme, solidarité et réalisme.
-It will try its best to reconcile ambition and solidarity with realism.

6772 **replier** **replicate|fold up**

vb

[ʁəplije]

Fixer la plaque et replier vers l'arrière à 90° l'extrémité libre du ruban.
-Fix the plate and fold back the free end of the tape at 90°.

6773 **bouillant** **boiling**

	adj [bujã]	Faire évaporer lentement l'éther de la fiole en plaçant celle-ci avec précaution dans un bain-marie bouillant. -Slowly evaporate the ether from the flask by carefully placing on a boiling water bath.
6774	**rendement** m [ʁãdmã]	**yield|efficiency** Ne confondez pas efficacité et rendement. -Don't confuse "efficacy" with "efficiency".
6775	**violoniste** m/f [vjɔlɔnist]	**violinist** Cette violoniste remarquable a joué dans de nombreux orchestres internationaux célèbres. -The outstanding violinist has performed with numerous famous international orchestras.
6776	**égorger** vb [egɔʁʒe]	**kill|slit throat** Ils vont l'égorger et la brûler. -They will slaughter and burn her.
6777	**accroché** adj [akʁɔʃe]	**hooked** C' est un sapin de Noël auquel nous avons accroché nos guirlandes de gadgets hors de prix. -It is a Christmas tree on which we have hung our wish list of expensive baubles.
6778	**sauvegarde** f[sovgaʁd]	**safeguard** En outre, il est important, en cas de faillite, de sauvegarder l'outil de production. -At the same time, in bankruptcies, it is important to safeguard productive assets.
6779	**leucémie** f [løsemi]	**leukemia** La chimio précédente a rendu la leucémie résistante. -It means the chemo from your first round of treatment has made the leukemia resistant.
6780	**congélateur** m [kɔ̃ʒelatœʁ]	**freezer** Le congélateur se trouve dans le garage. -The freezer's in the garage.
6781	**tora** f [tɔʁa]	**torah** La Tora nous ordonne de préserver la vie. -The torah commands us to preserve life.
6782	**passif** adj; m [pasif]	**passive; passive** Transport/interface, marchandises (entreposage actif ou passif), sécurité/sûreté. -Transport /interface, cargoes (active or passive storage), security and safety.
6783	**pénurie** f [penyʁi]	**shortage|scarcity** Étant donné la pénurie de main-d'oeuvre dans le pays, l'État encourage la natalité. -And in view of the national shortage of labour, the State encourages childbirth.
6784	**noisette** f; adj [nwazɛt]	**hazelnut; hazel** Elle a les yeux noisette. -She has hazel eyes.
6785	**pessimiste** adj; m/f [pesimist]	**pessimistic; pessimist** La situation est donc très différente selon que l'on est optimiste ou pessimiste. -This, in other words, is a question of whether you are an optimist or a pessimist.

6786	**ravage**	**havoc|ravage**
	m	Éteignez le feux qui ravage mon corps.
	[ʁavaʒ]	-Quench the fires that ravage my body.
6787	**fendu**	**split**
	adj	Tel un tigre sur un daim, le sabot fendu, et le bras cassé !
	[fɑ̃dy]	-Like a tiger on a deer, with a cloven hoof and with a broken arm!
6788	**synchronisation**	**synchronization**
	f	Ledit instant est ensuite utilisé pour la synchronisation.
	[sɛ̃kʁonizasjɔ̃]	-The at least one instant is subsequently used for time synchronization.
6789	**potage**	**soup**
	m	Il y a une couille dans le potage.
	[pɔtaʒ]	-There is a problem.
6790	**nostalgique**	**nostalgic**
	adj	Je trouve qu'il n'y a rien de nostalgique là-dedans.
	[nɔstalʒik]	-I submit that there is nothing nostalgic about it.
6791	**soumission**	**submission|tender**
	f[sumisjɔ̃]	Dernière date possible pour la soumission des offres. -This is the last possible date for submission of tenders.
6792	**planétaire**	**planetary; orrery**
	adj; m	Si le terrorisme est planétaire, notre réponse doit absolument être ferme, mais pareillement planétaire.
	[planetɛʁ]	-If terrorism is global, our response must be absolutely firm but likewise global.
6793	**approvisionnement**	**procurement|provision**
	m	La sécurité d'approvisionnement en gaz doit prévaloir.
	[apʁovizjɔnmɑ̃]	-Security of the gas supply must be the main consideration.
6794	**recoin**	**corner|recess**
	m	Il est impensable que la Commission puisse produire de bonnes normes pour tous les recoins de l'Europe.
	[ʁəkwɛ̃]	-It is impossible to imagine that the Commission would be capable of drafting good agricultural policy for every nook and cranny of Europe.
6795	**sacrer**	**consecrate|crown**
	vb	Depuis Henri Ier en 1027, les rois se font sacrer à Reims en mémoire de Clovis.
	[sakʁe]	-Starting with Henri I in 1027, French kings were crowned in Reims in memory of Clovis.
6796	**incomparable**	**incomparable**
	adj	De plus, la société russe connaît une tragédie démographique incomparable.
	[ɛ̃kɔ̃paʁabl]	-What is more, Russian society has experienced an incomparable demographic tragedy.
6797	**intervalle**	**interval**
	m	L'intervalle d'air entre l'échantillon et la paroi du tube doit être aussi petit que possible;
	[ɛ̃tɛʁval]	-The air gap between the sample and tubing wall should be as small as possible.
6798	**bricoler**	**tinker**
	vb	Je ne faisais que bricoler.
	[bʁikɔle]	-I was just tinkering around.
6799	**tricot**	**knitting**
	m	Jill ne connaît rien ni à la couture, ni au tricot.
	[tʁiko]	-Jill knows nothing of sewing or knitting.

6800	**affront**	**affront|outrage**
	m	Cette politique est un affront à l'humanité et doit donc être rejetée sans détour.
	[afʁɔ̃]	-This policy is an affront to humanity and must therefore be rejected outright.
6801	**formel**	**formal**
	adj	Il regroupe des plans spécifiques pour les secteurs formel, non formel et communautaire.
	[fɔʁmɛl]	-It compiles specific plans for the formal, non-formal and community-based sectors.
6802	**hareng**	**herring**
	m	L'industrie du hareng en bénéficierait certainement.
	[aʁɑ̃g]	-This would certainly be of benefit to the herring industry.
6803	**monteur**	**editor**
	m[mɔ̃tœʁ]	Monteur musique reconnu à Hollywood, Bos alterne souvent entre plusieurs applications. -As a top music editor in Hollywood, Bos often switches between multiple applications.
6804	**précéder**	**precede**
	vb	Il est bon que la proposition et la création d'un fonds laitier précèdent les mesures spécifiques visant à réformer le secteur des producteurs et des fabricants de lait.
	[pʁesede]	-It is good that the proposal for and creation of a milk fund come before specific actions to reform the milk producers' and processors' sector.
6805	**partiel**	**partial; midyear exam**
	adj; m	Un esai partiel défini par le service technique en fonction des modifications apportées.
	[paʁsjɛl]	-A partial test as defined by the Technical Service in relation to the modifications made.
6806	**étaler**	**spread out|display**
	vb	Ces mesures peuvent s'étaler dans le temps et avoir même un caractère partiel.
	[etale]	-Those measures could be implemented in phases, and even be partial in nature.
6807	**symboliser**	**symbolize**
	vb	Le lancement de l'opération Althea, conduite jusqu'à présent avec succès, symbolise cette ère nouvelle.
	[sɛ̃bɔlize]	-The launch of Operation Althea and its successful conduct so far epitomize this new era.
6808	**laitier**	**dairy; milkman**
	adj; m	Sans que Jack le sache, Jill couchait avec le laitier.
	[letje]	-Unbeknownst to Jack, Jill was having it off with the milkman.
6809	**écumer**	**skim|froth**
	vb	Les monopolistes écument le marché et rachètent des entreprises privées avec l'argent gagné grâce au monopole.
	[ekyme]	-The monopolists are combing the markets and buying up private companies with funds generated by the monopoly.
6810	**singulier**	**singular|strange; singular**
	adj; m	Je présume que vous pensez être plutôt singulier, n'est-ce pas ?
	[sɛ̃gylje]	-I guess you think you're pretty special, don't you?
6811	**infime**	**tiny**

adj
[ɛ̃fim]

Elle ne se penche que sur une partie infime d'un problème beaucoup plus grand.
 -It is an act that represents only a very small part of a much larger problem.

6812 opportun — **appropriate|timely**

adj
[ɔpɔʀtɛ̃]

Répondez comme vous l'estimez opportun et nous passerons à la question suivante.
 -Please reply as you feel appropriate and we shall move on to another question.

6813 caisson — **box**

m
[kɛsɔ̃]

U est le coefficient de déperdition thermique du caisson calorimétrique ou de la caisse isotherme, en W/°C,
 -where U is the heat leakage of the calorimeter box or insulated body, Watts/°C.

6814 glande — **gland**

f
[glɑ̃d]

Descartes pensait que l'esprit et le corps se rejoignaient dans la glande pinéale.
 -Descartes thought that the mind and body were joined in the pineal gland.

6815 cagoule — **hood**

f
[kagul]

Il ne portait pas de cagoule.
 -He wasn't wearing a mask.

6816 versement — **payment|installment**

m
[vɛʀsəmɑ̃]

Le versement de ces allocations s'entend sous réserve de l'autorisation du Président.
 -Payment of these allowances will be subject to authorization by the President.

6817 calé — **chock**

adj
[kale]

Ce phénomène est devenu plus visible en 2000-2001, quand le moteur a calé.
 -This became more apparent during 2000-2001 when the engine stalled.

6818 infiltration — **infiltration**

f
[ɛ̃filtʀasjɔ̃]

« […] par ruissellement et infiltration ou percolation directe dans le sol ».
 -"[…] by runoff on the ground and infiltration or direct percolation through soil".

6819 téléviser — **televise**

vb
[televize]

J'estime qu'il est judicieux de téléviser intégralement ce type de délibérations.
 -I agree that it is good practice to televise proceedings such as this from gavel to gavel.

6820 pareillement — **likewise**

adv
[paʀɛjmɑ̃]

Comme l'a dit Hamlet : C'était un homme, tout bien considéré, je ne retrouverai pas son pareil.
 -As Hamlet said: He was a man, take him for all in all; I shall not look upon his like again.

6821 miche — **loaf**

f
[miʃ]

Elle a acheté une miche de pain.
 -She bought a loaf of bread.

6822 tronçonneuse — **chain saw**

f
[tʀɔ̃sɔnøz]

Jack abattit l'arbre avec sa tronçonneuse.
 -Jack cut down the tree with his chainsaw.

6823 fissure — **crack|split**

f
[fisyʀ]

Le gaz s'échappait d'une fissure dans la conduite.
 -Gas was escaping from a crack in the pipe.

6824	**futile**	**futile|frivolous**
	adj	It would be futile to attempt to solve all the problems at once.
	[fytil]	-Il serait vain de s'efforcer de résoudre tous les problèmes en même temps.

6825	**excrément**	**excrement**
	m	Cette feuille est imperméable au liquide et capable de retenir un excrément humain.
	[ɛkskʁemã]	-The sheet is liquid impermeable and capable of retaining human excrement.

6826	**rallonge**	**extension**
	f	J'ai besoin d'une rallonge.
	[ʁalɔ̃ʒ]	-I need an extension cord.

6827	**interminable**	**endless**
	adj	À plusieurs reprises, cela a entraîné une ambiguïté et d'interminables procédures.
	[ɛ̃tɛʁminabl]	-In a number of cases, this has led to ambiguity and to endless procedures.

6828	**enflammer**	**ignite|inflame**
	vb	En séchant sur des vêtements ou des matières combustibles, ce produit peut s'enflammer.
	[ãflame]	-Drying of this product on clothing or combustible materials may cause fire.

6829	**acquisition**	**acquisition**
	f	Quand en avez-vous fait l'acquisition ?
	[akizisjɔ̃]	-When did make the acquisition?

6830	**idem**	**idem**
	adv	Idem - si le PCN est rédigé en caractères latins ou accompagné d'une traduction certifiée conforme (dans les deux cas).
	[idɛm]	-Ditto - if the DDP is in Roman type or accompanied by a certified translation (both cases).

6831	**macabre**	**macabre**
	adj	Malheureusement, il y a un contexte macabre qui l'explique.
	[makabʁ]	-Unfortunately, there is a macabre background to that.

6832	**emprisonner**	**imprison|trap**
	vb	Nous sommes disposés à emprisonner M. Taylor au Royaume-Uni s'il est condamné.
	[ãpʁizɔne]	-We stand ready to imprison Mr. Taylor in the United Kingdom if he is convicted.

6833	**blaguer**	**joke**
	vb	Je ne pense pas que la question de la pauvreté mondiale se prête aux blagues et aux jeux de mots.
	[blage]	-I do not believe that the issue of global poverty is a matter about which we should joke or make puns.

6834	**haie**	**hedge|hurdle**
	f	Il nous lorgne derrière la haie.
	[ɛ]	-He's watching us from behind the hedge.

6835	**rebord**	**flange|edge**
	m	Jack s'est assis sur le rebord de la fenêtre.
	[ʁəbɔʁ]	-Jack sat on the window sill.

6836	**terroriser**	**terrorize|bully**
	vb	L'usage disproportionné de la force vise à terroriser et à soumettre la population.
	[teʁɔʁize]	-The disproportionate use of force is designed to terrorize and subjugate the population.

| 6837 | **trouvaille** | **find** |

| | f | |
| | [tʁuvaj] | |

Malgré cette précaution, j'appris sa trouvaille.
-Despite this precaution, however, I got wind of his find.

6838 avorton runt

m
[avɔʁtɔ̃]

Et vous un petit avorton maigrichon.
-And you're a scrawny little runt.

6839 influent **influential**

adj[ɛ̃flyɑ̃]

Nous étions donc très heureux d'être un membre important et influent du Quartet. -We were then quite happy to be an important and influential member of the Quartet.

6840 tropical **tropical**

adj
[tʁɔpikal]

The prevailing climate is tropical and semi-tropical.
-Le climat y est essentiellement de type tropical et semi-tropical.

6841 roulement **rolling | rumbling**

m
[ʁulmɑ̃]

Assemblage de roulement a billes pour equipement a haute vitesse.
-The field of this invention is rolling ball bearing assemblies for high speed equipment.

6842 courtisan **courtier**

m
[kuʁtizɑ̃]

Il ne faut jamais oublier que les tâches des consultants sont celles du courtisan classique.
-We should always remember that the trade of the consultants is the trade of the classic courtesan.

6843 prédiction **prediction**

f
[pʁediksjɔ̃]

Le gouvernement n'a pas vraiment réagit à l'époque à cette prédiction.
-The government did not react at that time to that prediction in a substantive way.

6844 fascisme **fascism**

m
[faʃism]

La Serbie vit les dernières affres du fascisme en bordure de notre propre Union.
-Serbia is suffering the final pangs of fascism on the fringes of our own Union.

6845 éloge **eulogy | praise**

m
[elɔʒ]

Lors de son service commémoratif, l'éloge funèbre a été prononcé par son gendre, Bob Hughes.
-The eulogy at the memorial service was given by his son-in-law, Bob Hughes.

6846 schizophrénie **schizophrenia**

f
[skizɔfʁeni]

Tu ne seras jamais seule avec la schizophrénie.
-You will never be alone with schizophrenia.

6847 pizzeria **pizzeria**

f
[pizzʁija]

Ta pizzeria pourrait jouer contre Planet Express.
-Your pizzeria will play a game against Planet Express.

6848 hélium **helium**

m
[eljɔm]

L'hélium est particulièrement approprié à cet effet.
-Helium has been found to be particularly useful for this purpose.

6849 cholestérol **cholesterol**

m
[kɔlɛsteʁɔl]

Si seulement les œufs avaient une teneur en cholestérol moins élevée, j'en mangerais tous les jours !
-If only eggs had a lower cholesterol content, I'd eat them every day!

6850 médoc **medication**

m
[medɔk]

C'est l'heure de son médoc pour l'épilepsie.
-It's time for his seizure medication.

6851	**aigu**	**acute|shrill**
	adj	Par conséquent, il n'existe pas de risque aigu. C'est une mesure de
	[egy]	précaution.
		-Thus, there is no acute risk; it is a matter of precaution.
6852	**barricade**	**barricade|barrier**
	f[baʁikad]	Nous sommes tous du même côté de la barricade. -We are all standing on the
		same side of the barricade.
6853	**coopératif**	**cooperative; cooperator**
	adj; m	Le mouvement coopératif offre d'excellentes possibilités d'éradiquer la
	[kɔɔpeʁatif]	pauvreté.
		-The cooperative movement provided excellent opportunities to eradicate
		poverty.
6854	**adéquat**	**adequate**
	adj	Le reste de la carcasse de la voiture nécessite également un retraitement
	[adekwa]	adéquat.
		-What is left of the stripped vehicle also requires to be processed
		adequately.
6855	**fripouille**	**scoundrel**
	f	Tu sais que tu es une fripouille.
	[fʁipuj]	-You know you are a scoundrel.
6856	**incertain**	**uncertain**
	adj	Quant aux Baudelaires, leur avenir était incertain.
	[ɛ̃sɛʁtɛ̃]	-As for the Baudelaires, what lay ahead for them was unclear.
6857	**congédier**	**dismiss|discharge**
	vb	Ils veulent pouvoir congédier et blâmer quelque bureaucrate anonyme.
	[kɔ̃ʒedje]	-It will be some nameless, faceless bureaucrat they can fire and blame the
		problem on.
6858	**aviateur**	**aviator|pilot**
	m	La patronne exagère avec son aviateur.
	[avjatœʁ]	-Madame's gone too far over her aviator.
6859	**piquet**	**stake|picket**
	m	Les protestataires faisaient le piquet à l'extérieur du siège de la société.
	[pikɛ]	-Protesters were picketing outside the company's headquarters.
6860	**préavis**	**warning**
	m	J'ai été licencié sans préavis.
	[pʁeavi]	-I was discharged without notice.
6861	**aumônier**	**chaplain**
	m	Un aumônier est un fonctionnaire et un travailleur social dans une prison.
	[omonje]	-A chaplain is a public servant and social worker in prison.
6862	**merle**	**blackbird**
	m	Le merle bleu porte le ciel sur son dos.
	[mɛʁl]	-The blue blackbird carries the sky on his back.
6863	**dépanneur**	**repairman|convenience store**
	m	Je vais au dépanneur. Tu veux quelque chose?
	[depanœʁ]	-I'm going to the convenience store. Is there anything you want?
6864	**ronfler**	**snore**
	vb	Étais-je en train de ronfler ?
	[ʁɔ̃fle]	-Was I snoring?
6865	**grognement**	**grunt**
	m	Le grognement indique l'agression, cher collègue.
	[gʁɔɲmã]	-The grunting indicates aggression, my dear colleague.

6866	**figer**	**freeze**
	vb	Il ne ferait que figer le statu quo et ne répondrait pas à l'objectif du désarmement.
	[fiʒe]	-It will just freeze the status quo and not further the goal of disarmament.

6867	**chevaucher**	**lap**
	vb	Les échos reçus peuvent même chevaucher la bande de fréquence d'émission fondamentale.
	[ʃəvoʃe]	-The received echoes may even overlap the fundamental transmit frequency band.

6868	**décompte**	**count**
	m	Je dois dire à ce propos à la commissaire que j'ai procédé à un décompte au niveau du port de Bordeaux l'an dernier, donc après la catastrophe du Prestige.
	[dekɔ̃t]	-In this regard, I have to say to the Commissioner that I compiled a detailed account for the port of Bordeaux last year, after the Prestige disaster, that is.

6869	**volaille**	**poultry|fowl**
	f	Les oeufs de volaille infectée peuvent aussi être contaminés.
	[vɔlaj]	-Eggs from infected poultry could also be contaminated with the virus.

6870	**serein**	**serene; collection**
	adj; m	Ah ! Comme ce temple est serein !
	[səʁɛ̃]	-Ah! How serene is this temple!

6871	**balistique**	**ballistic; ballistics**
	adj; f	Vous avez déjà l'avantage balistique.
	[balistik]	-You guys are already zeroed for ballistic advantage.

6872	**flambeau**	**torch**
	m	Ensuite, nous passerons bien sûr le flambeau à nos successeurs au Luxembourg.
	[flɑ̃bo]	-Thereafter, we will, of course, be handing the torch to our successors in Luxembourg.

6873	**anticiper**	**anticipate**
	vb	Elle n'est pas en mesure de les prévenir, mais elle peut en anticiper les conséquences.
	[ɑ̃tisipe]	-It is unable to avoid them, but it can anticipate their consequences.

6874	**dévier**	**deviate**
	vb	Le panneau d'appui ne doit pas dévier plus de 100 mm ni subir de déformation ou de dommage permanents.
	[devje]	-The backrest shall not deflect more than 100 mm or suffer permanent deformation or damage.

6875	**moule**	**mold; mussel**
	m;f	Elle porte un jean ras-la-moule.
	[mul]	-She's wearing low-rise jeans.

6876	**flocon**	**flake**
	m	Je pense aussi trouver un flocon de chrome.
	[flɔkɔ̃]	-I think I found a chrome flake, too.

6877	**diabétique**	**diabetic; diabetic**
	adj; m/f	Le risque d'acidocétose diabétique, ou coma diabétique, est de 50 % plus élevé pour elles que pour les hommes.
	[djabetik]	-The risk of diabetic ketoacidosis, or diabetic coma, is 50% higher among women than men.

6878	**pakistanais**	**Pakistani**
	adj	Le "plombier polonais" d'hier sera demain chinois ou pakistanais.
	[pakistanɛ]	-Yesterday's 'Polish plumber' will tomorrow be Chinese or Pakistani.

6879	**stéroïde**	**steroid**
	m[steʁɔid]	La substance active est un stéroïde ayant la structure 4-ène-3-one. -The active material is a steroid having the 4-en-3-one structure.
6880	**déployer**	**deploy|display**
	vb [deplwaje]	Enfin, l'Uruguay prévoit de déployer la première unité fluviale en mai et juin. -Finally, Uruguay plans to deploy the first riverine unit during May and June.
6881	**tondre**	**mow|shear**
	vb [tɔ̃dʁ]	Il suffit tout simplement de tondre le gazon pour réclamer une subvention. -It is enough simply to mow the lawn and claim a subsidy.
6882	**décourager**	**discourage**
	vb [dekuʁaʒe]	Le Tribunal servira également à décourager les assassinats politiques à l'avenir. -The Tribunal will also serve to dsicourage future political assassinations.
6883	**historien**	**historian; historical**
	m; adj [istɔʁjɛ̃]	Il est historien. -He's a historian.
6884	**percevoir**	**levy**
	vb [pɛʁsəvwaʁ]	Nous, Parlementaires, avons du mal à percevoir les résultats positifs concrets qu'il est censé apporter. -We in Parliament find it difficult to see that this has led to any positive concrete results.
6885	**parjure**	**perjury**
	m [paʁʒyʁ]	Le système judiciaire et la presse étasuniennes sont rocambolesques : un jour vous êtes une pauvre mère de famille exemplaire victime d'un viol, le lendemain, une immigrée illégale parjure suspectée de blanchiment d'argent de la drogue. -The US judicial system and press are incredible: One day you're a poor examplary housewife, victim of a rape, the next, you're an illegal immigrant, having committed perjury and being suspected of whitewashing drug money.
6886	**aventurier**	**adventurer; aggressive**
	m; adj [avɑ̃tyʁje]	Né à Brouage en France, en 1567, Champlain était un jeune aventurier très talentueux et déterminé. -Born in Brouage, France, in 1567, Champlain was a talented and determined young adventurer.
6887	**accompli**	**accomplished**
	adj [akɔ̃pli]	Le salaire apparaît juridiquement comme la contrepartie du travail accompli. -In legal terms, salary is paid in consideration of work that has been accomplished.
6888	**effroi**	**terror**
	m [efʁwa]	Vous le dites avec un peu d'effroi. -You say that with some fear.
6889	**guillotiner**	**guillotine**
	vb [gijɔtine]	Campbell, un libéral, a dit que les néo-démocrates avaient guillotiné la démocratie. -Campbell, a Liberal, has said that the NDP have ``dropped the guillotine on democracy".
6890	**imposant**	**imposing|impressive**
	adj[ɛ̃pozɑ̃]	Contester une décision administrative imposant une mesure disciplinaire. - To appeal an administrative decision imposing a disciplinary measure.

6891	**taquin**	**teasing|playful; teaser**
	adj; m	Viens ici, espèce de petit taquin.
	[takɛ̃]	-Come here, you little tease.

6892	**tempo**	**tempo**
	m	It is the quality of the process that is crucial, not the tempo.
	[tãpo]	-La qualité du processus est déterminante, non sa cadence.

6893	**diffamation**	**defamation**
	f	La fille de l'envie est la diffamation.
	[difamasjɔ̃]	-The daughter of envy is defamation.

6894	**latitude**	**latitude**
	f	Vérifie chaque nombre comme latitude et longitude.
	[latityd]	-Kitt, check each number for latitude and longitude.

6895	**contretemps**	**setbacks**
	mpl	Le respect de l'ensemble de ces instructions permettra d'éviter tout contretemps.
	[kɔ̃tʁətã]	-Adherence to these instructions will help to avoid last-minute difficulties.

6896	**auguste**	**august**
	adj	En cette auguste occasion, voici un verset en Sanskrit...
	[ogyst]	-On this August occasion, here's a Sanskrit verse...

6897	**catastrophique**	**catastrophic**
	adj	Il y a eu une augmentation, mais elle n'est cependant pas catastrophique.
	[katastʁɔfik]	-There was an increase, but it did not appear to be a catastrophic increase.

6898	**faune**	**wildlife**
	f	Ils sont ainsi mieux à même de protéger la flore et la faune sur leur territoire.
	[fon]	-This strengthens their ability to preserve the flora and fauna within their boundaries.

6899	**détailler**	**detail**
	vb	On trouvera la ventilation détaillée des financements des projets à l'annexe 11 du document intitulé «Supporting documentation».
	[detaje]	-A detailed break down of project funding is contained in the "Supporting documentation", annex 11.

6900	**acolyte**	**acolyte**
	m	Mon acolyte est une télépathe noire canon.
	[akɔlit]	-And my sidekick is a hot black chick who can read minds.

6901	**poupe**	**stern|stern-post**
	f	Attachez-les aux taquets de la poupe.
	[pup]	-Now then, tie them to the stern cleats.

6902	**gobelet**	**cup**
	m	Jack montra à Jill comment faire bouillir de l'eau dans un gobelet en carton.
	[gɔblɛ]	-Jack showed Jill how to boil water in a paper cup.

6903	**frimer**	**show off**
	vb	Nous n'avons encore aucune raison de " frimer ", comme diraient certains chanteurs de variété.
	[fʁime]	-We cannot yet, as pop singers would perhaps suggest,'strut our stuff '.

6904	**chandail**	**sweater**
	m	Jack ne porte pas de chandail.
	[ʃãdaj]	-Jack is shirtless.

6905	**chimpanzé**	**chimpanzee**
	m	C'est Mokolo, notre chimpanzé pygmée.
	[ʃɛ̃pãze]	-That's Mokolo, our pygmy chimpanzee.

6906	**ourson**	**bear cub**

	m	L'ourson apprend à marcher.
	[uʁsɔ̃]	-The bear cub is just learning to walk.

6907 baume — balm | balsam

m
[bom]

Je ne mets pas de baume pour les lèvres.
-I don't wear chapstick.

6908 collecter — collect

vb
[kɔlɛkte]

L'OIT s'est efforcée d'améliorer la qualité des données qu'elle collecte et diffuse.
-The ILO has been working to improve the quality of the labour statistics they collect and disseminate.

6909 restant — remaining; remnant

adj; m
[ʁɛstɑ̃]

On a également signalé des cas de recrutement et d'emploi d'enfants par les forces restantes de l'Union des tribunaux islamiques.
-There are also reported cases of recruitment and use of children by remnant groups of UIC.

6910 horoscope — horoscope

m
[ɔʁɔskɔp]

Je ne crois pas en l'astrologie mais ça ne veut pas dire que je ne lis pas mon horoscope.
-I don't believe in astrology, but that doesn't mean that I don't read my horoscope.

6911 coquillage — shell

m
[kɔkijaʒ]

Cette moitié de coquillage appartenait à mon père.
-This half shell was my father's.

6912 moléculaire — molecular

adj
[mɔlekylɛʁ]

Ça devrait causer une réaction au niveau moléculaire.
-In theory, you should cause a chemical reaction at the molecular level.

6913 théorique — theoretical

adj
[teɔʁik]

À l'origine, ce rapport était relativement compliqué et théorique, trop théorique.
-Originally, this report was rather complex and quite theoretical, too theoretical, in fact.

6914 arthrite — arthritis

f
[aʁtʁit]

Ma femme souffre horriblement de son arthrite.
-My wife's suffering something wicked with the arthritis.

6915 purifier — purify

vb
[pyʁifje]

Les écosystèmes aident à purifier l'air que nous respirons et l'eau que nous buvons.
-Ecosystems help purify the air we breathe and the water we drink.

6916 poussette — stroller | crawl

f
[pusɛt]

Grayer doit traverser les avenues dans sa poussette.
-Grayer still must be in a stroller - when crossing Park or Madison.

6917 lagon — lagoon

m[lagɔ̃]

Dans d'autres cas, cette zone s'est développée pour devenir un lagon hypersalé. -In other cases, the supratidal zone has developed into a hyper-saline lagoon.

6918 païen — pagan; pagan

adj; m
[pajɛ̃]

Iconographie Chrétienne.. mais c'est aussi le symbole païen pour la Terre.
-Christian iconography.. but it's also the pagan symbol for Earth.

6919 mature — mature

adj
[matyʁ]

Only institutions that preserve the collective experience can mature.'
-Seules les institutions qui préservent l'expérience collective peuvent mûrir."

6920	**pirater**	**hack|pirate**
	vb	Vous avez pu pirater le mot de passe.
	[piʁate]	-You've had time to hack the password.
6921	**raton**	**north african|young rat**
	m	Voyez-vous le raton-laveur ?
	[ʁatɔ̃]	-Do you see the raccoon?
6922	**piétiner**	**trample on**
	vb	Il convient d'empêcher l'UE de les piétiner.
	[pjetine]	-The EU must not be allowed to trample all over these values.
6923	**luxueux**	**luxurious**
	adj	Il travaillait aussi parfois comme extra au luxueux hôtel Pressman.
	[lyksɥø]	-Tyler also works sometimes as a banquet waiter at the luxurious Pressman Hotel.
6924	**propager**	**propagate**
	vb	Nous avons réussi à propager le modèle démocratique européen à travers la paix.
	[pʁɔpaʒe]	-We have managed to propagate the European democratic model by peaceful means.
6925	**pendentif**	**pendant**
	m	Quand il nous donnera son pendentif.
	[pɑ̃dɑ̃tif]	-As soon as he gives us his pendant.
6926	**échauffer**	**warm**
	vb	Tu commences enfin à t'échauffer.
	[eʃofe]	-Finally starting to warm up.
6927	**filial**	**filial**
	adj	Je lui répète avec un abandon filial: Totus tuus!
	[filjal]	-To her I repeat with filial abandonment: Totus tuus!
6928	**manigancer**	**engineer**
	vb	Le but était-il de manigancer une confrontation sanglante ?
	[manigɑ̃se]	-Was this in order to engineer a bloody showdown?
6929	**boulon**	**bolt**
	m	Les scellés à boulon résistent bien aux tentatives d'effraction violentes.
	[bulɔ̃]	-Bolt seals can usually withstand substantial force without opening.
6930	**fade**	**bland|tasteless**
	adj	Ma délégation note que ce rapport constitue une compilation d'événements en grande partie statistique, une liste fade de réunions et de documents adoptés.
	[fad]	-My delegation notes that the report remains a largely statistical compilation of events, a bland listing of meetings and outcome documents.
6931	**frôler**	**graze**
	vb	Quand nous frôlons de trop près une voiture dans un parc de stationnement bondé, pourquoi déclenchons-nous tout un concert de sirènes, de sifflets et de klaxons ?
	[fʁole]	-Why, when we unwittingly brush against a car in a crowded parking lot, do we run the risk of setting off a chorus of sirens, whistles and klaxons?
6932	**coordination**	**coordination**
	f	L'information présentée dans l'article de Kelly sur la coordination des couleurs est considérée comme étant utile dans l'élaboration d'une théorie alternative.
	[kɔɔʁdinasjɔ̃]	-The information presented in Kelly's paper on color coordination is seen to be of use in building up an alternative theory.

6933 sculpteur
m
[skyltœʁ]

sculptor
Je m'appelle Sherwin Lemonde, sculpteur, peintre, barman à plein temps.
-My name is Sherwin Lemonde, sculptor, painter, full-time barista.

6934 joliment
adv
[ʒɔlimɑ̃]

nicely
Monsieur Hermann a bien joliment expliqué les tenants et les aboutissants de cette question.
-Mr. Hermann has very nicely explained the ins and outs of this question.

6935 borné
adj
[bɔʁne]

limited|narrow
J'espère que le Portugal, en particulier son nouveau gouvernement, sera moins borné que les socialistes et examinera au moins cette possibilité.
-I hope that Portugal, particularly with its new Government, will be less blinkered than the Socialists and at least give consideration to this prospect.

6936 devinette
f
[dəvinɛt]

riddle
Quelle est ta devinette ?
-What is your riddle?

6937 rougeole
f
[ʁuʒɔl]

measles
L'objectif du projet était d'éliminer et d'arrêter la transmission de la rougeole;
-The project's objective was to eliminate and stop the transmission of measles by 2008.

6938 pelle
f
[pɛl]

shovel
Avez-vous une pelle à neige ?
-Do you have a snow shovel?

6939 corail
m
[kɔʁaj]

coral
L'acidification de l'océan menacera, à un moment, l'existence même de la Grande Barrière de Corail.
-Acidification of the ocean will, in time, threaten the very existence of the Great Barrier Reef.

6940 prévenant
adj
[pʁevənɑ̃]

considerate
On nous a dit que l'intention de l'article 24.2 est de prévenir la fraude.
-We are told that the intent of section 24.2 is to prevent fraud.

6941 explorateur
m
[ɛksplɔʁatœʁ]

explorer
Sébastien Cabot était le fils de Jean Cabot et devient aussi un explorateur.
-Sebastian Cabot was John Cabot's son and also became an explorer.

6942 astéroïde
m[asteʁɔid]

asteroid
Qu'adviendrait-il si un gros astéroïde frappait la Terre ? -What would happen if a large asteroid struck the earth?

6943 désactiver
vb
[dezaktive]

deactivate
Cliquez ici pour désactiver le contexte et le style utilisé actuellement appliqués.
-Click here to remove the current context assigned to the selected style.

6944 reptile
adj; m
[ʁɛptil]

reptile; reptile
On compte 25 espèces endogènes de plantes et de reptiles sur les îles Caïmanes.
-The Islands have 25 endemic species of plants and reptiles.

6945 contester
vb
[kɔ̃tɛste]

challenge|contest
Personne au Canada ne peut contester le droit des Canadiens d'exprimer librement leur désaccord.
-No one in Canada can possibly dispute the right of Canadians to freely express dissent.

6946 déroute

rout

	f [deʁut]	Parfaitement coordonnée, elle a provoqué la déroute complète de l'armée Eurasienne. -Perfectly coordinated, it has resulted in the utter rout of the Eurasian Army.
6947	**interception** f [ɛ̃tɛʁsɛpsjɔ̃]	**interception** L'interception aura lieu dans deux heures. -Interception will take place in two hours' time.
6948	**typiquement** adv [tipikmɑ̃]	**typically** Je crois que nous sommes de fiers Canadiens d'origines mixtes typiquement canadiennes. -I believe that we are proud Canadians of typically Canadian mixed heritage.
6949	**déchaîner** vb [deʃene]	**unchain** Le racisme pouvait déchaîner les passions et la colère, voire menacer la paix. -Racism had the potential to unleash high emotions and anger, and even to threaten peace.
6950	**lycéen** m [liseɛ̃]	**high school student** Es-tu lycéen ? -Are you a high school student?
6951	**preux** adj [pʁø]	**doughty|gallant** J'ai 14 preux chevaliers à mes côtés. -I have 14 gallant kinghts with me.
6952	**saxon** adj; m/f [saksɔ̃]	**Saxon; Saxon** Pour certains aspects, la Communauté flamande se réfère plutôt au modèle anglo-saxon. -In certain aspects, the Flemish Community draws more on the Anglo-Saxon model.
6953	**lynx** m [lɛ̃ks]	**lynx** Il va essayer d'escalader la clôture, comme le lynx. -He'll probably try to climb over the fence, like that bobcat.
6954	**foret** m [fɔʁɛ]	**drill** Après affutage le foret est reintroduit dans le magasin. -After sharpening, the drill is brought back into the magazine.
6955	**profitable** adj [pʁɔfitabl]	**profitable** L' accord suit un arrangement qui était très profitable à l' Union européenne. -The agreement follows an arrangement that was very profitable for the European Union.
6956	**lilas** adj; m [lila]	**lilac; lilac** Or, au cours de la semaine, les règles portant le nom de code « Lilas bleu » ont été officiellement réintroduites. -However, during the current week the Blue Lilac rules had been reinstated.
6957	**rustre** adj; m [ʁystʁ]	**boor; boorish** Cet homme est un rustre, bien sûr. -The man's a boor, that's for sure.
6958	**narine** f [naʁin]	**nostril** Son bec est cependant doté d'une narine tubulaire. -Their beaks however have a tube-like nostril.
6959	**machette** f [maʃɛt]	**machete** Avec cette machette et vêtu de ces vêtements. -With that machete, in those clothes.
6960	**laitue**	**lettuce**

	f	Puis-je donner de la laitue à mon chien ?
	[lety]	-Is it OK to feed my dog lettuce?
6961	**civique**	**civic**
	adj	Instruction civique, assistance électorale et partis politiques (12,3 %);
	[sivik]	-Civil education, electoral support and political parties (12.3 per cent);
6962	**harpe**	**harp**
	f	Il s'est électrocuté en jouant de la harpe électrique.
	[aʀp]	-He was electrocuted while playing the electric harp.
6963	**pipeau**	**pipe**
	m	Il l'a séduite avec son pipeau.
	[pipo]	-He seduced her with his didgeridoo.
6964	**vaniteux**	**vain**
	adj	Nous sommes trop vaniteux pour observer un silence décent.
	[vanitø]	-We are too vain to remain decently silent.
6965	**paramètre**	**parameter**
	m	Le paramètre d'adsorption préféré suit un procédé Kubelka-Munk modifié.
	[paʀamɛtʀ]	-The parameter for the preferred adsorption follows from a modified Kubelka-Munk method.
6966	**macchabée**	**stiff**
	m	Ce "macchabée" est mon frère.
	[makʃabe]	-This "stiff" is my brother.
6967	**occurrence**	**occurrence**
	f	Naturellement, les gens du commun ne veulent pas de la guerre ; ni en Russie, ni en Angleterre, ni en Amérique, pas non plus en Allemagne, en l'occurrence, ça va de soi.
	[ɔkyʀɑ̃s]	-Naturally, the common people don't want war; neither in Russia nor in England nor in America, nor for that matter in Germany. That is understood.
6968	**inconfortable**	**uncomfortable**
	adj[ɛ̃kɔ̃fɔʀtabl]	La réalité en Bosnie-Herzégovine est aujourd'hui inconfortable à plusieurs égards. -Bosnia and Herzegovina's reality today is in many ways uncomfortable.
6969	**conversion**	**conversion**
	f	D'abord, des allongements importants des périodes transitoires de conversion.
	[kɔ̃vɛʀsjɔ̃]	-First, the transitional conversion periods are considerably extended.
6970	**inadmissible**	**inadmissible**
	adj	Il est inadmissible que la police considère la torture comme un procédé normal!
	[inadmisibl]	-It is unacceptable that the police consider torture a normal means to an end.
6971	**nicotine**	**nicotine**
	f	L'invention concerne également des compositions pharmaceutiques contenant des antagonistes du récepteur de la nicotine et soit un antidépresseur soit un médicament anxiolytique.
	[nikɔtin]	-The invention also includes related pharmaceutical compositions comprising nicotine receptor antagonists and either an anti-depressant or an anti-anxiety drug.
6972	**Guinée**	**Guinea**
	f	La Guinée a rejoint l'UNESCO le 2 février 1960.
	[gine]	-Guinea joined UNESCO on 2 February 1960.
6973	**armada**	**armada**

	f	La République envoie son armada pour reprendre les banques.
	[aʁmada]	-The Republic is sending its armada to take back the banks.
6974	**pseudonyme**	**pseudonym; pseudonymous**
	m; adj	Quel est votre pseudonyme ?
	[psødɔnim]	-What's your nickname?
6975	**miraculeux**	**miraculous**
	adj	Presque aussi miraculeux que le caramel dans la Caramilk.
	[miʁakylø]	-It is almost as miraculous as getting the milk inside the Caramilk bar.
6976	**pénicilline**	**penicillin**
	f	Le quatrième est la tétracycline, et le cinquième, la pénicilline.
	[penisilin]	-The fourth is tetracycline and the fifth is penicillin.
6977	**kamikaze**	**kamikaze**
	m	Je t'attaquerai tel un kamikaze.
	[kamikaz]	-I'll attack you like a suicide bomber...
6978	**corporel**	**corporal**
	adj	Il s'agit d'une réparation du préjudice corporel, moral et matériel.
	[kɔʁpɔʁɛl]	-Compensation is awarded for bodily injury and material and non-material damages.
6979	**patinoire**	**rink|ice rink**
	f	La patinoire intérieure est construite dans le cadre du Plan d'action économique du Canada.
	[patinwaʁ]	-The hockey rink is part of Canada's Economic Action Plan.
6980	**puberté**	**puberty**
	f	La puberté est le stade à partir duquel certaines communautés marient les enfants.
	[pybɛʁte]	-The stage at which certain communities begin to marry their children is puberty.
6981	**insurrection**	**insurrection|insurgency**
	f	Le lien entre l'insurrection et la culture du pavot est de plus en plus manifeste.
	[ɛ̃syʁɛksjɔ̃]	-There is increasing evidence of a link between the insurgency and poppy growing.
6982	**hérétique**	**heretic; heretical**
	m/f; adj	Une hérétique... suffit à pervertir tout un peuple.
	[eʁetik]	-a heretic... strong enough to mislead all of the people.
6983	**invoquer**	**invoke**
	vb	Invoquer le traité de Lisbonne est donc l'expression d'une arrogance inacceptable.
	[ɛ̃vɔke]	-To invoke the Treaty of Lisbon is therefore an expression of unacceptable arrogance.
6984	**reconstruction**	**reconstruction**
	f	Il ne peut y avoir de reconstruction sans paix ni de stabilité sans reconstruction.
	[ʁəkɔ̃stʁyksjɔ̃]	-There can be no reconstruction without peace and no stability without reconstruction.
6985	**procession**	**procession**
	f	Avancez en procession, s'il vous plaît.
	[pʁɔsesjɔ̃]	-Now, I need you all to line up... in the procession, please.
6986	**succomber**	**succumb**
	vb	En outre, les croyants ne sont pas enclins à succomber aux idéologies ou tendances dominantes.
	[sykɔ̃be]	

-Moreover, believers would not succumb readily to dominating ideologies or trends.

6987	**trompeter** vb [tʁɔ̃pte]	**trumpet** Je vais faire sonner cette trompette comme un trombone. -I will make this trumpet sound like a slide-trombone.
6988	**aumône** f [omon]	**alms** Ce financement ne doit pas ressembler à une aumône donnée par les riches aux pauvres. -This funding should not resemble alms given by the wealthy to the poor.
6989	**résonner** vb [ʁezɔne]	**resonate|resound** Ces cris pour la paix et la sécurité humaine continuent de résonner. -Those cries for peace and human security still resonate.
6990	**négligent** adj [negliʒɑ̃]	**negligent** À mon avis, le gouvernement du Canada de l'époque a été extrêmement négligent. -In my view the Government of Canada of the day was grossly negligent.
6991	**insolent** adj [ɛ̃sɔlɑ̃]	**insolent|cheeky** Comment bloquer les salaires "dans un esprit d'équité" alors que les profits font preuve d'une insolente exubérance ? -How can wages be restricted 'in a spirit of fairness' when profits reveal unashamed exuberance?
6992	**froussard** adj; m [fʁusaʁ]	**wimpy; coward** Ne sois pas un tel froussard ! -Don't be such a wimp!
6993	**sole** f[sɔl]	**sole** La sole commune capturée dans les casiers visés au paragraphe 1 est libérée immédiatement. -Common sole caught in cases referred to in paragraph 1 shall be released immediately.
6994	**hoquet** m [ɔkɛ]	**hiccup** Que devrais-je faire pour arrêter un hoquet ? -What should I do to stop hiccoughs?
6995	**trust** m [tʁœst]	**trust** Confidence-building measures are a powerful instrument for generating trust. -Les mesures de confiance sont un instrument puissant pour susciter la confiance.
6996	**préfecture** f [pʁefɛktyʁ]	**prefecture** J'ai des amis à la préfecture. -I have some friends in the police department.
6997	**amarrer** vb [amaʁe]	**moor|belay** Un navire marchand est au chômage lorsqu'il est amarré au port pour cause de manque de travail. -A merchant ship is laid up when it is moored in port because of lack of work.
6998	**mauve** adj; f [mov]	**mauve; mallow** Je me souviens des couleurs éclatantes qu'elle aimait porter, que ce soit son costume mauve ou jaune ou encore son vernis à ongles rouge vif. -I remember her zest for colour, the mauve or yellow suit and the shiny red nail polish.
6999	**chapiteau** m [ʃapito]	**tent** Maintenant, quittez calmement le chapiteau. -Now, please leave the tent in an orderly manner.

7000	**lutteur**	**wrestler; fighting**
	m; adj	Un lutteur, ce n'est pas une brute.
	[lytœʁ]	-There's a difference between a fighter and a bully!
7001	**glaçon**	**iceberg**
	m	Pas besoin de visiter ce glaçon.
	[glasɔ̃]	-Don't need visit this iceberg.
7002	**fourbe**	**deceitful**
	adj	Il est parfois difficile de traiter son adversaire de fourbe quand on a à
	[fuʁb]	négocier avec lui.
		-It is sometimes difficult to call our opponent deceitful when negotiating
		with them.
7003	**ermite**	**hermit**
	m	L'ermite vivait dans une cabane en bois.
	[ɛʁmit]	-The hermit lived in a wooden hut.
7004	**python**	**python**
	m	C'est presque comme un python.
	[pitɔ̃]	-It's almost like a python.
7005	**ponton**	**pontoon**
	m	Va décrocher les barques du ponton.
	[pɔ̃tɔ̃]	-Go untie the boats on the pontoon.
7006	**passionnément**	**passionately**
	adv[pasjɔnemã]	Le premier est celui dont bon nombre d'entre vous avez débattu
		passionnément. -First is the issue which has been quite passionately
		addressed by many of you.
7007	**écorce**	**bark**
	f	On presse l'orange et on jette l'écorce.
	[ekɔʁs]	-We squeeze the orange and throw away the rind.
7008	**simultanément**	**simultaneously**
	adv	Le Secrétariat travaille simultanément à l'établissement de quatre
	[simyltanemã]	Suppléments du Répertoire.
		-The Secretariat was concurrently working on four Supplements to the
		Repertoire.
7009	**différend**	**dispute**
	m	Les Parties au différend informent l'Organe exécutif de leur différend.
	[difeʁã]	-The parties to the dispute shall inform the Executive Body of their dispute.
7010	**relique**	**relic**
	f	En tant qu'instrument idéologique, le blocus est une relique d'une ère
	[ʁəlik]	révolue.
		-As an ideological tool, the embargo is a relic of a bygone era.
7011	**glacière**	**cooler**
	f	Je jetterai pas une bonne glacière.
	[glasjɛʁ]	-I'm not going to waste a perfectly good cooler.
7012	**givrer**	**frost**
	vb	L'invention concerne un appareil frigorifique avec un espace intérieur isolé
	[ʒivʁe]	dans lequel se trouve au moins un élément structurel refroidi dont la surface
		à tendance à givrer.
		-The invention relates to a refrigeration device, comprising an insulated
		interior, in which at least one cooled component is located, the surface of
		which tends to ice up.
7013	**oral**	**oral; oral**

	adj; m [ɔʀal]	J'aime toujours pas Cavalieri, Tonelli et Fubini... et demain j'ai déjà mon examen oral d'analyse. -I still don't like Cavalieri, Tonelli, or Fubini... and my oral calculus exam is already tomorrow.
7014	**antérieur** adj; m [ɑ̃teʀjœʀ]	**prior; antecessor** Mais toutes les entreprises n'ont pas retrouvé leur niveau d'activité antérieur. -But not all enterprises have been restored to their former level of activity.
7015	**copilote** m/f [kɔpilɔt]	**copilot** Tu te trompes... je ne suis que copilote. -It's not what you think. I'm just a copilot.
7016	**prestigieux** adj [pʀɛstiʒjø]	**prestigious** Il fait partie du prestigieux Comité sénatorial permanent des affaires étrangères. -He is a member of the prestigious Standing Senate Committee on Foreign Affairs.
7017	**typhon** m [tifɔ̃]	**typhoon** Le typhon a conduit l'école à fermer. -The typhoon led to the school being closed.
7018	**orateur** m [ɔʀatœʀ]	**speaker|orator** L'orateur devrait se tenir là où tout le monde peut le voir. -The speaker should stand where everyone can see him.
7019	**blanchisserie** f [blɑ̃ʃisʀi]	**laundry** À présent 20 étudiants travaillent dans la boulangerie et 10 dans la blanchisserie. -Presently 20 students are employed in the bakery unit and 10 in the Laundry.
7020	**décréter** vb [dekʀete]	**decree|order** Avant de décréter l'état d'urgence, le Président a consulté le Parlement. -Before declaring a state of emergency, the President consulted with the Parliament.
7021	**augure** m [ogyʀ]	**omen** Ce n'est pas de bon augure. -That does not bode well.
7022	**bride** f [bʀid]	**flange** Le film préféré de Jill est "Princess Bride". -Jill's favorite movie is The Princess Bride.
7023	**enchantement** m [ɑ̃ʃɑ̃tmɑ̃]	**enchantment** Nous savons tous qui de vous apporte enchantement à cette table. -Now, we all know which of you brings the enchantment to the table.
7024	**grappin** m [gʀapɛ̃]	**grapnel|holdfast** Quand quelqu'un met le grappin sur une personne âgée, on dirait que les autres accourent comme des vautours. -Once one gets its hooks into a senior citizen, the others seem to come in like vultures.
7025	**décomposition** f [dekɔ̃pozisjɔ̃]	**decay** Le temps venait à manquer pour les Terriens tandis que leur environnement planétaire était en décomposition. Le voyage spatial devint une nécessité. -Time was running out for the Earthlings as their planetary environment was in decay. Space travel became a necessity.
7026	**gazette**	**gazette**

f
[gazɛt]
Cette... C'est vrai, je n'avais pas terminé ma gazette.
-That's right, I didn't finish my gazette.

7027 épatant — splendid
adj
[epatã]
Ce serait épatant pour les enfants.
-It'd be wonderful for kids.

7028 advenir — happen
vb
[advəniʁ]
Nous nous demandons ce qu'il va advenir de l'emploi: telle est la grande inconnue.
-We wonder what will happen to employment and that is the million dollar question.

7029 submerger — overwhelm|submerge
vb
[sybmɛʁʒe]
En l'absence de personnel international, le personnel local pourrait être submergé.
-In the absence of international staff, the local staff may be overwhelmed.

7030 potin — titbit
m[pɔtɛ̃]
Ce n'est pas un potin, Blithe. -That's not gossip, Blithe.

7031 ferveur — fervor
f
[fɛʁvœʁ]
Votre soudaine ferveur religieuse est touchante, M. le maire.
-Your sudden religious fervor is most touching, Your Honor.

7032 mitaine — mitten
f
[mitɛn]
Cela fait ressembler son ancienne griffe à la mitaine de Mère Teresa.
-This makes his old claw look like Mother Teresa's mitten.

7033 précipitation — precipitation|haste
f
[pʁesipitasjɔ̃]
La précipitation efficace est la partie de la précipitation qui pénètre dans l'aquifère.
-In other words, it is total precipitation minus evaporation, surface runoff and vegetation.

7034 bretelle — shoulder strap
f
[bʁətɛl]
L'ensemble bretelle de soutien-gorge comprend une bretelle, un élément de réglage, et une paire d'éléments de fixation de bretelle portés par chaque extrémité de bretelle.
-The bra strap assembly comprises a strap, an adjustment member, and a pair of strap attachment members carried by each strap end.

7035 retaper — do up|retype
vb
[ʁətape]
Retaper le mot de passe : .
-Retype Password:.

7036 grammaire — grammar
f
[gʁamɛʁ]
Quelqu'un a-t il remarqué que dans la grammaire de l'espéranto, il n'est jamais question de ponctuation ?
-Has anyone noticed that in Esperanto grammars they never talk about punctuation?

7037 électoral — electoral
adj
[elɛktɔʁal]
Une réforme s'impose pour la simplification du système électoral.
-Electoral reform is necessary in order to simplify the electoral system.

7038 grogner — grumble
vb
[gʁɔɲe]
Il grogne toujours comme un ours.
-He always grumbles like a bear.

7039 agaçant — annoying|aggravating
adj
[agasã]
Je trouve donc très agaçante cette censure préventive dont le Premier ministre italien fait l'objet.

-I therefore find this preventive censure of the Italian Prime Minister very annoying.

7040 nullement
adv
[nylmã]

nothing

Mon intention aujourd'hui n'est nullement d'avoir le dernier mot dans ce débat.
-Today, I have no intention of attempting to record the final word in this debate.

7041 impulsif
adj
[ɛ̃pylsif]

impulsive

Tu as déjà vu un mutilateur rituel, tueur impulsif... se suicider ?
-Ever heard of a ritual mutilator, an impulsive serial-type killer...... committing suicide?

7042 carburateur
m[kaʁbyʁatœʁ]

carburetor

Le volume de la cuve du carburateur doit être dans une fourchette de 10 ml.
-The carburetor bowl fuel volume shall be within a * 10 millilitre range.

7043 tchèque
adj; m
[tʃɛk]

Czech; Czech

Bureaux durables − Réseau tchèque d'écoconsultation (République tchèque).
-Sustainable Offices - The Czech Eco-Counselling Network STEP (Czech Republic).

7044 encyclopédie
f
[ãsiklɔpedi]

encyclopedia

Il est ce qu'on appelle « une encyclopédie sur pattes ».
-He's what they call a walking encyclopedia.

7045 débloquer
vb
[deblɔke]

unblock

Nous croyons que les mesures de confiance peuvent réellement contribuer à débloquer le processus.
-We believe that confidence-building measures can truly help unblock the process.

7046 lingot
m
[lɛ̃go]

ingot

Le lingot émergent est refroidi par projection d'un fluide de refroidissement liquide sur sa surface extérieure.
-The emerging ingot is cooled by directing a liquid coolant onto its outer surface.

7047 retardement
m
[ʁətaʁdəmã]

delay

Cela entraîne un retard de l'enregistrement de la naissance.
-This delay in naming a child results in a delay in registering the birth.

7048 abdomen
m
[abdɔmɛn]

abdomen

L'abdomen se compose d'une partie centrale rigide recouverte de mousse.
-The abdomen consists of a rigid central part and a foam covering.

7049 frimeur
adj; m
[fʁimœʁ]

showy; show-off

Ne sois pas si frimeur, Barry.
-Don´t be such a show-off, Barry.

7050 ultimatum
m
[ÿltimatɔm]

ultimatum

Durant cette période, aucune partie n'a avancé de condition préalable ou d'ultimatum.
-No precondition or ultimatum was raised by either side during this period.

7051 adepte
m/f
[adɛpt]

supporter

La Commission est consciente des problèmes de harcèlement que les adeptes d'autres confessions font subir régulièrement aux minorités religieuses chrétiennes, notamment.
-The Commission is aware of the problems of harassment that the devotees of other faiths impose regularly on Christian religious minorities in particular.

7052 anonymat

anonymity

	m	J'aimerais garder l'anonymat.
	[anɔnima]	-I'd like to remain anonymous.

7053 fracture — fracture
f
[fʁaktyʁ]
La douleur de la fracture compliquée était presque insupportable.
-The pain of the compound fracture was almost unbearable.

7054 mortalité — mortality
f[mɔʁtalite]
La vie a un taux de mortalité de cent pour cent. -Life has a 100% fatality rate.

7055 euphémisme — euphemism
m
[øfemism]
Autrement, le mot permanence risque de devenir un euphémisme pour l'incompétence tolérée.
-Otherwise, tenure would become a euphemism for tolerated incompetence.

7056 cric — jack
m
[kʁik]
Même pas un cric pourrait le lever.
-Not even a jack would get it up.

7057 avare — miser; stingy
m/f; adj
[avaʁ]
Qui peut s'imaginer que l'on puisse construire une grande puissance européenne avec des États avares ?
-How can we imagine to build a grand European power with miserly States.

7058 synonyme — synonymous; synonym
adj; m
[sinɔnim]
La pauvreté chez les enfants est un synonyme politique commode de pauvreté familiale.
-Child poverty is a convenient political synonym for family poverty.

7059 infamie — infamy
f
[ɛ̃fami]
Les Nations Unies doivent se dresser ensemble contre une telle infamie.
-The United Nations must be united against such infamy.

7060 avidité — greed
f
[avidite]
Le pouvoir et l'avidité ne pourront jamais être prétexte au sacrifice d'enfants.
-Power and greed can never be an excuse for sacrificing children.

7061 méfait — wrongdoing;
m; adj
[mefɛ]
La disposition vise expressément un méfait bien précis.
-The provision specifically addresses a targeted mischief.

7062 gladiateur — gladiator
m
[gladjatœʁ]
Je voudrais voir un vrai gladiateur.
-I would like to see a real gladiator.

7063 chapitre — chapter
m
[ʃapitʁ]
Les implications de ces constats seront abordées dans le dernier chapitre (chapitre IV).
-The implications of these findings are discussed in the final chapter (chapter IV).

7064 revendication — claim
f
[ʁəvɑ̃dikasjɔ̃]
C' est notre revendication et la revendication du peuple du Tchad.
-That is our demand and it is the demand of the people of Chad.

7065 dépendant — dependent
adj
[depɑ̃dɑ̃]
Ne soyez pas trop dépendant des autres.
-Don't be too dependent on others.

7066 persévérance — perseverance
f
[pɛʁseveʁɑ̃s]
Ensuite, je souhaite évoquer la persévérance lors du sommet Afrique; quelqu'un en a parlé de la persévérance.
-Next, perseverance at the Africa summit; someone mentioned that, perseverance.

7067	**fuyant**	**elusive|receding**

7067 fuyant — **elusive\|receding**
adj [fɥijɑ̃]
Les droits de l'homme sont constamment bafoués et la démocratie demeure une utopie fuyante.
-Human rights are constantly disregarded and democracy remains an elusive utopia.

7068 tristement — **sadly**
adv [tʁistəmɑ̃]
En outre, la récente révision du tristement célèbre article 301 est une mesure positive.
-Moreover, the recent revision of the infamous Article 301 is a step forward.

7069 châssis — **chassis**
m [ʃasi]
Cet élévateur comprend un châssis mobile entraînant l'objet.
-The lift device includes a movable frame for raising and lowering the object.

7070 implacable — **implacable\|relentless**
adj [ɛ̃plakabl]
Ce texte avalise la logique implacable du dogmatisme libéral.
-This text supports the implacable logic of liberal dogmatism.

7071 antan — **of old\|bygone**
adj [ɑ̃tɑ̃]
Nous ne sommes pas retombés dans les vieux travers d'antan.
-We have not returned to the old ways of the old days.

7072 Sapristi! — **good heavens!**
int [sapʁisti!]
Mais, sapristi, il faut le persuader que le Parlement européen veut les financer!
-But, good heavens, he must be persuaded that the European Parliament wants to fund it!

7073 conquête — **conquest**
f [kɔ̃kɛt]
Le cheval est la plus noble conquête que l'homme ait jamais faite.
-The horse is the noblest conquest ever made by man.

7074 farceur — **jester**
m [faʁsœʁ]
C'est un grand farceur.
-He is a big prankster.

7075 contribuable — **taxpayer**
m/f [kɔ̃tʁibɥabl]
Il sait qu'un contribuable informé est un contribuable en colère.
-He knows that an informed taxpayer is an angry taxpayer.

7076 sanction — **sanction\|punishment**
f [sɑ̃ksjɔ̃]
Apple: Où l'attention au détail est sacrée et la sanction prompte.
-Apple: Where attention to detail is sacred, and punishment is swift.

7077 réparateur — **repairer; remedial**
m; adj [ʁepaʁatœʁ]
En outre, il y a quelque chose de positif et de potentiellement réparateur dans cette proposition.
-There is also a more positive, potentially restorative element to this proposal.

7078 injonction — **injunction**
f [ɛ̃ʒɔ̃ksjɔ̃]
J'obtiendrai un injonction contre elle.
-I'll get an injunction and stop her.

7079 tropique — **tropic**
m [tʁɔpik]
Un point précis sous le tropique.
-A precise point under the tropic.

7080 shampoing — **shampoo**
m [ʃɑ̃pwɛ̃g]
J'ai reçu du shampoing dans les yeux et ça fait mal. -I got shampoo in my eyes and it hurts.

7081 constellation — **constellation**

	f [kɔ̃stelasjɔ̃]	The constellation consists of six satellites with dual-frequency GPS receivers on board. -Cette constellation comprend six satellites équipés de récepteurs GPS bifréquence.
7082	**brouille** f [bʁuj]	**quarrel** Gaius et moi, avons eue une petite brouille. -Gaius and me, we had a bit of a falling out.
7083	**renne** m [ʁɛn]	**reindeer** En Suède, environ 2500 autochtones samis ont le droit d'élever le renne. -In Sweden, about 2500 Indigenous Samí people have the right to raise reindeer.
7084	**rallier** vb [ʁalje]	**rally** C'est peut-être notre dernière occasion de nous rallier derrière Nabucco. -This is possibly our last opportunity to rally behind Nabucco.
7085	**mongol** adj; m|mpl [mɔ̃gɔl]	**Mongolian; Mongol|retard** Il n'y aurait pas tout ce grabuge si les gens pensaient que ce mongol était normal. -There wouldn't be all this breast-beating if the folks thought the 'tard was normal.
7086	**idéaliste** adj; m/f [idealist]	**idealistic; idealist** On a dit tout à l'heure que je devais être l'idéaliste de service, le fabricant de rêves ! -Someone said earlier that I must be the idealist around here, the dream maker.
7087	**barricader** vb [baʁikade]	**barricade** Barricadez-vous dans mon bureau. -Barricade yourself in my office.
7088	**format** m [fɔʁma]	**format** FORMAT PDF Le Rapport du comité est disponible en format PDF (Portable Document Format). -PDF FORMAT The Committee report is available in PDF format (Portable Document Format).
7089	**glaive** m [glɛv]	**sword** Et le démon tomba sous son glaive... -And the demon fell beneath his sword...
7090	**pouffiasse** f [pufjas]	**bitch** C'est pas illégal, pouffiasse. -It's not illegal, bitch.
7091	**complexité** f [kɔ̃plɛksite]	**complexity** Cette différence tient à une complexité de la régulation, par opposition à une complexité structurelle. -The answer is that it is a complexity of regulation as opposed to a complexity of structure.
7092	**diamètre** m[djamɛtʁ]	**diameter** Formez des boules de 3 cm de diamètre et déposez-les sur une feuille de papier d'aluminium beurrée. -Make balls 3 centimeters in diameter and place them on a sheet of buttered aluminum foil.
7093	**prostate** f [pʁɔstat]	**prostate** Votre prostate ne m'inquiète pas. -And I'm not at all concerned about your prostate.
7094	**clitoris**	**clitoris**

m
[klitɔʁis]

Excision - ablation du clitoris et ablation partielle ou totale de la labia minora.
-Excision - removal of clitoris and part or total excision of the labia minora.

7095 **imam** **imam**

m
[imam]

J'ai été très occupé depuis que la communauté m'a nommé imam remplaçant.
-I have been very busy since the community named me fill-in imam.

7096 **confidentialité** **confidentiality**

f
[kɔ̃fidɑ̃sjalite]

Le principe de la confidentialité des communications client-avocat connaît toutefois des exceptions.
-There are certain exceptions to the principle of the confidentiality of solicitor-client communications, however.

7097 **considérablement** **greatly**

adv
[kɔ̃sideʁabləmɑ̃]

Troisièmement, l'aide publique au développement doit être considérablement accrue.
-Thirdly, official development assistance should be increased considerably.

7098 **visibilité** **visibility**

f
[vizibilite]

Impossible de la réparer sans visibilité.
-There was no way to do the repair without visibility.

7099 **prématuré** **premature**

adj
[pʁematyʁe]

Hoppenstedt a cité le premier débat sur l'euro, où l'euro a été appelé un bébé prématuré.
-Mr Hoppenstedt quoted from the first debate on the euro, in which the euro was called a premature baby.

7100 **bienfait** **kindness**

m
[bjɛ̃fɛ]

L'amitié d'un grand homme est un bienfait des dieux.
-The friendship of a great man is a gift from the gods.

7101 **argentin** **Argentine**

adj
[aʁʒɑ̃tɛ̃]

La Commission interaméricaine a accepté cette proposition du gouvernement argentin.
-The Commission accepted the proposal of the Argentine Government.

7102 **incision** **incision|cut**

f
[ɛ̃sizjɔ̃]

Nous débuterons par une incision elliptique ici.
-We'll probably start with an elliptical incision here.

7103 **sort** **whereabouts|fate**

m
[sɔʁ]

Les recherches concernant le sort du capitaine Speicher se poursuivent.
-Efforts to determine Captain Speicher's fate and whereabouts continue.

7104 **conjugal** **conjugal|marital**

adj
[kɔ̃ʒygal]

La supposition par exemple de l'obligation d'obéissance pour l'épouse limite les droits conjugaux et procréatifs de celle-ci et la rend vulnérable au viol conjugal.
-The assumption, for instance, of a wifely duty of obedience restricted the woman's marital and reproductive rights and left her open to marital rape.

7105 **laideur** **ugliness**

f
[lɛdœʁ]

La mode est une forme de laideur si intolérable que nous devons la changer tous les six mois.
-Fashion is a form of ugliness so intolerable that we have to alter it every six months.

7106 **aisé** **easy|fluent**

adj
[eze]

Notre pays a un bon système de soins de santé et sa population est généralement instruite et aisée.
-Our country has a good health care system and its population is generally educated and fairly well off.

7107	**multitude**	**multitude**
	f	Il existe une multitude d'organisations économiques, régionales et de coopération.
	[myltityd]	-There is a multitude of economic, regional and cooperation organizations.

7108	**faufiler**	**baste|dodge**
	vb	Existe -t-il une possibilité de se faufiler entre les catégories budgétaires?
	[fofile]	-Will there be possibilities for transferring between the budget categories?

7109	**rafle**	**raid**
	f	L'employeur de l'auteur était convaincu que la rafle avait eu lieu parce que la police avait un informateur parmi le personnel.
	[ʁafl]	-The employer believed that the raid occurred because there was a police informer among the staff.

7110	**amas**	**heap**
	m	Quand vous sauterez dans l'amas, vous serez désorientés.
	[ama]	-When you jump into the cluster, you will be disoriented.

7111	**impie**	**impious**
	adj	Et ceci est un repaire impie où toute forme de sortilège est possible.
	[ɛ̃pi]	-And this is an unholy lair where all manner of enchantment is possible.

7112	**grillage**	**roasting**
	m	Clôture d'enceinte, grillage en fil de fer et clôture en fil de fer barbelé, La Reforma
	[gʁijaʒ]	-Perimetre enclosure at the La Reforma penal centre, constructed of wire mesh and a barbed wire fence.

7113	**gober**	**swallow**
	vb	Tu crois que je vais gober ça ?
	[gɔbe]	-You think I will just swallow that?

7114	**affectueusement**	**fondly**
	adv	À son épouse, que nous appelions affectueusement Madi, je tiens aussi à exprimer mon affection.
	[afɛktɥøzmɑ̃]	-To his widow, whom we affectionately called Madi, I express as well my fondness.

7115	**reconstituer**	**reconstruct|put together**
	vb[ʁəkɔ̃stitɥe]	Il nous faudra du temps pour reconstituer nos forces de défense et de police.
		-It will take time for us to reconstitute the defence and police forces.

7116	**incertitude**	**uncertainty**
	f	Nous créons de l' incertitude et l' incertitude nuit au développement économique.
	[ɛ̃sɛʁtityd]	-We are creating uncertainty, and uncertainty is detrimental to economic development.

7117	**promoteur**	**sponsor**
	m	L'invention concerne un promoteur isolé du maïs.
	[pʁɔmɔtœʁ]	-The invention is directed to a promoter isolated from maize.

7118	**poutre**	**beam**
	f	Le retrait de la poutre porteuse a fragilisé la structure du bâtiment.
	[putʁ]	-The removal of the load-bearing beam compromised the structure of the building.

7119	**surplus**	**surplus**
	m	J'ai acheté un sac à dos au surplus militaire.
	[syʁply]	-I bought a backpack at the army surplus store.

7120	**rocheux**	**rocky**

| | | adj [ʁɔʃø] | Sa surface généralement plane présente de légères ondulations et quelques affleurements rocheux.
-Much of the country is flat with gentle undulations and occasional rocky outcrops. |

7121 tralala — splurge|blabla

int
[tʁalala]

Beaucoup de tralala pour rien... comme ces pièces du début du siècle.
-Big fuss over nothing... like all early 20th century Venetians.

7122 passionnant — exciting

adj
[pasjɔnɑ̃]

Je n'ai jamais pensé que ça serait aussi passionnant.
-I never thought it would be so exciting.

7123 clairière — clearing

f
[klɛʁjɛʁ]

Cette route conduit à la clairière.
-This road will take us straight through the clearing.

7124 périlleux — perilous|hazardous

adj
[peʁijø]

Les conditions de conduite sont extrêmement périlleuses dans toute la zone de la Mission.
-Extremely hazardous driving conditions exist throughout the Mission area.

7125 entracte — intermission; entr'acte

m; adj
[ɑ̃tʁakt]

Quand est-ce qu'est l'entracte ?
-When is the intermission?

7126 sanitaire — sanitary; sanitation

adj
[sanitɛʁ]

Je voudrais vous parler d'une initiative sanitaire critique...
-I wanted to talk to you about a critical health initiative...

7127 intriguer — intrigue

vb
[ɛ̃tʁige]

Ça s'est mis à m'intriguer.
-I became intrigued.

7128 exiler — exile

vb
[ɛgzile]

L'exiler serait une erreur aux conséquences incalculables.
-To exile him would be a mistake, with incalculable consequences.

7129 truck — truck

m
[tʁyk]

Je retournerai pas dans le truck.
-No, I'm not getting back in that truck.

7130 flairer — smell|scent

vb
[fleʁe]

Ils ont du flairer notre présence.
-They must have caught our scent.

7131 spontané — spontaneous

adj
[spɔ̃tane]

Le recours spontané à cette pratique se poursuit aujourd'hui contre les Hongrois.
-The spontaneous legacy of this practice continues today against Hungarians.

7132 congrégation — congregation

f
[kɔ̃gʁegasjɔ̃]

Congrégation russe de l'Église chrétienne pentecôtiste estonienne de Lasnamäe.
-Russian Congregation of the Estonian Christian Pentecostal Church in Lasnamäe;

7133 mollir — weaken|soften

vb
[mɔliʁ]

C'est pas le moment de mollir, Marchelier.
-It's not the time to soften up, Marchelier.

7134 créneau — niche

	m	Accordez-nous s'il vous plait un créneau de 20 à 30 minutes pour notre présentation.
	[kʁeno]	-Please give us a 20-30 min. time slot for our presentation.
7135	**tonalité**	**tone|tonality**
	f	Chantes-tu toujours cette chanson dans cette tonalité ?
	[tɔnalite]	-Do you always sing this song in this key?
7136	**climatique**	**climatic**
	adj	Nous avons la convention de Kyoto, qui vise à prévenir un changement climatique.
	[klimatik]	-We have the Kyoto agreement, which is aimed at preventing climatic change.
7137	**preste**	**nimble**
	adj	La travailleuse qui preste au moins 7 h 30 sur une journée a droit à deux pauses, à prendre en une ou deux fois.
	[pʁɛst]	-The female worker who works at least 7 1/2 hours in one day has the right to two breaks, to be taken together or separately.
7138	**péage**	**toll**
	m	Il vous faut la monnaie exacte pour payer le péage de l'autoroute.
	[peaʒ]	-You need to have exact change to pay the toll of the expressway.
7139	**patriotique**	**patriotic**
	adj	La seule femme candidate est Francisca Vaz Turpin de l'Union patriotique guinéenne.
	[patʁijɔtik]	-The only female candidate is Francisca Vaz Turpin of the Guinean Patriotic Union.
7140	**restriction**	**restriction**
	f	La restriction des prestations elles-mêmes est toutefois encore en discussion.
	[ʁɛstʁiksjɔ̃]	-The restriction of the services themselves is, however, still under discussion.
7141	**pécher**	**sin**
	vb	C'est inhabituel qu'un pécheur comblé soit malheureux de pécher.
	[peʃe]	-It's just so unusual for a successful sinner to be unhappy about sin.
7142	**étourdir**	**stun|surprise**
	vb	Ces éjections du Choujaio te permettront d'étourdir les démons que tu croiseras.
	[etuʁdiʁ]	-Daze and confuse demons with these Choujaio pop-up attacks.
7143	**corral**	**corral**
	m	The other side of the buffalo corral.
	[kɔʁal]	-De l'autre côté du corral à bisons.
7144	**écoutille**	**hatch|hatchway**
	f	Susan, emmenez-les à l'écoutille.
	[ekutij]	-Wait, Susan, you take everybody to the hatch.
7145	**irritable**	**irritable|prickly**
	adj	On indique souvent que l'enfant est moins irritable ou agressif, pleure moins et s'exprime mieux sur ses sentiments.
	[iʁitabl]	-Most likely to indicate child is less irritable or aggressive, cries less and can articulate feelings better.
7146	**passible**	**liable to**
	adj	Toute infraction à cet article est passible des peines prévues par la loi.
	[pasibl]	-Violation of this article is liable to punishment in accordance with the law".
7147	**légalité**	**legality**

	f	La légalité constitutionnelle de ces règlements municipaux a été contestée.
	[legalite]	-The constitutional legality of those laws was challenged.
7148	**persuasion**	**persuasion**
	f	Le respect des règlements scolaires par les enfants est obtenu par la persuasion.
	[pɛʁsɥazjɔ̃]	-The implementation of school rules by the children is achieved through persuasion.
7149	**dialecte**	**dialect**
	m	En général, un dialecte alémanique est utilisé dans la conversation.
	[djalɛkt]	-In general, an Alemannic dialect of German is used as the conversational language.
7150	**effronté**	**cheeky|brazen**
	adj	Son meurtrier s'est montré si effronté que les passants ont pris les balles pour des pétards.
	[efʁɔ̃te]	-So brazen was his killer, that passers-by mistook the bullets for firecrackers.
7151	**dada**	**hobbyhorse|pet subject**
	m	C'est le grand dada d'Andy.
	[dada]	-That's a big hobby with Andy.
7152	**désamorcer**	**defuse**
	vb	Il faut désamorcer les tensions suscitées par l'occupation et la colonisation.
	[dezamɔʁse]	-It was imperative to defuse the tension caused by the occupation and colonization.
7153	**conteneur**	**container**
	m	Remplacer "conteneur ou véhicule" par "véhicule, conteneur ou citerne".
	[kɔ̃tnœʁ]	-Replace "container or vehicle" with "vehicle, container or tank" (twice).
7154	**supercherie**	**deception|trickery**
	f	Ce serait presque amusant si ce n'était pas une telle supercherie.
	[sypɛʁʃəʁi]	-It would almost be funny if it was not such an act of deception.
7155	**recharge**	**recharge**
	f	Obtenez une prescription et vous aurez une recharge.
	[ʁəʃaʁʒ]	-Get a prescription, and you can have a refill.
7156	**extrémiste**	**extremist; extremist**
	adj; m/f	En outre est interdit la menée d'une activité extrémiste dans le cadre de réunions.
	[ɛkstʁemist]	-Also, the development of extremist activity in meetings is forbidden.
7157	**grappe**	**cluster**
	f	Il est incontestable que les munitions en grappe causent des préjudices humanitaires.
	[gʁap]	-The evidence of humanitarian damage caused by cluster munitions is compelling.
7158	**entailler**	**cut**
	vb	Je vais seulement t'entailler un peu.
	[ɑ̃taje]	-I'll just cut you a bit.
7159	**abaisser**	**lower|diminish**
	vb	Nous devons abaisser le statut opérationnel des armes nucléaires déployées.
	[abese]	-We need to lower the operational status of nuclear weapons that are deployed.
7160	**papoter**	**chatter|babble**
	vb	Je croyais papoter dans le vide.
	[papɔte]	-I thought I was talking to myself again.

7161	**vigile**	**watchman**
	m	Quelqu'un qui témoignera qu'il a poussé le vigile.
	[viʒil]	-And someone who will testify that he pushed the guard.
7162	**abstinence**	**abstinence**
	f	Moins de 10 % d'entre eux seulement pratiquent l'abstinence prônée par
	[apstinãs]	l'Église.
		-Catholics use church-approved periodic abstinence only in single digit percentages.
7163	**indicatif**	**indicative; indicative**
	adj; m	Dois-je également composer l'indicatif ?
	[ɛ̃dikatif]	-Do I have to dial the area code, too?
7164	**rayer**	**strike**
	vb	Je vais rayer « de la Commission ».
	[ʁeje]	-I will strike out "of the Commission".
7165	**repérage**	**tracking**
	m	Invisible pour vos systèmes de repérage.
	[ʁəpeʁaʒ]	-Invisible... to any of your tracking systems.
7166	**pénétration**	**penetration**
	f	L'expertise médicale prouve la pénétration.
	[penetʁasjɔ̃]	-And we do have medical evidence: no doubt about penetration.
7167	**prodiguer**	**give|lavish**
	vb[pʁɔdige]	Car je n'en ai aucun à te prodiguer. -Advice? Because I don't have any to give.
7168	**carapace**	**shell**
	f	Tandis que la carapace est molle, ils s'accouplent.
	[kaʁapas]	-While the shell is soft, they mate.
7169	**turbulence**	**turbulence**
	f	Nous traversons une zone de turbulence.
	[tyʁbylãs]	-Ladies and gentlemen, we're hitting a rough patch of turbulence here.
7170	**expéditeur**	**sender; dispatching**
	m; adj	J'ai directement recherché l'expéditeur.
	[ɛkspeditœʁ]	-I immediately tried to find out about the sender.
7171	**immigrant**	**immigrant; immigrant**
	adj; m	Elle est tombée en amour avec un immigrant russe.
	[imigʁã]	-She fell in love with a Russian immigrant.
7172	**lavande**	**lavender**
	f	De la lavande en fleur s'étendait à perte de vue.
	[lavãd]	-There was lavender in bloom as far as the eye could see.
7173	**aligner**	**align**
	vb	Align the test dummy's midsagittal plane with the centerline of the seat.
	[aliɲe]	-Aligner le plan sagittal médian du mannequin avec l'axe médian du siège.
7174	**convenablement**	**properly**
	adv	Elle nécessite un étalon de réflectance convenablement étalonné et entretenu.
	[kɔ̃vənabləmã]	-A properly calibrated and maintained reflectance standard is required.
7175	**dérobé**	**stolen|robbed**
	adj	Il a dérobé 4000 £ en tant que trésorier du club.
	[deʁɔbe]	-He pilfered 4,000 quid when acting as club treasure
7176	**insouciant**	**carefree|careless**
	adj	C'est un garçon si insouciant qu'il commet très souvent des erreurs.
	[ɛ̃susjã]	-He is such a careless boy that he makes mistakes very often.

7177	**rengainer**	**sheathe**
	vb	Et vous pouvez rengainer votre pistolet.
	[ʁɑ̃gene]	-And you can holster your gun.
7178	**présider**	**preside**
	vb	Madame la Présidente, c' est une satisfaction de vous voir présider cette séance.
	[pʁezide]	-Madam President, it is a joy to see you occupying the President' s chair.
7179	**adoptif**	**adoptive**
	adj	Pour un enfant mineur adoptif l'autorisation est accordée par le père adoptif ou la mère adoptive.
	[adɔptif]	-Permission for adopted minors shall be granted by the adoptive father or mother.
7180	**cheik**	**sheikh**
	m	Je préfère le dire au cheik, personnellement.
	[ʃɛk]	-Well, I'd rather tell that to the Sheik. Personally.
7181	**cote**	**odds|rating**
	f	Moody's et d'autres institutions avaient réduit notre cote de crédit.
	[kɔt]	-Our credit rating was being downgraded by Moody's and others.
7182	**démarrage**	**start-up**
	m	C'est un bon démarrage.
	[demaʁaʒ]	-That's a good start.
7183	**dirigeable**	**dirigible; airship**
	adj; m	De quoi un dirigeable a-t-il l'air ?
	[diʁiʒabl]	-What does an airship look like?
7184	**tourte**	**pie**
	f	Veux-tu une autre part de tourte ?
	[tuʁt]	-Will you have another slice of pie?
7185	**safari**	**safari**
	m	Rummler et moi, nous partons pour un long safari.
	[safaʁi]	-Rummler and I are going on a long safari.
7186	**chuchoter**	**whisper**
	vb	Personne ne doit tousser, éternuer, pleurer, ni même chuchoter.
	[ʃyʃɔte]	-Nobody coughs, nobody sneezes, nobody cries, nobody even whispers.
7187	**soutirer**	**extract**
	vb	Combien d'argent le ministre des Finances compte-t-il encore soutirer aux travailleurs ?
	[sutiʁe]	-How much more money will the minister rip off from workers before he is satisfied?
7188	**passant**	**elapsing; passer-by**
	adj; m	Un avion ne peut distinguer un soldat serbe d'un passant kosovar.
	[pasɑ̃]	-A plane cannot differentiate a Serb soldier from a Kosovar passer-by.
7189	**prédécesseur**	**predecessor**
	m	Comme son prédécesseur, la Constitution, il s'est heurté au mur de la démocratie.
	[pʁedesesœʁ]	-Like its predecessor, the Constitution, it foundered on the rock of democracy.
7190	**Cupidon**	**Cupid**
	nn	Je suis Cupidon, dieu de l'amour.
	[kypidɔ̃]	-I am Cupid, god of love.
7191	**grimace**	**grimace**

f
Denis peut faire la grimace la plus horrible de toute la ville.
[gʁimas]
-Dennis can make the ugliest face in town.

7192 **déficit**   **deficit**
m
Un énorme déficit dans le budget fédéral empoisonne l'économie américaine
[defisi]
depuis de nombreuses années.
-A huge federal budget deficit has been plaguing the American economy for
many years.

7193 **diva**   **diva**
f
La diva m'a offert un travail.
[diva]
-The diva has offered me a job.

7194 **mirage**   **mirage**
m
Mémoire temporelle, comme un mirage.
[miʁaʒ]
-It's time memory, like a mirage.

7195 **caler**   **stall**
vb
Augmente un peu la puissance pour ne pas caler.
[kale]
-Add a little power so we don't stall.

7196 **corset**   **corset**
m[kɔʁsɛ]
Si tu achetais la bonne taille de corset, je n'aurais pas à me tortiller. -If you
bought me the proper-sized corset, I wouldn't have to squirm.

7197 **mammouth**   **mammoth**
m
Voilà Oscar, notre mammouth colombien.
[mamut]
-This is Oscar, our Colombian mammoth.

7198 **rouquin**   **ginger**
adj
Vous êtes trop petit, rouquin.
[ʁukɛ̃]
-I guess you're too short, red.

7199 **rabaisser**   **belittle**
vb
Mes vis-à-vis rabaissent le processus parlementaire en posant des questions
[ʁabese]
aussi stupides.
-They belittle the parliamentary process by asking such inane questions.

7200 **superflu**   **superfluous|unnecessary**
adj
Certaines délégations ont estimé que ce paragraphe était superflu et qu'il
[sypɛʁfly]
devait être supprimé.
-Some delegations suggested that this paragraph was redundant and should
be deleted.

7201 **physicien**   **physicist**
m
En plus d'être un physicien reconnu, c'est un grand romancier.
[fizisjɛ̃]
-In addition to being a famous physicist, he is a great novelist.

7202 **propreté**   **cleanliness**
f
Il est obsédé par la propreté.
[pʁɔpʁəte]
-He's obsessed with cleanliness.

7203 **tribut**   **tribute**
m
Chaque galère romaine qui part de Brindes leur paye un tribut.
[tʁiby]
-Every Roman galley that sails out of Brundusium pays tribute to them.

7204 **kangourou**   **kangaroo**
m
Imagine que tu démontes le kangourou.
[kɑ̃guʁu]
-Imagine if you fight the kangaroo and beat it.

7205 **emblème**   **emblem**
m
Sélectionnez l'élément auquel vous souhaitez ajouter un emblème.
[ɑ̃blɛm]
-Select the item to which you want to add an emblem.

7206 **récompense**   **reward|award**

f
[ʁekɔ̃pɑ̃s]

Le BSCI note que « récompenser » ne signifie pas nécessairement « promouvoir ».
-OIOS notes that "reward" does not necessarily mean promotion.

7207 **interrogation**   **interrogation|query**

f
[ɛ̃tɛʁɔgasjɔ̃]

Le point d'accès est prévu pour transmettre sans fil des informations de produit dans une zone d'interrogation correspondante.
-The access point is arranged to wirelessly transmit the product information within a corresponding interrogation zone.

7208 **différencier**   **differentiate**

vb
[difeʁɑ̃sje]

La démocratie dans laquelle il est interdit de différencier selon les députés.
-In a democracy, giving preference to some Members over others is forbidden.

7209 **refroidissement**   **cooling**

m
[ʁəfʁwadismɑ̃]

Attendez le complet refroidissement du pain avant de déguster.
-Wait for the bread to completely cool down before eating it.

7210 **fréquentation**   **attendance**

f[fʁekɑ̃tasjɔ̃]

La fréquentation scolaire régulière est chose rare. -The cases of regular school attendance are quite sporadic.

7211 **harnais**   **harness**

m
[aʁnɛ]

Un ensemble harnais est connecté au siège.
-A harness assembly is connected to the seat member.

7212 **odorat**   **smell|sense of smell**

m
[ɔdɔʁa]

Nos yeux, nos oreilles, notre odorat, notre goût différents créent autant de vérités qu'il y a d'hommes sur la terre.
-Our eyes, our ears, our sense of smell, our taste create as many truths as there are men on earth.

7213 **interner**   **intern**

vb
[ɛ̃tɛʁne]

Tous, y compris les réfugiés, ont été internés comme des ennemis du pays.
-All, including the refugees, were interned as enemies of the nation.

7214 **secrétariat**   **secretariat|secretaryship**

m
[səkʁetaʁja]

M. Boulet appuie la suggestion du secrétariat.
-Mr. Boulet expressed support for the Secretariat's suggestion.

7215 **anecdote**   **anecdote**

f
[anɛkdɔt]

C'est peut-être une simple anecdote pour certains, mais c'est une réalité pour nous.
-While this may be a mere anecdote for some, it is a reality for us.

7216 **kérosène**   **kerosene**

m
[keʁozɛn]

On le stabilise dans du kérosène.
-We keep it in kerosene to stabilize it.

7217 **exhiber**   **produce**

vb
[ɛgzibe]

À trop exhiber son hardpower, on court le risque de ruiner son softpower.
-To show too much of one's 'hard power' is to run the risk of ruining one's 'soft power'.

7218 **index**   **index|index finger**

m
[ɛ̃dɛks]

Il a pris un papillon entre le pouce et l'index.
-He picked up a butterfly between his thumb and forefinger.

7219 **visée**   **sight**

f
[vize]

Dispositifs de visée et de vision nocturne, quel qu'en soit le système (passif ou à infrarouges).
-Aiming and night vision mechanisms, whatever their system (passive or infrared).

7220 **agile**   **agile**

		adj [aʒil]	Il s'efforce d'agir de façon stratégique, ciblée, novatrice, dynamique et agile. -The Agency strives to be strategic, focused, innovative, dynamic and agile.
7221	**intellect**	**intellect**	
		m [ɛ̃telɛkt]	Tu n'as jamais développé ton intellect. -That's because you have never developed your intellect.
7222	**organisateur**	**organizer**	
		m [ɔʁganizatœʁ]	Congdon est un orateur dynamique et un organisateur... -Although Congdon was a dynamic speaker and shrewd organizer…
7223	**fondamentalement**	**fundamentally**	
		adv [fɔ̃damãtalmã]	La mondialisation et le commerce international sont fondamentalement positifs. -Globalisation and international trade are fundamentally positive.
7224	**sésame**	**sesame**	
		m [sezam]	Sésame, ouvre-toi ! -Open Sesame!
7225	**carlin**	**pug**	
		m [kaʁlɛ̃]	Et puis, il ressemblait à un carlin. -Plus... it came out lookin' like a pug.
7226	**odyssée**	**odyssey**	
		f [ɔdise]	Jor-El savait qu'il t'envoyait pour une impossible odyssée... -Jor-El knew he was sending you on an impossible odyssey...
7227	**programmation**	**programming**	
		f [pʁɔgʁamasjɔ̃]	Les langages de programmation sont son hobby. -Programming languages are his hobby.
7228	**mondain**	**worldly; man about town**	
		adj; m [mɔ̃dɛ̃]	Tout le Paris, mondain et oisif. -All of Paris, worldly... and idle.
7229	**palet**	**puck**	
		m [palɛ]	Il est de la taille d'un palet. -They're about the same size as a puck.
7230	**concombre**	**cucumber**	
		m [kɔ̃kɔ̃bʁ]	Ce concombre est amer ? Jette-le ! -The cucumber is bitter? Then throw it away!
7231	**raquette**	**racket|bat**	
		f [ʁakɛt]	La nouvelle raquette y fait aussi. -The new racket does it too.
7232	**continuellement**	**continually**	
		adv [kɔ̃tinɥɛlmã]	Ce genre d'évaluation et de vigilance s'effectue continuellement. -That kind of evaluation and assessment is going on constantly.
7233	**manchette**	**cuff**	
		f [mãʃɛt]	On obtient une pluralité d'échantillons de pression lorsque la manchette se gonfle. -A plurality of pressure samples is obtained when the cuff is inflating.
7234	**composant**	**component; compound**	
		m; adj [kɔ̃pozã]	Un sous-formulaire est un " composant auxiliaire du formulaire principal ". -A subform is nothing more than an " additional component of the main form ".
7235	**instructif**	**instructive**	
		adj [ɛ̃stʁyktif]	Elle a été l'occasion d'un débat animé et instructif et a rempli son objectif. -It had generated a lively and informative discussion and fulfilled its objective.

| 7236 | **cinématographique** | **cinematographic** |
| | adj[sinematɔgʁafik] | Le soutien du gouvernement est crucial sur le marché international de l'industrie cinématographique. -Government support for film is crucial in the global market of the film industry. |

7237	**trimer**	**slave away**
	vb	On nous fait trimer, et au bout du compte...
	[tʁime]	-They make us slave away, and at the end...

7238	**ensorceler**	**bewitch**
	vb	ils diraient: "Vraiment nos yeux sont voilés. Mais plutôt, nous sommes des gens ensorcelés".
	[ɑ̃sɔʁsəle]	-They would say, "Our eyes are but spellbound; rather, we have been bewitched!"

7239	**détestable**	**detestable**
	adj	À cet égard, la situation des femmes en Afghanistan me paraît particulièrement détestable.
	[detɛstabl]	-In this respect, the situation of women in Afghanistan seems to me particularly detestable.

7240	**infidélité**	**infidelity**
	f	Layla a dû faire face à des années de maltraitance et d'infidélité.
	[ɛ̃fidelite]	-Layla had to cope with years of abuse and infidelity.

7241	**adversité**	**adversity**
	f	Nous devons apprendre à affronter l'adversité avec grâce.
	[advɛʁsite]	-We must learn to meet adversity gracefully.

7242	**docile**	**docile|obedient**
	adj	Il me semble qu'elle n'est pas aussi docile que certains le suggéraient ou l'espéraient au sein de la coalition.
	[dɔsil]	-It seems to me that it is not quite so docile as many in the coalition suggested or hoped.

7243	**potager**	**kitchen garden**
	m	Journées du potager au Chateau de Villandry 26 - 27 septembre 2009.
	[pɔtaʒe]	-The Kitchen Garden Festival 26 - 27 septembre 2009.

7244	**limpide**	**limpid**
	adj	Un message limpide, qui s'adresse également aux séparatistes.
	[lɛ̃pid]	-This sends a clear message to the parties concerned, and to the separatists too.

7245	**sécession**	**secession**
	f	La sécession du Haut-Karabakh de l'Azerbaïdjan a été pacifique, légale et juste.
	[sesesjɔ̃]	-Nagorny Karabakh's secession from Azerbaijan was peaceful, legal and just.

7246	**gâteux**	**senile; dotard**
	adj; m/f	Non, il est simplement gâteux.
	[gatø]	-No, he's just senile.

7247	**minéral**	**mineral; mineral**
	adj; m	Australasian Code for Reporting of Identified Mineral Resources and Mineral Ore Reserves.
	[mineʁal]	-Australasian Code for Reporting of Mineral Resources and Ore Reserves.

7248	**guimauve**	**marshmallow**
	f	Les adultes attendront la deuxième guimauve.
	[gimov]	-Well, adults will just wait for the second marshmallow.

| 7249 | **parenté** | **relationship\|kindred** |

	f	Jack a-t-il un lien de parenté avec Jill ?
	[paʁɑ̃te]	-Is Jack related to Jill?
7250	**partenariat**	**partnership**
	m	Le partenariat est une condition importante, y compris le partenariat avec les ONG.
	[paʁtənaʁja]	-Partnership is an important precondition, including partnership with NGOs.
7251	**régir**	**govern**
	vb	Cela représente une crise fondamentale des valeurs qui devraient régir le monde.
	[ʁeʒiʁ]	-That is a fundamental challenge to the values that should govern the world.
7252	**butte**	**mound | butt**
	f	Ne joue plus sur la butte.
	[byt]	-I don't want you playing out on the mound.
7253	**procuration**	**proxy**
	f	Représenter Okanagan-Centre comporte trois dimensions: mandat, procuration, tutelle.
	[pʁɔkyʁasjɔ̃]	-Being the representative of Okanagan Centre incorporates three dimensions, mandate, proxy and trusteeship.
7254	**brailler**	**bawl | scream**
	vb	Arrête de brailler et va dormir.
	[bʁaje]	-Stop hollering and go to bed.
7255	**dindon**	**turkey**
	m	On pourra y manger votre dindon.
	[dɛ̃dɔ̃]	-We can eat your turkey there.
7256	**bourdon**	**bee | drone**
	m	Certaines personnes acceptent leur statut de bourdon.
	[buʁdɔ̃]	-Some people accept their position as a drone.
7257	**gradin**	**bench | tier**
	m	Ce gradin provoque une usure accélérée localisée.
	[gʁadɛ̃]	-This step causes localized accelerated wear.
7258	**illumination**	**illumination**
	f	L'illumination n'arrive jamais ainsi.
	[ilyminasjɔ̃]	-Enlightenment will never come that way.
7259	**hublot**	**porthole**
	m	Il a choisi toute Ia cabine ou juste Ie hublot ?
	[yblo]	-Did he pick out the whole room or just the porthole?
7260	**éblouissant**	**dazzling**
	adj	L'affichage doit être muni d'un éclairage non éblouissant.
	[ebluisɑ̃]	-The display shall be provided with adequate non-dazzling lighting.
7261	**gallois**	**Welsh; Welsh**
	adj; m | mpl	Les établissements scolaires utilisent également le gallois dans l'enseignement.
	[galwa]	-Schools also use Welsh as the medium of teaching.
7262	**graphique**	**graphic; graph**
	adj; m[gʁafik]	Ce graphique détaille les différents postes de coûts impliqués dans la production de l'iPad. -This graph breaks down the different costs involved in producing the iPad.
7263	**morve**	**snot**
	f	La morve jaillit de mon nez.
	[mɔʁv]	-Snot is pouring out of my nose.
7264	**domino**	**domino**

	m	L'effet domino sur toutes les autres industries serait colossal.
	[dɔmino]	-The domino effect it would have on all other industries would be outrageous.
7265	**glander**	**screw around**
	vb	Il est occupé à glander à son poste.
	[glɑ̃de]	-He is busy loafing on the job.
7266	**hernie**	**hernia**
	f	Si les résultats sont bons, il sera opéré d'une hernie et d'une hydrocèle.
	[ɛʁni]	-If positive, he will then be operated upon for a hernia and hydrocele condition.
7267	**latrines**	**latrines**
	fpl	Frappe quand elle est aux latrines.
	[latʁin]	-Get her while she's on the latrine.
7268	**virement**	**transfer**
	m	Il montera une fois le virement passé.
	[viʁmɑ̃]	-We'll send him up... when the transfer is complete.
7269	**intersection**	**intersection**
	f	Les objets 3D n' autorisent pas les opérations de soustraction et d' intersection.
	[ɛ̃tɛʁsɛksjɔ̃]	-With 3D objects, subtraction and intersection operations are not possible.
7270	**conspirateur**	**conspirator; conspiratorial**
	m; adj	C'est le premier conspirateur à qui j'aie eu affaire.
	[kɔ̃spiʁatœʁ]	-He was the first conspirator that I ever dealt with.
7271	**individuel**	**individual|private**
	adj	Ils exerceront leurs fonctions à titre individuel et en toute indépendance.
	[ɛ̃dividɥɛl]	-They shall serve strictly in their personal capacity and enjoy full independence.
7272	**dard**	**dart|stinger**
	m	Le dard trouvé en vous a pu transporter les embryons de la créature.
	[daʁ]	-I believe the stinger we found in you may have carried the creature's embryos.
7273	**progressivement**	**progressively**
	adv	La langue portugaise est progressivement introduite dans le système scolaire.
	[pʁɔgʁesivmɑ̃]	-Portuguese language is progressively being introduced into the school system.
7274	**truffe**	**truffle**
	f[tʁyf]	Victor et lui sont comme deux cochons se disputant la même truffe. -He and Victor think so much alike now they're like two pigs reaching for the same truffle.
7275	**thermomètre**	**thermometer**
	m	Le thermomètre affiche 10 degrés.
	[tɛʁmɔmɛtʁ]	-The thermometer reads 10 degrees.
7276	**fraction**	**fraction**
	f	Cette glace couvre une fraction de nos besoins.
	[fʁaksjɔ̃]	-This ice represents a fraction of what we need to stay alive.
7277	**incarnation**	**incarnation**
	f	L'incarnation du corps, votre sherpa du suspense.
	[ɛ̃kaʁnasjɔ̃]	-The incarnation body, your sherpa of suspense.
7278	**tardif**	**late**

	adj	Je pensais à un dîner européen tardif.
	[taʁdif]	-I thought maybe he wanted to have a late European dinner.
7279	**redoubler**	**redouble**
	vb	La communauté internationale doit redoubler d'efforts dans ce domaine.
	[ʁəduble]	-The international community needed to redouble its efforts in that regard.
7280	**sarcasme**	**sarcasm**
	m	Dois-je entendre un sarcasme ?
	[saʁkasm]	-Do I detect sarcasm?
7281	**patinage**	**skating**
	m	Un des sports d'hiver que beaucoup de personnes apprécient est le patinage sur glace.
	[patinaʒ]	-A winter sport that many people enjoy is ice skating.
7282	**indigestion**	**indigestion**
	f	Cet après-midi, nous avons vu un exemple du genre d'indigestion que cela peut causer.
	[ɛ̃diʒɛstjɔ̃]	-This afternoon we have seen an example of some of the indigestion which that can cause.
7283	**gainer**	**sheathe**
	vb	Un mécanisme de gainage est configuré pour sertir et gainer totalement le dispositif implantable avant une procédure de déploiement.
	[gene]	-A sheathing mechanism is configured to crimp and fully sheathe the implantable device prior to a deployment procedure.
7284	**apôtre**	**apostle**
	m	Certainement parce qu'il se sentait une certaine affinité avec l'Apôtre des Gentils.
	[apotʁ]	-Certainly because he felt a special affinity with the Apostle of the Gentiles.
7285	**rejouer**	**replay**
	vb	Il nous a demandé de le rejouer et de le rejouer, six fois.
	[ʁəʒwe]	-He asked us to play again and again, six times.
7286	**aquatique**	**aquatic**
	adj	Il sera complété ultérieurement par un parc aquatique.
	[akwatik]	-In the future, the entertainment facility will be enhanced by an aqua park.
7287	**divinité**	**divinity**
	f[divinite]	En vérité, votre seul Dieu est Allah en dehors de qui il n'y a point de divinité. -Your only deity is Allah, other than Whom there is no deity.
7288	**trier**	**sort**
	vb	Définissez la colonne à trier (par ex. " Montant ") comme critère de tri et cliquez sur OK.
	[tʁije]	-In the dialog that appears, select the column to be sorted, e.g. " Amount ", as the sort criterion and click OK.
7289	**astronomie**	**astronomy**
	f	C'est un expert en astronomie.
	[astʁɔnɔmi]	-He is an expert in astronomy.
7290	**intensif**	**intensive**
	adj	Un programme intensif d'élaboration des politiques a alors été mis en route.
	[ɛ̃tɑ̃sif]	-Following this report, an intensive programme of policy development was started.
7291	**inconcevable**	**inconceivable**
	adj	Il est inconcevable qu'une femme accusée d'adultère soit toujours lapidée.
	[ɛ̃kɔ̃səvabl]	-It is inconceivable that a woman accused of adultery can still be stoned.
7292	**climatisation**	**air-conditioning**

f
[klimatizasjɔ̃]

Les bureaux n'ont pas encore de climatisation malgré l'approche de l'été.
-The offices had not yet been air-conditioned, despite the approaching summer heat.

7293 **store**
m
[stɔʁ]

blind | awning
Lorsque le store est fermé, les encoches sont recouvertes par la latte adjacente suivante.
-When the blind is closed, notches are covered by the next adjacent slat.

7294 **paradoxe**
m
[paʁadɔks]

paradox
J'appellerai cela le paradoxe suédois.
-I should like to call this a 'Swedish paradox'.

7295 **limace**
f
[limas]

slug
J'en ai assez d'être une limace.
-I am so sick of moving like a slug.

7296 **bookmaker**
m
[bɔɔkmake]

bookmaker
Le troisième est un bookmaker hassidique.
-Okay. The third is a Hasidic bookie.

7297 **scalp**
m
[skal]

scalp
Renard Roux veut son premier scalp.
-Red Fox wants to get his first scalp.

7298 **confidence**
f
[kɔ̃fidɑ̃s]

confidence
Il n'a pas mis le Parlement dans la confidence, ce qu'il aurait dû faire.
-He has not taken this House into his confidence, which he should have done.

7299 **gingembre**
m
[ʒɛ̃ʒɑ̃bʁ]

ginger
Poulet grillé aux herbes et purée de gingembre.
-Chicken on the grill with a celebration of local herbs, and ginger mash potato.

7300 **ranimer**
vb
[ʁanime]

revive | rekindle
Nous avons au contraire voulu ranimer le triangle institutionnel.
-On the contrary, we wanted to revive the institutional triangle.

7301 **fraîchement**
adv
[fʁɛʃmɑ̃]

freshly
Je me réjouis de voir des visages familiers et nouveaux dans ce Parlement fraîchement élu.
-It is good to see familiar faces and new faces alike in this new Parliament.

7302 **écouteur**
m
[ekutœʁ]

listener | earpiece
Un système et un écouteur sont également divulgués.
-A system and an earphone are also disclosed in the present invention.

7303 **couramment**
adv
[kuʁamɑ̃]

fluently
parle couramment l'anglais et le français et exerce le droit seul à Ottawa.
-Bilodeau is fluently bilingual and is a sole practitioner in Ottawa.

7304 **bronzé**
adj
[bʁɔ̃ze]

tanned | brown
Mon père était grand et bronzé.
-My dad was tall and tan.

7305 **planque**
f; adj
[plɑ̃k]

stash; plummy
Les flics recherchent la planque de la bande.
-The cops are looking for the gang's hideout.

7306 **chauffard**
m
[ʃofaʁ]

roadhog
Il prend son pied à conduire comme un chauffard.
-He gets a kick out of reckless driving.

7307 **sollicitude**

solicitude

f
[sɔlisityd]

Il tient ici à les remercier vivement pour leur sollicitude et leur compréhension.
-He would hereby like to thank them warmly for their concern and understanding.

7308 catéchisme   **catechism**

m
[kateʃism]

Nous étions en train de réviser notre catéchisme.
-We were just having a review of our catechism.

7309 embrayage   **clutch**

m
[ãbʀɛjaʒ]

En pressant de manière répétitive la pédale d'embrayage, j'ai quelque peu réussi à désolidariser l'embrayage de telle sorte que j'ai pu rouler pendant un moment.
-Repeatedly slamming the clutch pedal, I somehow managed to get the clutch disengaged so I could just about drive for the time being.

7310 ourse   **bear; ursine**

f; adj
[uʀs]

J'ai enfin trouvé ma maman ourse.
-It's like I finally found my lady bear.

7311 mesa   **mesa**

f
[mesa]

Placez les deux meilleurs tireurs en haut de la mesa.
-And position the two best marksmen we've got left on top of the mesa.

7312 péninsule   **peninsula**

f
[penɛ̃syl]

La déclunéarisation de la péninsule coréenne est cruciale pour la sécurité.
-Denuclearization of the Korean Peninsula is the key to security on the Peninsula.

7313 loulou   **spitz**

m
[lulu]

Et là, ton loulou veut te manger.
-Yes, now your booger is trying to eat you.

7314 tutelle   **guardianship|tutorship**

f
[tytɛl]

Ces personnes sont placées sous tutelle.
-A guardianship shall be established for such persons.

7315 érable   **maple**

m
[eʀabl]

Chaque pièce représente l'édifice du Centre dans une feuille d'érable stylisée.
-Each piece features an image of the Centre Block in a stylized maple leaf.

7316 occupant   **occupant; occupying**

m; adj
[ɔkypã]

Cette situation peut blesser l'occupant au niveau des côtes.
-This situation may cause injury to the occupant's ribs.

7317 aventurer   **venture**

vb
[avãtyʀe]

Pour aller chercher de l'eau, c'était tout une aventure qu'elles accomplissaient au péril de leur vie.
-To search for water is a huge trial that they risk their lives to undertake.

7318 paresse   **laziness**

f
[paʀɛs]

Il a été grondé par son instituteur pour sa paresse.
-He was scolded by his teacher for being lazy.

7319 contracter   **contract**

vb
[kɔ̃tʀakte]

Comme la saison froide s'installe, les gens qui ne sont pas en si bonne santé ont des chances de contracter des rhumes.
-As the cold season sets in, people who aren't so healthy are likely to catch colds.

7320 conventionnel   **conventional**

adj
[kɔ̃vãsjɔnɛl]

Le nombre conventionnel "d", indiquant le diamètre nominal de la jante;
-The conventional number "d" denoting the nominal rim diameter;

7321 preneur   **taker**

m
[pʁanɶʁ]

Le BSCI sait qu'un preneur de note établit les minutes des réunions et les distribue aux membres du Conseil de direction.
-OIOS is aware that a note taker prepares meeting minutes and distributes these to members of the Senior Management Group.

7322 **théoriquement** — **theoretically**

adv
[teɔʁikmã]

C'est théoriquement un grand progrès, mais la théorie ne se retrouve guère dans la pratique.
-This represents important progress in theory which has not amounted to much in practice.

7323 **radioactif** — **radioactive**

adj
[ʁadjoaktif]

Le nuage radioactif s'est arrêté à la frontière.
-The radioactive cloud stopped at the border.

7324 **abonnement** — **subscription**

m
[abɔnmã]

Combien coûte l'abonnement à ta salle de sport ?
-How much is the membership fee for your gym?

7325 **autodestruction** — **self-destruction**

f
[otodɛstʁyksjɔ̃]

L'expérience montre que l'autodestruction fonctionne et peut être quasi simultanée.
-Experience has shown that self-destruct works and can be near simultaneous.

7326 **corvette** — **corvette**

f
[kɔʁvɛt]

L'Indonésie, qui a fourni une corvette, est le seul nouveau contributeur au groupe.
-The contribution of a corvette by Indonesia marks the only new maritime contributor.

7327 **réanimation** — **resuscitation**

f
[ʁeanimasjɔ̃]

L'invention concerne des systèmes et procédés d'application d'une réanimation cardiopulmonaire guidée par compression-décompression active.
-Systems and methods for applying guided active compression decompression cardiopulmonary resuscitation are provided.

7328 **marmonnement** — **mumble**

m
[maʁmɔnmã]

Le marmonnement, c'est vraiment agaçant.
-The mumbling, that's really annoying.

7329 **dévaster** — **devastate|destroy**

vb
[devaste]

Le VIH/sida continue de dévaster des communautés dans tout le monde en développement.
-HIV/AIDS continues to devastate communities throughout the developing world.

7330 **roquette** — **rocket**

f
[ʁɔkɛt]

Chaque roquette tirée attise les risques de conflit.
-With each rocket that falls, the explosive potential for conflict rises.

7331 **bienheureux** — **blissful**

adj
[bjɛ̃nɶʁø]

Tu vas voir le bienheureux Simon ?
-You want to see the blessed Simon?

7332 **idéologie** — **ideology**

f
[ideɔlɔʒi]

Si cette idéologie est raciste, colonialiste et injuste, alors je crois qu'il faudrait la qualifier ainsi. Il faut appeler un chat un chat.
-If this ideology is racist, colonialist, and unjust, then I think that's what it must be called. You have to call a spade a spade.

7333 **bourgeoisie** — **bourgeoisie**

	f [buʁʒwazi]	Nous n'attendons rien d'autre d'une institution que la bourgeoisie a créée pour se protéger. -We expect nothing less from an institution created by the bourgeoisie for its own protection.
7334	**Bohême** f [bɔɛm]	**Bohemia** Alors nous attendons un Allemand de Bohême. -So we are to expect a German from Bohemia.
7335	**primordial** adj [pʁimɔʁdjal]	**primary|primordial** l'ADS présentait un intérêt primordial pour les pays en développement. -ADS was of prime importance for developing countries.
7336	**sanatorium** m [sanatɔʁjɔm]	**sanatorium** Je t'avais dit de dire que tu étais dans un sanatorium, pas un sanitaire. -I told you to tell 'em you was in a sanitarium, not sanitation.
7337	**chômeur** m [ʃomœʁ]	**unemployed** Un chômeur suicidaire m'aura égayé. -Then you, suicidal, unemployed, appear...
7338	**chaleureusement** adv [ʃalœʁøzmã]	**warmly|kindly** Je crois que nous pouvons très chaleureusement encourager cette initiative. -I believe that we can very heartily encourage this initiative.
7339	**cyclone** m [siklon]	**cyclone** Pour les victimes du cyclone Nargis, il ne s'agit pas de politique mais de survie. -For the victims of Cyclone Nargis, this is not an issue of politics, but of survival.
7340	**intensément** adv [ɛ̃tãsemã]	**deeply** Le Comité s'est employé intensément à résoudre diverses difficultés liées aux sanctions. -The Committee has worked intensely to address various challenging sanctions-related issues.
7341	**poire** f [pwaʁ]	**pear|sucker** Sur un poirier pousse une poire. -Upon a pear tree grows a pear.
7342	**descendance** f [desãdãs]	**descent** Ces filles finissent souvent dans la prostitution et leur descendance féminine suit le même parcours. -Such girls often ended as prostitutes, as did their female descendants.
7343	**baffe** f [baf]	**swipe** La jeune femme colla une baffe à l'homme qui lui avait pincé les fesses. -The young woman slapped the man who pinched her buttocks.
7344	**baïonnette** f [bajɔnɛt]	**bayonet** Mais mon vieux l'emporte avec sa baïonnette. -'Course, my old man will always have one on me with that bayonet.
7345	**périple** m [peʁipl]	**trek** Nous la suivrons à chaque instant, tout au long de ce périple important pour elle, bien sûr, pour le Canada et pour le Québec. -We will follow her moment by moment throughout this trip, of such importance to her, of course, and Canada and Quebec.
7346	**épilepsie** f; adj [epilɛpsi]	**epilepsy; epileptic** Mais pour l'épilepsie, il faut des médicaments. -But for epilepsy, the only treatment is medication, and this guy won't even listen to me.

7347	**ombrelle**	**umbrella**
	f	Avec cette chaleur, prends donc une ombrelle.
	[ɔ̃bʀɛl]	-With this heat, you should take an umbrella.
7348	**abomination**	**abomination**
	f	Même pour un ancien maoïste, le protectionnisme est une abomination.
	[abɔminasjɔ̃]	-Protectionism is an abomination - even for a former Maoist.
7349	**mammifère**	**mammal**
	m	Le mammifère est mort.
	[mamifɛʀ]	-The mammal is dead.
7350	**amputer**	**amputate|take off**
	vb	Les médecins ont été forcés d'amputer la jambe gauche d'Osher au cours d'une intervention chirurgicale.
	[ãpyte]	-Doctors were forced to amputate Osher's left leg during surgery.
7351	**pouilleux**	**lousy**
	adj[pujø]	Je me sentais moi-même plutôt pouilleux. -I was feeling pretty lousy myself.
7352	**gruau**	**groats**
	m	Quand il était jeune, il était pauvre et il vivait de gruau de riz.
	[gʀyo]	-When he was young, he was poor and had to live on rice gruel.
7353	**autodéfense**	**self-defense**
	f	Notre classe de karaté und autodéfense.
	[otodefãs]	-Und here is our class in karate und self-defence.
7354	**rôdeur**	**lurker; prowler**
	m; f	Juste un animal ou un rôdeur de nuit.
	[ʀodœʀ]	-It's surely an animal or night prowler.
7355	**transporteur**	**carrier|transporter**
	m	Les autorisations sont délivrées au nom du transporteur.
	[tʀãspɔʀtœʀ]	-Authorizations shall be issued in the name of the carrier.
7356	**fusible**	**fuse; fusible**
	m; adj	Le fusible a brûlé.
	[fyzibl]	-The fuse has blown.
7357	**aléatoire**	**aleatory**
	adj	Les enquêtes classiques par échantillonnage aléatoire ont été abandonnées.
	[aleatwaʀ]	-The otherwise normal random sample survey of crops on arable land was dropped.
7358	**viable**	**viable**
	adj	1999 Programme de construction écologiquement viable du Gouvernement finlandais
	[vjabl]	-1999 Finnish Government Programme for Ecologically Sustainable Construction.
7359	**combustion**	**combustion**
	f	Le monoxyde de carbone est une substance mortelle qui résulte de la combustion incomplète de composés carbonés.
	[kɔ̃bystjɔ̃]	-Carbon monoxide is a poisonous substance formed by the incomplete combustion of carbon compounds.
7360	**absurdité**	**absurdity**
	f	C'est une absurdité, et cette absurdité conduirait à d'autres absurdités.
	[apsyʀdite]	-This absurdity would lead to further absurdities.
7361	**perfide**	**perfidious|false**
	adj	L'utilisation de bombes à fragmentation s'est révélée particulièrement perfide.
	[pɛʀfid]	-The use of cluster bombs was particularly perfidious.

7362	**porridge**	**porridge**
	m	Children in primary schools in the area, and indeed throughout the country, are to be provided with a free lunch of porridge and milk.
	[pɔʁidʒ]	-Les enfants des écoles primaires de la région, et même du pays tout entier, recevront un repas de midi gratuit, à base de gruau d'avoine et de lait.
7363	**amiable**	**genial**
	adj	Il s'est dit optimiste quant aux perspectives de règlement amiable satisfaisant.
	[amjabl]	-He expressed optimism about the prospects for an amicable and satisfactory solution.
7364	**éboueur**	**garbage collector|scavenger**
	m	Un éboueur a trouvé quelque chose d'intéressant.
	[ebwœʁ]	-I got a garbage man here says he's got something you might want to see.
7365	**figue**	**fig**
	f	Mais je vous apporte une figue.
	[fig]	-Here? I brought you a fig.
7366	**gaulois**	**Gallic**
	adj	Permettez-moi de citer Astérix le Gaulois à ce propos: "Ils sont fous, ces Français!".
	[golwa]	-Let me quote Asterix the Gaul here: 'They must be crazy, the French!'
7367	**confins**	**confines**
	mpl	Je ne suis qu'un simple citoyen venant des confins de la Beauce.
	[kɔ̃fɛ̃]	-I am only a simple habitant from the borders of the Beauce.
7368	**érudit**	**scholar; erudite**
	m; adj	C'est un écrivain populaire plutôt qu'un érudit.
	[eʁydi]	-He is not so much a scholar as a popular writer.
7369	**devin**	**soothsayer**
	m	Rappelle donc et par la grâce de ton Seigneur tu n'es ni un devin ni un possédé;
	[dəvɛ̃]	-So preach and remind; by God's grace, you are not a soothsayer, nor a madman.
7370	**dignement**	**with dignity**
	adv	Un travail pour lequel on est traité dignement et les droits fondamentaux sont respectés.
	[diɲmɑ̃]	-Work in which they were treated decently and their basic rights were respected.
7371	**torrent**	**torrent**
	m	La petite rivière en bas était rouge: un torrent déchaîné de sang.
	[tɔʁɑ̃]	-The little river below was swollen red, a raging torrent of blood.
7372	**simuler**	**simulate|pretend**
	vb	Je peux la simuler.
	[simyle]	-I can fake it.
7373	**élixir**	**elixir**
	m	Trouvé une recette pour un élixir.
	[eliksiʁ]	-Found a recipe for an elixir.
7374	**écriteau**	**sign**
	m	Malgré l'écriteau « Défense de fumer », l'homme qui dirigeait le bateau fumait tout le temps sans se gêner.
	[ekʁito]	-Despite "No Smoking" signs, the boat operator was brazenly smoking all the time.
7375	**musique**	**music**

f

Ecoutons de la musique.

[myzik]
  -Let's listen to some music.

7376 **kidnappeur**   **kidnapper**

m

Je me rapproche du portable du kidnappeur.

[kidnapœʁ]
  -Finch, I'm closing in on the kidnapper's cell.

7377 **filtre**   **filter; filter**

adj; m

Dans les piscines, l'eau est continuellement pompée à travers un filtre.

[filtʁ]
  -In swimming pools, water is continuously pumped through a filter.

7378 **bienveillant**   **benevolent**

adj[bjɛ̃vɛjã]

Il ne s'agit pas de réforme coloniale, ni de colonialisme « contemporain » ou
« bienveillant ». -It was not colonial reform, or "contemporary" or
"benevolent" colonialism.

7379 **magouille**   **maneuvering**

f

On sait pour votre petite magouille.

[maguj]
  -We know about your little scam.

7380 **couronner**   **top|enthrone**

vb

La présidence a réussi à couronner l'ensemble de son agenda d'un nouveau
traité.

[kuʁɔne]
  -The Presidency has successfully managed to crown its full agenda with a
new treaty.

7381 **méchamment**   **nastily**

adv

Pour un végétarien, tu tires méchamment.

[meʃamã]
  -For a vegetarian, you're a mean shot!

7382 **désastreux**   **disastrous**

adj

Aux effets désastreux de la guerre s'est ajoutée une sécheresse prolongée.

[dezastʁø]
  -The disastrous effects of the war had been compounded by the protracted
drought.

7383 **phénix**   **phoenix**

m

Ceux qui touchent le phénix seront épargnés.

[feniks]
  -Those who touch the Phoenix, they will be spared.

7384 **escrimer**   **fight**

vb

Le Canada ne peut évidemment pas légiférer pour d'autres pays, ni dire à
ceux-ci quoi faire ou s'escrimer avec eux, tant et aussi longtemps qu'ils
observent les règles de l'OMC.

[ɛskʁime]
  -Canada obviously cannot write laws for other countries, or tell them what
to do or argue with them when they are staying within the WTO rules.

7385 **déploiement**   **deployment**

m

Elles ont sûrement beaucoup à faire avant son déploiement.

[deplwamã]
  -I'm sure they have a lot to take care of before deployment.

7386 **médiatique**   **media**

adj

L'environnement médiatique varie vraiment entre les différents pays.

[medjatik]
  -The media environment definitely varies between the individual countries.

7387 **vanner**   **winnow**

vb

On aime tous vanner les plombiers.

[vane]
  -Nothing like a good crack about a plumber.

7388 **respiratoire**   **respiratory**

adj

Irritation du système respiratoire en cas d'émission de poussières du produit

[ʁɛspiʁatwaʁ]
  -In case product dust is released, irritating to respiratory system.

7389 **mixer**   **mixer; blend**

m; vb

Vous pouvez monter et mixer simultanément, rappeler et conformer votre

[mikse]
automation facilement.

-You can Edit and Mix at the same time, recall all your automation and you can easily conform it."

7390	**zéphyr**	**zephyr**
	m[zefiʁ]	C'était une grosse rafale, un zéphyr. -It was one big gust, a zephyr.
7391	**noirceur**	**darkness**
	f [nwaʁsœʁ]	Arrêtez de fuir votre noirceur intérieure. -Stop trying to run from your inner darkness.
7392	**harem**	**harem**
	m [aʁɛm]	Il a été le harem, le harem signifie, les femmes. -It was the harem, the harem meant, women.
7393	**grêle**	**hail; thin**
	f; adj [gʁɛl]	«Help point Grêle» pour un règlement très rapide du sinistre. -«Hail Help Point» – for the quickest claim settlement possible.
7394	**trouer**	**pit**
	vb [TRUE]	Ça n'était pas assez puissant pour trouer la coque ou endommager le système hydraulique, mais suffisant pour tuer. -It wasn't powerful enough to puncture the hole or damage the hydraulic systems, just enough to kill.
7395	**fixation**	**fixing | attachment**
	f [fiksasjõ]	Dispositifs de fixation, notamment implants chirurgicaux. -The invention also relates to fixing devices, in particular, surgical implants.
7396	**collecteur**	**collector**
	m [kɔlɛktœʁ]	C'est un collecteur de fonds pour le parti Démocrate. -He's a Democrat fundraiser.
7397	**goujat**	**cad | boor**
	m [guʒa]	Ce n'est qu'un goujat. -He's nothing but a cad.
7398	**muraille**	**wall**
	f [myʁaj]	Qui va sur la grande muraille conquiert la bravitude. -Who walks on the Great Wall conquers bravitude.
7399	**bonze**	**monk**
	m [bõz]	La vie de bonze est plus tranquille. -I feel more at ease with being a monk.
7400	**impur**	**impure | tainted**
	adj [ɛ̃pyʁ]	Une forme impure, pas le cocktail synthétique... qui fait fureur chez les élites. -It was impure, not the engineered cocktail popular among the educated.
7401	**sceptre**	**scepter**
	m [sɛptʁ]	Que dire de la disparition d'un fils à qui on ne peut laisser son sceptre ? -What of the loss of a son to whom the sceptre cannot be left?
7402	**abracadabra**	**abracadabra**
	m [abʁakadabʁa]	Je crois que ce calmar est un drôle d'abracadabra, lui aussi. -You know, I think Mr. Squid was a little bit hocus-pocus himself.
7403	**prêcheur**	**preachy; preacher**
	adj; m [pʁɛʃœʁ]	Ils me traitent de prêcheur politique. -They say that I'm a political preacher.
7404	**nurse**	**nanny | governess**
	f [nyʁs]	Un bref aperçu avant que sa nurse l'emmène à l'église. -The odd glimpse as she's being swept off to church by her nurse.
7405	**flanquer**	**flank**

vb[flãke]

On peut tout de même pas flanquer Joe dehors. -We can't very well just kick Joe out.

7406 instance
f
[ɛ̃stɑ̃s]

authority

L'instance appropriée est incontestablement la Conférence du désarmement. -The appropriate forum for that is certainly the Conference on Disarmament.

7407 terreux
adj
[tɛʁø]

earthy

Quand je dis qu'un pinot noir a un goût luxueusement terreux avec une pointe de rhubarbe, je ne fais pas semblant. -When I say a Pinot Noir tastes luxuriously earthy with a hint of rhubarb, I'm not faking it.

7408 décamper
vb
[dekɑ̃pe]

decamp|run away

Celui qui voulait lui prendre avait besoin de le faire décamper. -Seems whoever wanted that space might have more motive to make him go away.

7409 firmament
m
[fiʁmamɑ̃]

firmament

Louez-le au firmament de sa puissance. -Praise him in the firmament of his power.

7410 éjecter
vb
[eʒɛkte]

eject|shed

Les munitions en grappe sont conçues pour éjecter des sous-munitions sur un objectif. -Cluster munitions are designed to eject submunitions over a target.

7411 clergé
m
[klɛʁʒe]

clergy

Le clergé est bien connu pour savoir ruser. -Well, clergy have always been noted for their guile.

7412 loque
f
[lɔk]

pile of rags|wreck

Je suis une loque. -I'm a wreck.

7413 étriper
vb
[etʁipe]

gut

Bev a engagé une armée d'avocats pour étriper cette firme. -Bev has hired an army of lawyers to gut this firm.

7414 radis
m
[ʁadi]

radish

Tout est politique, même la culture des radis. -Everything is political, including growing radishes.

7415 échappatoire
f
[eʃapatwaʁ]

evasion

Ce n'est pas une excuse ni une échappatoire. -That is not an excuse, it is not an evasion.

7416 snack
m
[snak]

snack

Maura, voici ton snack de la matinée. -Maura, here is your mid-morning snack.

7417 standing
m
[stɑ̃diŋ]

standing

Les chambres, de taille moyenne, sont confortablement meublées et d'un bon standing. -The medium-sized rooms are comfortably furnished, and of a good standard.

7418 exclusif
adj[ɛksklyzif]

exclusive

Pourquoi traiter l'existence de ces deux voix sur le mode exclusif de la déploration ? -I query whether the only way of dealing with these two views is to deplore them.

7419 effleurer

touch

vb
[eflœʁe]

Le risque avec ce règlement est que nous nous contentons d' effleurer ce problème.
-The risk is that with this particular regulation we are simply playing at the edges.

7420 **aérer**   **air|aerate**

vb
[aeʁe]

Aérer et nettoyer le fût afin d'en ôter tout résidu susceptible de fausser les résultats des essais suivants.
-Ventilate and clean the drum removing any residue likely to affect subsequent tests.

7421 **siamois**   **Siamese; Siamese**

adj; m|mpl
[sjamwa]

Raymour et son frère siamois, Flanigan.
-Raymour and his conjoined twin, Flanigan.

7422 **biceps**   **biceps**

m
[bisɛps]

M. gluteo biceps et tout le gras sous-cutané sont ensuite enlevés.
-The cap muscle (M. gluteo biceps) and all subcutaneous fat are further removed.

7423 **chaudron**   **cauldron**

m
[ʃodʁõ]

Il manque juste le chaudron au tableau.
-We only need a cauldron and we've got a witch's full house.

7424 **virtuel**   **virtual**

adj
[viʁtɥɛl]

Le concept de recensement virtuel s'est révélé être un succès aux Pays-Bas.
-The virtual census has proved to be a successful concept in the Netherlands.

7425 **bénévole**   **voluntary; volunteer**

adj; m
[benevɔl]

Ils apportent une assistance à titre bénévole et avec un appui institutionnel réduit.
-They provide counsel on a voluntary basis, with little institutional support.

7426 **minet**   **kitty**

m
[minɛ]

Prends soin d'elle, minet.
-All right. Kitty, take care of her.

7427 **appréhender**   **apprehend**

vb
[apʁeãde]

Je voudrais exhorter les autorités ougandaises à appréhender les meurtriers.
-I would call on the Ugandan authorities to apprehend the perpetrators of this crime.

7428 **extincteur**   **extinguisher; extinguishing**

m; adj
[ɛkstẽktœʁ]

N'oublie pas d'apporter ton extincteur.
-Just don't forget to bring your fire extinguisher.

7429 **forger**   **forge**

vb
[fɔʁʒe]

Une stratégie sera élaborée pour forger les partenariats nécessaires avec les principaux intervenants de l'aide au développement.
-A strategy will be developed to forge the necessary partnerships with the main actors involved in development aid.

7430 **jeûne**   **fasting**

m[ʒøn]

Je jeûne depuis ce matin en vue de Mulligan. -I've been fasting all day to save room for Mulligan's.

7431 **fascination**   **fascination**

f
[fasinasjõ]

Aussi longtemps que la guerre sera considérée comme perverse, elle aura toujours sa fascination. Quand elle sera considérée comme vulgaire, elle cessera d'être populaire.
-As long as war is regarded as wicked, it will always have its fascination. When it is looked upon as vulgar, it will cease to be popular.

7432 **croissant**   **growing; crescent**

adj; m
[kʁwasɑ̃]

Un sentiment centriste croissant menace de bouleverser le système bipartisan traditionnel des États-Unis d'Amérique.
-Growing centrist sentiment threatens to upset America's traditional two-party system.

7433 azote | **nitrogen**

m
[azɔt]

L'air que nous respirons est constituée d'oxygène et d'azote.
-The air we breathe consists of oxygen and nitrogen.

7434 capricieux | **capricious|whimsical**

adj
[kapʁisjø]

L'histoire s'écoule, capricieuse, au travers d'étranges dédales.
-History is capricious and is given to strange twists.

7435 marionnettiste | **puppeteer**

m/f
[maʁjɔnetist]

Elle est l'extension du marionnettiste.
-They're an extension of the puppeteer.

7436 bécane | **bike**

f
[bekan]

J'oubliais, tu n'as pas de bécane.
-I forgot you don't have a bike.

7437 accélération | **acceleration**

f
[akseleʁasjɔ̃]

Le détecteur d'accélération permet de déterminer les accélérations avec une très haute précision.
-The acceleration sensor is suitable for the highly accurate determination of accelerations.

7438 romarin | **rosemary**

m
[ʁɔmaʁɛ̃]

C'est l'heure d'entretenir le... romarin.
-It's time to trim the... Rosemary.

7439 lubrifier | **lubricate**

vb
[lybʁifje]

Elles doivent être lubrifiées ou réalisées en matériaux autolubrifiants.
-They shall either be lubricated or be constructed of self-lubricating materials.

7440 brunch | **brunch**

m
[bʁɛ̃ʃ]

Heidi Solomon organise un brunch dimanche.
-Heidi Solomon's having a brunch on Sunday.

7441 fellation | **blow job**

f
[felasjɔ̃]

Lorsque les femmes me disent quelles ont des problèmes avec la fellation...
-When women tell me that they have a problem with fellatio...

7442 statique | **static**

adj
[statik]

En outre, le film a des effets dissipatifs à la décharge statique.
-In addition, the film is dissipative to static discharge

7443 autocar | **coach|car**

m[otokaʁ]

Son métier est de conduire un autocar. -His job is driving a sight-seeing bus.

7444 conquérant | **conqueror**

m
[kɔ̃keʁɑ̃]

Un conquérant t'a dominé.
-Oppressed by a conqueror.

7445 bohémien | **Bohemian; Gypsy**

adj; m
[bɔemjɛ̃]

Le poète bohémien Adalbert Stifter, qui a travaillé en Bavière, en Haute-Autriche et en Bohème, unissant les peuples tchèque et allemand, fut une personnalité culturelle des plus éminentes.
-One of the greatest cultural figures was the Bohemian Forest poet Adalbert Stifter, who worked in Bavaria, Upper Austria and Bohemia and united Czech and German people.

7446 reconquérir | **regain|reconquer**

vb
[ʁəkɔ̃keʁiʁ]

Nous devons donc d'abord reconquérir notre identité, notre personnalité culturelle, artistique, linguistique.
-We first of all need to reconquer our own identity - our cultural, artistic and linguistic personality.

7447 sphinx sphinx

m
[sfɛ̃ks]

«Je vous laisserai passer en sécurité» dit le Sphinx, «si vous pouvez répondre à mon énigme.»
-"I will let you pass safely," the Sphinx said, "if you can answer my riddle."

7448 malfaisant evil

adj
[malfəzɑ̃]

Ceux qui mettent en avant des idées malfaisantes sont des hérétiques à l'islam.
-Those who put forward harmful ideas are heretics of Islam.

7449 calomnier slander

vb
[kalɔmnje]

Les députés sont trop occupés à chercher de nouveaux moyen plus imaginatifs de calomnier quelqu'un.
-They are too busy trying to figure out new and cute ways to slander somebody.

7450 fougueux fiery|spirited

adj
[fugø]

Je me suis toujours demandé comment les interprètes et les sténotypistes ont pu suivre le flot fougueux de ses paroles.
-I have always wondered how the interpreters and stenographers managed to follow his fiery speeches.

7451 réclamation complaint

f
[ʁeklamasjɔ̃]

Le Comité estime que la réclamation fait double emploi avec la réclamation chypriote.
-The Panel finds that the claim is a duplicate of the Cyprus claim.

7452 juriste lawyer|jurist

m/f
[ʒyʁist]

Elle a été admise à titre de juriste à la Cour supérieure du Zimbabwe en 1987.
-Was admitted as a legal practitioner of the High Court of Zimbabwe in 1987.

7453 coulant flowing; runner

adj; m
[kulɑ̃]

Il a confectionné un nœud coulant avec les draps de lit et s'est pendu dans sa cellule.
-He fashioned a noose out of the bed sheets and hung himself in his cell.

7454 péquenaud yokel

m[pekno]

Mec, tu cries comme un cochon pour le péquenaud. -Boy, you squeal like a piggy for the hillbilly man.

7455 fatigue fatigue|exhaustion

f
[fatig]

Mon travail me fatigue beaucoup.
-I'm very tired from work.

7456 accomplissement fulfillment|accomplishment

m
[akɔ̃plismɑ̃]

Elle est source d'encouragement pour nous dans l'accomplissement de notre mission ».
-It encourages us in the accomplishment of our mission", the President added.

7457 hérésie heresy

f
[eʁezi]

Il faut stopper les responsables de cette hérésie.
-The people responsible for this heresy need to be stopped in their tracks.

7458 simplet simple-minded

adj
[sɛ̃plɛ]

Il était trop sophistiqué pour un simplet comme Bellamy.
-It was far too sophisticated for anybody as simple as Bellamy.

7459 mémoriser — **memorize**
vb
[memɔʁize]
De nombreux étudiants en physique ne font que mémoriser leurs cours.
-Many physics students merely memorize their physics.

7460 explicite — **explicit**
adj
[ɛksplisit]
Elle doit indiquer de façon explicite que les soins sont temporaires et justifiés.
-The decision should make it explicit that the care is temporary and justified.

7461 gouttière — **gutter**
f
[gutjɛʁ]
De multiples ensembles sont disposés pour recouvrir une gouttière afin d'empêcher l'entrée de débris.
-Multiple assemblies are provided to overlie a gutter to preclude debris entry.

7462 relire — **read back**
vb
[ʁəliʁ]
Vous feriez mieux de relire les commentaires de votre professeur sur votre devoir.
-You had better read your teacher's comments on your compositions one more time.

7463 bénéficier — **gain**
vb
[benefisje]
Cela prouvera à la population qu'elle peut bénéficier de l'indépendance du Timor oriental.
-It will show the population that they gain in an independent East Timor.

7464 radioactivité — **radioactivity**
f
[ʁadjoaktivite]
"Radioactivité" est un terme de la chimie.
-Radioactivity' is a chemistry term.

7465 fleurir — **flower|flourish**
vb
[flœʁiʁ]
Mon bonsaï, qui est un cerisier, commence à fleurir.
-My bonsai, which is the cherry tree, is starting to bloom.

7466 opératoire — **operative**
adj[ɔpeʁatwaʁ]
Il y a eu d'autres annonces concernant la fermeture des services de fournitures médicales et le bloc opératoire de l'hôpital de Dalhousie. -There have been other announcements about cancelling the Dalhousie hospital supply stores and surgical unit.

7467 friture — **frying**
f
[fʁityʁ]
Aucune difficulté d'arrêter la friture après ça.
-No problem going easy on the fried food after this one.

7468 rhétorique — **rhetoric; rhetoric**
adj; f
[ʁetɔʁik]
On a entendu beaucoup de rhétorique et d'engagements, mais le monde ne nous jugera pas d'après la rhétorique.
-There has been much rhetoric and commitment, but the world will not judge us on rhetoric.

7469 indemnité — **allowance**
f
[ɛ̃dɛmnite]
Indemnité de maternité - il s'agit d'une indemnité de remplacement de revenu.
-Maternity leave allowance - this is an income replacement allowance.

7470 titane — **titanium**
m
[titan]
D'abord, j'ai été troublée par le titane.
-At first I was confused by titanium.

7471 sablier — **hourglass**
m
[sablije]
Jill est gaulée comme un sablier.
-Jill is hourglass-shaped.

7472 troll — **troll**

	m	Hans pense que les trolls peuvent être impliqués.
	[tʁɔl]	-Hans thinks it's troll related.

7473 lolo — milk

m
[lɔlo]
Je suis ton petit, et ça c'est mon lolo...
-I am your baby and this is my milk

7474 largeur — width|beam

f
[laʁʒœʁ]
Pour calculer le volume, il faut multiplier la longueur par la largeur puis par la hauteur.
-To calculate the volume, multiply the length by the width by the height.

7475 attachement — attachment

m
[ataʃmã]
Vous trouverez en attachement la facture de TVA correspondant à votre dernier achat.
-Attached you will find the VAT invoice for your recent purchase.

7476 potentiellement — potentially

adv
[pɔtãsjɛlmã]
Le risque d' irrégularités et de fraudes est donc potentiellement très élevé.
-The possibility of irregularities and abuse is therefore potentially very high.

7477 enrôler — enlist|enroll

vb
[ãʁole]
Ils auraient aussi menacé d'enrôler de force les 47 otages dans leurs rangs.
-The hijackers also threatened to forcibly enrol the 47 hostages into the SLM/A (AW) and JEM.

7478 doctrine — doctrine

f
[dɔktʁin]
Notre doctrine est une doctrine de réconciliation; la leur est une doctrine de mort.
-Ours is the doctrine of reconciliation; theirs is the doctrine of death.

7479 obstiné — obstinate|stubborn

adj[ɔpstine]
Jack est obstiné. -Jack is obstinate.

7480 célibat — celibacy

m
[seliba]
Ni leur jeune âge, ni des conceptions culturelles différentes en matière de célibat ne peuvent justifier ces actes de violence.
-Neither their young age, nor different cultural notions regarding celibacy could justify these acts of violence.

7481 cosmétique — cosmetic; cosmetic

adj; m
[kɔsmetik]
Application au traitement cosmétique de la peau.
-The invention is useful for cosmetic treatment of the skin.

7482 contraster — contrast

vb
[kõtʁaste]
Values from -100 % (no contrast at all) to +100 % (full contrast) are possible.
-Les valeurs admises sont comprises entre -100 % (aucun contraste) et +100 % (contraste complet).

7483 soulèvement — uprising|uplift

m
[sulɛvmã]
Le soulèvement hongrois était un soulèvement national, mais aussi politique, en faveur de la démocratie.
-The Hungarian uprising was an uprising for democracy; it was a national uprising, but also a political one.

7484 bienveillance — benevolence

f
[bjɛ̃vɛjãs]
Une certaine marque de sagesse est la réjouissante bienveillance que cela confère.
-A certain hallmark of wisdom is the cheerful benevolence it confers.

7485 éclatant — bright|brilliant

adj
[eklatã]
Elles sont d'un rouge éclatant et très sucrées.
-They're bright red and very sweet.

7486	**pittoresque**	**picturesque**
	adj	Au cœur du Marais animé et pittoresque.
	[pitɔʀɛsk]	-In the heart of the lively, picturesque Marais.

7487	**chaire**	**pulpit|professorship**
	f	LA popularité de la chaire en est venue à avoir une fausse signification.
	[ʃɛʀ]	-PULPIT popularity has come to have a false meaning.

7488	**guêpe**	**wasp**
	f	La guêpe est un insecte de l'ordre hyménoptère.
	[gɛp]	-A wasp is from the insect group hymenoptera.

7489	**adroit**	**skilful|adroit**
	adj	Il semble alors adroit d'avoir recours à l'instrument du règlement.
	[adʀwa]	-It seems a clever move to resort to a regulation.

7490	**autoritaire**	**authoritarian**
	adj	Le style autoritaire avec lequel le président Loekasjenko gouverne est inquiétant.
	[ɔtɔʀitɛʀ]	-President Lukashenko's authoritarian style of government gives cause for alarm.

7491	**errant**	**wandering; wanderer**
	adj; m	Mais cela lui permet d'échapper à ce brouillard oratoire pour aller à la recherche de son troupeau errant.
	[eʀã]	-It gives him a chance, however, to stop listening to the rhetorical fog and go trace his errant flock.

7492	**authenticité**	**authenticity**
	f[otãtisite]	..et l'authenticité des documents présentés par les requérants devant le Conseil. -..and the authenticity of the documents invoked by the complaints before the Board.

7493	**barbarie**	**barbarity**
	f	Ça illustre une nouvelle fois la barbarie humaine.
	[baʀbaʀi]	-You see, it's yet another example of mankind's barbarism.

7494	**délibérer**	**deliberate**
	vb	Il devra délibérer sur l'éventail le plus large de questions concernant l'information.
	[delibeʀe]	-It must deliberate on the broadest range of questions concerning information.

7495	**vulgarité**	**vulgarity**
	f	Le langage utilisé est souvent empreint d'argot, de cynisme, voire de vulgarité.
	[vylgaʀite]	-These terms are often infiltrated by slang, cynicism and even vulgarity.

7496	**paquebot**	**boat**
	m	Il revient avec un luxueux paquebot flottant sur un océan de whisky.
	[pakbo]	-He came back with a big luxury liner... floating on an ocean of whiskey and soda.

7497	**désorienter**	**disorient**
	vb	Ces organisations ont mené de vastes campagnes de propagande pour désorienter les Timorais.
	[dezɔʀjãte]	-These organizations conducted extensive propaganda campaigns to disorientate Timorese.

7498	**autobiographie**	**autobiography**
	f	Tu devrais écrire là-dessus dans ton autobiographie.
	[otobjɔgʀafi]	-You should definitely write about that in your autobiography.

| 7499 | **adverse** | **adverse\|opposing** |

	adj	Peut être qu'un avocat adverse cherchait un avantage.
	[advɛʁs]	-Maybe an opposing lawyer was angling for an advantage.
7500	**piratage**	**piracy**
	m	Le vol de la propriété intellectuelle est une forme de piratage particulièrement pernicieuse.
	[piʁataʒ]	-Intellectual property theft is a particularly pernicious form of piracy.
7501	**irriter**	**irritate**
	vb	Je n' aime pas irriter mes collègues en les interrompant, mais je réclame votre coopération.
	[iʁite]	-I do not like to irritate colleagues by interrupting them, but I must appeal for your support.
7502	**répugnant**	**repugnant**
	adj	Le terrorisme, quelles que soient ses manifestations est répugnant.
	[ʁepyɲɑ̃]	-Any manifestation of terrorism is abhorrent.
7503	**synthétique**	**synthetic; synthetic**
	adj; m	L'étude tentera d'utiliser les données pour présenter une image synthétique et identifier les lacunes.
	[sɛ̃tetik]	-The study will attempt to blend the various data into a synthesized picture and identify gaps.
7504	**trotter**	**trot**
	vb[tʁɔte]	Je vais trotter, galoper, pendant une heure. -I'm going to trot then gallop for an hour.
7505	**cynisme**	**cynicism**
	m	Le Parti réformiste a aidé à perpétuer ce cynisme.
	[sinism]	-The Reform Party has contributed to the continuation of this cynicism.
7506	**traumatique**	**traumatic**
	adj	Non, c'était plutôt traumatique.
	[tʁomatik]	-No, it was pretty traumatizing.
7507	**énervant**	**annoying**
	adj	C'est énervant.
	[enɛʁvɑ̃]	-That's annoying.
7508	**paternité**	**paternity**
	f	En fait, il s'agit surtout du père sur lequel pèse une présomption de paternité.
	[patɛʁnite]	-Mostly, these concern the father for whom there is a presumption of paternity.
7509	**trompeur**	**misleading; deceiver**
	adj; m	L'exemple souvent n'est qu'un miroir trompeur.
	[tʁɔ̃pœʁ]	-The example often is only a misleading mirror.
7510	**artisan**	**artisan**
	m	À l'œuvre, on connaît l'artisan.
	[aʁtizɑ̃]	-One recognizes the craftsman by his work.
7511	**lésion**	**lesion**
	f	Les tests ne révèlent aucune lésion médullaire ou cérébrale.
	[lezjɔ̃]	-Tests show no spinal cord injury, no cerebral lesions, no hemorrhage.
7512	**téléviseur**	**TV**
	m	Les jeunes passent beaucoup de temps devant le téléviseur ou l'ordinateur.
	[televizœʁ]	-Young people spend a lot of time in front of television screens or computer monitors.
7513	**sodomie**	**sodomy**
	f	C'est dangereux, la sodomie.
	[sɔdɔmi]	-It's a hazardous business, sodomy.

7514	**charrue**	**plow**
	f	Le bond entre la charrue et le tracteur n'est pas du tout le bond approprié.
	[ʃaʁy]	-The leap from plough to hi-tech tractor is not at all an appropriate one.

7515	**lande**	**moor**
	f	Ne traversez pas la lande seul.
	[lɑ̃d]	-You're not going to cross the moor alone, Sir Henry.

7516	**négociateur**	**negotiator**
	m	Vous êtes un négociateur avisé.
	[negɔsjatœʁ]	-You're one savvy negotiator.

7517	**pâturer**	**graze**
	vb	Empêcher le bétail de pâturer le gazon traité avec BASAGRAN herbicide liquide.
	[patyʁe]	-Do not allow livestock to graze on BASAGRAN Liquid Herbicide treated turf.

7518	**bourdonnement**	**buzz|hum**
	m [buʁdɔnmɑ̃]	Plus de bourdonnement dans nos têtes. -No more buzzing inside our heads.

7519	**déraper**	**skid**
	vb	Mais c'est là qu'on commence à déraper vers l'irréalisme, le pharisaïsme et l'intégrisme.
	[deʁape]	-This, however, is the start of the sideslip into lack of realism, self-righteousness and fundamentalism.

7520	**troc**	**barter|bartering**
	m	Tout gouvernement se fonde sur le compromis et le troc.
	[tʁɔk]	-All government is founded on compromise and barter.

7521	**mystérieusement**	**darkly**
	adv	Le contenu des conversations enregistrées circule mystérieusement dans les médias.
	[misteʁjøzmɑ̃]	-The contents of recorded conversations mysteriously circulate in the media.

7522	**attrister**	**sadden**
	vb	Pour nous, ton départ ne peut que nous attrister.
	[atʁiste]	-We are simply saddened by your leaving.

7523	**dessinateur**	**designer|draftsman**
	m	Ton prédécesseur était un grand dessinateur.
	[desinatœʁ]	-Guy who used to sit there was a great cartoonist.

7524	**éradiquer**	**eradicate**
	vb	Pour ce qui est de la tuberculose, le calcul est identique, mais la maladie est plus difficile à éradiquer.
	[eʁadike]	-As regards TB, the mathematics are similar but it is more difficult to eradicate.

7525	**pamplemousse**	**grapefruit**
	m	J'ai mangé un demi-pamplemousse pour le petit-déjeuner.
	[pɑ̃pləmus]	-I had half a grapefruit for breakfast.

Adjectives

Rank	French-PoS	Translation
5002	**préparé**-*adj*	prepared
5004	**faisable**-*adj*	feasible| doable
5006	**numérique**-*adj*	digital| numerical
5011	**tracé**-*m; adj*	route| course; tracing
5015	**diplomatique**-*adj*	diplomatic
5018	**immoral**-*adj*	immoral
5024	**sonore**-*f; adj*	sound; acoustic
5032	**conservateur**-*adj; m*	conservative; conservative
5034	**sadique**-*adj; m/f*	sadistic; sadist
5043	**gonflé**-*adj*	inflated
5044	**honoraire**-*adj; m*	honorary; honorarium
5051	**suffisant**-*adj*	sufficient
5053	**rassurant**-*adj*	reassuring
5065	**clandestin**-*adj*	clandestine
5084	**équivalent**-*adj; m*	equivalent; equivalent
5086	**culturel**-*adj*	cultural
5088	**locomotif**-*adj*	locomotive
5092	**débutant**-*m; adj*	beginner; novice
5094	**tranché**-*adj*	decided| cut
5095	**lunaire**-*adj*	lunar
5100	**exotique**-*adj*	exotic
5110	**attirant**-*adj*	attractive| appealing
5120	**miséricordieux**-*adj*	merciful
5129	**tact**-*m; adj*	tact; delicate
5131	**associé**-*adj; m*	associate; associate
5133	**viril**-*adj*	virile| manly
5134	**mathématique**-*adj*	mathematical
5136	**antarctique**-*adj*	Antarctic
5137	**cubain**-*adj*	Cuban
5139	**sournois**-*adj*	sneaky| sly
5141	**insignifiant**-*adj*	insignificant
5145	**malsain**-*adj*	unhealthy
5148	**gitan**-*adj; m*	Gypsy; Gypsy
5151	**universel**-*adj; m*	universal; universal
5153	**décent**-*adj*	decent
5154	**dynamique**-*adj; f*	dynamic; dynamics
5164	**optique**-*adj; f*	optical; optics
5170	**dandy**-*m; adj*	dandy; foppish
5172	**stérile**-*adj*	sterile| barren
5174	**émotionnel**-*adj*	emotional
5175	**mutuel**-*adj*	mutual
5180	**poétique**-*adj*	poetic
5192	**favorable**-*adj*	favorable
5197	**surnaturel**-*adj; m*	supernatural; occult
5198	**malhonnête**-*adj*	dishonest
5201	**vaudou**-*adj; m*	voodoo; voodoo
5209	**observateur**-*m; adj*	observer; observant
5213	**générique**-*adj*	generic
5214	**indiscret**-*adj*	indiscreet
5215	**démocratique**-*adj*	democratic
5217	**calmant**-*adj; m*	calming; tranquilizer
5223	**cosmique**-*adj*	cosmic
5227	**improbable**-*adj*	unlikely
5233	**subit**-*adj*	sudden
5234	**rêveur**-*m; adj*	dreamer; dreamy
5241	**collant**-*m; adj*	tights; adhesive
5245	**sédatif**-*adj; m*	sedative; sedative
5260	**martien**-*adj*	martian
5270	**agresseur**-*m; adj*	aggressor; assailant
5274	**boussole**-*adj; f*	compass; compass
5275	**affilé**-*adj*	sharp
5285	**prédateur**-*m; adj*	predator; predatory
5286	**funèbre**-*adj*	funeral
5287	**grincheux**-*adj; m*	grumpy; grumbler
5302	**choquant**-*adj*	shocking
5305	**démocrate**-*m/f; adj*	democrat; democratic
5312	**illustre**-*adj*	illustrious| illustrated
5320	**lucide**-*adj*	lucid| rational
5327	**mourant**-*adj*	dying
5328	**astucieux**-*adj*	clever| astute
5329	**vil**-*adj*	vile| base
5330	**paf**-*adj; int*	high; bam!
5335	**hilarant**-*adj*	hilarious
5337	**littéraire**-*adj*	literary
5341	**couché**-*adj; adv*	lying down; abed
5343	**ingénieux**-*adj*	ingenious
5353	**vétéran**-*m; adj*	veteran; old
5358	**mercenaire**-*adj; m*	mercenary; mercenary
5366	**voyant**-*m; adj*	seer; clairvoyant
5367	**boiteux**-*adj; m/f*	lame| limping; lame person
5372	**piètre**-*adj*	poor| mediocre
5393	**délinquant**-*m; adj*	offender; delinquent
5401	**impardonnable**-*adj*	unforgivable
5405	**bouseux**-*adj*	hick

5415	**millénaire**-*m; adj*	millennium| millennial; millenary
5416	**pieux**-*adj*	pious| devout
5424	**subconscient**-*adj*	subconscious
5429	**ardeur**-*f; adj*	ardor| heat; vehement
5432	**crevé**-*adj*	flat| all in| tired
5434	**vertébral**-*adj*	vertebral
5439	**innombrable**-*adj*	innumerable
5440	**appelant**-*adj; m*	appellant; appellant
5441	**impensable**-*adj*	unthinkable
5449	**palestinien**-*adj*	Palestinian
5450	**israélien**-*adj*	Israeli
5452	**fréquent**-*adj*	frequent
5457	**douillet**-*adj*	cozy| soft
5459	**étranglé**-*adj*	strangled
5461	**prévisible**-*adj*	predictable
5466	**imminent**-*adj*	imminent
5468	**bossu**-*m; adj*	hunchback; hunchbacked
5482	**intolérable**-*adj*	intolerable
5488	**fluide**-*adj; m*	fluid; fluid
5495	**parallèle**-*adj; m/f*	parallel; parallel
5497	**anxieux**-*adj*	anxious| worried
5501	**imprévu**-*adj; m*	unexpected; contingency
5506	**olympique**-*adj*	Olympic
5511	**sanglant**-*adj*	bloody
5513	**monétaire**-*adj*	monetary
5518	**lutin**-*m; adj*	pixie| leprechaun; impish
5525	**traditionnel**-*adj*	traditional
5528	**fertile**-*adj*	fertile| fruitful
5529	**mendiant**-*m; adj*	beggar; begging
5531	**taillé**-*adj*	tailored
5533	**stellaire**-*adj*	stellar
5537	**imperméable**-*adj; m*	impermeable; waterproof
5541	**effrayant**-*adj*	scary| frightening
5549	**superstitieux**-*adj*	superstitious
5551	**fâcheux**-*adj; m/f*	annoying; meddler
5552	**rival**-*adj; m*	rival; rival
5566	**cuisiné**-*adj*	cooked
5574	**spécifique**-*adj*	specific
5582	**douteux**-*adj*	doubtful
5586	**compétent**-*adj*	competent
5588	**vocal**-*adj*	vocal
5596	**charitable**-*adj*	charitable
5604	**caraïbe**-*adj*	Caribbean
5619	**collectif**-*adj*	collective
5623	**global**-*adj*	overall| global
5625	**métis**-*m; adj*	metis; colored
5628	**fascinant**-*adj*	fascinating
5629	**vertueux**-*adj*	virtuous
5631	**lisse**-*adj*	smooth| sleek
5634	**caractéristique**-*adj; f*	characteristic; characteristic
5635	**algue**-*f; adj*	alga; algoid
5637	**opérationnel**-*adj*	operational
5650	**apte**-*adj*	apt
5659	**percé**-*adj*	perforated
5660	**imprudent**-*adj*	imprudent| unwise
5663	**potable**-*adj*	potable
5674	**flagrant**-*adj*	flagrant| blatant
5682	**fainéant**-*adj; m*	lazy; lounger
5683	**stratégique**-*adj*	strategic
5690	**courtois**-*adj*	courteous
5692	**concret**-*adj; m*	concrete; concrete
5696	**stupéfiant**-*m; adj*	narcotic; amazing
5697	**arctique**-*adj*	Arctic
5703	**infaillible**-*adj*	infallible
5704	**souple**-*adj*	flexible| soft
5707	**naval**-*adj*	naval
5708	**manifestant**-*m; adj*	demonstrator; riotous
5714	**oriental**-*adj*	Oriental
5716	**basque**-*adj; f*	Basque; Basque
5721	**ardent**-*adj*	ardent| burning
5722	**effroyable**-*adj*	frightful| appalling
5726	**perspicace**-*adj*	perceptive| perspicacious
5727	**paternel**-*adj; m*	paternal; pater
5729	**auditeur**-*m; adj*	auditor; auditorial
5730	**défensive**-*adj*	defensive
5733	**conditionné**-*adj*	conditioned
5735	**destructeur**-*adj; m*	destructive; destroyer
5736	**intestin**-*adj; m*	intestine; intestine
5748	**brusque**-*adj*	sudden| brusque
5754	**australien**-*adj; m*	Australian; digger
5756	**poilu**-*adj*	hairy
5759	**avide**-*adj*	eager| greedy
5762	**cocu**-*m; adj*	cuckold; cheated on
5763	**vaillant**-*adj*	valiant| brave
5766	**considérable**-*adj*	considerable| significant

5767	**publicitaire**-*m/f; adj*	advertiser; advertising
5770	**rentable**-*adj*	profitable| cost-effective
5773	**plausible**-*adj*	plausible
5776	**anguille**-*f; adj*	eel; anguine
5780	**respectueux**-*adj*	respectful
5795	**stimulant**-*adj; m*	stimulating; stimulant
5804	**missionnaire**-*adj; m*	missionary; missionary
5814	**impair**-*adj; m*	odd; faux pas
5817	**psychique**-*adj*	psychic
5827	**brésilien**-*adj*	Brazilian
5839	**lugubre**-*adj*	dismal| lugubrious
5845	**tocard**-*adj; m*	tacky; loser
5862	**belge**-*adj*	Belgian
5863	**aval**-*m; adj*	approval; down-stream
5865	**barbu**-*adj; m*	bearded; bearded man
5874	**pesant**-*adj*	cumbersome
5875	**égyptien**-*adj*	Egyptian
5879	**manchot**-*m; adj*	penguin; one-handed
5880	**nabot**-*m; adj*	runt; dwarfish
5883	**symbolique**-*adj*	symbolic| nominal
5888	**marqué**-*adj*	marked
5891	**composé**-*adj; m*	compound; compound
5892	**mélancolique**-*adj; m/f*	melancholy; melancholiac
5899	**carré**-*adj; m*	square; square
5902	**fané**-*adj*	withered| dry
5904	**inimaginable**-*adj*	unimaginable
5907	**pascal**-*m; adj*	pascal; paschal
5913	**descendant**-*adj; m*	descending; descendant
5915	**propice**-*adj*	suitable
5917	**affectueux**-*adj*	affectionate
5918	**morbide**-*adj*	morbid
5929	**gaucher**-*m; adj*	left-hander; left-handed
5947	**maritime**-*adj*	maritime
5954	**puéril**-*adj*	childish
5955	**précoce**-*adj*	precocious
5961	**capitaliste**-*m/f; adj*	capitalist; capitalistic
5970	**cité**-*f; adj*	city-state; city
5971	**rationnel**-*adj; m*	rational; rational
5982	**pénal**-*adj*	penal
5986	**miniature**-*adj; f*	miniature; miniature
5989	**indemne**-*adj*	unscathed
5996	**élémentaire**-*adj*	elementary
5998	**miteux**-*adj*	shabby| seedy
6000	**verbal**-*adj; m*	verbal; verbal
6001	**fanatique**-*adj; m/f*	fanatic; fanatic
6002	**décisif**-*adj*	decisive
6011	**torride**-*adj*	torrid
6012	**sensass**-*adj*	sensational
6025	**infrarouge**-*adj*	infrared
6028	**juteux**-*adj*	juicy
6034	**glissant**-*adj*	sliding| slippery
6039	**valeureux**-*adj*	valorous| gallant
6040	**soucieux**-*adj*	concerned
6046	**sénile**-*adj*	senile
6061	**infernal**-*adj; m*	infernal; fiend
6063	**valide**-*adj*	valid| available
6067	**guéri**-*adj*	recovered
6076	**pointu**-*adj*	sharp
6078	**effectif**-*adj*	effective
6079	**dû**-*adj*	due
6080	**béat**-*adj*	smug
6083	**mémorable**-*adj*	memorable
6086	**coûteux**-*adj*	expensive
6087	**estropié**-*adj; m*	crippled; cripple
6092	**glacial**-*adj*	glacial
6095	**sceptique**-*adj; m/f*	skeptical; skeptic
6104	**durable**-*adj*	lasting| enduring
6110	**libéral**-*adj*	liberal
6112	**corsé**-*adj*	spicy
6116	**fiscal**-*adj*	tax
6120	**expérimental**-*adj*	experimental
6128	**comparable**-*adj*	comparable
6130	**intrépide**-*adj*	intrepid| bold
6132	**ignorant**-*adj; m*	ignorant; ignoramus
6135	**excessif**-*adj*	excessive| overdone
6143	**antibiotique**-*adj; m*	antibiotic; antibiotic
6145	**préservatif**-*m; adj*	condom; preservative
6153	**victorieux**-*adj*	victorious
6158	**saignant**-*adj*	bleeding
6159	**athée**-*m/f; adj*	atheist; atheistic
6163	**borgne**-*adj*	one-eyed
6165	**brûlant**-*adj*	burning
6167	**encourageant**-*adj*	encouraging
6168	**dingo**-*m; adj*	dingo; nuts

6172	**démoniaque**-*adj; m/f*	demonic; demoniac
6175	**scélérat**-*m; adj*	scoundrel; miscreant
6178	**troublant**-*adj*	disturbing
6179	**méprisable**-*adj*	contemptible
6180	**inhumain**-*adj*	inhuman
6184	**notoire**-*adj*	notorious
6189	**immature**-*adj*	immature
6194	**galactique**-*adj*	galactic
6207	**mécontent**-*adj*	dissatisfied| unhappy
6218	**externe**-*adj; m/f*	external; extern
6219	**hybride**-*m; adj*	hybrid; crossbred
6220	**superficiel**-*adj*	superficial
6225	**polaire**-*adj*	polar
6227	**éminent**-*adj*	eminent| learned
6229	**incompréhensible**-*adj*	incomprehensible
6231	**inaperçu**-*adj*	unseen
6238	**musclé**-*adj*	muscular
6241	**perplexe**-*adj*	puzzled
6245	**fatigant**-*adj*	tiring| fatiguing
6248	**originaire**-*adj*	native
6249	**présentable**-*adj*	presentable
6254	**prodigieux**-*adj*	prodigious
6259	**contraint**-*adj*	constrained
6263	**distant**-*adj*	distant
6264	**thermique**-*adj*	thermal
6266	**indestructible**-*adj*	indestructible
6267	**mesquin**-*adj*	mean| shabby
6271	**tracas**-*m; adj*	hassle; worry
6273	**transparent**-*adj*	transparent| clear
6274	**frappant**-*adj*	striking
6282	**pharmaceutique**-*adj*	pharmaceutical
6284	**tiède**-*adj*	lukewarm
6286	**invalide**-*adj; m/f*	invalid; invalid
6288	**robuste**-*adj*	robust| sturdy
6293	**énergétique**-*f; adj*	energetics; energizing
6295	**conforme**-*adj*	compliant
6314	**incurable**-*adj*	incurable
6326	**hydraulique**-*adj; f*	hydraulic; hydraulics
6330	**sondage**-*m; adj*	survey| poll; probing
6333	**inséparable**-*adj*	inseparable
6335	**infect**-*adj*	foul| vile
6336	**contesté**-*adj*	disputed
6344	**humanitaire**-*adj*	humanitarian
6348	**égocentrique**-*adj; m/f*	egocentric; egomania
6353	**somnambule**-*m; adj*	somnambulist; somnambulistic
6354	**bienfaiteur**-*adj; m*	benefactor; benefactor
6355	**inexplicable**-*adj*	inexplicable
6356	**gymnastique**-*f; adj*	gymnastics; gymnastic
6359	**oculaire**-*adj; m*	ocular; ocular
6371	**obèse**-*adj*	obese
6375	**infantile**-*adj*	infantile
6376	**funéraire**-*adj*	funerary
6381	**biblique**-*adj*	biblical
6383	**dégoûtant**-*adj*	disgusting
6385	**poivrot**-*m; adj*	boozer; rummy
6391	**directif**-*adj*	directive
6394	**ménager**-*adj; vb*	household; spare
6397	**roulant**-*adj*	rolling
6398	**auxiliaire**-*adj; m*	auxiliary; auxiliary
6408	**séducteur**-*m; adj*	seducer; seductive
6409	**nigaud**-*m; adj*	simpleton; stupid
6411	**vigilant**-*adj*	vigilant| watchful
6418	**commandant**-*m; adj*	commander; commanding
6422	**cannibale**-*adj; m/f*	cannibal; cannibal
6423	**incompétent**-*adj*	incompetent
6427	**adhésif**-*adj; m*	adhesive; adhesive
6429	**urbain**-*adj*	urban
6437	**organique**-*adj*	organic
6445	**visionnaire**-*adj; m*	visionary; visionary
6447	**gluant**-*adj*	sticky| slimy
6453	**défectueux**-*adj*	defective| deficient
6457	**commerçant**-*m; adj*	merchant; trading
6459	**déplaisant**-*adj*	unpleasant| distasteful
6460	**orthodoxe**-*adj*	orthodox
6462	**fossile**-*adj; m*	fossil; fossil
6463	**coupant**-*adj; m*	cutting; bolter
6464	**amnésique**-*m/f; adj*	amnesic; amnesiac
6465	**accessible**-*adj*	accessible| reachable
6466	**pourpre**-*adj*	purple
6467	**radieux**-*adj*	radiant| bright
6470	**approchant**-*adj*	approaching
6477	**matinal**-*adj*	morning
6489	**surprenant**-*adj*	surprising
6490	**agricole**-*adj*	agricultural
6493	**délégué**-*m; adj*	delegate; vicarious

6498	**somptueux**-*adj*	sumptuous| magnificent
6502	**trombone**-*m; adj*	trombone; annoyed
6503	**participant**-*m; adj*	participant; participating
6505	**évadé**-*f; m; adj*	escape; evader; escaped
6510	**inaccessible**-*adj*	inaccessible
6516	**charmeur**-*m; adj*	charmer; charming
6529	**inestimable**-*adj*	invaluable| inestimable
6533	**fondamental**-*adj; m*	fundamental; fundamental
6542	**méfiant**-*adj*	suspicious| distrustful
6544	**nuptial**-*adj*	nuptial| wedding
6550	**indulgent**-*adj*	indulgent| forgiving
6559	**présidentiel**-*adj*	presidential
6560	**rosbif**-*adj*	roast beef
6566	**régional**-*adj*	regional
6569	**bouddhiste**-*adj*	Buddhist
6575	**barré**-*adj*	crossed
6586	**crasseux**-*adj*	filthy| grimy
6588	**dense**-*adj*	dense
6590	**élastique**-*adj; m; f*	elastic; rubber band; elasticy
6596	**vietnamien**-*adj; m*	Vietnamese; Vietnamese
6601	**incorrigible**-*adj*	incorrigible
6607	**vengeur**-*m; adj*	avenger; vengeful
6608	**tenace**-*adj*	tenacious| persistent
6620	**pertinent**-*adj*	relevant| pertinent
6623	**métallique**-*adj*	metallic
6631	**underground**-*adj; m*	underground; underground
6636	**terne**-*adj*	dull| drab
6639	**apparent**-*adj*	apparent| obvious
6641	**sarcastique**-*adj*	sarcastic
6643	**chiche**-*adj; int*	stingy; I dare you
6644	**sanguinaire**-*adj*	bloody
6646	**lacté**-*adj*	milky
6648	**rigide**-*adj*	rigid| inflexible
6649	**intouchable**-*adj*	untouchable
6651	**véreux**-*adj*	shady| dubious
6652	**impec**-*adj*	impeccable
6655	**sacrilège**-*m; adj*	sacrilege; sacrilegious
6666	**pailleté**-*adj*	jeweled
6672	**gourmand**-*adj; m*	greedy| gourmand; gourmand
6676	**insolite**-*adj*	unusual
6677	**irréel**-*adj*	unreal
6678	**esquimau**-*adj; m*	Eskimo; Eskimo
6691	**piquant**-*adj; m*	spicy; spicyness
6692	**triché**-*adj*	cheated
6693	**insuffisant**-*adj*	insufficient| inadequate
6703	**imbattable**-*adj*	unbeatable
6705	**gracieux**-*adj*	gracious| graceful
6711	**rogue**-*adj*	rogue
6722	**héréditaire**-*adj*	hereditary
6727	**serbe**-*adj; m*	Serbian; Serbian
6732	**albanais**-*adj; m|mpl*	Albanian; Albanian
6740	**touristique**-*adj*	tourist
6741	**beige**-*adj; m*	beige; beige
6742	**diffus**-*adj*	diffuse
6752	**lépreux**-*adj; m*	leper; leper
6753	**irréprochable**-*adj*	unexceptionable
6760	**monotone**-*adj*	monotone
6764	**autonome**-*adj*	autonomous
6765	**continental**-*adj*	continental
6766	**mutilé**-*adj*	mutilated
6769	**judicieux**-*adj*	wise| sound
6773	**bouillant**-*adj*	boiling
6777	**accroché**-*adj*	hooked
6782	**passif**-*adj; m*	passive; passive
6784	**noisette**-*f; adj*	hazelnut; hazel
6785	**pessimiste**-*adj; m/f*	pessimistic; pessimist
6787	**fendu**-*adj*	split
6790	**nostalgique**-*adj*	nostalgic
6792	**planétaire**-*adj; m*	planetary; orrery
6796	**incomparable**-*adj*	incomparable
6801	**formel**-*adj*	formal
6805	**partiel**-*adj; m*	partial; midyear exam
6808	**laitier**-*adj; m*	dairy; milkman
6810	**singulier**-*adj; m*	singular| strange; singular
6811	**infime**-*adj*	tiny
6812	**opportun**-*adj*	appropriate| timely
6817	**calé**-*adj*	chock
6824	**futile**-*adj*	futile| frivolous
6827	**interminable**-*adj*	endless
6831	**macabre**-*adj*	macabre
6839	**influent**-*adj*	influential
6840	**tropical**-*adj*	tropical

6851	aigu-*adj*	acute| shrill
6853	coopératif-*adj; m*	cooperative; cooperator
6854	adéquat-*adj*	adequate
6856	incertain-*adj*	uncertain
6870	serein-*adj; m*	serene; collection
6871	balistique-*adj; f*	ballistic; ballistics
6877	diabétique-*adj; m/f*	diabetic; diabetic
6878	pakistanais-*adj*	Pakistani
6883	historien-*m; adj*	historian; historical
6886	aventurier-*m; adj*	adventurer; aggressive
6887	accompli-*adj*	accomplished
6890	imposant-*adj*	imposing| impressive
6891	taquin-*adj; m*	teasing| playful; teaser
6896	auguste-*adj*	august
6897	catastrophique-*adj*	catastrophic
6909	restant-*adj; m*	remaining; remnant
6912	moléculaire-*adj*	molecular
6913	théorique-*adj*	theoretical
6918	païen-*adj; m*	pagan; pagan
6919	mature-*adj*	mature
6923	luxueux-*adj*	luxurious
6927	filial-*adj*	filial
6930	fade-*adj*	bland| tasteless
6935	borné-*adj*	limited| narrow
6940	prévenant-*adj*	considerate
6944	reptile-*adj; m*	reptile; reptile
6951	preux-*adj*	doughty| gallant
6952	saxon-*adj; m/f*	Saxon; Saxon
6955	profitable-*adj*	profitable
6956	lilas-*adj; m*	lilac; lilac
6957	rustre-*adj; m*	boor; boorish
6961	civique-*adj*	civic
6964	vaniteux-*adj*	vain
6968	inconfortable-*adj*	uncomfortable
6970	inadmissible-*adj*	inadmissible
6974	pseudonyme-*m; adj*	pseudonym; pseudonymous
6975	miraculeux-*adj*	miraculous
6978	corporel-*adj*	corporal
6982	hérétique-*m/f; adj*	heretic; heretical
6990	négligent-*adj*	negligent
6991	insolent-*adj*	insolent| cheeky
6992	froussard-*adj; m*	wimpy; coward
6998	mauve-*adj; f*	mauve; mallow
7000	lutteur-*m; adj*	wrestler; fighting
7002	fourbe-*adj*	deceitful
7013	oral-*adj; m*	oral; oral
7014	antérieur-*adj; m*	prior; antecessor
7016	prestigieux-*adj*	prestigious
7027	épatant-*adj*	splendid
7037	électoral-*adj*	electoral
7039	agaçant-*adj*	annoying| aggravating
7041	impulsif-*adj*	impulsive
7043	tchèque-*adj; m*	Czech; Czech
7049	frimeur-*adj; m*	showy; show-off
7057	avare-*m/f; adj*	miser; stingy
7058	synonyme-*adj; m*	synonymous; synonym
7061	méfait-*m; adj*	wrongdoing;
7065	dépendant-*adj*	dependent
7067	fuyant-*adj*	elusive| receding
7070	implacable-*adj*	implacable| relentless
7071	antan-*adj*	of old| bygone
7077	réparateur-*m; adj*	repairer; remedial
7085	mongol-*adj; m|mpl*	Mongolian; Mongol| retard
7086	idéaliste-*adj; m/f*	idealistic; idealist
7099	prématuré-*adj*	premature
7101	argentin-*adj*	Argentine
7104	conjugal-*adj*	conjugal| marital
7106	aisé-*adj*	easy| fluent
7111	impie-*adj*	impious
7120	rocheux-*adj*	rocky
7122	passionnant-*adj*	exciting
7124	périlleux-*adj*	perilous| hazardous
7125	entracte-*m; adj*	intermission; entr'acte
7126	sanitaire-*adj*	sanitary; sanitation
7131	spontané-*adj*	spontaneous
7136	climatique-*adj*	climatic
7137	preste-*adj*	nimble
7139	patriotique-*adj*	patriotic
7145	irritable-*adj*	irritable| prickly
7146	passible-*adj*	liable to
7150	effronté-*adj*	cheeky| brazen
7156	extrémiste-*adj; m/f*	extremist; extremist
7163	indicatif-*adj; m*	indicative; indicative
7170	expéditeur-*m; adj*	sender; dispatching
7171	immigrant-*adj; m*	immigrant; immigrant
7175	dérobé-*adj*	stolen| robbed

7176	**insouciant**-*adj*	carefree| careless		7377	**filtre**-*adj; m*	filter; filter
7179	**adoptif**-*adj*	adoptive		7378	**bienveillant**-*adj*	benevolent
7183	**dirigeable**-*adj; m*	dirigible; airship		7382	**désastreux**-*adj*	disastrous
7188	**passant**-*adj; m*	elapsing; passer-by		7386	**médiatique**-*adj*	media
7198	**rouquin**-*adj*	ginger		7388	**respiratoire**-*adj*	respiratory
7200	**superflu**-*adj*	superfluous| unnecessary		7393	**grêle**-*f; adj*	hail; thin
7220	**agile**-*adj*	agile		7400	**impur**-*adj*	impure| tainted
7228	**mondain**-*adj; m*	worldly; man about town		7403	**prêcheur**-*adj; m*	preachy; preacher
				7407	**terreux**-*adj*	earthy
7234	**composant**-*m; adj*	component; compound		7418	**exclusif**-*adj*	exclusive
7235	**instructif**-*adj*	instructive		7421	**siamois**-*adj; m|mpl*	Siamese; Siamese
7236	**cinématographique**-*adj*	cinematographic		7424	**virtuel**-*adj*	virtual
				7425	**bénévole**-*adj; m*	voluntary; volunteer
7239	**détestable**-*adj*	detestable		7428	**extincteur**-*m; adj*	extinguisher; extinguishing
7242	**docile**-*adj*	docile| obedient		7432	**croissant**-*adj; m*	growing; crescent
7244	**limpide**-*adj*	limpid		7434	**capricieux**-*adj*	capricious| whimsical
7246	**gâteux**-*adj; m/f*	senile; dotard				
7247	**minéral**-*adj; m*	mineral; mineral		7442	**statique**-*adj*	static
7260	**éblouissant**-*adj*	dazzling		7445	**bohémien**-*adj; m*	Bohemian; Gypsy
7261	**gallois**-*adj; m|mpl*	Welsh; Welsh		7448	**malfaisant**-*adj*	evil
7262	**graphique**-*adj; m*	graphic; graph		7450	**fougueux**-*adj*	fiery| spirited
7270	**conspirateur**-*m; adj*	conspirator; conspiratorial		7453	**coulant**-*adj; m*	flowing; runner
				7458	**simplet**-*adj*	simple-minded
7271	**individuel**-*adj*	individual| private		7460	**explicite**-*adj*	explicit
7278	**tardif**-*adj*	late		7466	**opératoire**-*adj*	operative
7286	**aquatique**-*adj*	aquatic		7468	**rhétorique**-*adj; f*	rhetoric; rhetoric
7290	**intensif**-*adj*	intensive		7479	**obstiné**-*adj*	obstinate| stubborn
7291	**inconcevable**-*adj*	inconceivable		7481	**cosmétique**-*adj; m*	cosmetic; cosmetic
7304	**bronzé**-*adj*	tanned| brown		7485	**éclatant**-*adj*	bright| brilliant
7305	**planque**-*f; adj*	stash; plummy		7486	**pittoresque**-*adj*	picturesque
7310	**ourse**-*f; adj*	bear; ursine		7489	**adroit**-*adj*	skilful| adroit
7316	**occupant**-*m; adj*	occupant; occupying		7490	**autoritaire**-*adj*	authoritarian
7320	**conventionnel**-*adj*	conventional		7491	**errant**-*adj; m*	wandering; wanderer
7323	**radioactif**-*adj*	radioactive		7499	**adverse**-*adj*	adverse| opposing
7331	**bienheureux**-*adj*	blissful		7502	**répugnant**-*adj*	repugnant
7335	**primordial**-*adj*	primary| primordial		7503	**synthétique**-*adj; m*	synthetic; synthetic
7346	**épilepsie**-*f; adj*	epilepsy; epileptic		7506	**traumatique**-*adj*	traumatic
7351	**pouilleux**-*adj*	lousy		7507	**énervant**-*adj*	annoying
7356	**fusible**-*m; adj*	fuse; fusible		7509	**trompeur**-*adj; m*	misleading; deceiver
7357	**aléatoire**-*adj*	aleatory				
7358	**viable**-*adj*	viable				
7361	**perfide**-*adj*	perfidious| false				
7363	**amiable**-*adj*	genial				
7366	**gaulois**-*adj*	Gallic				
7368	**érudit**-*m; adj*	scholar; erudite				

Adverbs

Rank	French-PoS	Translation
5019	merveilleusement-adv	wonderfully
5036	mutuellement-adv	mutually
5040	quasi-adv	almost
5069	prudemment-adv	carefully
5112	proprement-adv	properly
5150	volontairement-adv	willingly
5178	longuement-adv	long
5194	violemment-adv	violently
5228	accidentellement-adv	accidentally
5293	publiquement-adv	publicly
5297	relativement-adv	relatively
5341	couché-adj; adv	lying down; abed
5346	difficilement-adv	with difficulty
5361	tendrement-adv	tenderly| fondly
5362	assurément-adv	certainly
5403	salement-adv	dirtily
5412	affreusement-adv	frightfully
5437	hautement-adv	highly
5475	ouvertement-adv	openly
5522	rudement-adv	roughly| harshly
5562	indéfiniment-adv	indefinitely
5600	nettement-adv	clearly| sharply
5614	poliment-adv	politely
5642	notamment-adv	in particular
5700	sévèrement-adv	severely
5758	essentiellement-adv; nn	essentially; essentiality
5835	politiquement-adv	politically
5836	illégalement-adv	illegally
5882	incognito-adv; m	incognito; incognito
5988	brièvement-adv	briefly
5995	paisiblement-adv	peacefully
6007	brutalement-adv	brutally
6019	curieusement-adv	funnily
6051	moralement-adv	morally
6055	humblement-adv	humbly
6149	véritablement-adv	truly| actually
6202	conformément-adv	in step
6325	périlleusement-adv	perilously
6343	inutilement-adv	uselessly
6349	aisément-adv	easily
6389	sagement-adv	wisely
6430	sauvagement-adv	savagely
6480	fièrement-adv	proudly
6481	approximativement-adv	approximately
6512	exclusivement-adv	exclusively
6630	lourdement-adv	heavily
6634	grandement-adv	sorely
6638	amont-adv	uphill
6650	amplement-adv	amply
6698	fixement-adv	fixedly
6820	pareillement-adv	likewise
6830	idem-adv	idem
6934	joliment-adv	nicely
6948	typiquement-adv	typically
7006	passionnément-adv	passionately
7008	simultanément-adv	simultaneously
7040	nullement-adv	nothing
7068	tristement-adv	sadly
7097	considérablement-adv	greatly
7114	affectueusement-adv	fondly
7174	convenablement-adv	properly
7223	fondamentalement-adv	fundamentally
7232	continuellement-adv	continually
7273	progressivement-adv	progressively
7301	fraîchement-adv	freshly
7303	couramment-adv	fluently
7322	théoriquement-adv	theoretically
7338	chaleureusement-adv	warmly| kindly
7340	intensément-adv	deeply
7370	dignement-adv	with dignity
7381	méchamment-adv	nastily
7476	potentiellement-adv	potentially
7521	mystérieusement-adv	darkly

Conjunctions

Rank	French-PoS	Translation
6029	**duquel**-*prn; con*	whose; whereof

Prepositions

Rank	French-PoS	Translation
5561	hormis-prp	except for

Pronouns

Rank	French-*PoS*	Translation
6029	**duquel**-*prn; con*	whose; whereof

Numerals

Rank	French-PoS	Translation	
5237	**huitième**-*num*	eighth	num
5467	**dixième**-*num*	tenth	num
5854	**neuvième**-*num*	ninth	num
6701	**cinquantaine**-*num; f*	fifties; middle age	num; f

Nouns

Rank	French-PoS	Translation
5001	**superviseur**-*m*	supervisor
5005	**ampoule**-*f*	bulb| ampoule
5007	**consentement**-*m*	consent
5008	**orientation**-*f*	orientation| guidance
5010	**pilotage**-*m; f*	control; piloting
5011	**tracé**-*m; adj*	route| course; tracing
5012	**aquarium**-*m*	aquarium
5013	**concession**-*f*	concession| dealership
5014	**rédaction**-*f*	writing| redaction
5016	**ravin**-*m*	ravine
5017	**venin**-*m*	venom
5020	**boulangerie**-*f*	bakery
5021	**maquette**-*f*	model
5023	**écharpe**-*f*	scarf
5024	**sonore**-*f; adj*	sound; acoustic
5025	**doctorat**-*m*	doctorate| phD
5026	**transition**-*f*	transition
5027	**watt**-*m*	watt
5029	**corvée**-*f*	corvee| chore
5030	**boutique**-*f*	shop| stall
5031	**tourisme**-*m*	tourism
5032	**conservateur**-*adj; m*	conservative; conservative
5033	**pingouin**-*m*	penguin
5034	**sadique**-*adj; m/f*	sadistic; sadist
5035	**lingerie**-*f*	lingerie
5037	**pointure**-*f*	size
5038	**Belgique**-*f*	Belgium
5041	**recommandation**-*f*	recommendation| reference
5042	**brève**-*f*	breve
5044	**honoraire**-*adj; m*	honorary; honorarium
5046	**croquis**-*m*	sketch
5047	**communion**-*f*	Communion
5048	**panda**-*m*	panda
5049	**débarquement**-*m*	landing| disembarkation
5050	**paragraphe**-*m*	paragraph
5054	**sabre**-*m*	saber| sword
5057	**maquereau**-*m*	mackerel| pimp
5058	**support**-*m*	support| bracket
5059	**négligence**-*f*	negligence| neglect
5061	**tyrannie**-*f*	tyranny
5062	**carrosse**-*m*	coach| carriage
5063	**soja**-*m*	soy
5066	**chaperon**-*m*	chaperon| coping
5067	**bluff**-*m*	bluff
5068	**blouse**-*f*	gown| blouse
5070	**perpétuité**-*f*	perpetuity
5072	**timing**-*m*	timing
5073	**dupe**-*f*	dupe
5074	**interrupteur**-*m*	switch
5075	**coursier**-*m*	steed| messenger
5076	**rubis**-*m*	ruby
5079	**bandeau**-*m*	headband
5080	**natation**-*f*	swimming| float
5081	**slogan**-*m*	slogan| tag
5082	**guichet**-*m*	window
5083	**kimono**-*m*	kimono
5084	**équivalent**-*adj; m*	equivalent; equivalent
5085	**prostitution**-*f*	prostitution
5087	**diplomate**-*m/f*	diplomat
5089	**cendrier**-*m*	ashtray
5090	**amendement**-*m*	amendment
5091	**gag**-*m*	gag
5092	**débutant**-*m; adj*	beginner; novice
5097	**rush**-*m*	rush
5099	**pantin**-*m*	puppet
5102	**ananas**-*m*	pineapple
5103	**spaghetti**-*m*	spaghetti
5104	**bison**-*f*	bison
5105	**vanille**-*f*	vanilla
5106	**bouillon**-*m*	broth| bouillon
5108	**hippie**-*f*	hippy
5109	**thérapeute**-*m/f*	therapist
5113	**réfrigérateur**-*m*	refrigerator
5118	**décence**-*f*	decency
5119	**curry**-*m*	curry
5122	**moustique**-*m*	mosquito
5126	**frustration**-*f*	frustration
5127	**morale**-*f*	morals| ethics
5128	**tournée**-*f*	tour| touring
5129	**tact**-*m; adj*	tact; delicate
5131	**associé**-*adj; m*	associate; associate
5132	**meute**-*f*	pack
5140	**terminus**-*m*	terminus
5142	**nageur**-*m*	swimmer
5143	**contremaître**-*m*	overseer
5144	**pêche**-*f*	fishing
5148	**gitan**-*adj; m*	Gypsy; Gypsy

5149	sanglot-*m*	sob
5151	universel-*adj; m*	universal; universal
5152	rancard-*m*	date
5154	dynamique-*adj; f*	dynamic; dynamics
5156	formalité-*f*	formality
5157	tuerie-*f*	killing
5158	samba-*f*	samba
5159	épice-*f*	spice
5160	été-*m*	summer
5161	sabotage-*m*	sabotage
5162	prodige-*m*	prodigy| wonder
5164	optique-*adj; f*	optical; optics
5165	coyote-*m*	coyote
5166	rubrique-*f*	rubric| column
5167	imitation-*f*	imitation
5168	nomination-*f*	appointment| nomination
5169	mayonnaise-*f*	mayonnaise
5170	dandy-*m; adj*	dandy; foppish
5171	paranoïaque-*m/f*	paranoid; paranoid
5173	gourou-*m*	guru
5179	campement-*m*	camp
5182	élevage-*m*	breeding| animal husbandry
5183	tornade-*f*	tornado
5185	antiquité-*f*	antiquity
5186	tournure-*f*	twist| turning
5187	pollution-*f*	pollution
5189	dague-*f*	dagger
5190	harcèlement-*m*	harassment| harassing
5191	trafiquant-*m*	trafficker
5193	parchemin-*m*	parchment| diploma
5196	stationnement-*m*	parking
5197	surnaturel-*adj; m*	supernatural; occult
5200	démence-*f*	dementia| madness
5201	vaudou-*adj; m*	voodoo; voodoo
5202	once-*f*	ounce
5203	Écosse-*f*	Scotland
5204	édifice-*m*	building| edifice
5205	plasma-*m*	plasma
5206	éventreur-*m*	ripper
5207	patin-*m*	skate
5208	détournement-*m*	misappropriation
5209	observateur-*m; adj*	observer; observant
5210	axe-*m*	axis
5211	pionnier-*m*	pioneer
5212	chiffon-*m*	cloth
5216	corporation-*f*	corporation
5217	calmant-*adj; m*	calming; tranquilizer
5218	déluge-*m*	downpour
5219	douane-*f*	customs
5221	désaccord-*m*	disagreement| odds
5222	fourrière-*f*	pound
5224	sterling-*m*	sterling
5225	swing-*m*	swing| stomp
5229	envie-*f*	desire
5230	perquisition-*f*	search
5231	vigueur-*f*	vigor| strength
5232	mutinerie-*f*	mutiny
5234	rêveur-*m; adj*	dreamer; dreamy
5235	hystérie-*f*	hysteria
5236	gouffre-*m*	gulf
5238	pantoufle-*f*	slipper
5239	moineau-*m*	sparrow
5240	paume-*f*	palm
5241	collant-*m; adj*	tights; adhesive
5242	chêne-*m*	oak
5243	capitalisme-*m*	capitalism
5244	critère-*m*	criterion
5245	sédatif-*adj; m*	sedative; sedative
5248	murmure-*m*	murmur
5250	citrouille-*f*	pumpkin
5252	stupidité-*f*	stupidity
5254	décret-*m*	decree| ordinance
5255	sable-*m*	sand| grittiness
5256	dicton-*m*	diction
5257	castor-*m*	beaver| beaver rat
5258	forfait-*m*	package
5259	lentille-*f*	lens
5262	entrepreneur-*m*	entrepreneur| contractor
5263	remerciement-*m*	thanks| appreciation
5264	célébration-*f*	celebration
5265	hibou-*m*	owl
5266	interruption-*f*	interruption
5267	rayure-*f*	stripe
5268	inauguration-*f*	inauguration
5270	agresseur-*m; adj*	aggressor; assailant
5271	mention-*f*	mention
5272	anxiété-*f*	anxiety
5274	boussole-*adj; f*	compass; compass
5276	distraction-*f*	distraction| entertainment

5277	**brutalité**-*f*	brutality
5278	**exclusivité**-*f*	exclusiveness
5279	**joyau**-*m*	jewel
5280	**rigolade**-*f*	fun| joke
5281	**supplément**-*m*	supplement
5282	**viole**-*f*	viol
5283	**gel**-*m*	gel| freezing
5284	**simulation**-*f*	simulation
5285	**prédateur**-*m; adj*	predator; predatory
5287	**grincheux**-*adj; m*	grumpy; grumbler
5289	**coussin**-*m*	cushion
5292	**boyau**-*m*	casing
5294	**croisement**-*m*	crossing
5295	**Madone**-*f*	Madonna
5298	**tribune**-*f*	gallery
5299	**parquet**-*m*	parquet
5301	**carabine**-*f*	carbine
5303	**viking**-*m*	viking
5304	**boulet**-*m*	ball| drag
5305	**démocrate**-*m/f; adj*	democrat; democratic
5306	**tempérament**-*m*	temperament| temper
5307	**expulsion**-*f*	expulsion| deportation
5308	**obéissance**-*f*	obedience
5309	**technicien**-*m*	technician
5310	**maternité**-*f*	maternity
5311	**superstition**-*f*	superstition
5313	**battement**-*m*	beat| beating
5314	**popularité**-*f*	popularity
5315	**magistrat**-*m*	magistrate
5316	**radeau**-*m*	raft
5317	**dépendance**-*f*	dependence| outbuilding
5319	**fleuriste**-*m*	florist
5321	**mosquée**-*f*	mosque
5322	**casque**-*m*	helmet
5323	**fragment**-*m*	fragment| piece
5324	**sonar**-*m*	sonar
5326	**caniveau**-*m*	gutter
5332	**nouveauté**-*f*	novelty
5334	**décennie**-*f*	decade
5336	**baril**-*m*	barrel| crater
5338	**renvoi**-*m*	return| reference
5340	**cartel**-*m*	cartel| coalition
5342	**lacet**-*m*	shoelace
5344	**financement**-*m*	funding
5347	**distinction**-*f*	distinction
5348	**entourage**-*m*	entourage
5349	**consolation**-*f*	consolation| comforting
5351	**truand**-*m*	hoodlum
5353	**vétéran**-*m; adj*	veteran; old
5354	**amnésie**-*f*	amnesia
5355	**vacarme**-*m*	racket| noise
5356	**annulation**-*f*	cancellation| annulment
5357	**avatar**-*m*	avatar
5358	**mercenaire**-*adj; m*	mercenary; mercenary
5359	**constance**-*f*	constancy
5360	**tonneau**-*m*	barrel| ton
5364	**pancarte**-*f*	placard
5365	**suture**-*f*	suture
5366	**voyant**-*m; adj*	seer; clairvoyant
5367	**boiteux**-*adj; m/f*	lame| limping; lame person
5368	**pie**-*f*	magpie
5369	**orgue**-*m*	organ
5370	**sifflement**-*m*	whistling| hiss
5374	**hurlement**-*m*	howl| yell
5375	**étagère**-*f*	shelf
5376	**exploration**-*f*	exploration
5377	**espérance**-*f*	hope| expectation
5378	**escouade**-*f*	squad
5379	**cachot**-*m*	dungeon
5380	**charpentier**-*m*	carpenter
5381	**bikini**-*m*	bikini
5382	**utérus**-*m*	uterus
5383	**logiciel**-*m*	software
5384	**geisha**-*f*	geisha
5385	**argile**-*f*	clay
5386	**clarté**-*f*	clarity| lightness
5387	**ogre**-*m*	ogre
5388	**chouchou**-*m*	pet
5389	**gland**-*m*	glans
5391	**pétition**-*f*	petition
5393	**délinquant**-*m; adj*	offender; delinquent
5394	**emballage**-*m*	packing| wrap
5395	**merlin**-*m*	marlin| poleaxe
5397	**migraine**-*f*	migraine
5398	**dictature**-*f*	dictatorship
5399	**caprice**-*m*	fancy
5402	**renverse**-*f*	inverse
5406	**tolérance**-*f*	tolerance
5407	**extraction**-*f*	extraction

5408	**zodiaque**-*m*	zodiac
5409	**expansion**-*f*	expansion
5410	**artère**-*f*	artery
5411	**hobby**-*m*	hobby
5413	**scrupule**-*m*	scruple| compunction
5414	**dynastie**-*f*	dynasty
5415	**millénaire**-*m; adj*	millennium| millennial; millenary
5417	**ravitaillement**-*m*	refueling
5418	**narrateur**-*m*	narrator
5419	**galop**-*m*	gallop
5420	**boucan**-*m*	racket| din
5422	**délégation**-*f*	delegation
5423	**candidature**-*f*	application| candidacy
5425	**sacoche**-*f*	pannier
5426	**navigateur**-*m*	navigator
5427	**jogging**-*m*	jogging
5428	**médaillon**-*m*	medallion
5429	**ardeur**-*f; adj*	ardor| heat; vehement
5433	**charlatan**-*m*	charlatan| quack
5440	**appelant**-*adj; m*	appellant; appellant
5442	**foule**-*f*	crowd| host
5443	**gouvernail**-*m*	rudder
5444	**guitariste**-*m/f*	guitarist
5446	**jaguar**-*m*	jaguar
5447	**sortilège**-*m*	spell
5448	**soucoupe**-*f*	saucer
5451	**fibre**-*f*	fiber| staple
5456	**prestige**-*m*	prestige
5458	**simplicité**-*f*	simplicity
5460	**tombeur**-*m*	ladykiller
5464	**criminalité**-*f*	criminality
5465	**coéquipier**-*m*	team mate
5468	**bossu**-*m; adj*	hunchback; hunchbacked
5469	**traîneau**-*m*	sled| drag
5470	**cadence**-*f*	pace
5471	**symphonie**-*f*	symphony
5472	**vison**-*m*	mink
5476	**shilling**-*m*	shilling
5478	**protéine**-*f*	protein
5479	**maintenance**-*f*	maintenance
5480	**dilemme**-*m*	dilemma
5481	**colon**-*m*	colon| settler
5483	**sculpture**-*f*	sculpture| sculpting
5484	**chaudière**-*f*	boiler
5487	**joujou**-*m*	toy
5488	**fluide**-*adj; m*	fluid; fluid
5489	**clairon**-*m*	bugle
5490	**biberon**-*m*	baby bottle
5491	**gaspillage**-*m*	waste| wastage
5492	**dictateur**-*m*	dictator
5493	**carcasse**-*f*	carcass
5494	**implant**-*m*	implant
5495	**parallèle**-*adj; m/f*	parallel; parallel
5496	**manucure**-*f*	manicure
5498	**cadenas**-*m*	padlock
5500	**clavier**-*m*	keyboard
5501	**imprévu**-*adj; m*	unexpected; contingency
5502	**virilité**-*f*	virility| manhood
5503	**bungalow**-*m*	bungalow
5504	**estimation**-*f*	estimate| rating
5505	**alphabet**-*m*	alphabet
5507	**bonne**-*f*	housemaid
5508	**dépêche**-*f*	dispatch| telegram
5509	**truie**-*f*	sow
5510	**tourbillon**-*m*	vortex| whirlwind
5512	**irruption**-*f*	irruption
5514	**verger**-*m*	orchard
5515	**diarrhée**-*f*	diarrhea
5516	**schéma**-*m*	schema| diagram
5517	**plaine**-*f*	plain
5518	**lutin**-*m; adj*	pixie| leprechaun; impish
5519	**chemisier**-*m*	blouse
5520	**oracle**-*m*	oracle
5521	**holocauste**-*m*	holocaust
5523	**raisonnement**-*m*	reasoning
5524	**déshonneur**-*m*	disgrace
5526	**gnôle**-*f*	hooch
5527	**hypothèque**-*f*	mortgage
5529	**mendiant**-*m; adj*	beggar; begging
5534	**excursion**-*f*	excursion| trip
5536	**application**-*f*	application
5537	**imperméable**-*adj; m*	impermeable; waterproof
5539	**croisade**-*f*	crusade
5542	**cabot**-*m*	pooch| mutt
5543	**emmerdeur**-*m*	pain in the neck
5544	**calamar**-*m*	squid
5545	**maturité**-*f*	maturity
5546	**renommée**-*f*	renown
5547	**sphère**-*f*	sphere| globe

5548	**plongeon**-*m*	dive| plunge	
5550	**hésitation**-*f*	hesitation	
5551	**fâcheux**-*adj; m/f*	annoying; meddler	
5552	**rival**-*adj; m*	rival; rival	
5553	**jockey**-*m*	jockey	
5554	**plomberie**-*f*	plumbing	
5555	**introduction**-*f*	introduction| listing	
5556	**liqueur**-*f*	liqueur	
5559	**fabricant**-*m*	manufacturer	
5560	**paranoïa**-*f*	paranoia	
5563	**rédemption**-*f*	redemption	
5565	**rai**-*m*	streak	
5567	**poulain**-*f*	foal	
5568	**veuf**-*m*	widower	
5570	**moniteur**-*m*	monitor	
5573	**déménagement**-*m*	move| removal	
5575	**expertise**-*f*	expertise| valuation	
5576	**hypocrisie**-*f*	hypocrisy	
5577	**nostalgie**-*f*	nostalgia	
5578	**décorateur**-*m*	decorator	
5579	**marguerite**-*f*	daisy	
5581	**trot**-*m*	trot	
5583	**anatomie**-*f*	anatomy	
5584	**fournisseur**-*m*	supplier| contractor	
5587	**engrais**-*m*	fertilizer	
5589	**psychiatrie**-*f*	psychiatry	
5590	**cochonnerie**-*f*	junk	
5591	**rejet**-*m*	rejection	
5592	**tonic**-*m*	tonic	
5593	**orthographe**-*f*	spelling	
5594	**lâcheté**-*f*	cowardice	
5595	**attente**-*f*	waiting| expectation	
5597	**apogée**-*m*	apogee| peak	
5598	**amertume**-*f*	bitterness| grief	
5601	**fiasco**-*m*	fiasco| failure	
5602	**lustre**-*m*	chandelier| luster	
5603	**réforme**-*f*	reform	
5605	**truite**-*f*	trout	
5606	**frousse**-*f*	jitters	
5607	**déclin**-*m*	decline	
5609	**diffusion**-*f*	diffusion| distribution	
5610	**trame**-*f*	weave	
5611	**éclaireur**-*m*	scout	
5612	**porcelaine**-*f*	porcelain	
5613	**paupière**-*f*	eyelid	
5615	**opium**-*m*	opium	

5617	**Pérou**-*m*	Peru
5618	**bûcher**-*m; vb*	pyre| slave; log
5620	**remorque**-*f*	trailer
5621	**dégoût**-*m*	disgust
5622	**cupidité**-*f*	greed
5625	**métis**-*m; adj*	metis; colored
5626	**terrien**-*m*	earthling| landlubber
5630	**magot**-*m*	hoard| loot
5633	**routier**-*vb; m*	truck; teamster
5634	**caractéristique**-*adj; f*	characteristic; characteristic
5635	**algue**-*f; adj*	alga; algoid
5636	**gamma**-*f*	gamma
5638	**créativité**-*f*	creativity
5639	**fesse**-*f*	buttock| bottom
5640	**astuce**-*f*	trick| cunning
5641	**méditation**-*f*	meditation
5643	**courtier**-*m*	broker
5644	**oseille**-*m*	money| dough
5648	**commotion**-*f*	shock| concussion
5649	**seigneurie**-*f*	lordship
5651	**motard**-*m*	outrider
5653	**pressing**-*m*	dry cleaning
5655	**admirateur**-*m*	admirer
5657	**zoom**-*m*	zoom
5662	**modestie**-*f*	modesty
5664	**conserve**-*f*	preserve
5665	**laverie**-*f*	laundry| laundromat
5666	**méchanceté**-*f*	wickedness
5667	**recrutement**-*m*	recruitment| recruiting
5669	**lieue**-*f*	league
5670	**horde**-*f*	horde
5671	**canton**-*m*	canton
5672	**urne**-*f*	urn
5673	**rotation**-*f*	rotation
5675	**instructeur**-*f*	instructor
5677	**accordéon**-*m*	accordion
5678	**insolence**-*f*	insolence
5679	**paddy**-*m*	paddy
5680	**glacier**-*m*	glacier
5682	**fainéant**-*adj; m*	lazy; lounger
5684	**chevet**-*m*	bedside
5685	**homosexualité**-*f*	homosexuality
5686	**supplice**-*m*	torture| ordeal
5687	**concerto**-*m*	concerto
5688	**transe**-*f*	trance

5689	**cratère**-*m*	crater
5691	**clodo**-*m*	bum
5692	**concret**-*adj; m*	concrete; concrete
5694	**citerne**-*f*	tank
5695	**grabuge**-*m*	mayhem
5696	**stupéfiant**-*m; adj*	narcotic; amazing
5698	**scooter**-*m*	scooter
5699	**crotte**-*f*	dung
5702	**boulanger**-*m*	baker
5706	**dévotion**-*f*	devotion
5708	**manifestant**-*m; adj*	demonstrator; riotous
5709	**label**-*m*	label
5710	**sornette**-*f*	fiddlestick
5711	**escale**-*f*	stop
5713	**punaise**-*f*	bug
5716	**basque**-*adj; f*	Basque; Basque
5718	**atrocité**-*f*	atrocity| outrage
5719	**mécano**-*m*	mechanic
5720	**cirage**-*m*	wax| polish
5723	**fondateur**-*m*	founder
5724	**démolition**-*f*	demolition
5725	**tabouret**-*m*	stool
5727	**paternel**-*adj; m*	paternal; pater
5729	**auditeur**-*m; adj*	auditor; auditorial
5731	**biographie**-*f*	biography
5734	**atome**-*m*	atom
5735	**destructeur**-*adj; m*	destructive; destroyer
5736	**intestin**-*adj; m*	intestine; intestine
5737	**molécule**-*f*	molecule
5738	**saveur**-*f*	flavor| taste
5739	**inculpation**-*f*	charge
5740	**orgie**-*f*	orgy
5741	**ivoire**-*m*	ivory
5742	**crampe**-*f*	cramp
5743	**dock**-*m*	dock
5744	**sabot**-*m*	shoe| hoof
5745	**style**-*m*	style| design
5746	**ruche**-*f*	hive
5747	**kiosque**-*m*	kiosk| newsstand
5752	**souche**-*f*	strain| stump
5753	**inflation**-*f*	inflation
5754	**australien**-*adj; m*	Australian; digger
5755	**allégeance**-*f*	allegiance
5757	**réincarnation**-*f*	reincarnation
5760	**minorité**-*f*	minority| infancy
5761	**anus**-*m*	anus
5762	**cocu**-*m; adj*	cuckold; cheated on
5764	**hospice**-*m*	hospice
5765	**twist**-*m*	twist
5767	**publicitaire**-*m/f; adj*	advertiser; advertising
5769	**orchidée**-*f*	orchid
5772	**plongeur**-*m*	diver
5774	**ardoise**-*f*	slate
5775	**panthère**-*f*	panther
5776	**anguille**-*f; adj*	eel; anguine
5778	**sérénité**-*f*	serenity
5779	**radiateur**-*m*	radiator
5781	**rite**-*m*	rite
5782	**potence**-*f*	gallows
5783	**étincelle**-*f*	spark
5784	**tablier**-*m*	apron
5785	**trio**-*m*	trio
5786	**charabia**-*m*	gibberish
5787	**jeton**-*m*	token
5788	**bobard**-*m*	lie
5789	**flair**-*m*	flair
5790	**craie**-*f*	chalk
5791	**actualité**-*f*	actuality
5792	**socialisme**-*m*	socialism
5793	**ingrédient**-*m*	ingredient
5795	**stimulant**-*adj; m*	stimulating; stimulant
5797	**solidarité**-*f*	solidarity
5798	**octave**-*m*	octave
5799	**waters**-*m*	bathroom| can
5800	**gouine**-*f*	dyke
5801	**bambou**-*m*	bamboo
5802	**indication**-*f*	indication
5803	**pornographie**-*f*	pornography
5804	**missionnaire**-*adj; m*	missionary; missionary
5805	**fente**-*f*	slot| slit
5806	**meneur**-*m*	leader
5807	**semence**-*f*	seed| seeds
5808	**mât**-*m*	mast
5809	**tramway**-*m*	streetcar
5810	**accélérateur**-*m*	accelerator
5811	**furie**-*f*	fury| she-cat
5812	**prévision**-*f*	forecast
5813	**camouflage**-*m*	camouflage
5814	**impair**-*adj; m*	odd; faux pas

5816	**gadget**-*m*	gadget	
5818	**tempe**-*f*	temple	
5820	**brick**-*m*	brig	
5822	**débauche**-*f*	debauchery	
5823	**gogo**-*m*	sucker	
5824	**fiesta**-*f*	shindig	
5826	**séduction**-*f*	seduction	
5828	**coroner**-*m*	coroner	
5829	**huissier**-*m*	bailiff	
5830	**attache**-*f*	clip	
5831	**éruption**-*f*	eruption| rash	
5832	**piment**-*m*	spice	
5834	**investigation**-*f*	investigation| inquiry	
5838	**tige**-*f*	stem| spindle	
5840	**gigolo**-*m*	gigolo	
5841	**tourment**-*m*	torment	
5842	**affectation**-*f*	assignment| allocation	
5843	**bobine**-*f*	coil| reel	
5844	**placement**-*m*	investment| placement	
5845	**tocard**-*adj; m*	tacky; loser	
5846	**harmonica**-*m*	harmonica	
5847	**pilier**-*m*	pillar| pier	
5850	**croquette**-*f*	croquette	
5851	**argenterie**-*f*	silverware	
5852	**coffret**-*m*	case	
5853	**banjo**-*m*	banjo	
5855	**shampooing**-*m*	shampoo	
5857	**stagiaire**-*m/f*	trainee	
5858	**délicatesse**-*f*	delicacy| sensitivity	
5860	**trèfle**-*m*	clover| shamrock	
5861	**donjon**-*m*	dungeon	
5863	**aval**-*m; adj*	approval; down-stream	
5865	**barbu**-*adj; m*	bearded; bearded man	
5866	**mitraillette**-*f*	submachine gun	
5868	**agressivité**-*f*	aggressiveness	
5870	**remboursement**-*m*	reimbursement| refund	
5871	**couvercle**-*m*	lid	
5873	**épuisement**-*m*	exhaustion| depletion	
5876	**encens**-*m*	incense	
5877	**aération**-*f*	aeration	
5878	**casserole**-*f*	pan	
5879	**manchot**-*m; adj*	penguin; one-handed	
5880	**nabot**-*m; adj*	runt; dwarfish	
5882	**incognito**-*adv; m*	incognito; incognito	
5884	**protestation**-*f*	protest| outcry	
5885	**stabilité**-*f*	stability| steadiness	
5886	**flan**-*m*	flan| pudding	
5887	**boudin**-*m*	black pudding| blood sausage	
5889	**cuvette**-*f*	bowl| basin	
5891	**composé**-*adj; m*	compound; compound	
5892	**mélancolique**-*adj; m/f*	melancholy; melancholiac	
5894	**domination**-*f*	domination	
5895	**blocage**-*m*	blocking	
5896	**caissier**-*m*	cashier	
5899	**carré**-*adj; m*	square; square	
5900	**dôme**-*m*	dome	
5903	**torchon**-*m*	tea towel	
5905	**rapidité**-*f*	speed| rapidity	
5906	**probation**-*f*	probation	
5907	**pascal**-*m; adj*	pascal; paschal	
5908	**exorcisme**-*m*	exorcism	
5909	**zèle**-*m*	zeal	
5910	**sandale**-*f*	sandal	
5911	**pli**-*m*	fold| ply	
5912	**avancement**-*m*	advancement| promotion	
5913	**descendant**-*adj; m*	descending; descendant	
5914	**pâtée**-*f*	mash| food	
5916	**oppression**-*f*	oppression	
5920	**cortège**-*m*	procession	
5922	**noyade**-*f*	drowning	
5923	**mentalité**-*f*	mentality	
5925	**véranda**-*f*	veranda| porch	
5927	**manipulation**-*f*	handling| rigging	
5928	**côtelette**-*f*	chop	
5929	**gaucher**-*m; adj*	left-hander; left-handed	
5930	**croiseur**-*m*	cruiser	
5931	**tram**-*m*	tram| car	
5932	**motion**-*f*	motion	
5933	**confrontation**-*f*	showdown	
5934	**talisman**-*m*	talisman	
5935	**uranium**-*m*	uranium	
5936	**vortex**-*m*	vortex	
5937	**branlette**-*f*	hand job	
5938	**extension**-*f*	extension| expansion	
5939	**catin**-*f*	trollop| whore	
5942	**délice**-*m*	delight	
5943	**indifférence**-*f*	indifference	

5944	**pif**-*m*	conk| snitch	6010	**partition**-*f*	partition| score
5945	**compensation**-*f*	compensation	6013	**toupet**-*m*	nerve| cheek
5949	**endurance**-*f*	endurance| stamina	6014	**bijouterie**-*f*	jewelry| jewelry store
5950	**cobaye**-*m*	guinea pig	6015	**châle**-*m*	shawl
5951	**reddition**-*f*	surrender	6017	**larbin**-*m*	stooge| flunkey
5952	**adolescence**-*f*	adolescence	6018	**pastèque**-*f*	watermelon
5953	**azur**-*m*	azure	6020	**habileté**-*f*	skill| cleverness
5956	**forain**-*m*	showman	6021	**navet**-*m*	turnip
5957	**jupon**-*m*	petticoat	6022	**météorite**-*f*	meteorite
5958	**marraine**-*f*	godmother	6023	**camelot**-*m*	hawker
5959	**romantisme**-*m*	romanticism	6027	**nappe**-*f*	tablecloth
5960	**cornichon**-*m*	gherkin| nincompoop			
5961	**capitaliste**-*m/f; adj*	capitalist; capitalistic			
5962	**diplomatie**-*f*	diplomacy			
5963	**gibbon**-*m*	gibbon			
5964	**pudeur**-*f*	modesty			
5965	**récréation**-*f*	recreation| recess			
5966	**fracas**-*m*	crash| smash			
5967	**tee**-*m*	tee			
5968	**plutonium**-*m*	plutonium			
5970	**cité**-*f; adj*	city-state; city			
5971	**rationnel**-*adj; m*	rational; rational			
5973	**luxure**-*f*	lust			
5974	**lavabo**-*m*	sink			
5975	**platine**-*m; f*	platinum; deck			
5976	**patriotisme**-*m*	patriotism			
5977	**choléra**-*m*	cholera			
5978	**titan**-*m*	titan			
5980	**prestation**-*f*	benefit			
5981	**conservatoire**-*m*	conservatory			
5983	**administrateur**-*m*	administrator			
5984	**graffiti**-*m*	graffiti			
5985	**veston**-*m*	jacket			
5986	**miniature**-*adj; f*	miniature; miniature			
5987	**peseta**-*f*	peseta			
5990	**louange**-*f*	praise			
5991	**amélioration**-*f*	improvement			
5992	**licorne**-*f*	unicorn			
5994	**sucrerie**-*f*	suger refinery			
5997	**mœurs**-*fpl*	manners			
5999	**idiotie**-*f*	idiocy			
6000	**verbal**-*adj; m*	verbal; verbal			
6001	**fanatique**-*adj; m/f*	fanatic; fanatic			
6004	**alligator**-*m*	alligator			
6008	**percée**-*f*	breakthrough			
6009	**pénitence**-*f*	penance			

Verbs

Rank	French-PoS	Translation
5003	**manœuvrer**-*vb*	maneuver| manipulate
5009	**connecter**-*vb*	log on
5022	**greffer**-*vb*	graft| engraft
5028	**enchaîner**-*vb*	enchain
5039	**équiper**-*vb*	equip| provide
5045	**inculper**-*vb*	charge
5052	**chatouiller**-*vb*	tickle
5055	**recouvrir**-*vb*	cover| re-cover
5056	**évoquer**-*vb*	evoke| recall
5060	**censurer**-*vb*	censor
5064	**diviser**-*vb*	divide| partition
5071	**bannir**-*vb*	banish
5077	**masquer**-*vb*	hide| mask
5078	**handicaper**-*vb*	handicap
5093	**croquer**-*vb*	crunch| eat
5096	**dégénérer**-*vb*	degenerate
5098	**déchiffrer**-*vb*	decipher
5101	**tourmenter**-*vb*	torment| plague
5107	**secourir**-*vb*	rescue
5111	**compromettre**-*vb*	compromise
5114	**râler**-*vb*	grumble| moan
5115	**aviser**-*vb*	inform
5116	**récolter**-*vb*	harvest| collect
5117	**hanter**-*vb*	haunt| spook
5121	**ressusciter**-*vb*	resurrect
5123	**redire**-*vb*	repeat
5124	**détecter**-*vb*	detect
5125	**enrichir**-*vb*	enrich
5130	**débarrer**-*vb*	unbar
5135	**détraquer**-*vb*	break down
5138	**réciter**-*vb*	recite
5146	**freiner**-*vb*	curb
5147	**cailler**-*vb*	curdle| clot
5155	**gouverner**-*vb*	govern| steer
5163	**truquer**-*vb*	rig| fake
5176	**apaiser**-*vb*	appease| soothe
5177	**flirter**-*vb*	flirt| spoon
5181	**recruter**-*vb*	recruit| rush
5184	**périr**-*vb*	perish
5188	**imprimer**-*vb*	print| print out
5195	**fouetter**-*vb*	whip| scourge
5199	**manier**-*vb*	handle| use
5220	**gâter**-*vb*	spoil| pamper
5226	**ramoner**-*vb*	sweep
5247	**surgir**-*vb*	arise| emerge
5249	**avorter**-*vb*	abort
5251	**surnommer**-*vb*	nickname
5253	**remédier**-*vb*	remedy
5261	**escalader**-*vb*	climb
5269	**démanger**-*vb*	itch
5273	**abriter**-*vb*	shelter
5288	**bombarder**-*vb*	bomb| bombard
5290	**émouvoir**-*vb*	move| stir
5291	**reconduire**-*vb*	renew
5296	**haler**-*vb*	tow
5300	**intimider**-*vb*	intimidate| frighten
5318	**ouïr**-*vb*	hear
5325	**piocher**-*vb*	pickax
5331	**agrandir**-*vb*	enlarge| extend
5333	**éclipser**-*vb*	eclipse| outshine
5339	**brandir**-*vb*	brandish
5345	**compenser**-*vb*	compensate| offset
5350	**diffuser**-*vb*	broadcast| spread
5352	**contribuer**-*vb*	contribute
5363	**vinaigrer**-*vb*	souse
5371	**damner**-*vb*	damn
5373	**réconcilier**-*vb*	reconcile
5390	**redonner**-*vb*	restore| give back
5392	**coiffer**-*vb*	style
5396	**crécher**-*vb*	chum
5400	**cirer**-*vb*	wax
5404	**croître**-*vb*	grow
5421	**éduquer**-*vb*	educate| teach
5430	**sanctifier**-*vb*	sanctify
5431	**guetter**-*vb*	await
5435	**lanterne**-*vb*	lantern
5438	**camer**-*vb*	dope
5445	**démonter**-*vb*	disassemble| dismantle
5453	**présager**-*vb*	predict| foresee
5454	**improviser**-*vb*	improvise
5455	**questionner**-*vb*	question
5462	**recueillir**-*vb*	collect| gather
5463	**intercepter**-*vb*	intercept
5473	**rédiger**-*vb*	rewrite
5474	**rouiller**-*vb*	rust
5477	**réviser**-*vb*	revise| review
5485	**collaborer**-*vb*	collaborate
5486	**percher**-*vb*	perch| hang

5499	**blasphémer**-*vb*	blaspheme	5777	**infliger**-*vb*	impose| mete
5530	**contredire**-*vb*	contradict	5794	**clarifier**-*vb*	clarify
5532	**contempler**-*vb*	contemplate	5796	**désobéir**-*vb*	disobey
5535	**polir**-*vb*	polish| buff	5815	**intituler**-*vb*	title
5538	**relaxer**-*vb*	relax	5819	**motiver**-*vb*	motivate
5540	**redresser**-*vb*	straighten| redress	5821	**prolonger**-*vb*	extend| prolong
5557	**aboyer**-*vb*	bark	5825	**rougir**-*vb*	blush| go red
5558	**déléguer**-*vb*	delegate| devolve	5833	**incliner**-*vb*	tilt| incline
5564	**duper**-*vb*	fool| deceive	5837	**cloner**-*vb*	clone
5569	**retomber**-*vb*	drop| relapse	5848	**neutraliser**-*vb*	neutralize| negative
5571	**mouler**-*vb*	mold| press	5856	**sangler**-*vb*	strap
5572	**comprimer**-*vb*	compress| jam	5859	**cerner**-*vb*	invest| bestow
5580	**dissuader**-*vb*	deter| put off	5864	**alimenter**-*vb*	feed
5585	**alerter**-*vb*	alert| warn	5867	**requérir**-*vb*	require
5599	**dégainer**-*vb*	unsheathe	5869	**cambrioler**-*vb*	burgle| rob
5608	**collectionner**-*vb*	collect	5872	**acquitter**-*vb*	pay| discharge
5616	**soufrer**-*vb*	sulfur| sulphurize	5881	**ravoir**-*vb*	get back
5618	**bûcher**-*m; vb*	pyre| slave; log	5890	**convertir**-*vb*	convert
5624	**brosser**-*vb*	brush	5893	**importuner**-*vb*	bother
5627	**tripoter**-*vb*	tamper| paw	5897	**rôder**-*vb*	prowl| lurk
5632	**hisser**-*vb*	hoist| pull up	5898	**sceller**-*vb*	seal| embed
5633	**routier**-*vb; m*	truck; teamster	5901	**saboter**-*vb*	sabotage
5645	**mâcher**-*vb*	chew| gum	5919	**déserter**-*vb*	desert
5646	**cane**-*vb*	cane	5921	**dépouiller**-*vb*	strip| skin
5647	**clouer**-*vb*	nail| tack	5924	**denteler**-*vb*	indent
5652	**combiner**-*vb*	combine| compound	5926	**bonder**-*vb*	cram
5656	**gaufrer**-*vb*	emboss	5940	**désarmer**-*vb*	disarm
5658	**travestir**-*vb*	travesty	5941	**décapiter**-*vb*	decapitate
5661	**pâtir**-*vb*	suffer	5946	**recoudre**-*vb*	sew| sew up
5668	**raffiner**-*vb*	refine	5948	**méditer**-*vb*	meditate| think
5676	**conjurer**-*vb*	conjure	5969	**contrer**-*vb*	counteract
5681	**projeter**-*vb*	project	5972	**vibrer**-*vb*	vibrate| thrill
5693	**expérimenter**-*vb*	experiment| experience	5979	**licencier**-*vb*	dismiss| fire
5701	**démontrer**-*vb*	demonstrate| reveal	5993	**refléter**-*vb*	reflect
5705	**confronter**-*vb*	confront	6003	**maquiller**-*vb*	make up
5712	**bousculer**-*vb*	hustle	6005	**peloter**-*vb*	grope
5715	**transpirer**-*vb*	sweat| transpire	6006	**frustrer**-*vb*	frustrate
5717	**maigrir**-*vb*	slim| become thin	6016	**gémir**-*vb*	moan| wail
5728	**diminuer**-*vb*	decrease| reduce	6024	**pomper**-*vb*	pump
5732	**prescrire**-*vb*	prescribe	6026	**léguer**-*vb*	will
5749	**pleurnicher**-*vb*	whimper| snivel	6030	**savourer**-*vb*	enjoy| glory
5750	**rouvrir**-*vb*	reopen	6031	**sombrer**-*vb*	sink
5751	**picoler**-*vb*	drink| booze	6035	**régaler**-*vb*	regale| feast
5768	**instruire**-*vb*	instruct| educate	6037	**spécialiser**-*vb*	specialize
5771	**contaminer**-*vb*	contaminate	6038	**engendrer**-*vb*	generate| give rise to
			6048	**gronder**-*vb*	scold| rumble

6053	**barder**-*vb*	bard	6372	**lister**-*vb*	list
6056	**riposter**-*vb*	hit back| retaliate	6378	**attribuer**-*vb*	assign| attribute
6058	**dévaliser**-*vb*	rob| raid	6380	**digérer**-*vb*	digest
6068	**encercler**-*vb*	circle| surround	6382	**recréer**-*vb*	recreate
6073	**épicer**-*vb*	spice	6384	**jaser**-*vb*	gossip| blab
6075	**refiler**-*vb*	palm off	6386	**suspecter**-*vb*	suspect
6088	**rider**-*vb*	wrinkle| ruffle	6387	**marchander**-*vb*	haggle| bargain
6094	**héberger**-*vb*	accommodate| harbor	6388	**dérober**-*vb*	steal
6096	**tatouer**-*vb*	tattoo	6392	**vénérer**-*vb*	revere| worship
6107	**aggraver**-*vb*	aggravate	6394	**ménager**-*adj; vb*	household; spare
6111	**expirer**-*vb*	expire| breathe out	6396	**blanchir**-*vb*	whiten| launder
6115	**skier**-*vb*	ski	6399	**inonder**-*vb*	flood| inundate
6148	**insinuer**-*vb*	insinuate| suggest	6403	**assigner**-*vb*	assign
6156	**bluffer**-*vb*	bluff	6404	**ajuster**-*vb*	adjust| tighten
6166	**percuter**-*vb*	ram	6414	**rimer**-*vb*	rhyme
6169	**limer**-*vb*	file	6417	**matraquer**-*vb*	club| cosh
6170	**taquiner**-*vb*	tease	6436	**rincer**-*vb*	rinse
6171	**démasquer**-*vb*	unmask| expose	6439	**moisir**-*vb*	mold
6183	**solder**-*vb*	settle	6440	**trébucher**-*vb*	stumble| stagger
6193	**cochonner**-*vb*	pig	6442	**resserrer**-*vb*	tighten
6197	**germer**-*vb*	germinate	6456	**shooter**-*vb*	shoot| shoot up
6206	**renouveler**-*vb*	renew	6468	**doter**-*vb*	endow
6209	**faucher**-*vb*	mow| reap	6469	**saccager**-*vb*	sack| ransack
6211	**fusiller**-*vb*	shoot	6475	**rivaliser**-*vb*	compete
6214	**feindre**-*vb*	pretend| put on	6499	**injecter**-*vb*	inject
6235	**disperser**-*vb*	disperse| spread	6501	**aboutir**-*vb*	lead
6247	**relancer**-*vb*	revive	6504	**absorber**-*vb*	absorb
6250	**seller**-*vb*	saddle	6508	**enfouir**-*vb*	bury
6253	**mijoter**-*vb*	simmer	6513	**masturber**-*vb*	masturbate
6269	**prêcher**-*vb*	preach| sermonize	6519	**déshonorer**-*vb*	dishonor
6285	**confisquer**-*vb*	confiscate| condemn	6520	**entamer**-*vb*	start| launch
6289	**déterrer**-*vb*	dig| unearth	6521	**regorger**-*vb*	abound
6294	**illuminer**-*vb*	illuminate| floodlight	6522	**dépanner**-*vb*	repair| debug
6297	**suer**-*vb*	sweat	6523	**pèlerinage**-*m; vb*	pilgrimage; streak
6302	**retraiter**-*vb*	reprocess	6524	**dégoter**-*vb*	find| dig up
6304	**dénicher**-*vb*	unearth	6525	**ressaisir**-*vb*	catch
6306	**expédier**-*vb*	send| dispatch	6526	**élaborer**-*vb*	elaborate| design
6308	**afficher**-*vb*	display	6528	**affoler**-*vb*	panic
6316	**étreindre**-*vb*	embrace| grasp	6531	**consommer**-*vb*	consume| use
6327	**grimer**-*vb*	make up| disguise	6545	**ligoter**-*vb*	bind| tie up
6334	**débrancher**-*vb*	unplug	6549	**purger**-*vb*	purge| bleed
6337	**piller**-*vb*	plunder| loot	6551	**incarner**-*vb*	embody| personify
6347	**léser**-*vb*	injure	6552	**basculer**-*vb*	toggle| tip
6350	**voûter**-*vb*	stoop| vault	6565	**renifler**-*vb*	sniff| smell
6357	**brouiller**-*vb*	blur| scramble	6576	**palpiter**-*vb*	throb| palpitate
6364	**inverser**-*vb*	reverse	6579	**grignoter**-*vb*	nibble

6597	esquiver-*vb*	dodge| avoid		6866	figer-*vb*	freeze
6599	repeindre-*vb*	repaint		6867	chevaucher-*vb*	lap
6605	souiller-*vb*	soil| defile		6873	anticiper-*vb*	anticipate
6612	omettre-*vb*	omit| pass over		6874	dévier-*vb*	deviate
6618	canneler-*vb*	groove		6880	déployer-*vb*	deploy| display
6619	inciter-*vb*	encourage| incite		6881	tondre-*vb*	mow| shear
6633	approprier-*vb*	appropriate		6882	décourager-*vb*	discourage
6658	pondre-*vb*	lay		6884	percevoir-*vb*	levy
6669	crucifier-*vb*	crucify		6889	guillotiner-*vb*	guillotine
6680	embarrasser-*vb*	embarrass| bother		6899	détailler-*vb*	detail
6688	élargir-*vb*	broaden| stretch		6903	frimer-*vb*	show off
6696	déballer-*vb*	unpack		6908	collecter-*vb*	collect
6700	déduire-*vb*	deduct| deduce		6915	purifier-*vb*	purify
6708	marmotter-*vb*	mutter		6920	pirater-*vb*	hack| pirate
6712	persister-*vb*	persist| continue		6922	piétiner-*vb*	trample on
6714	compléter-*vb*	complete| complement		6924	propager-*vb*	propagate
6715	patiner-*vb*	skate		6926	échauffer-*vb*	warm
6716	équilibrer-*vb*	balance| trim		6928	manigancer-*vb*	engineer
6717	lustrer-*vb*	polish		6931	frôler-*vb*	graze
6719	écœurer-*vb*	disgust		6943	désactiver-*vb*	deactivate
6720	aveugler-*vb*	blind		6945	contester-*vb*	challenge| contest
6724	préméditer-*vb*	premeditate		6949	déchaîner-*vb*	unchain
6725	marmiter-*vb*	strafe		6983	invoquer-*vb*	invoke
6733	nicher-*vb*	nest		6986	succomber-*vb*	succumb
6734	affaiblir-*vb*	weaken| reduce		6987	trompeter-*vb*	trumpet
6736	tâter-*vb*	feel		6989	résonner-*vb*	resonate| resound
6737	surpasser-*vb*	surpass| excel		6997	amarrer-*vb*	moor| belay
6739	initier-*vb*	initiate		7012	givrer-*vb*	frost
6748	fendre-*vb*	split| slit		7020	décréter-*vb*	decree| order
6756	triompher-*vb*	triumph		7028	advenir-*vb*	happen
6768	souligner-*vb*	emphasize| underline		7029	submerger-*vb*	overwhelm| submerge
6772	replier-*vb*	replicate| fold up		7035	retaper-*vb*	do up| retype
6776	égorger-*vb*	kill| slit throat		7038	grogner-*vb*	grumble
6795	sacrer-*vb*	consecrate| crown		7045	débloquer-*vb*	unblock
6798	bricoler-*vb*	tinker		7084	rallier-*vb*	rally
6804	précéder-*vb*	precede		7087	barricader-*vb*	barricade
6806	étaler-*vb*	spread out| display		7108	faufiler-*vb*	baste| dodge
6807	symboliser-*vb*	symbolize		7113	gober-*vb*	swallow
6809	écumer-*vb*	skim| froth		7115	reconstituer-*vb*	reconstruct| put together
6819	téléviser-*vb*	televise		7127	intriguer-*vb*	intrigue
6828	enflammer-*vb*	ignite| inflame		7128	exiler-*vb*	exile
6832	emprisonner-*vb*	imprison| trap		7130	flairer-*vb*	smell| scent
6833	blaguer-*vb*	joke		7133	mollir-*vb*	weaken| soften
6836	terroriser-*vb*	terrorize| bully		7141	pécher-*vb*	sin
6857	congédier-*vb*	dismiss| discharge		7142	étourdir-*vb*	stun| surprise
6864	ronfler-*vb*	snore				

7152	**désamorcer**-*vb*	defuse	7449	**calomnier**-*vb*	slander
7158	**entailler**-*vb*	cut	7459	**mémoriser**-*vb*	memorize
7159	**abaisser**-*vb*	lower| diminish	7462	**relire**-*vb*	read back
7160	**papoter**-*vb*	chatter| babble	7463	**bénéficier**-*vb*	gain
7164	**rayer**-*vb*	strike	7465	**fleurir**-*vb*	flower| flourish
7167	**prodiguer**-*vb*	give| lavish	7477	**enrôler**-*vb*	enlist| enroll
7173	**aligner**-*vb*	align	7482	**contraster**-*vb*	contrast
7177	**rengainer**-*vb*	sheathe	7494	**délibérer**-*vb*	deliberate
7178	**présider**-*vb*	preside	7497	**désorienter**-*vb*	disorient
7186	**chuchoter**-*vb*	whisper	7501	**irriter**-*vb*	irritate
7187	**soutirer**-*vb*	extract	7504	**trotter**-*vb*	trot
7195	**caler**-*vb*	stall	7517	**pâturer**-*vb*	graze
7199	**rabaisser**-*vb*	belittle	7519	**déraper**-*vb*	skid
7208	**différencier**-*vb*	differentiate	7522	**attrister**-*vb*	sadden
7213	**interner**-*vb*	intern	7524	**éradiquer**-*vb*	eradicate
7217	**exhiber**-*vb*	produce			
7237	**trimer**-*vb*	slave away			
7238	**ensorceler**-*vb*	bewitch			
7251	**régir**-*vb*	govern			
7254	**brailler**-*vb*	bawl| scream			
7265	**glander**-*vb*	screw around			
7279	**redoubler**-*vb*	redouble			
7283	**gainer**-*vb*	sheathe			
7285	**rejouer**-*vb*	replay			
7288	**trier**-*vb*	sort			
7300	**ranimer**-*vb*	revive| rekindle			
7317	**aventurer**-*vb*	venture			
7319	**contracter**-*vb*	contract			
7329	**dévaster**-*vb*	devastate| destroy			
7350	**amputer**-*vb*	amputate| take off			
7372	**simuler**-*vb*	simulate| pretend			
7380	**couronner**-*vb*	top| enthrone			
7384	**escrimer**-*vb*	fight			
7387	**vanner**-*vb*	winnow			
7389	**mixer**-*m; vb*	mixer; blend			
7394	**trouer**-*vb*	pit			
7405	**flanquer**-*vb*	flank			
7408	**décamper**-*vb*	decamp| run away			
7410	**éjecter**-*vb*	eject| shed			
7413	**étriper**-*vb*	gut			
7419	**effleurer**-*vb*	touch			
7420	**aérer**-*vb*	air| aerate			
7427	**appréhender**-*vb*	apprehend			
7429	**forger**-*vb*	forge			
7439	**lubrifier**-*vb*	lubricate			
7446	**reconquérir**-*vb*	regain| reconquer			

Alphabetical order

Rank	French-PoS	Translation
7159	abaisser-*vb*	lower| diminish
7048	abdomen-*m*	abdomen
6564	aboiement-*m*	bark
7348	abomination-*f*	abomination
7324	abonnement-*m*	subscription
6501	aboutir-*vb*	lead
5557	aboyer-*vb*	bark
7402	abracadabra-*m*	abracadabra
5273	abriter-*vb*	shelter
6504	absorber-*vb*	absorb
7162	abstinence-*f*	abstinence
7360	absurdité-*f*	absurdity
5810	accélérateur-*m*	accelerator
7437	accélération-*f*	acceleration
6465	accessible-*adj*	accessible| reachable
5228	accidentellement-*adv*	accidentally
6435	acclamation-*f*	acclamation| cheer
6887	accompli-*adj*	accomplished
7456	accomplissement-*m*	fulfillment| accomplishment
5677	accordéon-*m*	accordion
6777	accroché-*adj*	hooked
6900	acolyte-*m*	acolyte
6829	acquisition-*f*	acquisition
5872	acquitter-*vb*	pay| discharge
5791	actualité-*f*	actuality
7051	adepte-*m/f*	supporter
6854	adéquat-*adj*	adequate
6427	adhésif-*adj; m*	adhesive; adhesive
5983	administrateur-*m*	administrator
5655	admirateur-*m*	admirer
5952	adolescence-*f*	adolescence
7179	adoptif-*adj*	adoptive
7489	adroit-*adj*	skilful| adroit
7028	advenir-*vb*	happen
7499	adverse-*adj*	adverse| opposing
7241	adversité-*f*	adversity
5877	aération-*f*	aeration
7420	aérer-*vb*	air| aerate
6654	aérodrome-*m*	aerodrome
6734	affaiblir-*vb*	weaken| reduce
5842	affectation-*f*	assignment| allocation
7114	affectueusement-*adv*	fondly
5917	affectueux-*adj*	affectionate
6308	afficher-*vb*	display
5275	affilé-*adj*	sharp
6528	affoler-*vb*	panic
5412	affreusement-*adv*	frightfully
6747	affrontement-*m*	confrontation
6800	affront-*m*	affront| outrage
6686	affût-*m*	carriage
7039	agaçant-*adj*	annoying| aggravating
6107	aggraver-*vb*	aggravate
7220	agile-*adj*	agile
5331	agrandir-*vb*	enlarge| extend
5270	agresseur-*m; adj*	aggressor; assailant
5868	agressivité-*f*	aggressiveness
6490	agricole-*adj*	agricultural
6851	aigu-*adj*	acute| shrill
7106	aisé-*adj*	easy| fluent
6349	aisément-*adv*	easily
6404	ajuster-*vb*	adjust| tighten
6732	albanais-*adj; m|mpl*	Albanian; Albanian
7357	aléatoire-*adj*	aleatory
5585	alerter-*vb*	alert| warn
5635	algue-*f; adj*	alga; algoid
6617	alignement-*m*	alignment
7173	aligner-*vb*	align
5864	alimenter-*vb*	feed
6593	allégation-*f*	allegation
5755	allégeance-*f*	allegiance
6060	allergie-*f*	allergy
6004	alligator-*m*	alligator
6102	allumage-*m*	ignition
5505	alphabet-*m*	alphabet
6373	aluminium-*m*	aluminum
6527	amabilité-*f*	kindness
6997	amarrer-*vb*	moor| belay
7110	amas-*m*	heap
6415	amazone-*f*	amazon
5991	amélioration-*f*	improvement
5090	amendement-*m*	amendment
5598	amertume-*f*	bitterness| grief
7363	amiable-*adj*	genial
5354	amnésie-*f*	amnesia
6464	amnésique-*m/f; adj*	amnesic; amnesiac
6743	amnistie-*f*	amnesty

6638	amont-*adv*	uphill
6650	amplement-*adv*	amply
5005	ampoule-*f*	bulb| ampoule
7350	amputer-*vb*	amputate| take off
6066	amusement-*m*	fun
6191	analyste-*m/f*	analyst
5102	ananas-*m*	pineapple
5583	anatomie-*f*	anatomy
7215	anecdote-*f*	anecdote
5776	anguille-*f; adj*	eel; anguine
6117	animateur-*m*	animator
6129	annexe-*f*	annex| schedule
5356	annulation-*f*	cancellation| annulment
7052	anonymat-*m*	anonymity
7071	antan-*adj*	of old| bygone
5136	antarctique-*adj*	Antarctic
7014	antérieur-*adj; m*	prior; antecessor
6143	antibiotique-*adj; m*	antibiotic; antibiotic
6873	anticiper-*vb*	anticipate
5185	antiquité-*f*	antiquity
6174	antre-*m*	den
5761	anus-*m*	anus
5272	anxiété-*f*	anxiety
5497	anxieux-*adj*	anxious| worried
5176	apaiser-*vb*	appease| soothe
6252	apéritif-*m*	aperitif
6155	aplomb-*m*	aplomb
5597	apogée-*m*	apogee| peak
7284	apôtre-*m*	apostle
6639	apparent-*adj*	apparent| obvious
5440	appelant-*adj; m*	appellant; appellant
5536	application-*f*	application
7427	appréhender-*vb*	apprehend
6470	approchant-*adj*	approaching
6633	approprier-*vb*	appropriate
6793	approvisionnement-*m*	procurement| provision
6481	approximativement-*adv*	approximately
5650	apte-*adj*	apt
6407	aptitude-*f*	aptitude| fitness
5012	aquarium-*m*	aquarium
7286	aquatique-*adj*	aquatic
5697	arctique-*adj*	Arctic
5721	ardent-*adj*	ardent| burning

5429	ardeur-*f; adj*	ardor| heat; vehement
5774	ardoise-*f*	slate
5851	argenterie-*f*	silverware
7101	argentin-*adj*	Argentine
5385	argile-*f*	clay
6126	aristocrate-*m/f*	aristocrat
6973	armada-*f*	armada
5410	artère-*f*	artery
6914	arthrite-*f*	arthritis
7510	artisan-*m*	artisan
6403	assigner-*vb*	assign
5131	associé-*adj; m*	associate; associate
5362	assurément-*adv*	certainly
6942	astéroïde-*m*	asteroid
7289	astronomie-*f*	astronomy
5640	astuce-*f*	trick| cunning
5328	astucieux-*adj*	clever| astute
6159	athée-*m/f; adj*	atheist; atheistic
5734	atome-*m*	atom
5718	atrocité-*f*	atrocity| outrage
5830	attache-*f*	clip
7475	attachement-*m*	attachment
5595	attente-*f*	waiting| expectation
6473	attirance-*f*	attraction
5110	attirant-*adj*	attractive| appealing
6378	attribuer-*vb*	assign| attribute
7522	attrister-*vb*	sadden
5729	auditeur-*m; adj*	auditor; auditorial
7021	augure-*m*	omen
6896	auguste-*adj*	august
6988	aumône-*f*	alms
6861	aumônier-*m*	chaplain
5754	australien-*adj; m*	Australian; digger
7492	authenticité-*f*	authenticity
7498	autobiographie-*f*	autobiography
7443	autocar-*m*	coach| car
7353	autodéfense-*f*	self-defense
7325	autodestruction-*f*	self-destruction
6764	autonome-*adj*	autonomous
6729	autonomie-*f*	autonomy
7490	autoritaire-*adj*	authoritarian
6398	auxiliaire-*adj; m*	auxiliary; auxiliary
5863	aval-*m; adj*	approval; down-stream
5912	avancement-*m*	advancement| promotion

7057	**avare**-*m/f; adj*	miser; stingy
5357	**avatar**-*m*	avatar
7317	**aventurer**-*vb*	venture
6886	**aventurier**-*m; adj*	adventurer; aggressive
6720	**aveugler**-*vb*	blind
6858	**aviateur**-*m*	aviator| pilot
5759	**avide**-*adj*	eager| greedy
7060	**avidité**-*f*	greed
5115	**aviser**-*vb*	inform
5249	**avorter**-*vb*	abort
6838	**avorton**-*m*	runt
5210	**axe**-*m*	axis
7433	**azote**-*m*	nitrogen
5953	**azur**-*m*	azure

B

6689	**babouin**-*m*	baboon
6642	**bactérie**-*f*	bacterium
7343	**baffe**-*f*	swipe
7344	**baïonnette**-*f*	bayonet
6275	**balançoire**-*f*	swing
6240	**balayage**-*m*	scanning
6871	**balistique**-*adj; f*	ballistic; ballistics
5801	**bambou**-*m*	bamboo
5079	**bandeau**-*m*	headband
5853	**banjo**-*m*	banjo
6474	**bannière**-*f*	banner
5071	**bannir**-*vb*	banish
6136	**banquette**-*f*	bench| seat
7493	**barbarie**-*f*	barbarity
5865	**barbu**-*adj; m*	bearded; bearded man
6053	**barder**-*vb*	bard
5336	**baril**-*m*	barrel| crater
6575	**barré**-*adj*	crossed
6852	**barricade**-*f*	barricade| barrier
7087	**barricader**-*vb*	barricade
6483	**bascule**-*f*	rocker| weighing machine
6552	**basculer**-*vb*	toggle| tip
5716	**basque**-*adj; f*	Basque; Basque
5313	**battement**-*m*	beat| beating
6907	**baume**-*m*	balm| balsam
6412	**bavardage**-*m*	chat| chatting
6080	**béat**-*adj*	smug

7436	**bécane**-*f*	bike
6741	**beige**-*adj; m*	beige; beige
5862	**belge**-*adj*	Belgian
5038	**Belgique**-*f*	Belgium
7463	**bénéficier**-*vb*	gain
7425	**bénévole**-*adj; m*	voluntary; volunteer
6141	**benne**-*f*	dumpster| tub
6441	**béquille**-*f*	crutch
6091	**biais**-*m*	bias| angle
5490	**biberon**-*m*	baby bottle
6583	**bibliothécaire**-*m*	librarian
6381	**biblique**-*adj*	biblical
7422	**biceps**-*m*	biceps
6354	**bienfaiteur**-*adj; m*	benefactor; benefactor
7100	**bienfait**-*m*	kindness
7331	**bienheureux**-*adj*	blissful
7484	**bienveillance**-*f*	benevolence
7378	**bienveillant**-*adj*	benevolent
6014	**bijouterie**-*f*	jewelry| jewelry store
5381	**bikini**-*m*	bikini
5246	**Bing!**-*int*	Zap!
5731	**biographie**-*f*	biography
5104	**bison**-*f*	bison
6147	**bistrot**-*m*	pub
6833	**blaguer**-*vb*	joke
6396	**blanchir**-*vb*	whiten| launder
7019	**blanchisserie**-*f*	laundry
5499	**blasphémer**-*vb*	blaspheme
5895	**blocage**-*m*	blocking
5068	**blouse**-*f*	gown| blouse
6156	**bluffer**-*vb*	bluff
5067	**bluff**-*m*	bluff
5788	**bobard**-*m*	lie
5843	**bobine**-*f*	coil| reel
6345	**body**-*m*	body
7334	**Bohême**-*f*	Bohemia
7445	**bohémien**-*adj; m*	Bohemian; Gypsy
5367	**boiteux**-*adj; m/f*	lame| limping; lame person
5288	**bombarder**-*vb*	bomb| bombard
5926	**bonder**-*vb*	cram
5507	**bonne**-*f*	housemaid
7399	**bonze**-*m*	monk
7296	**bookmaker**-*m*	bookmaker
6163	**borgne**-*adj*	one-eyed

6935	**borné**-*adj*	limited| narrow
5468	**bossu**-*m; adj*	hunchback; hunchbacked
5420	**boucan**-*m*	racket| din
6569	**bouddhiste**-*adj*	Buddhist
5887	**boudin**-*m*	black pudding| blood sausage
6305	**bouée**-*f*	buoy
6773	**bouillant**-*adj*	boiling
5106	**bouillon**-*m*	broth| bouillon
5020	**boulangerie**-*f*	bakery
5702	**boulanger**-*m*	baker
5304	**boulet**-*m*	ball| drag
6929	**boulon**-*m*	bolt
7256	**bourdon**-*m*	bee| drone
7518	**bourdonnement**-*m*	buzz| hum
7333	**bourgeoisie**-*f*	bourgeoisie
5712	**bousculer**-*vb*	hustle
5405	**bouseux**-*adj*	hick
5274	**boussole**-*adj; f*	compass; compass
5030	**boutique**-*f*	shop| stall
5292	**boyau**-*m*	casing
7254	**brailler**-*vb*	bawl| scream
6616	**brancard**-*m*	stretcher
5339	**brandir**-*vb*	brandish
5937	**branlette**-*f*	hand job
5827	**brésilien**-*adj*	Brazilian
7034	**bretelle**-*f*	shoulder strap
5042	**brève**-*f*	breve
6757	**brevet**-*m*	patent| certificate
5820	**brick**-*m*	brig
6798	**bricoler**-*vb*	tinker
7022	**bride**-*f*	flange
5988	**brièvement**-*adv*	briefly
6425	**brigadier**-*m*	brigadier
6272	**brigand**-*m*	brigand
6610	**brio**-*m*	brillance
6131	**brochure**-*f*	brochure
7304	**bronzé**-*adj*	tanned| brown
5624	**brosser**-*vb*	brush
7082	**brouille**-*f*	quarrel
6357	**brouiller**-*vb*	blur| scramble
6165	**brûlant**-*adj*	burning
7440	**brunch**-*m*	brunch
5748	**brusque**-*adj*	sudden| brusque
6007	**brutalement**-*adv*	brutally
5277	**brutalité**-*f*	brutality
6341	**bûche**-*f*	log
5618	**bûcher**-*m; vb*	pyre| slave; log
6265	**bûcheron**-*m*	lumberjack
5503	**bungalow**-*m*	bungalow
6750	**buste**-*m*	bust
7252	**butte**-*f*	mound| butt

C

5542	**cabot**-*m*	pooch| mutt
5379	**cachot**-*m*	dungeon
5498	**cadenas**-*m*	padlock
5470	**cadence**-*f*	pace
6431	**caféine**-*f*	caffeine
6815	**cagoule**-*f*	hood
5147	**cailler**-*vb*	curdle| clot
5896	**caissier**-*m*	cashier
6813	**caisson**-*m*	box
5544	**calamar**-*m*	squid
6817	**calé**-*adj*	chock
7195	**caler**-*vb*	stall
5217	**calmant**-*adj; m*	calming; tranquilizer
7449	**calomnier**-*vb*	slander
6319	**calorie**-*f*	calorie
6393	**calvaire**-*m*	ordeal
5869	**cambrioler**-*vb*	burgle| rob
6023	**camelot**-*m*	hawker
6730	**cameraman**-*m*	cameraman
5438	**camer**-*vb*	dope
6472	**camisole de force**-*f*	straightjacket
5813	**camouflage**-*m*	camouflage
5179	**campement**-*m*	camp
6208	**canari**-*m*	canary
5423	**candidature**-*f*	application| candidacy
5646	**cane**-*vb*	cane
6154	**caniche**-*m*	poodle
5326	**caniveau**-*m*	gutter
6618	**canneler**-*vb*	groove
6422	**cannibale**-*adj; m/f*	cannibal; cannibal
5671	**canton**-*m*	canton
6281	**canular**-*m*	hoax
5243	**capitalisme**-*m*	capitalism
5961	**capitaliste**-*m/f; adj*	capitalist; capitalistic
6595	**cappuccino**-*m*	cappuccino
5399	**caprice**-*m*	fancy

7434	**capricieux**-*adj*	capricious| whimsical
6455	**capteur**-*m*	sensor
6278	**captivité**-*f*	captivity
5301	**carabine**-*f*	carbine
5634	**caractéristique**-*adj; f*	characteristic; characteristic
5604	**caraïbe**-*adj*	Caribbean
7168	**carapace**-*f*	shell
6491	**carat**-*m*	carat
7042	**carburateur**-*m*	carburetor
5493	**carcasse**-*f*	carcass
7225	**carlin**-*m*	pug
6098	**carpe**-*f*	carp
5899	**carré**-*adj; m*	square; square
5062	**carrosse**-*m*	coach| carriage
5340	**cartel**-*m*	cartel| coalition
6069	**carter**-*m*	housing| casing
6216	**cascade**-*f*	cascade
6362	**cascadeur**-*m*	stuntman
5322	**casque**-*m*	helmet
5878	**casserole**-*f*	pan
5257	**castor**-*m*	beaver| beaver rat
6897	**catastrophique**-*adj*	catastrophic
7308	**catéchisme**-*m*	catechism
5939	**catin**-*f*	trollop| whore
5264	**célébration**-*f*	celebration
7480	**célibat**-*m*	celibacy
5089	**cendrier**-*m*	ashtray
5060	**censurer**-*vb*	censor
5859	**cerner**-*vb*	invest| bestow
6369	**chacal**-*m*	jackal
7487	**chaire**-*f*	pulpit| professorship
6015	**châle**-*m*	shawl
7338	**chaleureusement**-*adv*	warmly| kindly
6424	**chambellan**-*m*	chamberlain
6904	**chandail**-*m*	sweater
5066	**chaperon**-*m*	chaperon| coping
6999	**chapiteau**-*m*	tent
7063	**chapitre**-*m*	chapter
5786	**charabia**-*m*	gibberish
5596	**charitable**-*adj*	charitable
5433	**charlatan**-*m*	charlatan| quack
6226	**charlot**-*m*	clown
6516	**charmeur**-*m; adj*	charmer; charming
5380	**charpentier**-*m*	carpenter
7514	**charrue**-*f*	plow
7069	**châssis**-*m*	chassis
6744	**chasteté**-*f*	chastity
5052	**chatouiller**-*vb*	tickle
5484	**chaudière**-*f*	boiler
7423	**chaudron**-*m*	cauldron
7306	**chauffard**-*m*	roadhog
6568	**cheeseburger**-*m*	cheeseburger
7180	**cheik**-*m*	sheikh
5519	**chemisier**-*m*	blouse
5242	**chêne**-*m*	oak
6346	**chenille**-*f*	caterpillar
6867	**chevaucher**-*vb*	lap
6292	**chevelure**-*f*	hair
5684	**chevet**-*m*	bedside
6643	**chiche**-*adj; int*	stingy; I dare you
5212	**chiffon**-*m*	cloth
6212	**chimiste**-*m*	chemist
6905	**chimpanzé**-*m*	chimpanzee
5977	**choléra**-*m*	cholera
6849	**cholestérol**-*m*	cholesterol
7337	**chômeur**-*m*	unemployed
5302	**choquant**-*adj*	shocking
5388	**chouchou**-*m*	pet
7186	**chuchoter**-*vb*	whisper
6657	**cidre**-*m*	cider
6667	**cil**-*m*	eyelash
7236	**cinématographique**-*adj*	cinematographic
6701	**cinquantaine**-*num; f*	fifties; middle age
5720	**cirage**-*m*	wax| polish
5400	**cirer**-*vb*	wax
5970	**cité**-*f; adj*	city-state; city
5694	**citerne**-*f*	tank
5250	**citrouille**-*f*	pumpkin
6106	**civière**-*f*	litter| stretcher
6961	**civique**-*adj*	civic
7123	**clairière**-*f*	clearing
5489	**clairon**-*m*	bugle
5065	**clandestin**-*adj*	clandestine
6758	**claquette**-*f*	tap
5794	**clarifier**-*vb*	clarify
5386	**clarté**-*f*	clarity| lightness
6402	**classement**-*m*	classification
5500	**clavier**-*m*	keyboard
6239	**clebs**-*m*	mutt

7411	**clergé**-*m*	clergy	5111	**compromettre**-*vb*	compromise
6182	**clic**-*m*	click| snip	5687	**concerto**-*m*	concerto
7136	**climatique**-*adj*	climatic	5013	**concession**-*f*	concession| dealership
7292	**climatisation**-*f*	air-conditioning	7230	**concombre**-*m*	cucumber
7094	**clitoris**-*m*	clitoris	6584	**concorde**-*f*	concord| amity
5691	**clodo**-*m*	bum	5692	**concret**-*adj; m*	concrete; concrete
5837	**cloner**-*vb*	clone	5733	**conditionné**-*adj*	conditioned
5647	**clouer**-*vb*	nail| tack	7298	**confidence**-*f*	confidence
6557	**coalition**-*f*	coalition	7096	**confidentialité**-*f*	confidentiality
5950	**cobaye**-*m*	guinea pig	7367	**confins**-*mpl*	confines
5590	**cochonnerie**-*f*	junk	6285	**confisquer**-*vb*	confiscate| condemn
6193	**cochonner**-*vb*	pig	6295	**conforme**-*adj*	compliant
5762	**cocu**-*m; adj*	cuckold; cheated on	6202	**conformément**-*adv*	in step
5465	**coéquipier**-*m*	team mate	5933	**confrontation**-*f*	showdown
5852	**coffret**-*m*	case	5705	**confronter**-*vb*	confront
5392	**coiffer**-*vb*	style	6857	**congédier**-*vb*	dismiss| discharge
6572	**collaborateur**-*m*	collaborator| contributer	6780	**congélateur**-*m*	freezer
5485	**collaborer**-*vb*	collaborate	7132	**congrégation**-*f*	congregation
5241	**collant**-*m; adj*	tights; adhesive	7104	**conjugal**-*adj*	conjugal| marital
6908	**collecter**-*vb*	collect	5676	**conjurer**-*vb*	conjure
7396	**collecteur**-*m*	collector	5009	**connecter**-*vb*	log on
5619	**collectif**-*adj*	collective	7444	**conquérant**-*m*	conqueror
5608	**collectionner**-*vb*	collect	7073	**conquête**-*f*	conquest
6312	**collectionneur**-*m*	collector	5007	**consentement**-*m*	consent
5481	**colon**-*m*	colon| settler	5032	**conservateur**-*adj; m*	conservative; conservative
5652	**combiner**-*vb*	combine| compound	5981	**conservatoire**-*m*	conservatory
7359	**combustion**-*f*	combustion	5664	**conserve**-*f*	preserve
6418	**commandant**-*m; adj*	commander; commanding	5766	**considérable**-*adj*	considerable| significant
6457	**commerçant**-*m; adj*	merchant; trading	7097	**considérablement**-*adv*	greatly
5648	**commotion**-*f*	shock| concussion	5349	**consolation**-*f*	consolation| comforting
5047	**communion**-*f*	Communion	6710	**consommateur**-*m*	consumer
6128	**comparable**-*adj*	comparable	6531	**consommer**-*vb*	consume| use
6514	**compas**-*m*	compass	7270	**conspirateur**-*m; adj*	conspirator; conspiratorial
5945	**compensation**-*f*	compensation	5359	**constance**-*f*	constancy
5345	**compenser**-*vb*	compensate| offset	7081	**constellation**-*f*	constellation
5586	**compétent**-*adj*	competent	6507	**contamination**-*f*	contamination
6714	**compléter**-*vb*	complete| complement	5771	**contaminer**-*vb*	contaminate
7091	**complexité**-*f*	complexity	5532	**contempler**-*vb*	contemplate
7234	**composant**-*m; adj*	component; compound	7153	**conteneur**-*m*	container
5891	**composé**-*adj; m*	compound; compound	6336	**contesté**-*adj*	disputed
6770	**compote**-*f*	compote	6945	**contester**-*vb*	challenge| contest
5849	**compréhensif**-	comprehensive	6765	**continental**-*adj*	continental
5572	**comprimer**-*vb*	compress| jam			

7232	**continuellement**-*adv*	continually	7453	**coulant**-*adj; m*	flowing; runner
7319	**contracter**-*vb*	contract	6463	**coupant**-*adj; m*	cutting; bolter
6059	**contradiction**-*f*	contradiction	6413	**couplet**-*m*	verse
6259	**contraint**-*adj*	constrained	7303	**couramment**-*adv*	fluently
7482	**contraster**-*vb*	contrast	6581	**couronnement**-*m*	coronation| crowning
5530	**contredire**-*vb*	contradict	7380	**couronner**-*vb*	top| enthrone
5143	**contremaître**-*m*	overseer	5075	**coursier**-*m*	steed| messenger
5969	**contrer**-*vb*	counteract	5643	**courtier**-*m*	broker
6895	**contretemps**-*mpl*	setbacks	6842	**courtisan**-*m*	courtier
7075	**contribuable**-*m/f*	taxpayer	5690	**courtois**-*adj*	courteous
5352	**contribuer**-*vb*	contribute	5289	**coussin**-*m*	cushion
6695	**controverse**-*f*	controverse	6086	**coûteux**-*adj*	expensive
7174	**convenablement**-*adv*	properly	5871	**couvercle**-*m*	lid
7320	**conventionnel**-*adj*	conventional	5165	**coyote**-*m*	coyote
6969	**conversion**-*f*	conversion	5790	**craie**-*f*	chalk
5890	**convertir**-*vb*	convert	5742	**crampe**-*f*	cramp
6853	**coopératif**-*adj; m*	cooperative; cooperator	6586	**crasseux**-*adj*	filthy| grimy
6606	**coopérative**-*f*	cooperative| cooperation	5689	**cratère**-*m*	crater
6932	**coordination**-*f*	coordination	5638	**créativité**-*f*	creativity
7015	**copilote**-*m/f*	copilot	5396	**crécher**-*vb*	chum
6911	**coquillage**-*m*	shell	7134	**créneau**-*m*	niche
6939	**corail**-*m*	coral	5432	**crevé**-*adj*	flat| all in| tired
6361	**Coran**-*m*	Koran	7056	**cric**-*m*	jack
6279	**cordonnier**-*m*	shoemaker	5464	**criminalité**-*f*	criminality
5960	**cornichon**-*m*	gherkin| nincompoop	6571	**crique**-*f*	creek
5828	**coroner**-*m*	coroner	5244	**critère**-*m*	criterion
5216	**corporation**-*f*	corporation	5539	**croisade**-*f*	crusade
6978	**corporel**-*adj*	corporal	5294	**croisement**-*m*	crossing
7143	**corral**-*m*	corral	5930	**croiseur**-*m*	cruiser
6303	**corridor**-*m*	corridor	7432	**croissant**-*adj; m*	growing; crescent
6112	**corsé**-*adj*	spicy	5404	**croître**-*vb*	grow
7196	**corset**-*m*	corset	5093	**croquer**-*vb*	crunch| eat
5920	**cortège**-*m*	procession	5850	**croquette**-*f*	croquette
5029	**corvée**-*f*	corvee| chore	5046	**croquis**-*m*	sketch
7326	**corvette**-*f*	corvette	5699	**crotte**-*f*	dung
6416	**cosaque**-*m*	Cossack	6443	**cruche**-*f*	jug| pitcher
7481	**cosmétique**-*adj; m*	cosmetic; cosmetic	6669	**crucifier**-*vb*	crucify
5223	**cosmique**-*adj*	cosmic	6718	**crucifix**-*m*	crucifix
7181	**cote**-*f*	odds| rating	6567	**crypte**-*f*	crypt
5928	**côtelette**-*f*	chop	5137	**cubain**-*adj*	Cuban
6280	**cottage**-*m*	cottage	6763	**cuiller**-*f*	spoon
5341	**couché**-*adj; adv*	lying down; abed	5566	**cuisiné**-*adj*	cooked
6298	**couchette**-*f*	bed	5086	**culturel**-*adj*	cultural
			5622	**cupidité**-*f*	greed
			7190	**Cupidon**-*m*	Cupid
			6019	**curieusement**-*adv*	funnily

5119	**curry**-*m*	curry
5889	**cuvette**-*f*	bowl| basin
7339	**cyclone**-*m*	cyclone
7505	**cynisme**-*m*	cynicism

D

7151	**dada**-*m*	hobbyhorse| pet subject
5189	**dague**-*f*	dagger
6188	**daim**-*m*	suede
6632	**damnation**-*f*	damnation
5371	**damner**-*vb*	damn
5170	**dandy**-*m; adj*	dandy; foppish
7272	**dard**-*m*	dart| stinger
6696	**déballer**-*vb*	unpack
5049	**débarquement**-*m*	landing| disembarkation
5130	**débarrer**-*vb*	unbar
5822	**débauche**-*f*	debauchery
7045	**débloquer**-*vb*	unblock
6334	**débrancher**-*vb*	unplug
5092	**débutant**-*m; adj*	beginner; novice
6192	**décalage**-*m*	lag| shift
7408	**décamper**-*vb*	decamp| run away
5941	**décapiter**-*vb*	decapitate
5118	**décence**-*f*	decency
5334	**décennie**-*f*	decade
5153	**décent**-*adj*	decent
6949	**déchaîner**-*vb*	unchain
5098	**déchiffrer**-*vb*	decipher
6002	**décisif**-*adj*	decisive
5607	**déclin**-*m*	decline
7025	**décomposition**-*f*	decay
6868	**décompte**-*m*	count
5578	**décorateur**-*m*	decorator
6882	**décourager**-*vb*	discourage
7020	**décréter**-*vb*	decree| order
5254	**décret**-*m*	decree| ordinance
6496	**dédicace**-*f*	dedication
6318	**déduction**-*f*	deduction
6700	**déduire**-*vb*	deduct| deduce
6659	**défaillance**-*f*	failure
6453	**défectueux**-*adj*	defective| deficient
5730	**défensive**-*adj*	defensive
7192	**déficit**-*m*	deficit
5599	**dégainer**-*vb*	unsheathe

5096	**dégénérer**-*vb*	degenerate
6524	**dégoter**-*vb*	find| dig up
6383	**dégoûtant**-*adj*	disgusting
5621	**dégoût**-*m*	disgust
5422	**délégation**-*f*	delegation
6493	**délégué**-*m; adj*	delegate; vicarious
5558	**déléguer**-*vb*	delegate| devolve
7494	**délibérer**-*vb*	deliberate
5858	**délicatesse**-*f*	delicacy| sensitivity
5942	**délice**-*m*	delight
5393	**délinquant**-*m; adj*	offender; delinquent
6543	**délivrance**-*f*	deliverance| release
5218	**déluge**-*m*	downpour
5269	**démanger**-*vb*	itch
7182	**démarrage**-*m*	start-up
6171	**démasquer**-*vb*	unmask| expose
5573	**déménagement**-*m*	move| removal
5200	**démence**-*f*	dementia| madness
5305	**démocrate**-*m/f; adj*	democrat; democratic
5215	**démocratique**-*adj*	democratic
5724	**démolition**-*f*	demolition
6172	**démoniaque**-*adj; m/f*	demonic; demoniac
5445	**démonter**-*vb*	disassemble| dismantle
5701	**démontrer**-*vb*	demonstrate| reveal
6304	**dénicher**-*vb*	unearth
6588	**dense**-*adj*	dense
6438	**densité**-*f*	density
5924	**denteler**-*vb*	indent
6675	**dentier**-*m*	denture
6522	**dépanner**-*vb*	repair| debug
6863	**dépanneur**-*m*	repairman| convenience store
5508	**dépêche**-*f*	dispatch| telegram
5317	**dépendance**-*f*	dependence| outbuilding
7065	**dépendant**-*adj*	dependent
6459	**déplaisant**-*adj*	unpleasant| distasteful
7385	**déploiement**-*m*	deployment
6880	**déployer**-*vb*	deploy| display
5921	**dépouiller**-*vb*	strip| skin
7519	**déraper**-*vb*	skid
7175	**dérobé**-*adj*	stolen| robbed
6388	**dérober**-*vb*	steal
6946	**déroute**-*f*	rout

5221	**désaccord**-*m*	disagreement| odds	5609	**diffusion**-*f*	diffusion| distribution
6943	**désactiver**-*vb*	deactivate	6380	**digérer**-*vb*	digest
7152	**désamorcer**-*vb*	defuse	7370	**dignement**-*adv*	with dignity
5940	**désarmer**-*vb*	disarm	5480	**dilemme**-*m*	dilemma
7382	**désastreux**-*adj*	disastrous	5728	**diminuer**-*vb*	decrease| reduce
7342	**descendance**-*f*	descent	7255	**dindon**-*m*	turkey
5913	**descendant**-*adj; m*	descending; descendant	6168	**dingo**-*m; adj*	dingo; nuts
5919	**déserter**-*vb*	desert	5087	**diplomate**-*m/f*	diplomat
6223	**déserteur**-*m*	deserter	5962	**diplomatie**-*f*	diplomacy
5524	**déshonneur**-*m*	disgrace	5015	**diplomatique**-*adj*	diplomatic
6519	**déshonorer**-*vb*	dishonor	6391	**directif**-*adj*	directive
6041	**désign**-*m*	design	7183	**dirigeable**-*adj; m*	dirigible; airship
5796	**désobéir**-*vb*	disobey	6093	**discrimination**-*f*	discrimination
7497	**désorienter**-*vb*	disorient	6235	**disperser**-*vb*	disperse| spread
7523	**dessinateur**-*m*	designer| draftsman	5580	**dissuader**-*vb*	deter| put off
5735	**destructeur**-*adj; m*	destructive; destroyer	6263	**distant**-*adj*	distant
6899	**détailler**-*vb*	detail	5347	**distinction**-*f*	distinction
5124	**détecter**-*vb*	detect	5276	**distraction**-*f*	distraction| entertainment
6395	**détection**-*f*	detection	7193	**diva**-*f*	diva
6289	**déterrer**-*vb*	dig| unearth	7287	**divinité**-*f*	divinity
7239	**détestable**-*adj*	detestable	5064	**diviser**-*vb*	divide| partition
6663	**détonation**-*f*	detonation	6577	**divorce**-*m*	divorce
5208	**détournement**-*m*	misappropriation	5467	**dixième**-*num*	tenth
5135	**détraquer**-*vb*	break down	7242	**docile**-*adj*	docile| obedient
6058	**dévaliser**-*vb*	rob| raid	5743	**dock**-*m*	dock
7329	**dévaster**-*vb*	devastate| destroy	5025	**doctorat**-*m*	doctorate| phD
6874	**dévier**-*vb*	deviate	7478	**doctrine**-*f*	doctrine
6936	**devinette**-*f*	riddle	5900	**dôme**-*m*	dome
7369	**devin**-*m*	soothsayer	5894	**domination**-*f*	domination
5706	**dévotion**-*f*	devotion	7264	**domino**-*m*	domino
6419	**diabète**-*m*	diabetes	5861	**donjon**-*m*	dungeon
6877	**diabétique**-*adj; m/f*	diabetic; diabetic	6468	**doter**-*vb*	endow
7149	**dialecte**-*m*	dialect	5219	**douane**-*f*	customs
7092	**diamètre**-*m*	diameter	5457	**douillet**-*adj*	cozy| soft
5515	**diarrhée**-*f*	diarrhea	5582	**douteux**-*adj*	doubtful
5492	**dictateur**-*m*	dictator	6079	**dû**-*adj*	due
5398	**dictature**-*f*	dictatorship	6082	**dune**-*f*	dune
5256	**dicton**-*m*	diction	5073	**dupe**-*f*	dupe
6309	**diesel**-*m*	diesel	5564	**duper**-*vb*	fool| deceive
6893	**diffamation**-*f*	defamation	6029	**duquel**-*prn; con*	whose; whereof
7208	**différencier**-*vb*	differentiate	6104	**durable**-*adj*	lasting| enduring
7009	**différend**-*m*	dispute	5154	**dynamique**-*adj; f*	dynamic; dynamics
5346	**difficilement**-*adv*	with difficulty	5414	**dynastie**-*f*	dynasty
6742	**diffus**-*adj*	diffuse			
5350	**diffuser**-*vb*	broadcast| spread		**E**	

7260	**éblouissant**-*adj*	dazzling	7205	**emblème**-*m*	emblem
7364	**éboueur**-*m*	garbage collector| scavenger	6324	**embouteillage**-*m*	bottling
7415	**échappatoire**-*f*	evasion	7309	**embrayage**-*m*	clutch
6665	**échappement**-*m*	exhaust| escapement	6227	**éminent**-*adj*	eminent| learned
5023	**écharpe**-*f*	scarf	5543	**emmerdeur**-*m*	pain in the neck
6926	**échauffer**-*vb*	warm	5174	**émotionnel**-*adj*	emotional
6331	**échéance**-*f*	term	5290	**émouvoir**-*vb*	move| stir
5611	**éclaireur**-*m*	scout	6578	**empoisonnement**-*m*	poisoning
7485	**éclatant**-*adj*	bright| brilliant	6032	**emprisonnement**-*m*	imprisonment
5333	**éclipser**-*vb*	eclipse| outshine	6832	**emprisonner**-*vb*	imprison| trap
6719	**écœurer**-*vb*	disgust	5876	**encens**-*m*	incense
7007	**écorce**-*f*	bark	6068	**encercler**-*vb*	circle| surround
5203	**Écosse**-*f*	Scotland	5028	**enchaîner**-*vb*	enchain
7302	**écouteur**-*m*	listener| earpiece	7023	**enchantement**-*m*	enchantment
7144	**écoutille**-*f*	hatch| hatchway	6167	**encourageant**-*adj*	encouraging
7374	**écriteau**-*m*	sign	6234	**encouragement**-*m*	encouragement
6809	**écumer**-*vb*	skim| froth	7044	**encyclopédie**-*f*	encyclopedia
5204	**édifice**-*m*	building| edifice	5949	**endurance**-*f*	endurance| stamina
5421	**éduquer**-*vb*	educate| teach	6293	**énergétique**-*f; adj*	energetics; energizing
6078	**effectif**-*adj*	effective	7507	**énervant**-*adj*	annoying
7419	**effleurer**-*vb*	touch	6828	**enflammer**-*vb*	ignite| inflame
5541	**effrayant**-*adj*	scary| frightening	6452	**enflure**-*f*	swelling
6888	**effroi**-*m*	terror	6508	**enfouir**-*vb*	bury
7150	**effronté**-*adj*	cheeky| brazen	6038	**engendrer**-*vb*	generate| give rise to
5722	**effroyable**-*adj*	frightful| appalling	5587	**engrais**-*m*	fertilizer
6348	**égocentrique**-*adj; m/f*	egocentric; egomania	5125	**enrichir**-*vb*	enrich
6090	**égoïsme**-*m*	selfishness	7477	**enrôler**-*vb*	enlist| enroll
6776	**égorger**-*vb*	kill| slit throat	7238	**ensorceler**-*vb*	bewitch
5875	**égyptien**-*adj*	Egyptian	7158	**entailler**-*vb*	cut
7410	**éjecter**-*vb*	eject| shed	6520	**entamer**-*vb*	start| launch
6526	**élaborer**-*vb*	elaborate| design	6062	**entité**-*f*	entity
6688	**élargir**-*vb*	broaden| stretch	5348	**entourage**-*m*	entourage
6590	**élastique**-*adj; m; f*	elastic; rubber band; elasticy	7125	**entracte**-*m; adj*	intermission; entr'acte
7037	**électoral**-*adj*	electoral	6299	**entrave**-*f*	obstacle| interference
6668	**électricien**-*m*	electrician	5262	**entrepreneur**-*m*	entrepreneur| contractor
5996	**élémentaire**-*adj*	elementary	6506	**envahisseur**-*m*	invader
5182	**élevage**-*m*	breeding| animal husbandry	6137	**envergure**-*f*	span
6582	**élimination**-*f*	elimination	5229	**envie**-*f*	desire
7373	**élixir**-*m*	elixir	6681	**envol**-*m*	flight
6845	**éloge**-*m*	eulogy| praise	6405	**épaisseur**-*f*	thickness
5394	**emballage**-*m*	packing| wrap	7027	**épatant**-*adj*	splendid
6680	**embarrasser**-*vb*	embarrass| bother	5159	**épice**-*f*	spice
			6073	**épicer**-*vb*	spice
			6379	**épicier**-*m*	grocer

7346	**épilepsie**-*f; adj*	epilepsy; epileptic	6512	**exclusivement**-*adv*	exclusively
6320	**épinard**-*m*	spinach	5278	**exclusivité**-*f*	exclusiveness
6173	**épine**-*f*	thorn	6825	**excrément**-*m*	excrement
6113	**épouvantail**-*m*	scarecrow	5534	**excursion**-*f*	excursion	trip
5873	**épuisement**-*m*	exhaustion	depletion	7217	**exhiber**-*vb*	produce
6101	**équation**-*f*	equation	7128	**exiler**-*vb*	exile
6716	**équilibrer**-*vb*	balance	trim	5908	**exorcisme**-*m*	exorcism
6374	**équipée**-*f*	escape	5100	**exotique**-*adj*	exotic
5039	**équiper**-*vb*	equip	provide	5409	**expansion**-*f*	expansion
5084	**équivalent**-*adj; m*	equivalent; equivalent	6306	**expédier**-*vb*	send	dispatch
7315	**érable**-*m*	maple	7170	**expéditeur**-*m; adj*	sender; dispatching
7524	**éradiquer**-*vb*	eradicate	6120	**expérimental**-*adj*	experimental
7003	**ermite**-*m*	hermit	5693	**expérimenter**-*vb*	experiment	experience
7491	**errant**-*adj; m*	wandering; wanderer	5575	**expertise**-*f*	expertise	valuation
7368	**érudit**-*m; adj*	scholar; erudite	6111	**expirer**-*vb*	expire	breathe out
5831	**éruption**-*f*	eruption	rash	7460	**explicite**-*adj*	explicit
5261	**escalader**-*vb*	climb	6941	**explorateur**-*m*	explorer
5711	**escale**-*f*	stop	5376	**exploration**-*f*	exploration
6230	**escargot**-*m*	snail	5307	**expulsion**-*f*	expulsion	deportation
5378	**escouade**-*f*	squad	5938	**extension**-*f*	extension	expansion
7384	**escrimer**-*vb*	fight	6637	**extermination**-*f*	extermination
5377	**espérance**-*f*	hope	expectation	6218	**externe**-*adj; m/f*	external; extern
6678	**esquimau**-*adj; m*	Eskimo; Eskimo	7428	**extincteur**-*m; adj*	extinguisher; extinguishing
6597	**esquiver**-*vb*	dodge	avoid	6713	**extorsion**-*f*	extortion
5758	**essentiellement**-*adv; nn*	essentially; essentiality	5407	**extraction**-*f*	extraction
5504	**estimation**-*f*	estimate	rating	7156	**extrémiste**-*adj; m/f*	extremist; extremist
6087	**estropié**-*adj; m*	crippled; cripple	6611	**extrémité**-*f*	end	extremity
5375	**étagère**-*f*	shelf			
6806	**étaler**-*vb*	spread out	display		**F**	
5160	**été**-*m*	summer			
6670	**éther**-*m*	ether	5559	**fabricant**-*m*	manufacturer
5783	**étincelle**-*f*	spark	5551	**fâcheux**-*adj; m/f*	annoying; meddler
6548	**étiquette**-*f*	label| etiquette	6930	**fade**-*adj*	bland| tasteless
7142	**étourdir**-*vb*	stun	surprise	5682	**fainéant**-*adj; m*	lazy; lounger
5459	**étranglé**-*adj*	strangled	5004	**faisable**-*adj*	feasible	doable
6316	**étreindre**-*vb*	embrace	grasp	6517	**faisceau**-*m*	beam
7413	**étriper**-*vb*	gut	6001	**fanatique**-*adj; m/f*	fanatic; fanatic
7055	**euphémisme**-*m*	euphemism	5902	**fané**-*adj*	withered	dry
6505	**évadé**-*f; m; adj*	escape; evader; escaped	7074	**farceur**-*m*	jester
5206	**éventreur**-*m*	ripper	5628	**fascinant**-*adj*	fascinating
6290	**éventualité**-*f*	eventuality	7431	**fascination**-*f*	fascination
5056	**évoquer**-*vb*	evoke	recall	6844	**fascisme**-*m*	fascism
6135	**excessif**-*adj*	excessive	overdone	6536	**fatalité**-*f*	fatality
7418	**exclusif**-*adj*	exclusive	6245	**fatigant**-*adj*	tiring	fatiguing

7455	**fatigue**-*f*	fatigue| exhaustion	6876	**flocon**-*m*	flake
6033	**fat**-*m*	smug person	5488	**fluide**-*adj; m*	fluid; fluid
6209	**faucher**-*vb*	mow| reap	6533	**fondamental**-*adj; m*	fundamental; fundamental
7108	**faufiler**-*vb*	baste| dodge	7223	**fondamentalement**-*adv*	fundamentally
6898	**faune**-*f*	wildlife			
5192	**favorable**-*adj*	favorable	5723	**fondateur**-*m*	founder
6214	**feindre**-*vb*	pretend| put on	6138	**fondement**-*m*	foundation
7441	**fellation**-*f*	blow job	6449	**footballeur**-*m*	footballer
6748	**fendre**-*vb*	split| slit	6627	**forage**-*m*	drilling| digging
6787	**fendu**-*adj*	split	5956	**forain**-*m*	showman
5805	**fente**-*f*	slot| slit	6954	**foret**-*m*	drill
5528	**fertile**-*adj*	fertile| fruitful	5258	**forfait**-*m*	package
7031	**ferveur**-*f*	fervor	7429	**forger**-*vb*	forge
5639	**fesse**-*f*	buttock| bottom	5156	**formalité**-*f*	formality
6200	**feuilleton**-*m*	serial	7088	**format**-*m*	format
5601	**fiasco**-*m*	fiasco| failure	6801	**formel**-*adj*	formal
5451	**fibre**-*f*	fiber| staple	6160	**forum**-*m*	forum
6097	**fief**-*m*	fief| fee	6462	**fossile**-*adj; m*	fossil; fossil
6480	**fièrement**-*adv*	proudly	5195	**fouetter**-*vb*	whip| scourge
5824	**fiesta**-*f*	shindig	7450	**fougueux**-*adj*	fiery| spirited
6866	**figer**-*vb*	freeze	5442	**foule**-*f*	crowd| host
7365	**figue**-*f*	fig	7002	**fourbe**-*adj*	deceitful
6728	**figurant**-*m*	extra| dummy	5584	**fournisseur**-*m*	supplier| contractor
6277	**filature**-*f*	spinning	6682	**fourniture**-*f*	supply
6927	**filial**-*adj*	filial	5222	**fourrière**-*f*	pound
6444	**filon**-*m*	vein	5966	**fracas**-*m*	crash| smash
6150	**filou**-*m*	trickster	7276	**fraction**-*f*	fraction
7377	**filtre**-*adj; m*	filter; filter	7053	**fracture**-*f*	fracture
5344	**financement**-*m*	funding	5323	**fragment**-*m*	fragment| piece
6108	**finesse**-*f*	fineness| delicacy	7301	**fraîchement**-*adv*	freshly
7409	**firmament**-*m*	firmament	6731	**fraîcheur**-*f*	freshness| coolness
6116	**fiscal**-*adj*	tax	6274	**frappant**-*adj*	striking
6823	**fissure**-*f*	crack| split	5146	**freiner**-*vb*	curb
7395	**fixation**-*f*	fixing| attachment	5452	**fréquent**-*adj*	frequent
6698	**fixement**-*adv*	fixedly	7210	**fréquentation**-*f*	attendance
5674	**flagrant**-*adj*	flagrant| blatant	6458	**friandise**-*f*	delicacy| treat
7130	**flairer**-*vb*	smell| scent	6903	**frimer**-*vb*	show off
5789	**flair**-*m*	flair	7049	**frimeur**-*adj; m*	showy; show-off
6872	**flambeau**-*m*	torch	6855	**fripouille**-*f*	scoundrel
5886	**flan**-*m*	flan| pudding	7467	**friture**-*f*	frying
7405	**flanquer**-*vb*	flank	6931	**frôler**-*vb*	graze
6679	**flaque**-*f*	puddle	6992	**froussard**-*adj; m*	wimpy; coward
7465	**fleurir**-*vb*	flower| flourish	5606	**frousse**-*f*	jitters
5319	**fleuriste**-*m*	florist	5126	**frustration**-*f*	frustration
5177	**flirter**-*vb*	flirt| spoon	6006	**frustrer**-*vb*	frustrate
6558	**flirt**-*m*	flirting	5286	**funèbre**-*adj*	funeral

6376	**funéraire**-*adj*	funerary
5811	**furie**-*f*	fury| she-cat
7356	**fusible**-*m; adj*	fuse; fusible
6211	**fusiller**-*vb*	shoot
6824	**futile**-*adj*	futile| frivolous
7067	**fuyant**-*adj*	elusive| receding

G

5816	**gadget**-*m*	gadget
5091	**gag**-*m*	gag
6406	**gaieté**-*f*	cheerfulness
7283	**gainer**-*vb*	sheathe
6194	**galactique**-*adj*	galactic
7261	**gallois**-*adj; m|mpl*	Welsh; Welsh
5419	**galop**-*m*	gallop
5636	**gamma**-*f*	gamma
6256	**garderie**-*f*	nursery
5491	**gaspillage**-*m*	waste| wastage
5220	**gâter**-*vb*	spoil| pamper
7246	**gâteux**-*adj; m/f*	senile; dotard
5929	**gaucher**-*m; adj*	left-hander; left-handed
5656	**gaufrer**-*vb*	emboss
7366	**gaulois**-*adj*	Gallic
6706	**gazelle**-*f*	gazelle
7026	**gazette**-*f*	gazette
5384	**geisha**-*f*	geisha
5283	**gel**-*m*	gel| freezing
6016	**gémir**-*vb*	moan| wail
5213	**générique**-*adj*	generic
6246	**génocide**-*m*	genocide
6134	**géographie**-*f*	geography
6328	**gerbe**-*f*	sheaf
6197	**germer**-*vb*	germinate
5963	**gibbon**-*m*	gibbon
5840	**gigolo**-*m*	gigolo
7299	**gingembre**-*m*	ginger
6609	**girafe**-*f*	giraffe
5148	**gitan**-*adj; m*	Gypsy; Gypsy
7012	**givrer**-*vb*	frost
6092	**glacial**-*adj*	glacial
7011	**glacière**-*f*	cooler
5680	**glacier**-*m*	glacier
7001	**glaçon**-*m*	iceberg
7062	**gladiateur**-*m*	gladiator

7089	**glaive**-*m*	sword
6814	**glande**-*f*	gland
7265	**glander**-*vb*	screw around
5389	**gland**-*m*	glans
6034	**glissant**-*adj*	sliding| slippery
5623	**global**-*adj*	overall| global
6447	**gluant**-*adj*	sticky| slimy
5526	**gnôle**-*f*	hooch
6902	**gobelet**-*m*	cup
7113	**gober**-*vb*	swallow
5823	**gogo**-*m*	sucker
5043	**gonflé**-*adj*	inflated
6258	**goudron**-*m*	tar
5236	**gouffre**-*m*	gulf
5800	**gouine**-*f*	dyke
7397	**goujat**-*m*	cad| boor
6672	**gourmand**-*adj; m*	greedy| gourmand; gourmand
5173	**gourou**-*m*	guru
7461	**gouttière**-*f*	gutter
5443	**gouvernail**-*m*	rudder
5155	**gouverner**-*vb*	govern| steer
5695	**grabuge**-*m*	mayhem
6705	**gracieux**-*adj*	gracious| graceful
7257	**gradin**-*m*	bench| tier
5984	**graffiti**-*m*	graffiti
7036	**grammaire**-*f*	grammar
6634	**grandement**-*adv*	sorely
7262	**graphique**-*adj; m*	graphic; graph
7157	**grappe**-*f*	cluster
7024	**grappin**-*m*	grapnel| holdfast
5022	**greffer**-*vb*	graft| engraft
7393	**grêle**-*f; adj*	hail; thin
6579	**grignoter**-*vb*	nibble
7112	**grillage**-*m*	roasting
7191	**grimace**-*f*	grimace
6327	**grimer**-*vb*	make up| disguise
5287	**grincheux**-*adj; m*	grumpy; grumbler
6865	**grognement**-*m*	grunt
7038	**grogner**-*vb*	grumble
6048	**gronder**-*vb*	scold| rumble
7352	**gruau**-*m*	groats
7488	**guêpe**-*f*	wasp
6067	**guéri**-*adj*	recovered
6428	**guérilla**-*f*	guerrilla
6186	**guérisseur**-*m*	healer

5431	**guetter**-*vb*	await
5082	**guichet**-*m*	window
6709	**guidage**-*m*	guidance
6889	**guillotiner**-*vb*	guillotine
6532	**gui**-*m*	mistletoe
7248	**guimauve**-*f*	marshmallow
6972	**Guinée**-*f*	Guinea
5444	**guitariste**-*m/f*	guitarist
6356	**gymnastique**-*f; adj*	gymnastics; gymnastic

H

6020	**habileté**-*f*	skill| cleverness
6834	**haie**-*f*	hedge| hurdle
5296	**haler**-*vb*	tow
6221	**hamster**-*m*	hamster
5078	**handicaper**-*vb*	handicap
5117	**hanter**-*vb*	haunt| spook
5190	**harcèlement**-*m*	harassment| harassing
7392	**harem**-*m*	harem
6802	**hareng**-*m*	herring
5846	**harmonica**-*m*	harmonica
7211	**harnais**-*m*	harness
6962	**harpe**-*f*	harp
5437	**hautement**-*adv*	highly
6585	**havre**-*m*	haven
6094	**héberger**-*vb*	accommodate| harbor
6488	**hélice**-*f*	propeller| screw
6848	**hélium**-*m*	helium
6722	**héréditaire**-*adj*	hereditary
7457	**hérésie**-*f*	heresy
6982	**hérétique**-*m/f; adj*	heretic; heretical
7266	**hernie**-*f*	hernia
6500	**héroïsme**-*m*	heroism
5550	**hésitation**-*f*	hesitation
5265	**hibou**-*m*	owl
6043	**hiérarchie**-*f*	hierarchy
5335	**hilarant**-*adj*	hilarious
5108	**hippie**-*f*	hippy
5632	**hisser**-*vb*	hoist| pull up
6883	**historien**-*m; adj*	historian; historical
5411	**hobby**-*m*	hobby
5521	**holocauste**-*m*	holocaust
5685	**homosexualité**-*f*	homosexuality

5044	**honoraire**-*adj; m*	honorary; honorarium
6994	**hoquet**-*m*	hiccup
5670	**horde**-*f*	horde
5561	**hormis**-*prp*	except for
6910	**horoscope**-*m*	horoscope
5764	**hospice**-*m*	hospice
6057	**hostilité**-*f*	hostility
7259	**hublot**-*m*	porthole
6653	**huile**-*f*	oil| big shot
5829	**huissier**-*m*	bailiff
5237	**huitième**-*num*	eighth
6344	**humanitaire**-*adj*	humanitarian
6055	**humblement**-*adv*	humbly
5374	**hurlement**-*m*	howl| yell
6219	**hybride**-*m; adj*	hybrid; crossbred
6326	**hydraulique**-*adj; f*	hydraulic; hydraulics
5576	**hypocrisie**-*f*	hypocrisy
5527	**hypothèque**-*f*	mortgage
5235	**hystérie**-*f*	hysteria

I

6049	**iceberg**-*m*	iceberg
7086	**idéaliste**-*adj; m/f*	idealistic; idealist
6830	**idem**-*adv*	idem
7332	**idéologie**-*f*	ideology
5999	**idiotie**-*f*	idiocy
6132	**ignorant**-*adj; m*	ignorant; ignoramus
5836	**illégalement**-*adv*	illegally
7258	**illumination**-*f*	illumination
6294	**illuminer**-*vb*	illuminate| floodlight
5312	**illustre**-*adj*	illustrious| illustrated
7095	**imam**-*m*	imam
6703	**imbattable**-*adj*	unbeatable
5167	**imitation**-*f*	imitation
6189	**immature**-*adj*	immature
7171	**immigrant**-*adj; m*	immigrant; immigrant
5466	**imminent**-*adj*	imminent
5018	**immoral**-*adj*	immoral
5814	**impair**-*adj; m*	odd; faux pas
5401	**impardonnable**-*adj*	unforgivable
6652	**impec**-*adj*	impeccable
5441	**impensable**-*adj*	unthinkable
6228	**impératif**-*m*	imperative

5537	**imperméable**-*adj; m*	impermeable; waterproof	
7111	**impie**-*adj*	impious	
7070	**implacable**-*adj*	implacable| relentless	
5494	**implant**-*m*	implant	
6146	**implication**-*f*	involvement	
5893	**importuner**-*vb*	bother	
6890	**imposant**-*adj*	imposing| impressive	
5501	**imprévu**-*adj; m*	unexpected; contingency	
6321	**imprimerie**-*f*	printing house	
5188	**imprimer**-*vb*	print| print out	
5227	**improbable**-*adj*	unlikely	
5454	**improviser**-*vb*	improvise	
5660	**imprudent**-*adj*	imprudent| unwise	
6694	**impuissance**-*f*	impotence| helplessness	
7041	**impulsif**-*adj*	impulsive	
7400	**impur**-*adj*	impure| tainted	
6510	**inaccessible**-*adj*	inaccessible	
6970	**inadmissible**-*adj*	inadmissible	
6231	**inaperçu**-*adj*	unseen	
5268	**inauguration**-*f*	inauguration	
6045	**incapacité**-*f*	inability| disability	
7277	**incarnation**-*f*	incarnation	
6551	**incarner**-*vb*	embody| personify	
6856	**incertain**-*adj*	uncertain	
7116	**incertitude**-*f*	uncertainty	
7102	**incision**-*f*	incision| cut	
6619	**inciter**-*vb*	encourage| incite	
5833	**incliner**-*vb*	tilt| incline	
5882	**incognito**-*adv; m*	incognito; incognito	
6796	**incomparable**-*adj*	incomparable	
6339	**incompétence**-*f*	incompetence	
6423	**incompétent**-*adj*	incompetent	
6229	**incompréhensible**-*adj*	incomprehensible	
7291	**inconcevable**-*adj*	inconceivable	
6968	**inconfortable**-*adj*	uncomfortable	
6601	**incorrigible**-*adj*	incorrigible	
5739	**inculpation**-*f*	charge	
5045	**inculper**-*vb*	charge	
6314	**incurable**-*adj*	incurable	
5562	**indéfiniment**-*adv*	indefinitely	
5989	**indemne**-*adj*	unscathed	
7469	**indemnité**-*f*	allowance	

6266	**indestructible**-*adj*	indestructible
7218	**index**-*m*	index| index finger
7163	**indicatif**-*adj; m*	indicative; indicative
5802	**indication**-*f*	indication
5943	**indifférence**-*f*	indifference
7282	**indigestion**-*f*	indigestion
5214	**indiscret**-*adj*	indiscreet
7271	**individuel**-*adj*	individual| private
6492	**indulgence**-*f*	indulgence
6550	**indulgent**-*adj*	indulgent| forgiving
6529	**inestimable**-*adj*	invaluable| inestimable
6355	**inexplicable**-*adj*	inexplicable
5703	**infaillible**-*adj*	infallible
7059	**infamie**-*f*	infamy
6375	**infantile**-*adj*	infantile
6335	**infect**-*adj*	foul| vile
6061	**infernal**-*adj; m*	infernal; fiend
7240	**infidélité**-*f*	infidelity
6818	**infiltration**-*f*	infiltration
6811	**infime**-*adj*	tiny
5753	**inflation**-*f*	inflation
5777	**infliger**-*vb*	impose| mete
6839	**influent**-*adj*	influential
6025	**infrarouge**-*adj*	infrared
5343	**ingénieux**-*adj*	ingenious
5793	**ingrédient**-*m*	ingredient
6180	**inhumain**-*adj*	inhuman
5904	**inimaginable**-*adj*	unimaginable
6268	**initiation**-*f*	initiation
6739	**initier**-*vb*	initiate
6499	**injecter**-*vb*	inject
7078	**injonction**-*f*	injunction
5439	**innombrable**-*adj*	innumerable
6140	**inondation**-*f*	flood
6399	**inonder**-*vb*	flood| inundate
6333	**inséparable**-*adj*	inseparable
5141	**insignifiant**-*adj*	insignificant
6148	**insinuer**-*vb*	insinuate| suggest
5678	**insolence**-*f*	insolence
6991	**insolent**-*adj*	insolent| cheeky
6676	**insolite**-*adj*	unusual
6614	**insomnie**-*f*	insomnia
7176	**insouciant**-*adj*	carefree| careless
7406	**instance**-*f*	authority
5675	**instructeur**-*f*	instructor

7235	**instructif**-*adj*	instructive
5768	**instruire**-*vb*	instruct| educate
6693	**insuffisant**-*adj*	insufficient| inadequate
6539	**insuline**-*f*	insulin
6981	**insurrection**-*f*	insurrection| insurgency
7221	**intellect**-*m*	intellect
7340	**intensément**-*adv*	deeply
7290	**intensif**-*adj*	intensive
5463	**intercepter**-*vb*	intercept
6947	**interception**-*f*	interception
6142	**interférence**-*f*	interference
6827	**interminable**-*adj*	endless
6311	**internat**-*m*	internship| boarding school
7213	**interner**-*vb*	intern
7207	**interrogation**-*f*	interrogation| query
5074	**interrupteur**-*m*	switch
5266	**interruption**-*f*	interruption
7269	**intersection**-*f*	intersection
6797	**intervalle**-*m*	interval
5736	**intestin**-*adj; m*	intestine; intestine
5300	**intimider**-*vb*	intimidate| frighten
5815	**intituler**-*vb*	title
5482	**intolérable**-*adj*	intolerable
6649	**intouchable**-*adj*	untouchable
6130	**intrépide**-*adj*	intrepid| bold
7127	**intriguer**-*vb*	intrigue
5555	**introduction**-*f*	introduction| listing
6343	**inutilement**-*adv*	uselessly
6286	**invalide**-*adj; m/f*	invalid; invalid
6364	**inverser**-*vb*	reverse
5834	**investigation**-*f*	investigation| inquiry
6983	**invoquer**-*vb*	invoke
6677	**irréel**-*adj*	unreal
6753	**irréprochable**-*adj*	unexceptionable
7145	**irritable**-*adj*	irritable| prickly
7501	**irriter**-*vb*	irritate
5512	**irruption**-*f*	irruption
5450	**israélien**-*adj*	Israeli
5741	**ivoire**-*m*	ivory

J

5446	**jaguar**-*m*	jaguar
6555	**jardinage**-*m*	gardening

6433	**jargon**-*m*	jargon
6384	**jaser**-*vb*	gossip| blab
6656	**jasmin**-*m*	jasmine
5787	**jeton**-*m*	token
7430	**jeûne**-*m*	fasting
5553	**jockey**-*m*	jockey
5427	**jogging**-*m*	jogging
6934	**joliment**-*adv*	nicely
5487	**joujou**-*m*	toy
5279	**joyau**-*m*	jewel
6769	**judicieux**-*adj*	wise| sound
6563	**judo**-*m*	judo
5957	**jupon**-*m*	petticoat
7452	**juriste**-*m/f*	lawyer| jurist
6421	**justesse**-*f*	accuracy| appropriateness
6118	**justicier**-*m*	justiciary| vigilante
6028	**juteux**-*adj*	juicy

K

6203	**kaiser**-*m*	Kaiser
6977	**kamikaze**-*m*	kamikaze
7204	**kangourou**-*m*	kangaroo
7216	**kérosène**-*m*	kerosene
7376	**kidnappeur**-*m*	kidnapper
5083	**kimono**-*m*	kimono
5747	**kiosque**-*m*	kiosk| newsstand

L

5709	**label**-*m*	label
5342	**lacet**-*m*	shoelace
5594	**lâcheté**-*f*	cowardice
6646	**lacté**-*adj*	milky
6917	**lagon**-*m*	lagoon
7105	**laideur**-*f*	ugliness
6808	**laitier**-*adj; m*	dairy; milkman
6960	**laitue**-*f*	lettuce
6767	**lambeau**-*m*	shred
7515	**lande**-*f*	moor
5435	**lanterne**-*vb*	lantern
6017	**larbin**-*m*	stooge| flunkey
6683	**largage**-*m*	dropping
7474	**largeur**-*f*	width| beam
6761	**larve**-*f*	larva

6894	**latitude**-*f*	latitude	
7267	**latrines**-*fpl*	latrines	
5974	**lavabo**-*m*	sink	
7172	**lavande**-*f*	lavender	
5665	**laverie**-*f*	laundry| laundromat	
6291	**laveur**-*m*	mop	
7147	**légalité**-*f*	legality	
6026	**léguer**-*vb*	will	
5259	**lentille**-*f*	lens	
6752	**lépreux**-*adj; m*	leper; leper	
6347	**léser**-*vb*	injure	
7511	**lésion**-*f*	lesion	
6779	**leucémie**-*f*	leukemia	
6139	**libellule**-*f*	dragonfly	
6110	**libéral**-*adj*	liberal	
6635	**licenciement**-*m*	termination| redundancy	
5979	**licencier**-*vb*	dismiss| fire	
5992	**licorne**-*f*	unicorn	
5669	**lieue**-*f*	league	
6545	**ligoter**-*vb*	bind| tie up	
6956	**lilas**-*adj; m*	lilac; lilac	
7295	**limace**-*f*	slug	
6169	**limer**-*vb*	file	
7244	**limpide**-*adj*	limpid	
5035	**lingerie**-*f*	lingerie	
7046	**lingot**-*m*	ingot	
5556	**liqueur**-*f*	liqueur	
5631	**lisse**-*adj*	smooth| sleek	
6372	**lister**-*vb*	list	
5337	**littéraire**-*adj*	literary	
6377	**livret**-*m*	book	
6673	**lobe**-*m*	lobe	
6541	**localisation**-*f*	location| tracking	
5088	**locomotif**-*adj*	locomotive	
5383	**logiciel**-*m*	software	
6723	**logis**-*m*	dwelling	
6329	**logo**-*m*	logo	
7473	**lolo**-*m*	milk	
5178	**longuement**-*adv*	long	
7412	**loque**-*f*	pile of rags| wreck	
6317	**lotion**-*f*	lotion	
6187	**lotus**-*m*	lotus	
5990	**louange**-*f*	praise	
7313	**loulou**-*m*	spitz	
6630	**lourdement**-*adv*	heavily	

7439	**lubrifier**-*vb*	lubricate
5320	**lucide**-*adj*	lucid| rational
5839	**lugubre**-*adj*	dismal| lugubrious
5095	**lunaire**-*adj*	lunar
6547	**lunette**-*f*	lens
5602	**lustre**-*m*	chandelier| luster
6717	**lustrer**-*vb*	polish
5518	**lutin**-*m; adj*	pixie| leprechaun; impish
7000	**lutteur**-*m; adj*	wrestler; fighting
6923	**luxueux**-*adj*	luxurious
5973	**luxure**-*f*	lust
6950	**lycéen**-*m*	high school student
6953	**lynx**-*m*	lynx

M

6831	**macabre**-*adj*	macabre
6966	**macchabée**-*m*	stiff
5645	**mâcher**-*vb*	chew| gum
6959	**machette**-*f*	machete
6310	**maçon**-*m*	mason
5295	**Madone**-*f*	Madonna
5315	**magistrat**-*m*	magistrate
6749	**magnéto**-*f*	magneto
6222	**magnétophone**-*m*	tape recorder
5630	**magot**-*m*	hoard| loot
7379	**magouille**-*f*	maneuvering
5717	**maigrir**-*vb*	slim| become thin
5479	**maintenance**-*f*	maintenance
6574	**malaria**-*f*	malaria
7448	**malfaisant**-*adj*	evil
5198	**malhonnête**-*adj*	dishonest
5145	**malsain**-*adj*	unhealthy
7349	**mammifère**-*m*	mammal
7197	**mammouth**-*m*	mammoth
7233	**manchette**-*f*	cuff
5879	**manchot**-*m; adj*	penguin; one-handed
6215	**manette**-*f*	lever| controller
6390	**mangeur**-*m*	eater
5199	**manier**-*vb*	handle| use
5708	**manifestant**-*m; adj*	demonstrator; riotous
6928	**manigancer**-*vb*	engineer
5927	**manipulation**-*f*	handling| rigging
6420	**manœuvre**-*f*	maneuver| move

5003	**manœuvrer**-*vb*	maneuver| manipulate
5496	**manucure**-*f*	manicure
5057	**maquereau**-*m*	mackerel| pimp
5021	**maquette**-*f*	model
6003	**maquiller**-*vb*	make up
6387	**marchander**-*vb*	haggle| bargain
5579	**marguerite**-*f*	daisy
7435	**marionnettiste**-*m/f*	puppeteer
5947	**maritime**-*adj*	maritime
6725	**marmiter**-*vb*	strafe
7328	**marmonnement**-*m*	mumble
6708	**marmotter**-*vb*	mutter
5888	**marqué**-*adj*	marked
6755	**marquise**-*f*	marquise
5958	**marraine**-*f*	godmother
5260	**martien**-*adj*	martian
6185	**martinet**-*m*	swift
6123	**mascarade**-*f*	masquerade
6036	**mascotte**-*f*	mascot
5077	**masquer**-*vb*	hide| mask
6164	**masturbation**-*f*	masturbation
6513	**masturber**-*vb*	masturbate
5310	**maternité**-*f*	maternity
5134	**mathématique**-*adj*	mathematical
6477	**matinal**-*adj*	morning
5808	**mât**-*m*	mast
6417	**matraquer**-*vb*	club| cosh
6919	**mature**-*adj*	mature
5545	**maturité**-*f*	maturity
6998	**mauve**-*adj; f*	mauve; mallow
5169	**mayonnaise**-*f*	mayonnaise
5719	**mécano**-*m*	mechanic
7381	**méchamment**-*adv*	nastily
5666	**méchanceté**-*f*	wickedness
6207	**mécontent**-*adj*	dissatisfied| unhappy
5428	**médaillon**-*m*	medallion
7386	**médiatique**-*adj*	media
5641	**méditation**-*f*	meditation
5948	**méditer**-*vb*	meditate| think
6850	**médoc**-*m*	medication
7061	**méfait**-*m; adj*	wrongdoing;
6707	**méfiance**-*f*	mistrust
6542	**méfiant**-*adj*	suspicious| distrustful
6105	**mélancolie**-*f*	melancholy
5892	**mélancolique**-*adj; m/f*	melancholy; melancholiac
6083	**mémorable**-*adj*	memorable
7459	**mémoriser**-*vb*	memorize
6394	**ménager**-*adj; vb*	household; spare
5529	**mendiant**-*m; adj*	beggar; begging
5806	**meneur**-*m*	leader
5923	**mentalité**-*f*	mentality
5271	**mention**-*f*	mention
6179	**méprisable**-*adj*	contemptible
5358	**mercenaire**-*adj; m*	mercenary; mercenary
6862	**merle**-*m*	blackbird
5395	**merlin**-*m*	marlin| poleaxe
5019	**merveilleusement**-*adv*	wonderfully
7311	**mesa**-*f*	mesa
6267	**mesquin**-*adj*	mean| shabby
6100	**mess**-*m*	mess
6623	**métallique**-*adj*	metallic
6537	**météore**-*m*	meteor
6022	**météorite**-*f*	meteorite
5625	**métis**-*m; adj*	metis; colored
5132	**meute**-*f*	pack
6821	**miche**-*f*	loaf
6052	**microscope**-*m*	microscope
5397	**migraine**-*f*	migraine
6253	**mijoter**-*vb*	simmer
5415	**millénaire**-*m; adj*	millennium| millennial; millenary
7247	**minéral**-*adj; m*	mineral; mineral
7426	**minet**-*m*	kitty
5986	**miniature**-*adj; f*	miniature; miniature
5760	**minorité**-*f*	minority| infancy
6975	**miraculeux**-*adj*	miraculous
7194	**mirage**-*m*	mirage
5120	**miséricordieux**-*adj*	merciful
5804	**missionnaire**-*adj; m*	missionary; missionary
7032	**mitaine**-*f*	mitten
5998	**miteux**-*adj*	shabby| seedy
5866	**mitraillette**-*f*	submachine gun
7389	**mixer**-*m; vb*	mixer; blend
6065	**mobilier**-*m*	suite
5662	**modestie**-*f*	modesty
6446	**modification**-*f*	modification
5997	**mœurs**-*fpl*	manners

5239	**moineau**-*m*	sparrow
6439	**moisir**-*vb*	mold
6251	**moisson**-*m*	harvest
6912	**moléculaire**-*adj*	molecular
5737	**molécule**-*f*	molecule
7133	**mollir**-*vb*	weaken| soften
6662	**monarchie**-*f*	monarchy
7228	**mondain**-*adj; m*	worldly; man about town
5513	**monétaire**-*adj*	monetary
7085	**mongol**-*adj; m|mpl*	Mongolian; Mongol| retard
5570	**moniteur**-*m*	monitor
6760	**monotone**-*adj*	monotone
6803	**monteur**-*m*	editor
6243	**monture**-*f*	mount
5127	**morale**-*f*	morals| ethics
6051	**moralement**-*adv*	morally
5918	**morbide**-*adj*	morbid
7054	**mortalité**-*f*	mortality
6621	**mortier**-*m*	mortar
6054	**morue**-*f*	cod
7263	**morve**-*f*	snot
5321	**mosquée**-*f*	mosque
5651	**motard**-*m*	outrider
5932	**motion**-*f*	motion
5819	**motiver**-*vb*	motivate
6603	**mouette**-*f*	seagull
6875	**moule**-*m;f*	mold; mussel
5571	**mouler**-*vb*	mold| press
5327	**mourant**-*adj*	dying
6556	**mousquetaire**-*m*	musketeer
5122	**moustique**-*m*	mosquito
6400	**muffin**-*m*	muffin
6244	**mulet**-*m*	mule| mullet
7107	**multitude**-*f*	multitude
7398	**muraille**-*f*	wall
5248	**murmure**-*m*	murmur
6238	**musclé**-*adj*	muscular
7375	**musique**-*f*	music
6766	**mutilé**-*adj*	mutilated
5232	**mutinerie**-*f*	mutiny
5175	**mutuel**-*adj*	mutual
5036	**mutuellement**-*adv*	mutually
6685	**myrtille**-*f*	blueberry
7521	**mystérieusement**-*adv*	darkly
6161	**mythologie**-*f*	mythology

N

5880	**nabot**-*m; adj*	runt; dwarfish
5142	**nageur**-*m*	swimmer
6027	**nappe**-*f*	tablecloth
6958	**narine**-*f*	nostril
5418	**narrateur**-*m*	narrator
5080	**natation**-*f*	swimming| float
5707	**naval**-*adj*	naval
6021	**navet**-*m*	turnip
5426	**navigateur**-*m*	navigator
6626	**nectar**-*m*	nectar
5059	**négligence**-*f*	negligence| neglect
6990	**négligent**-*adj*	negligent
7516	**négociateur**-*m*	negotiator
6684	**néné**-*m*	tit
5600	**nettement**-*adv*	clearly| sharply
5848	**neutraliser**-*vb*	neutralize| negative
5854	**neuvième**-*num*	ninth
6733	**nicher**-*vb*	nest
6971	**nicotine**-*f*	nicotine
6409	**nigaud**-*m; adj*	simpleton; stupid
7391	**noirceur**-*f*	darkness
6784	**noisette**-*f; adj*	hazelnut; hazel
5168	**nomination**-*f*	appointment| nomination
6255	**norme**-*f*	standard
5577	**nostalgie**-*f*	nostalgia
6790	**nostalgique**-*adj*	nostalgic
5642	**notamment**-*adv*	in particular
6184	**notoire**-*adj*	notorious
5332	**nouveauté**-*f*	novelty
5922	**noyade**-*f*	drowning
6604	**nudité**-*f*	nudity
7040	**nullement**-*adv*	nothing
5006	**numérique**-*adj*	digital| numerical
6544	**nuptial**-*adj*	nuptial| wedding
7404	**nurse**-*f*	nanny| governess

O

6352	**oasis**-*f*	oasis
5308	**obéissance**-*f*	obedience
6371	**obèse**-*adj*	obese

5209	**observateur**-*m; adj*	observer; observant
6754	**observatoire**-*m*	observatory
7479	**obstiné**-*adj*	obstinate| stubborn
6450	**obstruction**-*f*	obstruction| blockage
7316	**occupant**-*m; adj*	occupant; occupying
6967	**occurrence**-*f*	occurrence
5798	**octave**-*m*	octave
6359	**oculaire**-*adj; m*	ocular; ocular
7212	**odorat**-*m*	smell| sense of smell
7226	**odyssée**-*f*	odyssey
6121	**ogive**-*f*	warhead
5387	**ogre**-*m*	ogre
6157	**olivier**-*m*	olive
5506	**olympique**-*adj*	Olympic
7347	**ombrelle**-*f*	umbrella
6612	**omettre**-*vb*	omit| pass over
5202	**once**-*f*	ounce
5637	**opérationnel**-*adj*	operational
7466	**opératoire**-*adj*	operative
5615	**opium**-*m*	opium
6812	**opportun**-*adj*	appropriate| timely
5916	**oppression**-*f*	oppression
6704	**optimisme**-*m*	optimism
5164	**optique**-*adj; f*	optical; optics
5520	**oracle**-*m*	oracle
7013	**oral**-*adj; m*	oral; oral
7018	**orateur**-*m*	speaker| orator
5769	**orchidée**-*f*	orchid
6437	**organique**-*adj*	organic
7222	**organisateur**-*m*	organizer
6401	**orge**-*f*	barley
5740	**orgie**-*f*	orgy
5369	**orgue**-*m*	organ
5714	**oriental**-*adj*	Oriental
5008	**orientation**-*f*	orientation| guidance
6248	**originaire**-*adj*	native
6460	**orthodoxe**-*adj*	orthodox
5593	**orthographe**-*f*	spelling
5644	**oseille**-*m*	money| dough
5318	**ouïr**-*vb*	hear
7310	**ourse**-*f; adj*	bear; ursine
6906	**ourson**-*m*	bear cub
5475	**ouvertement**-*adv*	openly
5654	**OVNI**-*abr*	UFO

P

5679	**paddy**-*m*	paddy
5330	**paf**-*adj; int*	high; bam!
6918	**païen**-*adj; m*	pagan; pagan
6666	**pailleté**-*adj*	jeweled
5995	**paisiblement**-*adv*	peacefully
6878	**pakistanais**-*adj*	Pakistani
5449	**palestinien**-*adj*	Palestinian
7229	**palet**-*m*	puck
6647	**palier**-*m*	bearing
6313	**palmier**-*m*	palm
6576	**palpiter**-*vb*	throb| palpitate
7525	**pamplemousse**-*m*	grapefruit
5364	**pancarte**-*f*	placard
5048	**panda**-*m*	panda
5775	**panthère**-*f*	panther
5099	**pantin**-*m*	puppet
5238	**pantoufle**-*f*	slipper
7160	**papoter**-*vb*	chatter| babble
7496	**paquebot**-*m*	boat
7294	**paradoxe**-*m*	paradox
5050	**paragraphe**-*m*	paragraph
5495	**parallèle**-*adj; m/f*	parallel; parallel
6276	**paralysie**-*f*	paralysis
6965	**paramètre**-*m*	parameter
5560	**paranoïa**-*f*	paranoia
5171	**paranoïaque**-*m/f*	paranoid; paranoid
6233	**parcelle**-*f*	parcel| plot
5193	**parchemin**-*m*	parchment| diploma
6820	**pareillement**-*adv*	likewise
7249	**parenté**-*f*	relationship| kindred
7318	**paresse**-*f*	laziness
6885	**parjure**-*m*	perjury
6119	**paroi**-*f*	wall
5299	**parquet**-*m*	parquet
7250	**partenariat**-*m*	partnership
6503	**participant**-*m; adj*	participant; participating
6805	**partiel**-*adj; m*	partial; midyear exam
6010	**partition**-*f*	partition| score
5907	**pascal**-*m; adj*	pascal; paschal
7188	**passant**-*adj; m*	elapsing; passer-by
6509	**passeur**-*m*	ferryman| smuggler
7146	**passible**-*adj*	liable to
6782	**passif**-*adj; m*	passive; passive

7122	**passionnant**-*adj*	exciting	
7006	**passionnément**-*adv*	passionately	
6018	**pastèque**-*f*	watermelon	
5914	**pâtée**-*f*	mash| food	
5727	**paternel**-*adj; m*	paternal; pater	
7508	**paternité**-*f*	paternity	
7281	**patinage**-*m*	skating	
6715	**patiner**-*vb*	skate	
5207	**patin**-*m*	skate	
6979	**patinoire**-*f*	rink| ice rink	
5661	**pâtir**-*vb*	suffer	
6671	**patrimoine**-*m*	heritage	
7139	**patriotique**-*adj*	patriotic	
5976	**patriotisme**-*m*	patriotism	
6629	**pâturage**-*m*	pasture| grazing	
7517	**pâturer**-*vb*	graze	
5240	**paume**-*f*	palm	
5613	**paupière**-*f*	eyelid	
7138	**péage**-*m*	toll	
5144	**pêche**-*f*	fishing	
7141	**pécher**-*vb*	sin	
6726	**pègre**-*f*	underworld	
6523	**pèlerinage**-*m; vb*	pilgrimage; streak	
6242	**pèlerin**-*m*	pilgrim	
6938	**pelle**-*f*	shovel	
6005	**peloter**-*vb*	grope	
5982	**pénal**-*adj*	penal	
6925	**pendentif**-*m*	pendant	
6479	**penderie**-*f*	wardrobe	
7166	**pénétration**-*f*	penetration	
6697	**péniche**-*f*	barge| houseboat	
6976	**pénicilline**-*f*	penicillin	
7312	**péninsule**-*f*	peninsula	
6009	**pénitence**-*f*	penance	
6674	**pensionnat**-*m*	boarding school	
6783	**pénurie**-*f*	shortage| scarcity	
7454	**péquenaud**-*m*	yokel	
5659	**percé**-*adj*	perforated	
6008	**percée**-*f*	breakthrough	
6884	**percevoir**-*vb*	levy	
5486	**percher**-*vb*	perch| hang	
6166	**percuter**-*vb*	ram	
7361	**perfide**-*adj*	perfidious| false	
6325	**périlleusement**-*adv*	perilously	
7124	**périlleux**-*adj*	perilous| hazardous	
7345	**périple**-*m*	trek	

5184	**périr**-*vb*	perish	
6434	**périscope**-*m*	periscope	
5617	**Pérou**-*m*	Peru	
5070	**perpétuité**-*f*	perpetuity	
6241	**perplexe**-*adj*	puzzled	
5230	**perquisition**-*f*	search	
7066	**persévérance**-*f*	perseverance	
6712	**persister**-*vb*	persist| continue	
5726	**perspicace**-*adj*	perceptive| perspicacious	
7148	**persuasion**-*f*	persuasion	
6620	**pertinent**-*adj*	relevant| pertinent	
5874	**pesant**-*adj*	cumbersome	
5987	**peseta**-*f*	peseta	
6785	**pessimiste**-*adj; m/f*	pessimistic; pessimist	
6640	**pétale**-*m*	petal	
5391	**pétition**-*f*	petition	
6282	**pharmaceutique**-*adj*	pharmaceutical	
6340	**pharmacien**-*m*	pharmacist	
7383	**phénix**-*m*	phoenix	
6690	**phoque**-*m*	seal	
7201	**physicien**-*m*	physicist	
6645	**pian**-*m*	yaws	
5751	**picoler**-*vb*	drink| booze	
5368	**pie**-*f*	magpie	
6922	**piétiner**-*vb*	trample on	
5372	**piètre**-*adj*	poor| mediocre	
6338	**pieuvre**-*f*	octopus	
5416	**pieux**-*adj*	pious| devout	
5944	**pif**-*m*	conk| snitch	
5847	**pilier**-*m*	pillar| pier	
6613	**pillage**-*m*	looting| pillage	
6337	**piller**-*vb*	plunder| loot	
5010	**pilotage**-*m; f*	control; piloting	
5832	**piment**-*m*	spice	
6047	**pinceau**-*m*	brush	
5033	**pingouin**-*m*	penguin	
6287	**pinte**-*f*	pint	
5325	**piocher**-*vb*	pickax	
5211	**pionnier**-*m*	pioneer	
6963	**pipeau**-*m*	pipe	
6691	**piquant**-*adj; m*	spicy; spicyness	
6859	**piquet**-*m*	stake| picket	
7500	**piratage**-*m*	piracy	
6920	**pirater**-*vb*	hack| pirate	
6580	**piston**-*m*	piston| valve	

7486	**pittoresque**-*adj*	picturesque		6204	**poulailler**-*m*	hen house
6847	**pizzeria**-*f*	pizzeria		5567	**poulain**-*f*	foal
5844	**placement**-*m*	investment| placement		6901	**poupe**-*f*	stern| stern-post
5517	**plaine**-*f*	plain		6466	**pourpre**-*adj*	purple
6792	**planétaire**-*adj; m*	planetary; orrery		6916	**poussette**-*f*	stroller| crawl
7305	**planque**-*f; adj*	stash; plummy		7118	**poutre**-*f*	beam
5205	**plasma**-*m*	plasma		6860	**préavis**-*m*	warning
5975	**platine**-*m; f*	platinum; deck		6804	**précéder**-*vb*	precede
5773	**plausible**-*adj*	plausible		6269	**prêcher**-*vb*	preach| sermonize
5749	**pleurnicher**-*vb*	whimper| snivel		7403	**prêcheur**-*adj; m*	preachy; preacher
5911	**pli**-*m*	fold| ply		7033	**précipitation**-*f*	precipitation| haste
5554	**plomberie**-*f*	plumbing		5955	**précoce**-*adj*	precocious
5548	**plongeon**-*m*	dive| plunge		5285	**prédateur**-*m; adj*	predator; predatory
5772	**plongeur**-*m*	diver		7189	**prédécesseur**-*m*	predecessor
5968	**plutonium**-*m*	plutonium		6843	**prédiction**-*f*	prediction
5180	**poétique**-*adj*	poetic		6996	**préfecture**-*f*	prefecture
6600	**poignée**-*f*	handle| handful		6687	**préjudice**-*m*	prejudice| injury
5756	**poilu**-*adj*	hairy		7099	**prématuré**-*adj*	premature
6076	**pointu**-*adj*	sharp		6724	**préméditer**-*vb*	premeditate
5037	**pointure**-*f*	size		7321	**preneur**-*m*	taker
7341	**poire**-*f*	pear| sucker		5002	**préparé**-*adj*	prepared
6385	**poivrot**-*m; adj*	boozer; rummy		5453	**présager**-*vb*	predict| foresee
6225	**polaire**-*adj*	polar		6257	**prescription**-*f*	prescription
5614	**poliment**-*adv*	politely		5732	**prescrire**-*vb*	prescribe
5535	**polir**-*vb*	polish| buff		6249	**présentable**-*adj*	presentable
5835	**politiquement**-*adv*	politically		6144	**présentateur**-*m*	presenter
5187	**pollution**-*f*	pollution		6145	**préservatif**-*m; adj*	condom; preservative
6358	**pommade**-*f*	ointment		6559	**présidentiel**-*adj*	presidential
6024	**pomper**-*vb*	pump		7178	**présider**-*vb*	preside
6658	**pondre**-*vb*	lay		5653	**pressing**-*m*	dry cleaning
7005	**ponton**-*m*	pontoon		5980	**prestation**-*f*	benefit
5314	**popularité**-*f*	popularity		7137	**preste**-*adj*	nimble
5612	**porcelaine**-*f*	porcelain		5456	**prestige**-*m*	prestige
6071	**porcherie**-*f*	pigsty		7016	**prestigieux**-*adj*	prestigious
5803	**pornographie**-*f*	pornography		6570	**prêteur**-*m*	lender
7362	**porridge**-*m*	porridge		6721	**prêtresse**-*f*	priestess
6074	**posture**-*f*	posture		6951	**preux**-*adj*	doughty| gallant
5663	**potable**-*adj*	potable		6940	**prévenant**-*adj*	considerate
6789	**potage**-*m*	soup		5461	**prévisible**-*adj*	predictable
7243	**potager**-*m*	kitchen garden		5812	**prévision**-*f*	forecast
5782	**potence**-*f*	gallows		7335	**primordial**-*adj*	primary| primordial
7476	**potentiellement**-*adv*	potentially		6064	**probabilité**-*f*	probability
7030	**potin**-*m*	titbit		5906	**probation**-*f*	probation
7090	**pouffiasse**-*f*	bitch		6985	**procession**-*f*	procession
7351	**pouilleux**-*adj*	lousy		7253	**procuration**-*f*	proxy

5162	**prodige**-*m*	prodigy| wonder
6254	**prodigieux**-*adj*	prodigious
7167	**prodiguer**-*vb*	give| lavish
6955	**profitable**-*adj*	profitable
6351	**progéniture**-*f*	offspring
7227	**programmation**-*f*	programming
6602	**progression**-*f*	progression
7273	**progressivement**-*adv*	progressively
6210	**prohibition**-*f*	prohibition
5681	**projeter**-*vb*	project
5821	**prolonger**-*vb*	extend| prolong
7117	**promoteur**-*m*	sponsor
6924	**propager**-*vb*	propagate
5915	**propice**-*adj*	suitable
6738	**proportion**-*f*	proportion| rate
5112	**proprement**-*adv*	properly
7202	**propreté**-*f*	cleanliness
6594	**propulsion**-*f*	propulsion
7093	**prostate**-*f*	prostate
5085	**prostitution**-*f*	prostitution
5478	**protéine**-*f*	protein
5884	**protestation**-*f*	protest| outcry
6495	**proue**-*f*	bow| head
6410	**provocation**-*f*	provocation
5069	**prudemment**-*adv*	carefully
6366	**prune**-*f*	plum
6974	**pseudonyme**-*m; adj*	pseudonym; pseudonymous
5589	**psychiatrie**-*f*	psychiatry
5817	**psychique**-*adj*	psychic
6561	**psychose**-*f*	psychosis
6980	**puberté**-*f*	puberty
6363	**publication**-*f*	publication| issue
5767	**publicitaire**-*m/f; adj*	advertiser; advertising
5293	**publiquement**-*adv*	publicly
5964	**pudeur**-*f*	modesty
5954	**puéril**-*adj*	childish
6232	**pulsion**-*f*	drive| pulse
5713	**punaise**-*f*	bug
6485	**pupille**-*f*	pupil
6482	**purgatoire**-*m*	purgatory
6549	**purger**-*vb*	purge| bleed
6915	**purifier**-*vb*	purify
6322	**putois**-*m*	skunk
7004	**python**-*m*	python

Q

5040	**quasi**-*adv*	almost
6151	**querelle**-*f*	quarrel| feud
5455	**questionner**-*vb*	question
6070	**quincaillerie**-*f*	hardware

R

6072	**rabais**-*m*	discount
7199	**rabaisser**-*vb*	belittle
6484	**racisme**-*m*	racism
6181	**racket**-*m*	racketeering
5316	**radeau**-*m*	raft
5779	**radiateur**-*m*	radiator
6467	**radieux**-*adj*	radiant| bright
7323	**radioactif**-*adj*	radioactive
7464	**radioactivité**-*f*	radioactivity
7414	**radis**-*m*	radish
5668	**raffiner**-*vb*	refine
6077	**raffut**-*m*	racket
7109	**rafle**-*f*	raid
6494	**raie**-*f*	ray| parting
5565	**rai**-*m*	streak
5523	**raisonnement**-*m*	reasoning
5114	**râler**-*vb*	grumble| moan
7084	**rallier**-*vb*	rally
6826	**rallonge**-*f*	extension
5226	**ramoner**-*vb*	sweep
5152	**rancard**-*m*	date
6114	**rand**-*m*	rand
7300	**ranimer**-*vb*	revive| rekindle
5905	**rapidité**-*f*	speed| rapidity
7231	**raquette**-*f*	racket| bat
6699	**rasage**-*m*	shaving
5053	**rassurant**-*adj*	reassuring
5971	**rationnel**-*adj; m*	rational; rational
6921	**raton**-*m*	north african| young rat
6786	**ravage**-*m*	havoc| ravage
5016	**ravin**-*m*	ravine
6624	**ravisseur**-*m*	abductor| ravisher
5417	**ravitaillement**-*m*	refueling
5881	**ravoir**-*vb*	get back
7164	**rayer**-*vb*	strike

5267	**rayure**-*f*	stripe	6035	**régaler**-*vb*	regale| feast
6771	**réalisme**-*m*	realism	6554	**régal**-*m*	treat
7327	**réanimation**-*f*	resuscitation	6566	**régional**-*adj*	regional
6835	**rebord**-*m*	flange| edge	7251	**régir**-*vb*	govern
6300	**réceptionniste**-*m/f*	receptionist	6270	**régisseur**-*m*	steward
6109	**receveur**-*m*	recipient| conductor	6521	**regorger**-*vb*	abound
7155	**recharge**-*f*	recharge	6262	**réhabilitation**-*f*	rehabilitation
6448	**récif**-*m*	reef	5757	**réincarnation**-*f*	reincarnation
6535	**récital**-*m*	recital	5591	**rejet**-*m*	rejection
5138	**réciter**-*vb*	recite	7285	**rejouer**-*vb*	replay
7451	**réclamation**-*f*	complaint	6247	**relancer**-*vb*	revive
6794	**recoin**-*m*	corner| recess	5297	**relativement**-*adv*	relatively
5116	**récolter**-*vb*	harvest| collect	5538	**relaxer**-*vb*	relax
5041	**recommandation**-*f*	recommendation| reference	7010	**relique**-*f*	relic
7206	**récompense**-*f*	reward| award	7462	**relire**-*vb*	read back
6553	**réconciliation**-*f*	reconciliation	5870	**remboursement**-*m*	reimbursement| refund
5373	**réconcilier**-*vb*	reconcile	5253	**remédier**-*vb*	remedy
5291	**reconduire**-*vb*	renew	5263	**remerciement**-*m*	thanks| appreciation
7446	**reconquérir**-*vb*	regain| reconquer	5620	**remorque**-*f*	trailer
7115	**reconstituer**-*vb*	reconstruct| put together	6360	**remplacement**-*m*	replacement| displacement
6984	**reconstruction**-*f*	reconstruction	6774	**rendement**-*m*	yield| efficiency
5946	**recoudre**-*vb*	sew| sew up	7177	**rengainer**-*vb*	sheathe
5055	**recouvrir**-*vb*	cover| re-cover	6565	**renifler**-*vb*	sniff| smell
5965	**récréation**-*f*	recreation| recess	7083	**renne**-*m*	reindeer
6382	**recréer**-*vb*	recreate	5546	**renommée**-*f*	renown
5667	**recrutement**-*m*	recruitment| recruiting	6206	**renouveler**-*vb*	renew
5181	**recruter**-*vb*	recruit| rush	5770	**rentable**-*adj*	profitable| cost-effective
5462	**recueillir**-*vb*	collect| gather	5402	**renverse**-*f*	inverse
6089	**récupération**-*f*	recovery| retrieval	5338	**renvoi**-*m*	return| reference
5014	**rédaction**-*f*	writing| redaction	7077	**réparateur**-*m; adj*	repairer; remedial
5951	**reddition**-*f*	surrender	6599	**repeindre**-*vb*	repaint
5563	**rédemption**-*f*	redemption	7165	**repérage**-*m*	tracking
5473	**rédiger**-*vb*	rewrite	6772	**replier**-*vb*	replicate| fold up
5123	**redire**-*vb*	repeat	6323	**repli**-*m*	withdrawal| fold
5390	**redonner**-*vb*	restore| give back	6124	**répression**-*f*	repression
7279	**redoubler**-*vb*	redouble	6944	**reptile**-*adj; m*	reptile; reptile
6546	**redoute**-*f*	redoubt	7502	**répugnant**-*adj*	repugnant
6476	**redressement**-*m*	recovery| redress	5867	**requérir**-*vb*	require
5540	**redresser**-*vb*	straighten| redress	6261	**résident**-*m*	resident
6075	**refiler**-*vb*	palm off	6989	**résonner**-*vb*	resonate| resound
5993	**refléter**-*vb*	reflect	5780	**respectueux**-*adj*	respectful
5603	**réforme**-*f*	reform	7388	**respiratoire**-*adj*	respiratory
5113	**réfrigérateur**-*m*	refrigerator	6525	**ressaisir**-*vb*	catch
7209	**refroidissement**-*m*	cooling	6442	**resserrer**-*vb*	tighten

5121	ressusciter-*vb*	resurrect	
6909	restant-*adj; m*	remaining; remnant	
6085	restauration-*f*	restoration| restaurant	
7140	restriction-*f*	restriction	
6332	rétablissement-*m*	recovery| restoration	
7035	retaper-*vb*	do up| retype	
7047	retardement-*m*	delay	
5569	retomber-*vb*	drop| relapse	
6302	retraiter-*vb*	reprocess	
7064	revendication-*f*	claim	
6201	révérence-*f*	reverence| bow	
5234	rêveur-*m; adj*	dreamer; dreamy	
5477	réviser-*vb*	revise| review	
6534	révision-*f*	revision	
7468	rhétorique-*adj; f*	rhetoric; rhetoric	
6237	rhinocéros-*m*	rhinoceros	
6088	rider-*vb*	wrinkle| ruffle	
6648	rigide-*adj*	rigid| inflexible	
5280	rigolade-*f*	fun| joke	
6414	rimer-*vb*	rhyme	
6436	rincer-*vb*	rinse	
6056	riposter-*vb*	hit back| retaliate	
5781	rite-*m*	rite	
5552	rival-*adj; m*	rival; rival	
6475	rivaliser-*vb*	compete	
6288	robuste-*adj*	robust| sturdy	
6540	roche-*f*	rock	
7120	rocheux-*adj*	rocky	
5897	rôder-*vb*	prowl| lurk	
7354	rôdeur-*m; f*	lurker; prowler	
6711	rogue-*adj*	rogue	
5959	romantisme-*m*	romanticism	
7438	romarin-*m*	rosemary	
6864	ronfler-*vb*	snore	
7330	roquette-*f*	rocket	
6560	rosbif-*adj*	roast beef	
6152	rossignol-*m*	nightingale	
5673	rotation-*f*	rotation	
6176	rouble-*m*	ruble	
6937	rougeole-*f*	measles	
5825	rougir-*vb*	blush| go red	
5474	rouiller-*vb*	rust	
6397	roulant-*adj*	rolling	
6841	roulement-*m*	rolling| rumbling	
7198	rouquin-*adj*	ginger	

5633	routier-*vb; m*	truck; teamster	
5750	rouvrir-*vb*	reopen	
5076	rubis-*m*	ruby	
5166	rubrique-*f*	rubric| column	
5746	ruche-*f*	hive	
5522	rudement-*adv*	roughly| harshly	
6454	rugby-*m*	rugby	
5097	rush-*m*	rush	
6957	rustre-*adj; m*	boor; boorish	

S

6315	sabbat-*m*	Sabbath	
5255	sable-*m*	sand| grittiness	
7471	sablier-*m*	hourglass	
5161	sabotage-*m*	sabotage	
5901	saboter-*vb*	sabotage	
5744	sabot-*m*	shoe| hoof	
5054	sabre-*m*	saber| sword	
6469	saccager-*vb*	sack| ransack	
6432	sachet-*m*	bag	
5425	sacoche-*f*	pannier	
6795	sacrer-*vb*	consecrate| crown	
6655	sacrilège-*m; adj*	sacrilege; sacrilegious	
5034	sadique-*adj; m/f*	sadistic; sadist	
7185	safari-*m*	safari	
6389	sagement-*adv*	wisely	
6158	saignant-*adj*	bleeding	
6661	salami-*m*	salami	
5403	salement-*adv*	dirtily	
5158	samba-*f*	samba	
7336	sanatorium-*m*	sanatorium	
5430	sanctifier-*vb*	sanctify	
7076	sanction-*f*	sanction| punishment	
5910	sandale-*f*	sandal	
5511	sanglant-*adj*	bloody	
5856	sangler-*vb*	strap	
5149	sanglot-*m*	sob	
6190	sangsue-*f*	leech	
6644	sanguinaire-*adj*	bloody	
7126	sanitaire-*adj*	sanitary; sanitation	
7072	Sapristi!-*int*	good heavens!	
7280	sarcasme-*m*	sarcasm	
6641	sarcastique-*adj*	sarcastic	
6283	satin-*m*	satin| demon	

6205	**Saturne**-*m*	Saturn	7421	**siamois**-*adj; m|mpl*	Siamese; Siamese
6461	**sauterelle**-*f*	grasshopper	5370	**sifflement**-*m*	whistling| hiss
6430	**sauvagement**-*adv*	savagely	7458	**simplet**-*adj*	simple-minded
6778	**sauvegarde**-*f*	safeguard	5458	**simplicité**-*f*	simplicity
5738	**saveur**-*f*	flavor| taste	5284	**simulation**-*f*	simulation
6030	**savourer**-*vb*	enjoy| glory	7372	**simuler**-*vb*	simulate| pretend
6952	**saxon**-*adj; m/f*	Saxon; Saxon	7008	**simultanément**-*adv*	simultaneously
6370	**scalpel**-*m*	scalpel	6810	**singulier**-*adj; m*	singular| strange; singular
7297	**scalp**-*m*	scalp	6368	**sketch**-*m*	sketch
6175	**scélérat**-*m; adj*	scoundrel; miscreant	6115	**skier**-*vb*	ski
5898	**sceller**-*vb*	seal| embed	6538	**skipper**-*m*	skipper
6095	**sceptique**-*adj; m/f*	skeptical; skeptic	5081	**slogan**-*m*	slogan| tag
7401	**sceptre**-*m*	scepter	7416	**snack**-*m*	snack
5516	**schéma**-*m*	schema| diagram	5792	**socialisme**-*m*	socialism
6846	**schizophrénie**-*f*	schizophrenia	7513	**sodomie**-*f*	sodomy
6660	**scolarité**-*f*	schooling	5063	**soja**-*m*	soy
5698	**scooter**-*m*	scooter	6183	**solder**-*vb*	settle
5413	**scrupule**-*m*	scruple| compunction	6993	**sole**-*f*	sole
6933	**sculpteur**-*m*	sculptor	5797	**solidarité**-*f*	solidarity
5483	**sculpture**-*f*	sculpture| sculpting	7307	**sollicitude**-*f*	solicitude
7245	**sécession**-*f*	secession	6031	**sombrer**-*vb*	sink
5107	**secourir**-*vb*	rescue	6353	**somnambule**-*m; adj*	somnambulist; somnambulistic
6589	**secousse**-*f*	shock| shake	6498	**somptueux**-*adj*	sumptuous| magnificent
7214	**secrétariat**-*m*	secretariat| secretaryship	5324	**sonar**-*m*	sonar
5245	**sédatif**-*adj; m*	sedative; sedative	6330	**sondage**-*m; adj*	survey| poll; probing
6408	**séducteur**-*m; adj*	seducer; seductive	5024	**sonore**-*f; adj*	sound; acoustic
5826	**séduction**-*f*	seduction	5710	**sornette**-*f*	fiddlestick
5649	**seigneurie**-*f*	lordship	5447	**sortilège**-*m*	spell
6260	**séisme**-*m*	earthquake	7103	**sort**-*m*	whereabouts| fate
6250	**seller**-*vb*	saddle	6125	**sosie**-*f*	double
6478	**semelle**-*f*	sole	5752	**souche**-*f*	strain| stump
5807	**semence**-*f*	seed| seeds	6040	**soucieux**-*adj*	concerned
6046	**sénile**-*adj*	senile	5448	**soucoupe**-*f*	saucer
6012	**sensass**-*adj*	sensational	6301	**Soudan**-*m*	Sudan
6084	**sentinelle**-*f*	sentinel	5616	**soufrer**-*vb*	sulfur| sulphurize
6127	**séquence**-*f*	sequence	6605	**souiller**-*vb*	soil| defile
6727	**serbe**-*adj; m*	Serbian; Serbian	7483	**soulèvement**-*m*	uprising| uplift
6870	**serein**-*adj; m*	serene; collection	6768	**souligner**-*vb*	emphasize| underline
5778	**sérénité**-*f*	serenity	6791	**soumission**-*f*	submission| tender
7224	**sésame**-*m*	sesame	5704	**souple**-*adj*	flexible| soft
5700	**sévèrement**-*adv*	severely	5139	**sournois**-*adj*	sneaky| sly
7080	**shampoing**-*m*	shampoo	7187	**soutirer**-*vb*	extract
5855	**shampooing**-*m*	shampoo	5103	**spaghetti**-*m*	spaghetti
5476	**shilling**-*m*	shilling	6037	**spécialiser**-*vb*	specialize
6456	**shooter**-*vb*	shoot| shoot up			

5574	**spécifique**-*adj*	specific	5281	**supplément**-*m*	supplement
5547	**sphère**-*f*	sphere| globe	5686	**supplice**-*m*	torture| ordeal
7447	**sphinx**-*m*	sphinx	5058	**support**-*m*	support| bracket
6497	**sponsor**-*m*	sponsor	6103	**supposition**-*f*	assumption| guess
7131	**spontané**-*adj*	spontaneous	5247	**surgir**-*vb*	arise| emerge
6625	**spore**-*f*	spore	5197	**surnaturel**-*adj; m*	supernatural; occult
6050	**squaw**-*f*	squaw	5251	**surnommer**-*vb*	nickname
5885	**stabilité**-*f*	stability| steadiness	6737	**surpasser**-*vb*	surpass| excel
5857	**stagiaire**-*m/f*	trainee	7119	**surplus**-*m*	surplus
7417	**standing**-*m*	standing	6489	**surprenant**-*adj*	surprising
5196	**stationnement**-*m*	parking	6386	**suspecter**-*vb*	suspect
7442	**statique**-*adj*	static	5365	**suture**-*f*	suture
5533	**stellaire**-*adj*	stellar	5225	**swing**-*m*	swing| stomp
6195	**stéréo**-*f*	stereo	5883	**symbolique**-*adj*	symbolic| nominal
5172	**stérile**-*adj*	sterile| barren	6807	**symboliser**-*vb*	symbolize
5224	**sterling**-*m*	sterling	5471	**symphonie**-*f*	symphony
6879	**stéroïde**-*m*	steroid	6562	**synagogue**-*f*	synagogue
6451	**steward**-*m*	steward	6788	**synchronisation**-*f*	synchronization
5795	**stimulant**-*adj; m*	stimulating; stimulant	7058	**synonyme**-*adj; m*	synonymous; synonym
6628	**stockage**-*m*	storage| stocking	6735	**synthèse**-*f*	synthesis
7293	**store**-*m*	blind| awning	7503	**synthétique**-*adj; m*	synthetic; synthetic
5683	**stratégique**-*adj*	strategic	6598	**syphilis**-*f*	syphilis
6196	**string**-*m*	string| thong			
5696	**stupéfiant**-*m; adj*	narcotic; amazing		**T**	
5252	**stupidité**-*f*	stupidity			
5745	**style**-*m*	style| design	6236	**tablette**-*f*	tablet
5424	**subconscient**-*adj*	subconscious	5784	**tablier**-*m*	apron
5233	**subit**-*adj*	sudden	5725	**tabouret**-*m*	stool
7029	**submerger**-*vb*	overwhelm| submerge	5129	**tact**-*m; adj*	tact; delicate
6487	**substitut**-*m*	surrogate| substitute	5531	**taillé**-*adj*	tailored
6986	**succomber**-*vb*	succumb	6081	**taille**-*f*	size| height
6762	**sucette**-*f*	lollipop| pacifier	5934	**talisman**-*m*	talisman
6515	**suceur**-*m*	nozzle	6745	**tanière**-*f*	lair
5994	**sucrerie**-*f*	suger refinery	6224	**tapage**-*m*	noise| fuss
6297	**suer**-*vb*	sweat	6891	**taquin**-*adj; m*	teasing| playful; teaser
5051	**suffisant**-*adj*	sufficient	6170	**taquiner**-*vb*	tease
7154	**supercherie**-*f*	deception| trickery	7278	**tardif**-*adj*	late
6220	**superficiel**-*adj*	superficial	6736	**tâter**-*vb*	feel
7200	**superflu**-*adj*	superfluous| unnecessary	6096	**tatouer**-*vb*	tattoo
6471	**supériorité**-*f*	superiority	7043	**tchèque**-*adj; m*	Czech; Czech
6042	**superstar**-*m*	superstar	5309	**technicien**-*m*	technician
5549	**superstitieux**-*adj*	superstitious	5967	**tee**-*m*	tee
5311	**superstition**-*f*	superstition	6573	**teinture**-*f*	dyeing
5001	**superviseur**-*m*	supervisor	6746	**télégraphe**-*m*	telegraph
			6342	**téléspectateur**-*m*	viewer

6819	**téléviser**-*vb*	televise	7184	**tourte**-*f*	pie
7512	**téléviseur**-*m*	TV	6271	**tracas**-*m; adj*	hassle; worry
5818	**tempe**-*f*	temple	5011	**tracé**-*m; adj*	route| course; tracing
5306	**tempérament**-*m*	temperament| temper	6296	**tract**-*m*	leaflet
6892	**tempo**-*m*	tempo	5525	**traditionnel**-*adj*	traditional
6608	**tenace**-*adj*	tenacious| persistent	6162	**traducteur**-*m*	translator
5361	**tendrement**-*adv*	tenderly| fondly	5191	**trafiquant**-*m*	trafficker
5140	**terminus**-*m*	terminus	5469	**traîneau**-*m*	sled| drag
6636	**terne**-*adj*	dull| drab	7121	**tralala**-*int*	splurge| blabla
7407	**terreux**-*adj*	earthy	5610	**trame**-*f*	weave
5626	**terrien**-*m*	earthling| landlubber	5931	**tram**-*m*	tram| car
6486	**terrier**-*m*	terrier	5809	**tramway**-*m*	streetcar
6836	**terroriser**-*vb*	terrorize| bully	5094	**tranché**-*adj*	decided| cut
6913	**théorique**-*adj*	theoretical	5688	**transe**-*f*	trance
7322	**théoriquement**-*adv*	theoretically	5026	**transition**-*f*	transition
5109	**thérapeute**-*m/f*	therapist	6273	**transparent**-*adj*	transparent| clear
6264	**thermique**-*adj*	thermal	5715	**transpirer**-*vb*	sweat| transpire
7275	**thermomètre**-*m*	thermometer	7355	**transporteur**-*m*	carrier| transporter
6284	**tiède**-*adj*	lukewarm	7506	**traumatique**-*adj*	traumatic
5838	**tige**-*f*	stem| spindle	6759	**traverse**-*f*	crossing| going through
6133	**tigresse**-*f*	tigress	5658	**travestir**-*vb*	travesty
5072	**timing**-*m*	timing	6440	**trébucher**-*vb*	stumble| stagger
7470	**titane**-*m*	titanium	5860	**trèfle**-*m*	clover| shamrock
5978	**titan**-*m*	titan	6702	**trésorier**-*m*	treasurer
5845	**tocard**-*adj; m*	tacky; loser	5298	**tribune**-*f*	gallery
6044	**tôle**-*f*	sheet metal| slammer	7203	**tribut**-*m*	tribute
5406	**tolérance**-*f*	tolerance	6692	**triché**-*adj*	cheated
5460	**tombeur**-*m*	ladykiller	6799	**tricot**-*m*	knitting
7135	**tonalité**-*f*	tone| tonality	7288	**trier**-*vb*	sort
6881	**tondre**-*vb*	mow| shear	6751	**tri**-*m*	sorting
5592	**tonic**-*m*	tonic	7237	**trimer**-*vb*	slave away
5360	**tonneau**-*m*	barrel| ton	5785	**trio**-*m*	trio
6781	**tora**-*f*	torah	6756	**triompher**-*vb*	triumph
5903	**torchon**-*m*	tea towel	5627	**tripoter**-*vb*	tamper| paw
5183	**tornade**-*f*	tornado	7068	**tristement**-*adv*	sadly
7371	**torrent**-*m*	torrent	7520	**troc**-*m*	barter| bartering
6011	**torride**-*adj*	torrid	7472	**troll**-*m*	troll
6013	**toupet**-*m*	nerve| cheek	6502	**trombone**-*m; adj*	trombone; annoyed
5510	**tourbillon**-*m*	vortex| whirlwind	6198	**tromperie**-*f*	deception
5031	**tourisme**-*m*	tourism	6987	**trompeter**-*vb*	trumpet
6740	**touristique**-*adj*	tourist	7509	**trompeur**-*adj; m*	misleading; deceiver
5101	**tourmenter**-*vb*	torment| plague	6822	**tronçonneuse**-*f*	chain saw
5841	**tourment**-*m*	torment	6840	**tropical**-*adj*	tropical
5128	**tournée**-*f*	tour| touring	7079	**tropique**-*m*	tropic
6365	**tournevis**-*m*	screwdriver	5581	**trot**-*m*	trot
5186	**tournure**-*f*	twist| turning			

7504	**trotter**-*vb*	trot
6178	**troublant**-*adj*	disturbing
7394	**trouer**-*vb*	pit
6837	**trouvaille**-*f*	find
5351	**truand**-*m*	hoodlum
7129	**truck**-*m*	truck
7274	**truffe**-*f*	truffle
5509	**truie**-*f*	sow
5605	**truite**-*f*	trout
5163	**truquer**-*vb*	rig| fake
6995	**trust**-*m*	trust
6307	**tuberculose**-*f*	tuberculosis
5157	**tuerie**-*f*	killing
6591	**tulipe**-*f*	tulip
7169	**turbulence**-*f*	turbulence
7314	**tutelle**-*f*	guardianship| tutorship
5765	**twist**-*m*	twist
7017	**typhon**-*m*	typhoon
6948	**typiquement**-*adv*	typically
5061	**tyrannie**-*f*	tyranny

U

7050	**ultimatum**-*m*	ultimatum
5436	**ultra-**-*pfx*	ultra-
6518	**unanimité**-*f*	unanimity
6631	**underground**-*adj; m*	underground; underground
5151	**universel**-*adj; m*	universal; universal
5935	**uranium**-*m*	uranium
6429	**urbain**-*adj*	urban
5672	**urne**-*f*	urn
5382	**utérus**-*m*	uterus

V

5355	**vacarme**-*m*	racket| noise
5763	**vaillant**-*adj*	valiant| brave
6039	**valeureux**-*adj*	valorous| gallant
6063	**valide**-*adj*	valid| available
6426	**valve**-*f*	valve
5105	**vanille**-*f*	vanilla
6964	**vaniteux**-*adj*	vain
7387	**vanner**-*vb*	winnow
6213	**variété**-*f*	variety| choice
5201	**vaudou**-*adj; m*	voodoo; voodoo

6392	**vénérer**-*vb*	revere| worship
6607	**vengeur**-*m; adj*	avenger; vengeful
5017	**venin**-*m*	venom
6199	**ventilateur**-*m*	fan
6177	**ventilation**-*f*	ventilation
5925	**véranda**-*f*	veranda| porch
6000	**verbal**-*adj; m*	verbal; verbal
6622	**verbe**-*m*	vb
6651	**véreux**-*adj*	shady| dubious
5514	**verger**-*m*	orchard
6149	**véritablement**-*adv*	truly| actually
6592	**verrouillage**-*m*	locking
6816	**versement**-*m*	payment| installment
6511	**verset**-*m*	verse
5434	**vertébral**-*adj*	vertebral
5629	**vertueux**-*adj*	virtuous
6122	**vessie**-*f*	bladder
5985	**veston**-*m*	jacket
5353	**vétéran**-*m; adj*	veteran; old
5568	**veuf**-*m*	widower
7358	**viable**-*adj*	viable
5972	**vibrer**-*vb*	vibrate| thrill
6153	**victorieux**-*adj*	victorious
6596	**vietnamien**-*adj; m*	Vietnamese; Vietnamese
6411	**vigilant**-*adj*	vigilant| watchful
7161	**vigile**-*m*	watchman
6530	**vigne**-*f*	vine
5231	**vigueur**-*f*	vigor| strength
5303	**viking**-*m*	viking
5329	**vil**-*adj*	vile| base
5363	**vinaigrer**-*vb*	souse
5282	**viole**-*f*	viol
5194	**violemment**-*adv*	violently
6775	**violoniste**-*m/f*	violinist
7268	**virement**-*m*	transfer
5133	**viril**-*adj*	virile| manly
5502	**virilité**-*f*	virility| manhood
7424	**virtuel**-*adj*	virtual
7219	**visée**-*f*	sight
6587	**viseur**-*m*	viewfinder
7098	**visibilité**-*f*	visibility
6445	**visionnaire**-*adj; m*	visionary; visionary
5472	**vison**-*m*	mink
5588	**vocal**-*adj*	vocal
6615	**voilier**-*m*	yacht

6869	**volaille**-*f*	poultry| fowl
5150	**volontairement**-*adv*	willingly
6099	**volt**-*m*	volt
5936	**vortex**-*m*	vortex
6350	**voûter**-*vb*	stoop| vault
5366	**voyant**-*m; adj*	seer; clairvoyant
6367	**voyeur**-*m*	voyeur
7495	**vulgarité**-*f*	vulgarity

W

5799	**waters**-*m*	bathroom| can
5027	**watt**-*m*	watt

Y

6664	**yaourt**-*m*	yogurt

Z

5909	**zèle**-*m*	zeal
7390	**zéphyr**-*m*	zephyr
6217	**zinc**-*m*	zinc
5408	**zodiaque**-*m*	zodiac
5657	**zoom**-*m*	zoom

Contact, Further Reading and Resources

For more tools, tips & tricks visit our site www.mostusedwords.com. We publish various language learning resources.

If you have a great idea you want to pitch us, please send an e-mail to info@mostusedwords.com.

Frequency Dictionaries

Frequency Dictionaries in this series:

French Frequency Dictionary 1 – Essential Vocabulary – 2500 Most Common French Words
French Frequency Dictionary 2 - Intermediate Vocabulary – 2501-5000 Most Common French Words
French Frequency Dictionary 3 - Advanced Vocabulary – 5001-7500 Most Common French Words
French Frequency Dictionary 4 - Master Vocabulary – 7501-10000 Most Common French Words

Please visit our website www.mostusedwords.com/frequency-dictionary/french-english for more information.

Our goal is to provide language learners with frequency dictionaries for every major and minor language worldwide. You can view our selection on www.mostusedwords.com/frequency-dictionary

Bilingual books

We're creating a selection of parallel texts, and our selection is ever expanding.

To help you in your language learning journey, all our bilingual books come with a dictionary included, created for that particular book.

Current bilingual books available are English, Spanish, Portuguese, Italian, German, and French.

For more information, check www.mostusedwords.com/parallel-texts. Check back regularly for new books and languages.

Other language learning methods

You'll find reviews of other 3rd party language learning applications, software, audio courses, and apps. There are so many available, and some are (much) better than others.

Check out our reviews at www.mostusedwords.com/reviews.

Contact

If you have any questions, you can contact us through e-mail info@mostusedwords.com.

www.ingramcontent.com/pod-product-compliance
Lightning Source LLC
Chambersburg PA
CBHW080126150626
46550CB00017B/2692